The Encyclopedia
of Decorative Arts 1890–1940

Edited by Philippe Garner
*Sotheby's expert in twentieth-century applied arts
and the history of photography.*

The history of the decorative arts in the first half of
the twentieth century is one of revolutions and
vivid contrasts in style and taste. It embraces such
decorative opposites as the tubular steel furniture
of the Bauhaus and the Modern Movement – whose
ideals still inspire much contemporary design – and
the elaborate and individual craftsmanship of the
creations of the great French Art Nouveau and Art
Deco stylists. The refined constructions of Gropius
and Marcel Breuer seem a far remove from the
asymmetrical curves of *le style Guimard* and the
rich ornamentation of much Art Deco.

There have been many books on the individual
movements and figures of the decorative arts of this
century, but *The Encyclopedia of Decorative Arts
1890–1940* is the first to provide a comprehensive
and authoritative account of all the classic
movements in design of the modern period.
Historically, the various essays span the period
from the end of the nineteenth century to the
Second World War, thus tracing the development
of the applied arts and design from the beginnings
and rapid flowering of Art Nouveau and its
national variants to the widespread application of
the ideals of the Modern Movement to the design
of everyday objects and interiors.

Every section of this encyclopedia has been
written by an expert in that particular field. The
editor of the volume is Philippe Garner, an expert
at the London auction house of Sotheby Parke
Bernet and head of the department of modern
decorative arts and photography at Sotheby's
Belgravia.

CONTRIBUTING AUTHORS

Philippe Garner, the consultant editor of the
encyclopedia, has published several works on
modern decorative arts, including *Edwardiana,
Art Nouveau for Collectors* and the standard
critical work on the French glass artist, Emile
Gallé. He has also published articles in *The
Connoisseur* magazine on Eileen Gray, Jean Dunand
and Pierre Legrain.

Roger-Henri Guerrand teaches at the Ecole
Supérieure des Beaux-Arts in Paris. His books
include *L'Art Nouveau en Europe.*

Martin Battersby is both a theatre designer and
painter, as well as being a leading authority on
international Art Nouveau and Art Deco. His most
notable books are *The Decorative Twenties* and
The Decorative Thirties.

Gillian Naylor is an acknowledged expert on the
Modern Movement in design and is currently
writing a book on the subject. Her books include
The Arts and Crafts Movement and *The Bauhaus.*

Malcolm Haslam is currently working on a book
about the Martin Brothers, art potters. His
previous publications include *English Art Pottery
1865–1915, Marks and Monograms of the Modern
Movement* and *The Real World of the Surrealists.*

Stuart Durant is Senior Lecturer in the History
of Design at Kingston Polytechnic, London. He
has published a book on *Victorian Ornamental
Design* and has organised numerous exhibitions on
the decorative arts.

Lynne Thornton was formerly an expert with
Sotheby's, specialising in Art Nouveau. She is now
a recognised expert for the major Paris auction
rooms and has made a speciality of the study of late
nineteenth- and early twentieth-century ceramics.

Ian Bennett is the author of numerous books on
the fine and applied arts, including the recently
published *Rugs and Carpets of the World.* He is also
a keen collector of modern art ceramics.

Isabelle Anscombe, after a period spent working
for a London decorative arts business, now
devotes herself entirely to writing on the modern
applied arts. Her book on the *Arts and Crafts
Movement in America* is to be published in 1978.

Ada Polak is the Deputy Curator in Britain of the
Arts and Crafts Museum of Norway. She has
published articles on the decorative arts in a
number of journals, and her book *Modern Glass* is
one of the standard works on the subject.

Marina Henderson, who has contributed a
special essay on the relationship between the fine
and applied arts of the twentieth century, is the
author of a book on Dante Gabriel Rossetti.

The Encyclopedia
of
Decorative Arts
1890–1940

THE
ENCYCLOPEDIA
OF
DECORATIVE
ARTS
1890-1940

Edited by Philippe Garner

 VAN NOSTRAND REINHOLD COMPANY
NEW YORK   CINCINNATI   TORONTO   LONDON   MELBOURNE

A Quarto Book

Copyright © 1978 by Quarto Limited

Library of Congress Catalog Card Number 78-7479

ISBN 0-442-22577-6

Published in 1979 by Van Nostrand Reinhold Company
A division of Litton Educational Publishing, Inc.
135 West 50th Street, New York, NY 10020, U.S.A.

Van Nostrand Reinhold Limited
1410 Birchmount Road
Scarborough, Ontario M1P 2E7, Canada

1 3 5 7 9 11 13 15 16 14 12 10 8 6 4 2

Library of Congress Cataloging in Publication Data
Main entry under title:

The Encyclopedia of decorative arts, 1890–1940.

   Bibliography: p.
   Includes index.
   1. Art, Decorative – History – 19th century –
Dictionaries. 2. Art, Decorative – History – 20th
century – Dictionaries. I. Garner, Philippe.
NK775.E63   745'.09'04   78-7479
ISBN 0-442-22577-6

This book was designed and produced by
Quarto Publishing Limited,
13, New Burlington Street, London W1

Managing Editor: Robert Adkinson
Art Editor: Roger Daniels
Designers: Gillian Allan, Peter Laws, Linda Nash
Editorial Assistant: Corinne Molesworth
Picture Research: Annette Brown

Phototypeset in England by
Filmtype Services Limited, Scarborough

Colour illustrations originated in Italy by
Starf Photolitho SRL, Rome

Printed in Hong Kong by
Leefung-Asco Printers Limited

Endpapers
Decorative details on the façade of the church of the
Sagrada Familia, Barcelona, by Antoni Gaudí.

Frontispiece
Bronze bust by Alphonse Mucha, *c.* 1900.

Contents

Introduction

THE LAST TEN YEARS have witnessed a strong awakening of interest in the decorative arts of the period 1890–1940, as a result of which there has been a flood of books and articles on aspects of the period. There has been a confusing proliferation of reference works on specific topics; confusing, because it detracts from the appreciation of the overall picture and the fluidity of design history, the often subtle phases of transition from one style to another; confusing, also, because of the inability of certain authors to agree on points of terminology – one author's Modernism can easily become another's Art Deco.

The aim of this encyclopedia has been to cover the whole period in detail from the dual viewpoints of style and theory and of actual production. The introductory chapters, through both their text and illustrations, should establish distinctly the predominant styles and trends around which evolved the detailed history of the period. It has been particularly satisfying to see, at last, Art Deco identified and isolated as the exotic and elusive style it was, a peculiarly French swansong to femininity, luxury and refinement before the onslaught of the international Modernist style.

It has also proved interesting, in discussing certain schools or theorists or designers, to realise how the pen can prove mightier than the craftsman's tasks and the artifacts can fall short of their theoretical ideals. In German design, for instance, the history of design school theory and administration has proved often more relevant to the history of decorative art than the artifacts themselves.

Perhaps the most valid driving force behind the encyclopedia, however, has been the enthusiasm for the period felt by all those involved in its production, an enthusiasm which hopefully this work will help to communicate.

PHILIPPE GARNER

PART ONE

STYLES
AND
INFLUENCES
IN THE
DECORATIVE
ARTS

1890-1940

Art Nouveau *by Roger-Henri Guerrand*

The birth of a modern style

THE STYLE IN THE decorative arts which eventually came to be known as Art Nouveau was made possible by a number of outstanding writers on aesthetics during the nineteenth century, notably John Ruskin and William Morris in Britain, and Léon de Laborde and Eugène-Emmanuel Viollet-le-Duc in France. What these writers had in common was a rejection of the crass materialism which had reached its apogee in many of the exhibits at the Great Exhibition held in London in 1851. The long-forgotten truth that art should be in harmony with·the age which produces it was rediscovered around 1850 by these men whose love of the past was, nevertheless, beyond dispute.

In the field of aesthetics Ruskin especially was responsible for numerous advances. He rejected the fine distinction between the so-called major and minor arts; interior decoration, therefore, which had formerly been entirely in the hands of artisans, now took on the dimensions of a major social and artistic mission to be accomplished. According to Ruskin, the decorative arts should once again assume the central position in artistic concern they had occupied at the time of the Renaissance. Lecturing at Bradford in 1859, he reminded his audience that Correggio's finest work is to be found in the domes of two churches he decorated in Padua, that Michelangelo's mas-

Portrait of John Ruskin by T. B. Wirgman.

terpiece is the decorated ceiling of the Pope's private chapel, that Tintoretto decorated the ceiling and walls of a benevolent society in Venice.

It was also Ruskin who called on architects to draw their inspiration from the lessons taught by nature, a concept which was to be central to movements in the decorative arts at the end of the nineteenth century. The ambition to translate the secret truths of nature in architecture and interior design can be seen in the works of Horta in Brussels, of Guimard in Paris and of Gaudí in Barcelona.

At the first international industrial exhibition of modern times, the Great Exhibition of 1851 held in London, there were 1,756 French participants, many of whom gained awards. This success delighted French officialdom, with the exception of Count Léon de Laborde, who had been in charge of organising French participation in the exhibition. In his report on the exhibition, published in 1856, he made a number of criticisms which show him to have been one of the most perceptive men of his time and one of the prophets of future developments in the decorative arts.

Léon de Laborde was an eminent archaeologist, a member of the Institut and director of the Archives Nationales during the Second Empire. He had travelled widely and studied the great monuments of antiquity. Unlike some of his contemporaries, however, he did not make a cult of the past and roundly criticized artists who killed art by making a fetish of copying the masterpieces of past ages. At the beginning of his report on the Great Exhibition he made the following revolutionary statement: 'The future of the Arts, of the Sciences and of Industry lies in their association'. According to Laborde, artists should concern themselves much more with the settings and surroundings of everyday life; we should be able to attend concerts or plays in auditoriums decorated by Ingres or Delacroix. In the creation of fine architecture, fine streets and the organisation of performances and manifestations, the government would introduce town dwellers to the beauties of nature.

The report of Count de Laborde was not unfamiliar to those who supported the idea of an artistic revolution in which the state would play an important role. The Belgian workers party, for instance, included the promotion of art in its programme at the end of the nineteenth century, and its leader Emile Vandervelde, regularly attended the social gatherings given by the daughter of William Morris. In Brussels Victor Horta constructed the first 'cathedral of socialism' in the form of the new Maison du Peuple. Laborde

Parisian silverwork exhibited at
the 1851 Great Exhibition.

Above French bronze
vide-poche, c. 1900.

Right Silver and cast glass
pendant-brooch by René
Lalique, *c.* 1900.

would have appreciated this incarnation of his dreams which was so far removed from the Neo-classical monuments so much favoured during his lifetime.

Only the restoration work carried out by Viollet-le-Duc and his writings on Gothic art have been the subject of serious study hitherto. Little remains to be said about the way he was virtually possessed by the Gothic style. His discussions of the nature of architecture are, however, amazingly clear-sighted. His *Entretiens sur l'Architecture* appeared between 1863 and 1872 and were translated into English between 1877 and 1881. They were to become key works for all those who wished a change in the accepted attitude to architecture and the decorative arts in the nineteenth century. 'It is barbarous,' he suggested, 'to reproduce a Greek temple in Paris or London, for a transplanted imitation of this monument reveals an ignorance of the basic principles governing its construction, and ignorance is barbarism.'

On the subject of interior decoration, Viollet-le-Duc, who was to teach for several years in the Ecole des Arts Décoratifs in Paris, professed exactly the same ideas as Ruskin and Laborde: 'Interior decoration', he wrote, 'has lost any semblance of unity. The architect never gives a

Gilt and silver-bronze
statuette by E. Barrias, 'La
Nature se dévoilant devant
La Science', 1890s.

DE LA COUR DU CHATEAU DE CHARLEVAL

Above Illustration from Viollet-le-Duc's *Entretiens sur l'Architecture,* 1863–72.

Above right German advertisement for Samuel Bing's Maison de l'Art Nouveau, 1895.

Right Vaulted hall from Viollet-le-Duc's *Entretiens sur l'Architecture.*

second thought to what sort of paintings are to decorate the rooms he has designed, the painter never takes into consideration the architecture of the rooms where he hangs his works, the furniture-maker completely ignores what both the painter and the architect have done, and the man who supplies the curtains takes great pains to ensure that his products are all that you notice in a room.'

The twenty *Entretiens sur l'Architecture* run to about a thousand pages in which Viollet-le-Duc reveals an extensive knowledge of the architecture of the past, while offering countless new ideas. He did not, however, succeed in shaking the faith of his established colleagues who, for many more years, continued to copy the methods of past architecture and persisted in their attempt to dress up modern building programmes in classical forms.

Thanks to Ruskin, Laborde and Viollet-le-Duc, however, the artistic expression of life in the nineteenth century was soon to appear in the social landscape. Through their writings they had a determining influence on the formation of the new modern style for which they had so passionately pleaded. Although they often contradicted themselves they had the great merit of trying to resolve the dichotomy between Art and Industry, which

Above left Hotel Solvay in Brussels by Victor Horta, 1894–8.

Above centre Antoni Gaudí, Barcelona, Casa Milá, 1905–7.

Left Antoni Gaudí, Barcelona, detail of window, Casa Milá, 1905–7.

Above right Paris Métro, Victor Hugo, by Hector Guimard, 1900.

Right Paris Métro, Bois de Boulogne, by Hector Guimard, 1900.

Printed fabric designed by
Alphonse Mucha, *c.* 1900.

was the major problem of their age.

Samuel Bing, the well-known expert on Far-Eastern Art, did not invent the expression 'Art Nouveau' when he chose it as the name of the shop he opened, at the end of December 1895, in the Rue de Provence in Paris. The term had already been coined by the Belgian lawyers, Octave Maus and Edmond Picard, who created the review *L'Art Moderne* in 1881.

As early as 1884 these two men proclaimed themselves 'believers in Art Nouveau,' an art which refused to accept the prevailing cult of the past. At first they attached the label to the works of painters who rejected academicism. The more specialised use of the term, for architecture and art objects, was only to come later when the painters were given various other labels. At the same time different countries were quick to create their own specific version of the term: Jugendstil, Sezessionstill, Modern Style, Arte Joven, Nieuwe Kunst, Style Liberty.

These movements have a number of common features which can be grouped under four major headings or aspirations.

First of all, there was a total rejection of the academic traditions which dominated teaching in art schools throughout the whole of the nineteenth century. For anyone wishing to create 'Art Nouveau' the cult of classical antiquity was a thing of the past and only to be found in the work of careerists. The Parisian Métro is a perfect illustration of this point. Jules Formigé, who built the overhead lines in a neo-doric style was covered with honours and made a member of the Institut, while Hector Guimard, who created a distinctive organic style for the stations, suffered the misfortune of seeing his work defaced – something which has continued to the present day – and being considered unworthy of mention in reference books for many years to come.

The rejection of antiquity went hand in hand with a return to the observation and imitation of nature. This was the advice given by Horta to Guimard when the latter came to visit him in Brussels. It was also one of the principles governing Gaudí's architecture, Morris's wallpapers, and Gallé's vases. It meant that the straight line was abandoned in favour of the curve and that there was a considerable vogue for Gothic or Japanese forms. These innovations were soon to become new conventions for second-rate artists.

Finally, many of the designers and architects of 1900 wished to take part in the movement for social reform and to join in the struggle of the European working class. Jean Lahor, a French disciple of William Morris, became the apostle of cheap housing, the creation of which would have kept Art Nouveau artists more than busy. Some of these men actually became members of socialist parties while others professed their sympathy to the socialist cause.

Thus it seemed possible that a form of art in keeping with a democratic society might now emerge, transforming the streets, the décor of the home, and everyday objects. Perhaps the wish expressed by Viollet-le-Duc could now come true: 'It is only possible for the Arts to find their true place, to develop and to progress in the living heart of the nation...'

Left Necklace in gold and pearls by Edward Colonna for Samuel Bing, *c.* 1900.

Below left Tiffany peacock lamp, *c.* 1900; Tiffany glass and lamps were promoted in Europe by Samuel Bing in his Rue de Provence shop in Paris.

Art Deco *by Martin Battersby*

The triumph of 1925

THE INTERNATIONAL EXHIBITION of Decorative and Industrial Arts held in Paris during the summer of 1925 was the occasion for a number of publications by leading French art critics and historians dealing with various aspects of contemporary applied arts. From these it is possible to trace the emergence and development of the style known today as 'Art Deco', a name bestowed as a result of the exhibition held at the Musée des Arts Décoratifs in 1966 entitled 'Les Années 1925'. The style was not so named during its existence when it was referred to as 'moderne' or 'contemporain' for, as is usually the case, a definitive name was applied only long after in retrospect.

Enamelled glass flask with stopper by Delvaux, *c.* 1920.

The general consensus among these writers, Gabriel Mourey, Gaston Quénioux, Emile Bayard and Emile Sedeyn and others was that Art Nouveau became 'une fantaisie passagère, tôt démodée, vouée au bienfaisant oubli' as early as 1901 when, due to the inevitable commercialisation and consequent decline in artistic standards following the 1900 Exhibition, the style was abruptly dropped by both the influential patrons and the majority of artists and craftsmen who had championed its cause with such energy a few years before.

While this categorical statement was in the main true, Art Nouveau lingered on in favour for some years with those not in the inner circles of taste-makers. A number of buildings in Paris, some dated as late as 1913, show typical Art Nouveau motifs incorporating whiplash curves and floral motifs, and Louis Majorelle continued creating designs for furniture with elaborate decorations of carving and gilt-bronze appliques on themes of waterlilies and orchids which have been dated well after 1901. There is justification however for the contemporary comment that between 1901 and 1910 there was little or no original work produced and that for the most part decorative artists were working 'dans l'ombre'.

Art Nouveau had exerted a liberating influence in freeing design from the historicism which had debased so much of nineteenth-century creative activity, but the fact of its having no links with the past (the occasional references to Louis-Quinze and Louis-Seize styles can be discounted) proved to be a disadvantage. Art Nouveau could only be seen at its best in a complete ensemble, something only a limited number of patrons desired or could afford. Single pieces did not harmonise with furniture of previous periods in the way that, for instance, those of the eighteenth century did, even if in different styles. It is difficult to see how Art Nouveau could have developed logically with the passage of time as the works of past epochs had done, for the alternatives were either greater eccentricity or a simplicity which would have destroyed its essence.

This lack of a natural development, combined with its abandonment by artists and patrons alike, left many wary of novelty and, to the pleasure and profit of antique dealers and the many manufacturers of reproduction eighteenth-century furniture who had been bitter opponents of Art Nouveau from the start, the trend in interior decoration turned to versions of Louis-Quinze and Louis-Seize styles which, if lacking in originality, were pleasing and guaranteed not to become

Lalique glass figure,
'Suzanne au bain', *c.* 1925.

Centre Bronze hand
mirror by René Lalique,
c. 1915.

Below Lithograph by Jean
Dupas for *Toi*, an
advertisement for Fourrures
Max, *c.* 1925.

unfashionable overnight – a serious matter in taste-conscious Paris. During this period, when design seemed almost to lie fallow, a number of critics advocated a return to the principles of the last period of French design, that of about 1820, when there had been a logical development of taste before the growing mass-production had combined with showy pastiches of past historical styles to atrophy original inspiration. The dangers of slavish imitation were recognised and what was advocated was a development of 1820 styles as though the intervening years had not existed, at the same time recognising and adapting the technical improvements of the last eighty years.

A complaint often voiced in the previous two decades had been of the lack of co-operation between designers and manufacturers. Even more serious were the lamentably low standards of tuition in the decorative arts in technical schools. Equal concern was expressed at the vast quantities of low-priced German imports such as lighting fixtures from Nuremberg, furnishing fabrics from Gladbach and Leipzig and furniture from Darmstadt and Munich. These imports seriously threatened French manufacturers and imperilled the vaunted supremacy of Paris as the arbiter of taste. This influx of German goods had started even before the founding in 1907 of the Munich Deutscher Werkbund, with its aim of bringing together artists, craftsmen and manufacturers for the production of well-designed and inexpensive products for the home market and for export to other countries.

This purpose had been spelled out in the introduction to the catalogue for the Munich Werkbund Exhibition of 1909 in Brussels. In the hope that similar collaboration could result from the German example and that French designers and manufacturers could profit to their mutual advantage, an invitation was extended to the Munich Werkbund to exhibit in Paris at the 1910 Salon d'Automne. An important element in the creation of Art Deco was the result of this exhibition.

French critics were at best lukewarm in their comments on the rooms and objects displayed. Cultured Parisian taste, chauvinistic to the last, had never found much to admire in German design and not without reason. In this case, the verdict on the furniture was that it lacked elegance and was too obviously derived from the more cumbersome types of Biedermeier – itself a style flourishing about 1820 – while the colour schemes were found to be garish. However, the more observant visitors were impressed by a general unity of concept, a sincerity of purpose and the benefits of a collaboration between the artist and the manufacturer. The influential writer Gabriel Mourey commented that the greatest merit of German decorative art was that it was 'profoundly and congenitally German', and from it the lesson could be drawn that it was the duty of French decorative art to be as French as possible and that nothing should be neglected in accentuating this quality. In other words, the qualities of craftsmanship, elegance and originality which had characterised the best of the eighteenth-century work should be renewed.

The lesson of co-operation was quickly learned

and, as a result of this exhibition, several large Parisian department stores opened specialised departments under the direction of established designers for the sale of contemporary furniture, textiles and artifacts manufactured in quantity, but stamped by the personal taste of the designer and his collaborators. These shops within shops were important in introducing Art Deco to a much wider public.

Paradoxically, it was yet another foreign influence – and the most important – which crystallised the Frenchness of Art Deco. Again to quote Gabriel Mourey, 'there is no doubt that the influence of the Ballets Russes not only in the arts of the theatre but the arts of the book, textiles, in fact on all the decorative arts, appeared as dominating as that of Japanese art in former years'.

Paris had little or no knowledge of Russian decorative art of any period before the arrival of Serge Diaghilev and his compatriots in 1909. Since the early years of the eighteenth century the traffic had been in the opposite direction with French architects, sculptors and painters being sought after by Russian royalty and aristocracy and with news of the latest Parisian fashions being eagerly awaited in the Russian capital. The impact therefore of the Ballets Russes was all the greater on an audience knowing little or nothing of contemporary artistic trends in Russia. The greatest sensation was caused by the ballets on Oriental themes and the premières of *Schéhérazade* and *Thamar* caused a furore with their blending of unfamiliar music, exciting choreography and the performances of inspired dancers interpreting erotic and sadistic tales, so different from the badly danced and insipid ballets to which Parisian audiences were accustomed at the Paris Opera House.

Apart from the genius of the leading dancers, the most significant impact upon the audiences were the designs of Léon Bakst (the more restrained but no less brilliant work of Alexandre

Above Stone sculpture by Joseph Bernard, included in the 1925 Paris Exhibition.

Left André Groult: Chambre de Madame in the Pavillon d'un Ambassadeur at the 1925 Paris Exhibition.

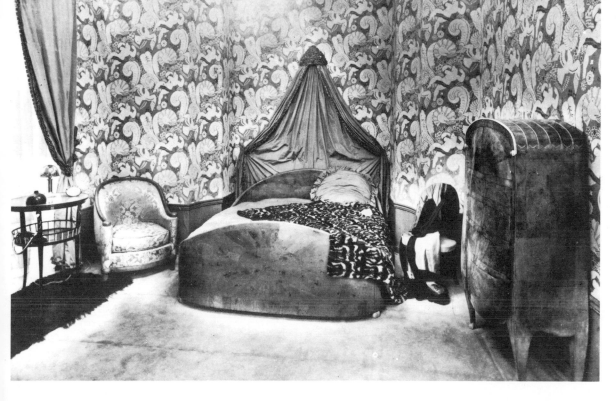

Below Walnut *chiffonnier* by Süe et Mare, made in 1923 and exhibited in the Rotonde du Pavillon de la Compagnie des Arts Français at the Paris 1925 Exhibition.

Right Marquetry panel designed for the Compagnie Internationale des Wagons-Lits, 1920s.

Benois tended to be overshadowed) and overnight the pale subdued tones – 'la chanson grise' – which were a legacy of Art Nouveau were swept away by a dazzling spectrum of jewel colours, vermilion, violet, citron, crimson, orange, emerald and ultramarine enhanced by a liberal use of gold and silver. Equally exciting were the combinations of clashing colours, red with orange, blue with green or violet with yellow, all considered vulgar and unused since the heyday of the Second Empire. Bakst's interpretations of a legendary Orient opened exciting prospects for artists and designers.

In 1910 Paul Poiret was at the outset of a brilliant though chequered career as a couturier, decorator and patron of the arts. Two years previously he had revolutionised fashion and fashion illustration with his production in a limited edition of *Les Robes de Paul Poiret* illustrated by drawings by the young Paul Iribe in which an Oriental influence can be seen. This was intensified in the volume presented by Poiret in 1911 which had even more spectacular illustrations by Georges Lepape. The new craze which swept Paris for all things Persian and reminiscent of the Arabian Nights Entertainments exactly coincided with Poiret's own tastes. In a ceaseless search for new ideas, Poiret toured Germany and

Austria visiting art schools, exhibitions, theatres and studios and meeting the leading figures in avant-garde circles. At the Wiener Werkstätte he met Josef Hoffmann, Bruno Paul, Gustav Klimt, he exchanged ideas with Max Reinhardt and his company of actors and designers and was welcomed by Prince Eitel, the cultured and informed third son of the German Kaiser.

He found much to admire and emulate, and returned from his travels replete with ideas to be transmuted into French terms. Impressed by the high standards and the results of the training in German and Austrian art schools and technical colleges, he nevertheless deplored the somewhat pedantic approach to teaching and in 1911 put his own ideas into practice by founding the Atelier Martine where the pupils, completely untrained young girls, were encouraged to express their individuality in designs for textiles, wallpapers and furniture. Their lack of technical knowledge was made up for by skilled overseers who translated their designs into practical terms, carefully preserving the original concept. In addition, he encouraged the young and still unsuccessful painter Raoul Dufy to embark on textile design as a result of seeing his woodcut illustrations for *Le Bestiaire* of Guillaume Apollinaire with the happy

Above left Printed fabric border by André Mare, *c.* 1920.

Above Fabric by Edouard Benedictus, *c.* 1928.

result that Dufy created some of the most beautiful printed fabrics of this century, first for Poiret and later for the firm of Bianchini-Férier.

A similar use of untrained talent was made in the studio organised in Paris by François Ducharne in 1922, under the leadership of the brilliant designer Michel Dubost. Some thirty young boys and girls were maintained to produce sketches and ideas and again their freshness and spontaneity were considered to benefit from not being hampered by the technical needs of the actual processes of silk weaving, and technicians in Lyons adapted their ideas with successful results.

The accent on youth was characteristic of the generation of versatile designers mostly in their early twenties who, through the encouragement and active patronage of Paul Poiret, Lucien Vogel the publisher and others, created Art Deco. In the four years preceding the First World War, Paris was the brilliant centre of European culture at a time of feverish activity. It was as though French society was obeying an instinct to enjoy every aspect of life to the full.

Artists and designers were given opportunities for exercising their versatility which they generally seized with enthusiasm. To take only one example, Paul Iribe revolutionised fashion illustration in his work for Poiret, designed beautiful fabrics, which can still be seen at the Musée des Tissus in Lyons, furniture for the discriminating couturier Jacques Doucet, who had been Poiret's mentor, and even wallpapers and jewellery. His 'rose Iribe' was widely imitated and in its various transformations became a key motif in the ornamental repertoire of Art Deco – a repertoire which drew from the colours of the Ballets Russes, the forms of early nineteenth-century furniture and applied ornament, and which in turn owed a lot to the Viennese designers. All these elements were welded together and transformed by a characteristic French sense of style and elegance.

Iribe's rose, a highly conventionalised version of the bloom, bears a close resemblance to a similar treatment found in the work of Viennese designers. This in turn was derived from the roses of Charles Rennie Mackintosh and his followers of the Glasgow School. Mackintosh had a considerable influence in Austria and Germany in the early years of the century although when exhibited in Paris his work had met with minimal appreciation.

Very different from the slightly morbid and sometimes even sinister blooms of Art Nouveau, the conventionalised Art Deco roses, marguerites, dahlias and zinnias appear as a constant theme, sometimes as an allover design, sometimes in an oval panel (the oval itself being a favourite shape), or in a swag of drapery with ropes of pearls, ribbons, doves, fawns and formalised fountains. The spiral is a recurring motif, especially in ironwork. During the war years Iribe's rose became more than just a decorative motif: it symbolised the spirit of France. In 1930, when Art Deco was no longer fashionable, Iribe mourned the passing of his rose with the words 'for thousands the flower is as necessary as the machine – shall we sacrifice the flower on the altar of cubism and the machine?'

It was in 1911 that the term *ensemblier* appeared and with it the indication that a new factor in

Above right Cabinet in macassar ebony and inlaid ivory by Emile-Jacques Ruhlmann, 1919.

Right Interior by Primavera, *c.* 1920.

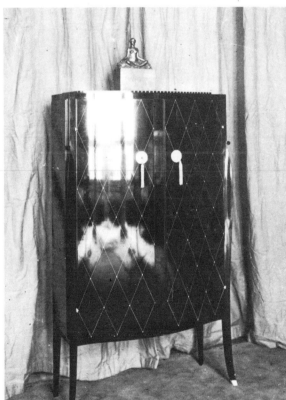

Above left Commemorative silver medallion for the Paris 1925 Exhibition by P. Turin.

Above Metal-mounted, decorated pottery vase, marked 'd'Argyl', *c.* 1925.

Far left Cabinet in macassar ebony by Emile-Jacques Ruhlmann, early 1920s.

Left Wrought-iron mirror frame by Edgar Brandt, *c.* 1925.

Below Silvered bronze clock designed by Paul Follot for Pomone at the Bon Marché, *c.* 1925.

La Soie, Boulogne glazed pottery figure by Marcel Renard, exhibited at the Paris 1925 Exhibition.

interior decoration had emerged, to have a definite effect on designers and patrons alike. For the greater part of the nineteenth century fashionable styles of furniture and decoration had ceased to develop in a logical and orderly manner. With the coming of the Industrial Revolution, the rise of new social classes and the increasing use of machinery, taste veered to uninspired pastiches, however inappropriate to their function, of the previous centuries. These *ameublements de style* were largely mass-produced and were supplied from firms of *tapissier-décorateurs*. Art Nouveau itself had been a revolt against this obsession with historicism and from it one concept remained: the interior or *ensemble* contemporary in feeling, original in design, with no references to the past and preferably the creation of either a single designer or a group working in close collaboration. It was this lesson that the French designers had to relearn from the example of the Munich Werkbund.

The foremost upholders of this principle were Paul Follot and Maurice Dufrêne. Both had worked in the Art Nouveau manner for Julius Meier-Graefe's La Maison Moderne and both had reacted strongly against Art Nouveau soon after the 1900 Exhibition. Dufrêne was particularly vehement in his condemnation in the introduction to the catalogue of his exhibits at the Salon des Décorateurs in 1906. While both designers sought new idioms of expression, each developed in a different way. Follot's inclination was towards rich surface ornament applied to simple and elegant forms using rare figured veneers, lacquer and gilded carvings. As versatile as any of his contemporaries, he designed wallpapers, metalwork, ceramics and textiles, which formed part of his ensembles, and in 1923 his prolific talents were employed at Pomone, a department at the Bon Marché devoted to his work. Dufrêne on the other hand was less interested in the luxurious aspects of interior decoration, favouring an almost rustic simplicity in much of his work which increasingly showed his interest in the application of industrial techniques to furniture. In 1921 he set up a special shop, La Maîtrise, at the Galeries Lafayette.

The painter André Mare turned his attention to interior decoration in 1910 and, after working with the architect Louis Süe on the decorations to celebrate the end of the war in 1918, they founded the Compagnie des Arts Français, working with Boutet de Monval, the painter, Gustave-Louis Jaulmes, who specialised in tapestry design and mural paintings, Paul Véra, a versatile painter, sculptor and wood engraver, Maurice Marinot, a distinguished glass worker, and André Marty, a graphic artist whose work was much in demand for fashion periodicals such as *La Gazette du Bon Ton*, *Vogue* and *Fémina* among others. This group was concerned less with creating startling and fashionable interiors than with an adherence to traditional values of sobriety and elegance. It dispersed in 1928 when Art Deco had given way to a starker idiom of decoration alien to their ideas.

Léon Jallot had been the director of Bing's Art Nouveau workshops and like many of his contemporaries rebelled against the style when he opened his own studio in 1903 after Bing's death. He was joined by his son Maurice after the war in the creation of furniture characterised by simplicity of line enlivened by rich surface textures of veneers and lacquer.

Undoubtedly the most celebrated of the designers working along traditional lines was Emile-Jacques Ruhlmann, who first won attention in 1913 and soon became known for the luxurious elegance and exquisite craftsmanship of his furniture which could compare with that of the greatest *ébenistes* of the eighteenth century. Fortunate in very soon acquiring an extremely rich clientèle to appreciate the magnificent quality of his work, he produced until his death in 1933 furniture restrained in shape and veneered in exotic and rare woods, enhanced by delicate inlays of ivory combined with shagreen and tooled leather. Designed in collaboration with other craftsmen of the first rank, Edgar Brandt, Jean Dunand, René Lalique and Stephany, the Hôtel d'un Collectionneur Ruhlmann created for the 1925 Exhibition proved the most notable representative of the best of contemporary French decorative art.

The outbreak of war in 1914 did not necessarily mean a complete stoppage of artistic activity in Paris, but shortages of materials and labour diminished production considerably. But despite the continuing shortages after the end of the war, the major concern was to reassert the position of Paris and French craftsmanship in every field of decorative art, now that the threat of German competition had been removed. Apart from being a matter of national pride, the export of French luxury goods brought into the country extremely large amounts of money and was a mainstay of the economy. With little or no competition, France was in a position to dictate to the rest of the world and to supply luxury and style for which there was an increasing demand after the grim war years. Paris was a magnet for the rich and pleasure-seeking from every continent who flocked to buy from the great French design houses.

There was no immediate change of direction as far as the decorative arts were concerned. On demobilisation some artists resumed where they had left off in 1914; for those who had not been involved in the war it had been a period of marking time. Two significant art movements now arose: Dada in Switzerland and De Stijl in Holland, but in 1919 they were little known in Paris beyond a limited circle and no one could foresee that they were to contribute to the counter movement which would sweep away Art Deco. In the meantime, the creative artists who had made their mark before the war still ruled as arbiters of taste, notably Paul Poiret whose elaborate styles typified the fashions of the first five years of the 1920s. Once again, the Ballets Russes appeared to renew the excitements of prewar seasons, reviving the repertoire which had made such an impression and adding new productions designed principally by French painters.

Immediately after the war new names appeared in the art journals – names of designers trained before the war and now qualified to satisfy in their individual manner the growing demands, such as the two metalworkers, Raymond Subes and Edgar Brandt, the latter working to the designs of his partner Louis Favart and making major contributions to the 1925 Exhibition.

In 1920 the highly individual worker in metal and lacquer, Armand-Albert Rateau opened his own studio and during the next ten years produced a body of work for illustrious clients which was inspired by the patinated bronzes of Pompeii and the Near Eastern countries. In 1922 Jules Leleu followed suit, specialising in furniture entirely veneered in blond shagreen ornamented with a version of the Iribe rose. In the same year André Domin and Marcel Genevrière combined to open the firm of Dominique and René Joubert and Philippe Petit opened D.I.M. (Décoration Intérieure Moderne).

The majority of illustrations of interiors of this period were not of actual houses but of the temporary installations at the annual Salons des Artistes-Décorateurs and the Salons d'Automne where, in addition to the work of the *ensembliers,* that of specialised designers and craftsmen was exhibited. Ceramics by René Buthaud, Emile Decoeur, Raoul Lachenal and Emile Lenoble, metalwork by Luc Lanel for the firm of Christofle, Raymond Subes and Paul Kiss, glass by Gabriel Argy-Rousseau, Maurice Marinot, François Décorchemont, Marcel Goupy, Jean Luce and the firms of Daum, Baccarat and, pre-eminently, Lalique, bookbindings by Rose Adler, Paul Bonet and Pierre Legrain – also a creator of individual pieces of furniture – textiles and carpets by Eric Bagge, Sonia Delaunay, and Hélène Henry and jewellery by Cartier, Boucheron, Lacloche, Jean and Georges Bastard. Many more could be cited to witness the galaxy of original talent working in the Art Deco style, the apotheosis of which was the 1925 Exhibition. It was also its swan song – a curious parallel with the demise of Art Nouveau soon after the 1900 Exhibition.

The element of change was an essential factor in the structure of fashion in Paris. Just as women's fashions changed from season to season so did the fashions in interior decoration, but necessarily at a slower tempo: elegant women could change their clothes more rapidly than their surroundings. Two new enthusiasms, Cubism and Negro Art, were important factors in the decline of Art Deco. The former had been the subject of experiment before the war in a very limited circle of painters, but in the early twenties began to acquire a certain chic not unconnected with the new craze for jazz music which had been introduced into France in 1919. Negro art had been known and admired by a number of artists before the war, but they were mostly unrecognised at the time and it took the 1922 exhibition of art from the French colonies to awaken a wider interest in a form of expression totally alien to the refined elegance of Art Deco. But the latter had been in vogue for a number of years, while the new angular forms had the attraction of novelty. Other factors rendered Art Deco unfashionable after 1925: women's clothes became simpler as they began to take a more active role in life and indulged in sports of which they had previously been spectators; machines and especially automobiles came to symbolise the new doctrines of functionalism, and the new and revolutionary steel furniture began to appear from the Bauhaus. The elegance of Art Deco with its gracious curves and pretty ornaments of flowers and garlands was replaced by the hard chic of steel and angular and unadorned surfaces.

Modernism *by Gillian Naylor*

An international style

FOR THE PURPOSES of this survey, the roots of Modernism must be located in the nineteenth-century consolidation and questioning of Enlightenment attitudes. For the ideal of progress, the cult of individualism, the celebration of nature, and the challenge of science and technology, which all contribute, to a greater or lesser degree, to nineteenth-century theories of design, are protean and ambiguous concepts, their impact and interpretation varied from country to country, and from generation to generation; their acceptance or rejection depended on social, political and philosophical developments.

Several generalisations, however, can be made about nineteenth-century attitudes which are relevant to the emerging concept of 'modernity'; for the major theorists of the nineteenth century were concerned, above all, with the problem of 'style', and in their investigations and recommendations certain themes or obsessions emerge that were to be developed and, in some cases, transformed by their twentieth-century successors. On the most simplistic level, the preoccupation with a new focus for commitment was prompted by the rejection, or reinterpretation of the classical canons of form and beauty; and this assault on classicism, or more specifically, on the rule of the academies, was conducted on various fronts.

A growing sense of nationalism had contributed to the re-interpretation and celebration of the Gothic, and Gothic, the native style of Northern Europe, was promoted on both moral and rational grounds (most typically by Ruskin in England and Viollet-le-Duc in France – Ruskin celebrating its humanistic virtues, while Viollet-le-Duc demonstrated the style's allegiance to the laws of structural necessity). And at the same time, Darwin's evolutionary theories, reinforced by botanists' and biologists' investigations into the determinants for organic growth and form, prompted similar investigations into the nature and development of style. Style, which obviously varied according to country and culture, could now be seen to be determined by the nature and availability of materials and techniques, as well as by social and symbolic needs.

Two conflicting ideologies emerged from this concentration on objective analysis, as well as on social and symbolic priorities. For while the 'scientific attitude' led to demands for a new architecture to meet the needs of a new age, the growing dissatisfaction with the materialism of the nineteenth century led to that nostalgia for the past and celebration of the vernacular associated with the British Arts and Crafts Movement's ideals for design reform.

Following Nikolaus Pevsner's seminal works, most historians of modern design locate the initial impulse for reform in the theory and practice of British designers in the nineteenth century. For their crusade in the cause of craftsmanship established an ideal of commitment which no subsequent generation could ignore. Starting from the premise that man-made forms both reflect and shape society's values, they campaigned for a new humanism in design. This concern for the ethics as well as the aesthetics of design involved first an attempt to revive the philosophies of service, apprenticeship and quality that were associated with the medieval guild system; second, a respect for natural and organic form, and third the conviction that the designer should promote spiritual rather than commercial values. Such ideals, however quixotic, led to a renaissance in British design that was admired and imitated throughout Europe. The various 'secessions' in Europe looked to Britain for a lead in both the theory and practice of design reform.

The British approach to design tended to be emotional and empirical, while Continental designers were heirs to a more rigorously intellectual tradition. Both Viollet-le-Duc and Semper, whose books formed the corner-stone of Continental theory, were analytical and objective in their assessments of the nature of design. Their observations were based on attempts to define the laws of structure and the nature of materials, and their definitions of design were related to scientific rather than spiritual 'truths'. Designers attempting to forge a 'modern' style at the turn of the century inherited, then, a complex set of values from their nineteenth-century predecessors – values that were reflected in the ambiguous achievements of Art Nouveau. For in their search for new and symbolic forms of expression, Art Nouveau architects, while remaining faithful to the spirit of Viollet-le-Duc, demonstrated revolutionary concepts of space, form and structure; and the designers, drawing inspiration from nature, from the discovery, or re-discovery of earlier or alien cultures as well as from their determination to demonstrate craftsmanship as an art, achieved the now familiar transformation and fusion of form and decoration. At the same time, however, the majority of the designers and architects associated with Art Nouveau acknowledged social as well as aesthetic priorities. Their campaign was for beauty in the service of humanity, so that the cost, and inevitable élitism of the style had either to be justified or avoided.

Several strategies were evolved in order to overcome the problem. In France, for example,

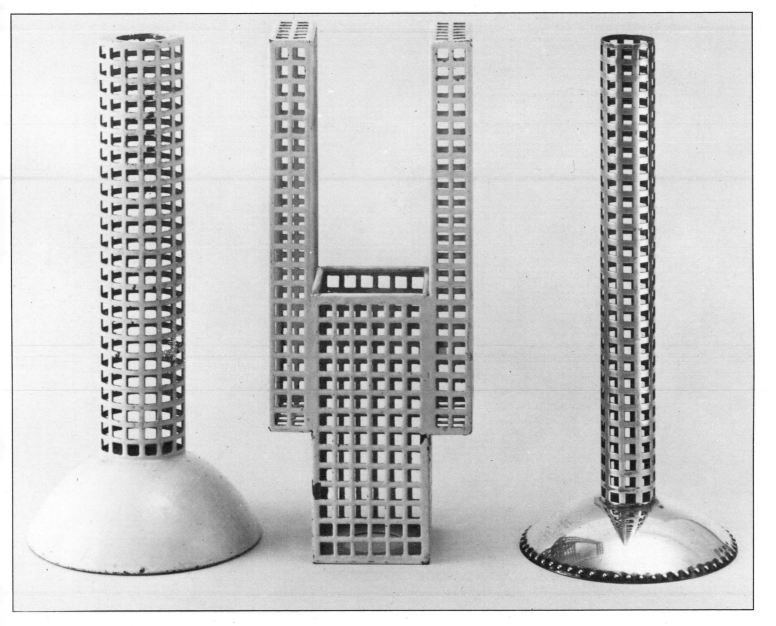

Metal baskets designed by
Josef Hoffmann *c.* 1905,
which strongly anticipate
the stylistic preoccupations
of the Modernist designers
of the twenties and thirties.

Hector Guimard had demonstrated in his designs for the Métro stations how individuality of form and expression could be reconciled with mass-production techniques. In Austria Otto Wagner, who had been appointed head of the School of Architecture in the Vienna Academy of Fine Art as well as artistic adviser to the Viennese Transport Commission in 1894, was involved with similar problems. Wagner, however, believed that 'modern' problems required 'modern' solutions, and his inaugural address to the academy (*Moderne Architektur*, 1895) was based on this theme. 'All modern forms', he stated, 'must reflect the new materials and the new requirements of our time: if they are to meet the needs of modern man, they must express our improved, democratic, clear-thinking selves. . . .'

Wagner was, of course, the *éminence grise* of the Vienna Secession movement, and the Wiener Werkstätte (1903), whose founder members included his pupil Josef Hoffmann, was the most prestigious of the various guilds, societies and artists' collaboratives that were set up throughout Europe at the turn of the century.

The majority of these were inspired by British Arts and Crafts precedents, and the Wiener Werkstätte was originally modelled on C. R. Ashbee's Guild of Handicraft (1888). Hoffmann, however, did not share the Arts and Crafts anxiety about designing for an élite. From the outset the workshops served a rich, sophisticated and cosmopolitan clientèle, producing furniture, fabrics, metalware and ceramics in forms and patterns that anticipate the stylistic preoccupations of the 1920s and 1930s.

Similar workshops had been established in Germany during the 1880s and 1890s; their subsequent development, however, was very different from that of their Viennese counterpart. From the turn of the century, German craft societies, unlike those in Britain, were concerned with the problem of serial, as opposed to craft production. Within a few years of helping to found the Werkstätte in Munich in 1897, for example, Richard Riemerschmid was designing furniture from standardised components (Typenmöbel), and the Deutscher Werkbund (1907), whose founder members included industrialists as well as representatives from the Werkstätte, was established with the specific programme of promoting standards for industrial design.

The establishment of the Werkbund marks a watershed in the history of modern design, for in the bitter debates that surrounded its formation all

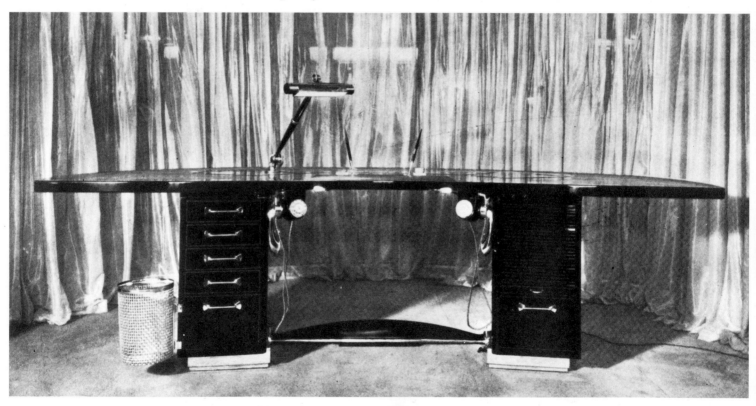

Above Emile-Jacques Ruhlmann: modernist desk, *c.* 1930.

Right Adjustable *chaise longue* with a steel tube frame, designed by Le Corbusier and manufactured by Thonet Brothers, 1928.

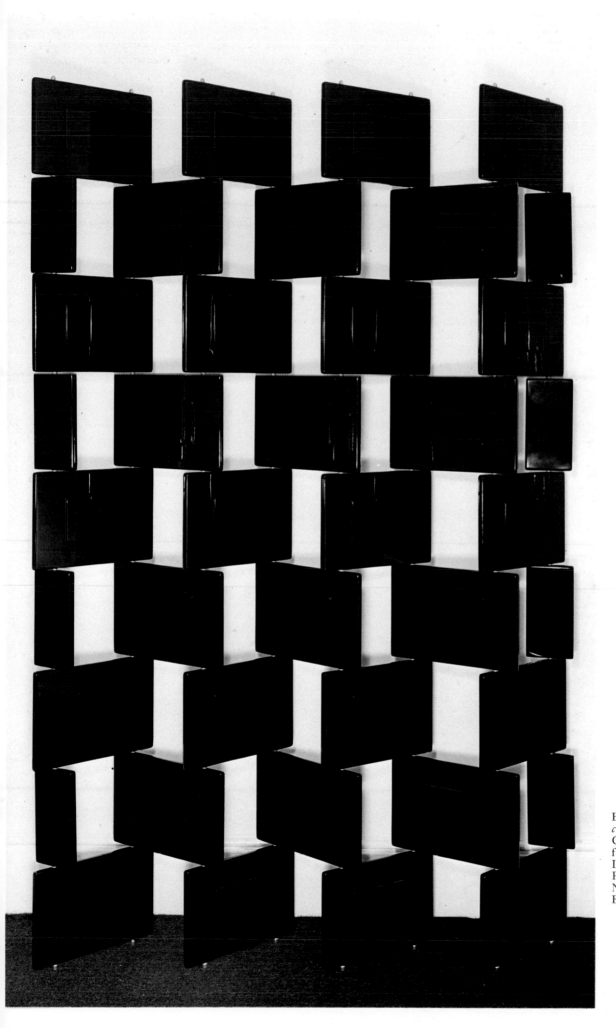

Black lacquer screen,
c. 1924, designed by Eileen
Gray, whose lacquer
furniture was exhibited by
Le Corbusier in the
Pavillon de l'Esprit
Nouveau at the 1925 Paris
Exhibition.

the conflicting ideologies that underlie twentieth-century design theory were either aired or anticipated. The first and most controversial issue involved the need to define the nature and role of the designer: should he continue to consolidate the British tradition and work as an artist and an individualist, or should he dedicate himself to the service of industry, evolving a style and a standard for mass-production? Each point of view had its champion within the organisation, and the issue came to a head in 1914 in the now famous debate between Henry van de Velde and Hermann Muthesius.

By this time, however, Van de Velde seemed to be fighting a rear-guard action, and the practical as well as ideological implications of Muthesius' theories were reflected in design developments throughout Europe. For in the decade leading up to the First World War, European countries were recognising the need to establish or improve standards in industrial design, and it is significant that during this period several organisations with similar aims were established. Austria, for example, set up its Werkbund in 1910, and a Swiss Werkbund was founded in 1913; the Svenska Slöjdföreningen was reorganised along Werkbund lines during the war, and the British Design and Industries Association was founded in 1915.

These organisations were primarily concerned with the practical problems of improving standards for mass production, and each country evolved its own methods and ideals for training designers and proselytizing industry. But the problem of form, or style, remained, and definitions of style were complicated by moral and aesthetic imperatives as well as practical considerations. As Muthesius put it in 1911, in a speech outlining the aims of the Werkbund: 'Higher than purpose, material and technique stands form. The first three aspects [of design] might be impeccably achieved, but if form is

ignored we are still living in a brutish world.' For Muthesius, as for several of his contemporaries at this time, the concept of 'ideal form' had obvious platonic, or classical connotations, and the 'call to order' which followed in the wake of Art Nouveau frequently involved a return to classical forms or a renewed interest in classical canons of order and harmony. At the same time, however, such preoccupations, paradoxically enough, were reinforced by a widespread admiration for what Le Corbusier was to call the 'Engineer's Aesthetic' in *Towards a New Architecture*. For ships, locomotives and aircraft were designed in a 'style' that was both determined by and expressive of function and materials. Modern life was, in fact, according to Le Corbusier, creating 'its own objects: its costume, its fountain pen, its eversharp pencil, its typewriter, its telephone, its admirable office furniture, its plate glass, and its "innovation" trunks, the safety razor and the briar pipe, the bowler hat and the limousine, the steamship and the airplane.'

The conviction that design should be determined by need and function, and at the same time achieve that 'state of platonic grandeur, mathematical order, speculation [and] the perception of the harmony that lies in emotional relationships' was fundamental to Modern Movement theory during the 1920s and 1930s. It was, of course, clearly expressed in Le Corbusier's work during this period, and was also latent in the teaching at the Bauhaus (1919–33). Although Walter Gropius, who assumed the directorship of Van de Velde's Craft School in Weimar in 1918, maintained that the school never sought to achieve or to express a 'style', its work, both at Weimar and Dessau, reflects the school's preoccupation with the formal expression, or interpretation, of a platonic ideal of architecture and design. For, following the post-war 'Expressionist' period, in which materials were used to demonstrate per-

Interior of the Berlin apartment designed by Marcel Breuer in 1927 for Piscator, one of the leading avant-garde theatrical directors of the twenties.

The spread of the
International Style: an
American Modernist
interior, *c.* 1930.

sonal, and in some cases, idiosyncratic ideologies, the school embarked on its now familiar crusade for 'the creation of standard types for all the practical commodities of everyday use'; and its programme produced a 'style', or form-language similar to that achieved by avant-garde designers throughout Europe during this period. For designers from within both the Russian and Dutch Constructivist movements formulated similar ideals and a similar aesthetic. It is significant, however, that the Dutch had no reservations about conducting their campaign under the banner of 'style', or, more specifically 'the style' (De Stijl), defined by Theo van Doesburg, the movement's most active theorist, as 'the universal, collective manner of expression.'

These aspirations towards unity and universality, however, were challenged on various levels during the 1920s and 1930s. From within the Bauhaus itself, Hannes Meyer, the Swiss architect who was appointed as successor to Gropius in 1928, campaigned for a more rigidly functionalist approach to architecture and design, and for the elimination of the 'stylistic' preoccupations of 'inbred theories', which 'closed every approach to right living'. 'Thus my tragi-comic situation arose: as Director of the Bauhaus I fought against the Bauhaus style. I fought constructively through my teaching: Let all life be a striving for oxygen + carbon + sugar + starch + protein. All design, therefore, should be firmly anchored in the world of reality . . .'.

The 'world of reality', however, especially in the post-Freudian era, could never be satisfactorily defined or expressed in terms of economy, efficiency and logic, for as Salvador Dali pointed out: 'The subconscious has a symbolic language that is a truly universal language, for it speaks with the vocabulary of the great vital constants – sexual instincts, feeling of death, physical notions of the enigma of space – those vital constants are echoed in every human being.' And the Surrealist vision, with its subversive questioning and undermining of the contemporary striving for efficiency and competence, re-invested the object with those ambiguous levels of meaning that had been inherent in Art Nouveau design, and in the Utopian ideals formulated by Expressionist architects and designers following the First World War. 'Has the useful ever made us happy?' wrote Bruno Taut in his *Alpine Architecture* (1919), 'Comfort, Convenience, Good Living, Education, knife and fork, railways and water-closets: and then – guns, bombs, instruments for killing! . . . We must

Chaise longue in laminated beech and plywood, designed by Marcel Breuer for the Isokon furniture company of London, 1935.

Left The influence of the Bauhaus: armchair in tubular steel and canvas manufactured *c*. 1931 by PEL (Practical Equipment Ltd.) of London.

Below Bar table in glass and steel from the villa Le Roc at Cannes, designed for the Marquis of Cholmondely, 1934.

always strive for the unattainable if we are to reach the attainable.'

In their striving for the unattainable, however, Expressionist architects and designers demonstrated their ideas in forms that were either crystalline or amorphous, and these 'crystalline' visions were expressed in shapes and suggested structures that are now associated with the Modernist style in decorative design. The use of shiny materials, angular or geometric forms and exaggerated symmetries became stylistic clichés among the 'Modernist' (as opposed to 'modern') designers of the 1920s and 1930s.

The existence of what was felt to be a 'pseudo-modern' style of design first became apparent in the 1925 Exhibition in Paris, which, according to its sponsors, was 'open to all manufacturers whose produce is artistic in character and shows clearly modern tendencies'. These 'clearly modern tendencies', however, could be and were, widely interpreted. For, apart from Corbusier's Pavillon de l'Esprit Nouveau, a number of French exhibits revealed a spurious and superficial 'modernity'.

'It was the ominous Paris Exhibition of 1925 which must be held responsible for the introduction of bad "Modernism" into the trade', wrote Nikolaus Pevsner in his *An Enquiry into Industrial Art in England*, published in 1937. The majority of promoters of 'good' design in the 1920s and 1930s shared Pevsner's conviction that 'Modernism' in its 'jazz forms' had 'spoiled the market for serious modern work.' The assumption that 'nothing of vital energy and beauty can be created unless it be fit for its purpose, clear, straightforward and simple' had, as we have seen, a long pre-history. It was founded on the fallacy of progress, the conviction that man is capable of achieving an ordered and efficient society and that such order and efficiency could be expressed in the forms he created. Such optimism, of course, was to be challenged by twentieth-century realities.

Surrealism and Neo-Baroque *by Martin Battersby*

Reaction to Modernism

THE 1929 EDITION of *Répertoire du Goût Moderne*, an album with coloured drawings of interiors and accessories by Pierre Chareau, Dominique, Guévrékian, André Lurçat, Mallet-Stevens and Louis Sognot, amply demonstrates the full extent of the reaction against Art Deco. The interiors illustrated are devoid of any decoration in the sense the word would have possessed a few years before. The furniture has become angular, with no mouldings or carving, and in many cases incorporates tubular metal elements; paintings and ornaments have been reduced to a minimum and often the only note of relief from the predominating severity is a rug of geometrical design.

This cult of simplicity, so alien to the principles of Art Deco, had been advocated as early as 1920 in the first issue of the avant-garde manifesto *L'Esprit Nouveau*, and was followed in 1921 by Le Corbusier's famous dictum, 'une maison est une machine à habiter'. Functional simplicity and harmony were the aims of the new generation of architects and decorators for whom *L'Esprit Nouveau* was the spokesman. L'Union des Artistes Modernes, an association with Robert Mallet-Stevens, Pierre Chareau, René Herbst and François Jourdain as leading figures, was equally firm in the belief that the interior of the future should be suited to the needs of contemporary life – as they imagined it to be – with no concession to unnecessary ornament to distract from functionalism. The tubular steel furniture originating from the Bauhaus designs of Marcel Breuer had its imitators in France even before the exhibition of work from the Bauhaus at the Salon des Artistes-Décorateurs in 1930, some French writers even claiming the concept as being French.

The machine, particularly that type of machine giving an impression of pent-up power and speed, had a fascination for many designers and they expressed this preoccupation in abstract geometrical terms with straight lines or circles arranged in interlocking patterns. The desire to dissociate their work from any trace of traditional design is obvious.

This new idiom of decoration with its emphasis on plain unadorned surfaces, sombre or neutral colours relieved only by the use of mirrors or the sharp glitter of chromium plate, undoubtedly by reason of its novelty had its followers in both France and England. For one thing, this modernistic effect could be obtained relatively inexpensively, which was an important consideration in the early 1930s when the effects of the depression following the Wall Street crash of 1929 made economy a necessity. It was in harmony with the

current fashions dictated by Parisian couturiers with their emphasis on elongation and the use of the bias cut in the new long skirts, mandatory for both day and evening wear.

Yet the financial stringencies which made this simplicity a fashion also meant that Modernism was comparatively little used in private houses and was mainly to be found in public buildings such as hotels, showrooms and restaurants. Also, just as there had been those resistant to the attractions of Art Nouveau and Art Deco, so there were many who found Modernism without charm.

Although Baroque painters had to wait until after the war to receive academic approval on a large scale, the architecture and sculpture began to find adherents about 1930. As far back as 1909 the Ballets Russes had presented *Le Pavillon d'Armide* with Louis-Quatorze décor and costumes by Alexandre Benois on their first appearance in Paris, but the more exotic Oriental fantasies of Léon Bakst had overshadowed this production. The brilliant revival of *La Belle au Bois Dormant* by Diaghilev in 1921, with its masterly designs by Bakst in the most lavish and exuberant Baroque style, had been a short-lived failure, and was only produced in London. However, music lovers were attracted to the Mozart festivals at Salzburg and were exploring the Baroque monasteries and churches in Austria.

This combination of circumstances gave an impetus to the reversal of taste against Modernism – an impetus fostered by the growing number of interior decorators, the majority of whom could no longer be classed as *ensembliers* designing every element in an interior. The new type of decorator was more versed in commercialising his personal taste, choosing antiques and fabrics to form a pleasing décor. As the opportunities for any kind of training in interior decoration were at that time non-existent, decorators were not adept at designing either furniture or decorations and consequently relied upon the use of antiques rather than modern furniture.

The apartment in Paris of Carlos de Bestigui demonstrates the trend away from Modernism to a more decorative treatment incorporating neo-Baroque motifs. In the early 1930s de Bestigui had commissioned Le Corbusier to design an apartment near the Arc de Triomphe in Paris. Consisting of a drawing room, dining room, bedroom and a roof garden, with, of course, a bathroom and kitchen, it was on two floors. Le Corbusier's treatment resulted in plain white walls, large windows from floor to ceiling, and a free-standing spiral staircase connecting the upper and lower

Drawing room in the Paris apartment of Carlos de Bestigui, designed by Le Corbusier, showing the spiral staircase, before 1936.

floors, positioned in the living room.

Figures of blackamoors fashionable in the eighteenth century and revived in the sixties and seventies of the nineteenth century became extremely popular in the 1930s. Christian Bérard ranged them against the blood-red colonnades in the second scene of the 1936 ballet *Symphonie Fantastique*. Beyond the columns could be seen winged sphinxes – another much collected ornament. These were not the Egyptian type but based on eighteenth-century models which were coquettish portraits of contemporary beauties – La Belle Omorphi, mistress of Louis XV, or Camargo the dancer.

Two further theatrical productions reflected this new interest in the Baroque. In 1932 Charles B. Cochran presented the Max Reinhardt production of Offenbach's operetta, renamed *Helen*, with designs by Oliver Messel which owed inspiration to the work of the Bibbienna family. The all-white bedroom – an innovation in theatrical décor – was particularly praised. Max Reinhardt had a strong preference for the Baroque as he demonstrated in his film version of *A Midsummer Night's Dream*, again inspired by the Bibbiennas and Tiepolo and with Surrealist touches in the treatment of the fairy scenes. Incidentally, Hollywood designers also favoured Baroque elements, particularly in décors for musicals, the best example being the spectacular sequence designed by John Harkrider for the film of *The Great Ziegfeld* in 1936.

The second major theatrical production was Rex Whistler's décor for the ballet *The Wise Virgins* in 1940 which confirmed the masterly command of period interpretation, design and draughtsmanship which had already been revealed by his previous graphic work and mural paintings, which incorporated references to the Baroque.

The Surrealist exhibitions held in London and New York in 1936 and in Paris two years later caused a furore of praise and abuse. Surrealism was not a new movement in 1936 – it had its origins, according to some, before the First World War – but the exhibition revealed to an astonished public a large quantity of work previously known only to limited circles. Anyone who attended the opening in London will remember the mingled delight and repulsion forcibly expressed by those present, together with the realisation that there were surreal elements in so much of the artistic creativity of the past. The fantastic dream-like works of William Blake, Hieronymus Bosch, 'Douanier' Rousseau, Arcimboldo, Fuseli and a host of others were claimed as forerunners of the movement.

Furthered by publicity stunts by Salvador Dali, Surrealism was taken up by advertising, photographers, window dressers and interior decorators. In fashion, Elsa Schiaparelli interpreted designs by Dali and Cocteau, creating the much publicised but little-worn hats in the form of a shoe, a hen sitting on a nest and a lamb cutlet with a paper frill. Dali's version of the Venus de Milo as a chest of drawers became a walking suit with *trompe l'oeil* drawer fronts, and for evening wear, a series of short jackets were beautifully embroidered with Surrealist motifs. With the more macabre and hallucinatory aspects removed, Surrealism invaded interior decoration in the shape of Mae

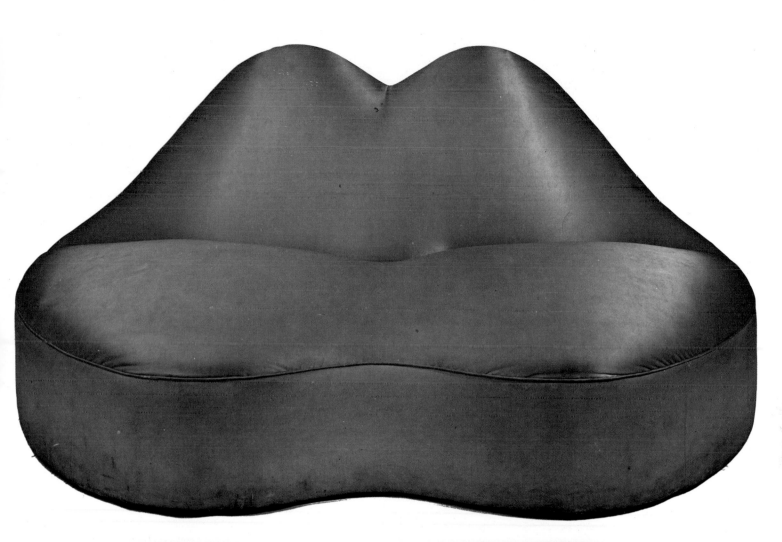

Above Mae West lips sofa by Salvador Dali, 1936.

Left Setting for *The Great Ziegfeld*, 1936.

Far left top Roof garden of Carlos de Bestigui's apartment.

Far left centre Rex Whistler's design for the setting of the ballet *The Wise Virgins*, 1940.

Far left Room setting exhibited at the Surrealist exhibition held in Paris in 1938.

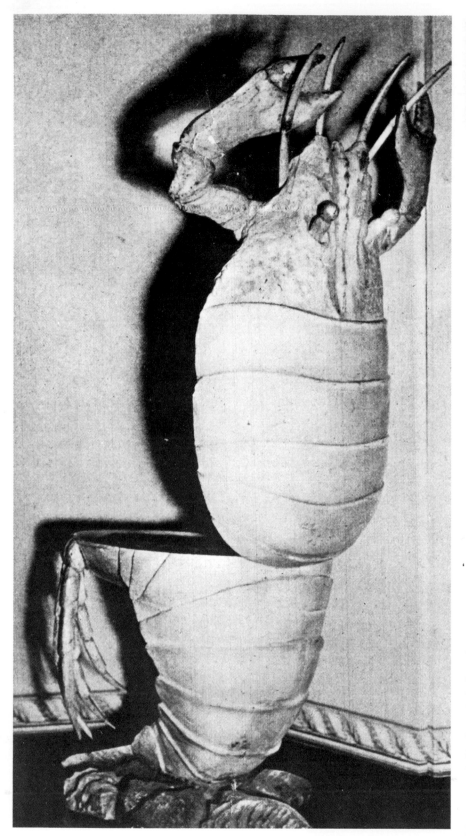

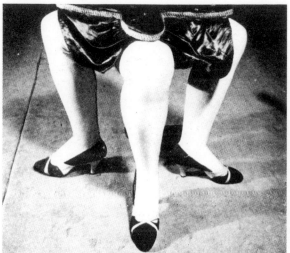

Above Lobster chair, mid–1930s.

Above right The 'Ultra-meuble' by Kurt Seligmann, exhibited at the Paris Surrealist Exhibition of 1938.

West's mouth made into a settee, tables supported by giant hands or stools with three lifelike legs of acrobats. Hands as a motif were to be seen in fashion photographs, holding jewels, cosmetics – in fact anything a hand could hold. Victorian marble hands created as souvenirs or *memento mori* were brought once more to light and occupied places of honour, often with the nails varnished in the fashionable shade of shocking pink.

Other Victorian bric-à-brac, such as marble obelisks and glass domes, encasing the stranger products of nineteenth-century imagination, were eagerly sought after in the newly discovered Caledonian Market in London and the flea market in Paris, both these markets having been found to be fruitful sources for the fashionable Baroque and mid-nineteenth century pieces. With the break-up of many large houses as a result of the depression of the early thirties the contents of attics and drawing rooms alike flooded the market and could be found at extremely low prices.

The main sources for spreading this fashion, which combined Surrealism, Baroque and Victoriana, were the fashion magazines. *Vogue* with its supplement on decorating – issued separately as *House and Garden* at a later date – and *Harper's Bazaar* all influenced taste and fashion by the editorial text and by the advertising more than any other periodicals. Both looked to Paris for ideas, as they were primarily concerned with fashion. Paris was still the leader in this field and both employed the best photographers and artists to illustrate fashion, the rivalry between the two periodicals ensuring that only the most original and imaginative treatment was used by each. To add variety to the editorial text, the best of interior decoration was included and as one succeeded in obtaining an exclusive coverage of a house decorated by Elsie de Wolfe the other would reply by an article on Syrie Maugham.

Vogue had an advantage in the services of Christian Bérard, acknowledged as an arbiter of taste in Parisian society. From his fertile imagination there issued designs for covers of the magazine, evocative drawings of the important fashions from the leading couturiers as well as original ideas for interior decoration, needlework or printed fabrics. His romantic outlook, preference for period derivations and exquisite sense of colour cannot be underestimated as an influence on taste in the period before the war.

Revivalism *by Malcolm Haslam*

Alternative styles and tastes

WHAT OCCURRED DURING the period 1890–1940 was a rare event in the history of art: the emergence of styles which depended hardly at all on precedent. Even the Renaissance, as its name implies, was to a large extent a historical revival. Perhaps the advent of Gothic in the twelfth and thirteenth centuries had been the last time that an entirely modern style had appeared, as it were, from nowhere.

All the art historical glamour of the last decade of the nineteenth and the first half of the twentieth century belongs to the designers and architects celebrated in Nikolaus Pevsner's *Pioneers of Modern Design* and it is easy to forget that Modernism was regarded by a vast majority of their contemporaries with suspicion and scorn, and that much the greater part of the architecture and decorative art produced during the period was traditional in style – or rather styles.

It is not to be supposed that every Modernist rejected out of hand his entire artistic heritage. On the contrary many had a profound understanding of past styles and applied their knowledge to their art. The pottery of William de Morgan, a close friend and disciple of William Morris, seemed and still seems today something original and progressive; but in 1888 De Morgan wrote to his partner from Italy: 'I hope to find when I come back a mine of pots that might be Greek, Sicilian, Etruscan, Moorish, Italian Renaissance – anything but Staffordshire.' De Morgan's remark indicates an attitude shared by many of the avant-garde decorative artists: that considerations of manufacture and materials came above style. The corollary, which was recognised by a small but increasing number of architects, designers and craftsmen was that style *depended* on materials and manufacture, and this idea became an integral principle of the Bauhaus ideology.

At the same time there were all those who regretted this down-grading of style – in the art historical sense – and who turned with a defensive ardour to the traditional criteria of good taste. Even some Modernists seem to have looked askance at the monsters they had spawned; for instance Josef Maria Olbrich was apparently only saved by an early death from dedicating himself entirely to a revived Rococo, and Arthur Heygate Mackmurdo, one of the creators of Art Nouveau, had effectively bowed out of the Modern Movement by the turn of the century with a series of designs in imitation of Wren or Sansovino.

The inversion of this process, which can hardly be documented, involves all those young art-school dreamers whose Modernist aspirations were soon drowned in the very muddy waters of commercialism and financial necessity and profit.

There were many designers who accepted their clients' taste, whether their client was a private patron or the public at large. Outside a small circle of enlightened individuals, men like Güell or Rathenau, most people clung to the styles they understood or, more importantly, the styles which had the 'correct' national, social or economic significance. Over the last hundred years Modernism in art and design has so often been identifiable with radical opinion that a healthy demand for historical styles from those wishing to declare their ideological orthodoxy, or simply their wealth, has always been maintained. From Morris to Le Corbusier the ethos of Modernism often demanded a socialist orientation in politics. The world would only become a more beautiful place when the poor were richer and the rich were less vulgar.

At the Great Exhibition of 1851, however, Prince Albert had helped to establish Renaissance as the style of commercial prosperity. Baron Haussmann had rebuilt Paris for Napoleon III in the styles of the periods during which the French monarchy had enjoyed its greatest degree of absolutism; he had made the boulevards too wide to be barricaded by a discontented populace.

Similarly, the Ringstrasse in Vienna had been planned by Franz Josef in order to avert any recurrence of the events of 1848 when the vulnerability of the imperial residence had become frighteningly apparent. The Ringstrasse had created a quasi-moat between the imperial government and the proletarians who lived in Vienna's suburbs. The new road had been lined along its inner edge by government offices, which were in effect fortresses, built in a variety of historical styles recalling the might and majesty of the Hapsburg Emperors.

Seldom during the period under review was there a public building erected in an avant-garde style. It is also noticeable how often Modernism flourished in provincial cities, away from the seat of national government. Art Nouveau, for instance was nurtured in Nancy, Barcelona, Glasgow, Turin, Munich and Chicago, cities with a degree of commercial prosperity but with something less than awe for the central administration. It does not seem fanciful to argue that the more authoritarian governments were the more relentlessly opposed to Modernism was the style of their buildings. Henry Bacon's Lincoln Memorial, Washington D.C., completed in 1917, and Sir Edward Lutyens' Viceroy's House, New Delhi, completed in 1931 were both as frankly revivalist as Albert

Right The Lincoln Memorial, Washington DC, designed in classical style by Henry Bacon, 1917.

Far right English Edwardian revivalism in the staircase of Belfast City Hall, designed by Sir A. Brumwell Thomas, 1906.

Below The Neo-Baroque domed hall of the World Exhibition, Paris, 1889.

Speer's model for a new Berlin or Marcello Piacentini's Terza Roma.

The antipathy to Modernism which characterised totalitarian governments is endorsed by the Nazis' closure of the Bauhaus and by the Kremlin's promulgation of Social Realism. If this argument seems a little exaggerated it is only putting in terms of political history the innate conservatism of the higher echelons in society, which is neatly expressed by the wording of a 1908 advertisement for a leading firm of British cabinet-makers: 'Persons of taste who desire to furnish their town houses or country houses in the English or French Period Styles may entrust themselves with complete confidence to the guidance of Warings', Decorators to H. M. the King'. Even in the early twentieth century much western art remained in one important respect the same as it had been since the middle ages – it was art designed for courtiers.

What styles, then, were revived between 1890 and 1940? The brief answer is any if not all. 'Eclecticism' is the English word applied to Victorian revivalism of the latter half of the nineteenth century and there is no reason why it should not be used for the continuation of the same phenomenon in the twentieth century. It is less descriptive than the German term 'Historismus', but its innuendo of selection from a repertoire is more revealing about contemporary attitudes, one of which claimed that the biological analogy of 'natural selection' invalidated any fundamental break with earlier modes.

The bible of British eclecticism was for at least half a century Owen Jones' *Grammar of Ornament*, first published in 1856. Here, presented in fine chromo-lithographic plates, is a wide choice of historical styles of decoration ranging from ancient Greek and Celtic to Louis Quinze and late Stuart; there are even illustrations by Christopher Dresser of the geometrical adaptation of flowers, but that is the book's only concession to Modernism, and the Baroque, Rococo, Adam, Louis Seize, Empire and Regency were omitted because their frivolity offended mid-Victorian high-mindedness. But Thackeray's novels and the architecture of Nesfield and Shaw cast a more demure light over the eighteenth century so that by 1890 the designer's range of choice was practically comprehensive.

Similarly in France, during the reign of Emperor Napoleon III, as we have seen, those styles most readily identifiable with autocracy had been reinstated after decades of neglect following the Revolution of 1789. As Germany moved towards unification the principal criterion operating in choice of historical style was nationalism, tempered only by a perennial infatuation with the classicism of the south. In America, where the country's own artistic past would hardly be appreciated until the twentieth century, a catholicity of taste reflected the variety of European nations from which the immigrants hailed.

This rapid survey shows that during the period under review the designer's (or his client's) choice was practically unlimited, or at least that the permissible certainly outweighed the taboo. Moreover the formalisation of architectural training, which occurred in most nations of the western world at the turn of the century and was due to the

Left A Neo-classical cabinet made in England, *c.* 1905.

Below An English Edwardian interior in the Neo-classical style.

ever increasing amount of technical and legal information to be assimilated by the student, produced a breed of architect versed not only in the minutiae of plumbing and electric lifts but also in the niceties of the acanthus scroll and the gargoyle.

Thorstein Veblen in his book *Theory of the Leisure Class* published in 1899 coined the phrase 'conspicuous waste' to describe the ostentatious affluence of the European and American rich, and it is a phrase which may be neatly applied to so much of the architecture and the decorative arts produced during the two decades before the First World War. 'Edwardian' and 'Wilhelminisch' have entered their respective languages as pejorative terms implying profligate luxury; this was *la Belle Epoque* or, as it became known in Veblen's America, the Gilded Age.

Nowhere was the waste more conspicuous than in New York. Along Fifth Avenue there sprang up the palaces which were ironically labelled 'houses' – Senator Clark house, William K. Vanderbilt house, A. T. Stewart house, Andrew Carnegie house, John Jacob Astor house and more.

Their style was usually that of the grandest seventeenth- or eighteenth-century French *châteaux* and American architects like Richard M. Hunt, who had attended the Ecole des Beaux-Arts

in Paris, France, were much in demand. Even when Duveen was in full flight it was not possible to furnish these mansions throughout with more or less genuine antiques, so all over Europe and America craftsmen were at work making replicas or creating period pieces. The Franco-British Exhibition at the White City, London, in 1908 included immaculate reproductions by Edouard Poteau of Oeben and Riesener furniture and a complete Marie Antoinette boudoir. H. C. Marillier, writing in the *Illustrated Review of the Exhibition*, compared these reproductions with 'the new art,' and no doubt expressed conventional opinion on both sides of the Channel and on both sides of the Atlantic when he concluded: '. . . . but in common honesty I am bound to confess that of the two, I am more inclined to admire the splendid workmanship exhibited by these copies of the antique than the striving after original effects exhibited by the new school'.

It is too easy to forget that Tiffany's iridescent glass was only a sideline and that far greater resources went into the manufacture of such objects as the Adams vase presented in 1895 by the stockholders and directors of the American Cotton Oil Company to Edward Dean Adams, chairman of the board. An elaborate confection in the manner of Cellini, it inspires statistical rather

The John Jacob Astor house on Fifth Avenue, New York, designed in French château style, 1898.

than aesthetic appreciation; for instance, three draughtsmen, fifteen modellers, eighteen goldsmiths, twenty-one chasers, twelve finishers, four moulders, three turners, two enamellers, three stonecutters and two lapidaries were involved in its production.

Opulence and Rococo splendour had not been unknown during the second half of the nineteenth century. The Rothschilds, for example, in London, Paris and Vienna had established Louis Quinze as a style *de luxe* and the firms catering for the taste of the wealthy had provided the bankers and their imitators with appropriate accessories. But the American tycoons of the Gilded Age outstripped their European counterparts in the lavish grandeur of the surroundings which they demanded. They came to Europe to acquire the heirlooms of a declining aristocracy and on their sallies into the old continent in search of tapestries or titled marriage partners they had to be accommodated in hotels built in the manner to which they were accustomed. Thus, beside Green Park in London rose the Ritz, designed by the Anglo-French partnership of Davis and Mewès, the latter supplying the inevitable Beaux-Arts panache.

In Paris and on the Riviera the same sort of monuments appeared, and to ferry the 'Innocents' across the Atlantic, liners were built which had public rooms fitted out like Renaissance or Baroque palaces such as those designed by Gustavo Pulitzer Finali for the Italia Line. Before the industrial buildings of America began to impinge on progressive architects, before Hollywood spectaculars had begun to flicker on the screens of European cinemas and before jazz imprinted its crazy rhythms on the culture of the Old World, the first wave of transatlantic influence was an imposing heap of flotsam and jetsam, in styles which were elaborately historical but unmistakably Yankee.

At the same time other, less sumptuous styles were being revived. In France, despite rapid assimilation of iron and ferro-concrete technology, decorative art appeared in the styles associated with most of the French monarchs from François Premier to Louis Seize; particularly favoured round the turn of the century was the Rococo of Louis Quinze, as curly and flippant as Art Nouveau without being offensively modern. But almost everywhere Art Nouveau itself provoked a flight to the more sober styles of the past.

Sir Reginald Blomfield was typical of a generation of English architects bred in the neo-gothic tradition who despised 'the swirl and the blob' (to quote his description of Art Nouveau), and turned to a rather jaded Georgian. The 'Wrenaissance' which had begun in the 1880s was still a style sometimes preferred to Georgian for office buildings, either commercial or municipal, and for some domestic work. Generally, however, 'Jacobethan' remained the popular style for private houses, occasionally on a grand scale when Sir Edward Lutyens used it for some of his country mansions, but mostly in a more modest version which particularly found favour with the garden-city planners. The style was taken up by speculators who built in the suburbs of most large English cities, and a huge market was created for the appropriate furnishings.

In an age when nationalism pervaded all levels of society, vernacular styles were in vogue not only in England but throughout most of Europe. In Scotland, the Scottish Baronial prevailed; Mackintosh's original development of the style was a mutation which met with very limited approval. Similarly, the Dutch architect Berlage transformed the medievalism of the Rundbogenstil into something modern, but for every Berlage there were several others happy to follow historical detail with the pedantry of P. J. H. Cuypers whose Rijksmuseum and railway-station in Amsterdam had established the popularity of the revival.

Nowhere was the reaction against Art Nouveau more vehement than in Germany, where the new style was known as Jugendstil. C. F. Schinkel's architecture, the most severely monumental style with a claim to being considered national, was an appropriate corrective. Peter Behrens and a few others could doff their caps to Schinkel and still design factories and electrical fittings that were truly modern, but many more were happy to retrieve their pattern-books and recreate the world of Frederick Wilhelm III. Among the latter, Heinrich von Tessenow was to be Speer's tutor, and Wilhelm Kreis and Paul Ludwig Troost were, like the style in which they were adepts, to have a new lease of life during the 1930s.

Cultivated German taste which disapproved of Jugendstil but found the Neo-classical monotonous and frighteningly plain, sought relief in the northern Baroque, the old standby which always afforded the ornamental carver plenty of opportunity for *angst*-ridden intricacies of decoration; and the furniture in this style was more solid, more *burgerlich*.

The Rundbogenstil also had its followers in Germany and a notable construction was the Wertheim department store in the Leipziger Strasse, Berlin, designed by Adolf Messel and completed in 1899; on a framework of iron and hung in places with enormous plate-glass windows the full height of the façade, the building was liberally spread with Gothic carved stone decoration, but the elevations were articulated in a Schinkelesque repetition of unitary bays, and the edifice was topped off with mansard roofs. It looked like the plates from a history of German architecture, superimposed one over another.

In Scandinavia the same sort of historicisms appeared as were being perpetrated by architects and designers in the rest of Europe. Martin Nyrop's Town Hall, Copenhagen, built between 1892 and 1902 is in the revived Rundbogenstil which prevailed in Holland and Germany during the 1890s, and Ragnar Ostberg's Town Hall, Stockholm, was built between 1909 and 1923 in the local version of Baroque (with Gothic embellishments).

A revival of Romantic Classicism which started in Denmark round 1910 and in Sweden about a decade later has affinities with neo-Schinkelism in Germany. Just as an admiration for Schinkel led some German designers to a severe functionalism, so Romantic Classicism in Scandinavia was gradually transformed into the international Modern Style of the late 1920s. In Denmark the revival included an enthusiasm for Sheraton's furniture designs, which lies behind the elegance of modern

Right The swimming bath at the Royal Automobile Club building, London, built in 1908–11 to designs by Arthur J. Davis and Charles Mewès.

Below Revivalist styles were widely used in the interior designs for the great transatlantic liners; the main lounge of the Italia Line's *Conte di Savoia* (1932), designed by Gustavo Pulitzer Finali, was a combination of Neo-classical and Baroque elements which contrasted strangely with the 'modern' covering of the furniture.

Danish furniture, perhaps the country's most felicitous contribution to the Modern Movement.

Gradually during the 1920s and 1930s Modernism became more acceptable in Europe and America. The Bauhaus message was disseminated, and the attention of the world was caught at the 1925 Exhibition in Paris. But reviewing this exhibition the Surrealist poet Louis Aragon commented: 'Well, personally, after all, I prefer *le Grand Art*'. The barren geometry of modern design put off many less profound critics than Aragon; they clung tenaciously to the more homely, less sophisticated styles of their forbears or the more pompous, less restrained styles which bore authority's seal of approval – just as the Surrealists might yearn for decoration which was more the stuff that dreams are made of. Hybrids began to appear: Palladian windows with Crittal metal frames, bakelite boxes with classical reliefs moulded on the lid. Sometimes it is called Kitsch and it has had its own revival in the recent past.

Times were changing. But Liberty's, the London department store, must have reassured those who felt that progress was inexorably swift. In 1924 they opened their new (if that is the right word) premises on Great Marlborough Street. It was a pious offering to the buccaneering genius of the Elizabethan era, the spirit of commercial

Left The Neo-classical design of the Royal Automobile Club's swimming bath was repeated by Davis and Mewès in their design for the German liner *Vaterland*.

Below The tea foyer at the Ritz Hotel, London, designed in 1904 by Arthur J. Davis and Charles Mewès.

enterprise which had made Britain so rich and powerful. The half-timbered façade, the oak-beamed interior and the shopgirls' medieval uniforms testified to the middle-class's undying faith in the right-mindedness of their yeomen forbears. One wonders whether it was a deliberate touch of irony to have had carved, on the keystone of the archway bearing the famous clock, this couplet:

> *No minute gone comes ever back again*
> *Take heed and see ye nothing do in vain.*

Perhaps since 1920 stylistic revivals have changed in character. One cannot be quite sure whether Libertys' Tudor building of 1924 was historical revivalism or nostalgia for happier days before the First World War. The same doubt is raised when considering Hitler's classicism; was it an evocation of the Roman Republic or a reminiscence of the pride of Germany before the Second Reich collapsed? Perhaps a new category of revivalism had emerged. There had been the antiquarianism of the earlier nineteenth-century revivals; then there had been the political, social or economic symbolism of most revivals up to the First World War; and now there were revivals induced by nostalgia, which seem to have begun between the Wars and are still with us now.

Above Reception room by Wilhelm Kreis, Bremen, 1911; reproduced in the Deutscher Werkbund yearbook for 1912.

Right and below Sculpted window surrounds by Karl Gross, Dresden, 1911; reproduced in the Deutscher Werkbund yearbook for 1912.

Above Cabinet made in the workshops of Liberty & Co., *c*. 1908.

Right Liberty & Co. dress, made *c*. 1929.

Industrial Design 1890–1940 *by Stuart Durant*

An aesthetic for technology

IN 1890 THE STEAM AGE was drawing to its close. The exalted position of steam, which had seemed so permanent at the time of the 1851 Exhibition, was to be usurped in barely more than a generation. At its zenith, steam could propel screw or paddle ships, a single steam engine could turn many lathes or operate many looms. The steam locomotive had appeared early in its final and perfect form, but within a short time steam had ceased to be the prime field for the innovator. With the exception of the development of the steam turbine in the 1880s and 1890s, steam technology had changed remarkably little throughout the whole steam age.

The advance of nineteenth-century technology was so swift that by 1879 Werner von Siemens was able to demonstrate electric traction with his miniature passenger-carrying railway at the Berlin Trade Fair. The death knell had sounded for steam. In December 1879, Thomas Edison, having perfected the carbon filament lamp, demonstrated the practicability of electric lighting to New Yorkers. Electricity was clean, it could be produced at centralised generating stations and, above all, it was versatile. It could provide motive power, illumination and heat. By 1884 Siemens and his partner Halske had constructed an electric

tramway between Frankfurt-am-Main and Offenbach. The earliest of the London electric underground railways was begun in 1887.

Over twenty-five million people witnessed the marvels of electricity at the Paris Universal Exhibition of 1889. The electric beacon at the top of Gustave Eiffel's three-hundred-metre tower – the centre-piece of the exhibition – was seen from vantage points on the cathedral of Orléans, some seventy miles distant. Searchlights on the Eiffel Tower picked out buildings over six miles away on the outskirts of Paris. At the Telephone Pavilion visitors listened to singers performing at the Opéra, or the Opéra Comique – a clumsy foretaste of the radio broadcast some thirty years away. Electrically-driven viewing gantries gave visitors an aerial view of the unprecedented array of machinery displayed along the length of Ferdinand Dutert's Palace of Machines, the largest nineteenth-century steel and glass building. The 1889 Exhibition was entirely illuminated by electricity and had its own generating stations operated by rival contractors. There were 20,000 Edison electric lamps in the Palace of Machines alone. In England the gardens of the Royal Horticultural Society in South Kensington had been illuminated with 9,700 electric lights for the

Far left A contemporary impression of the electric searchlights placed on the Eiffel Tower for the 1889 Paris Universal Exhibition.

Left The Palace of Machines at the 1889 Paris Universal Exhibition by Contamin and Dutert, showing the curtain wall of stained glass.

Colonial and Indian Exhibition of 1886.

The invention of the petrol-powered internal combustion engine, together with the introduction of the electric motor, was to prove an important factor in the eventual displacement of the steam engine. The precursor of the petrol engine was the gas engine in which a mixture of gas and air was combusted by an electric spark. The Parisian engineer Etienne Lenoir had succeeded in producing such an engine in 1859. Lenoir's engine was, however, too expensive to be operated commercially. But, in 1878, the German Nikolaus Otto developed a four-stroke gas engine that was comparatively economical to run. In principle Otto's gas engine is close to the modern petrol engine. At the 1889 Exhibition, one of the electricity-generating stations was operated with Otto engines. In 1885 Gottlieb Daimler fitted a high-speed petrol engine of his own design to a rudimentary motor car.

Henry Ford brought the motor car within reach of considerable sections of the American proletariat. Ford achieved this not by making improvements to the design of the motor car itself, but by concentrating on bringing down the costs of production. Ford reduced costs by the introduction of production-line assembly, first introduced for the Model T Ford in 1913, although the car itself had been first launched in 1908.

It is ironical that the Great War could not have been fought upon the vast and terrifying scale which it was, had it not been for the adoption of assembly-line production by manufacturers of military equipment. The obverse side of this dispiriting picture was that mass-production soon made it possible for many ordinary people to possess mechanical domestic equipment which made their lives a good deal more enjoyable. In *Vers une Architecture* (1923) Le Corbusier could speak of houses 'built on the same principles as the Ford car'. He looked forward to the coming of the 'house-machine' – 'the mass-production house, healthy – and morally so too – and beautiful'.

Ford and his methods epitomise the unfettered spirit of American industry. American industry had, in fact, been making spectacular progress since the middle of the nineteenth century, this was amply confirmed by the scale of the great American industrial exhibitions – the Philadelphia Centennial Exhibition of 1876, the World's Columbian Exhibition of Chicago of 1893 and the St. Louis Exhibition of 1904.

However impressive was American industrial growth, that of Germany was equally so. German mercantilism was, like America's, allied to a vigorous technology. The rise of Germany as an industrial giant is readily demonstrated by a few statistics. During the years 1881–5, Britain's share of world trade was approximately 38 per cent while Germany's share was just over 17 per cent. By 1913, however, the gap had narrowed and Britain's share of world trade had fallen to just over 27 per cent while Germany's had risen to nearly 22 per cent. The German figures for steel production are especially impressive, for by 1913 Germany's steel production was within sight of being three times that of Britain's. By 1914 Germany's national wealth had surpassed Britain's. These figures were achieved despite the facts that Germany lacked a ready-made imperial market and that she had emerged late as a unified nation. Much of Germany's industrial progress can be attributed to the importance which she attached to scientific and technological research.

The Germans responded not only to the technological challenges of industrialization but also to its aesthetic challenges. Although Britain, as exemplified by Richard Redgrave's *Supplementary Report on Design (1852)*, a critical assessment of the art manufactures at the Great Exhibition, had been concerned at a comparatively early date with mass-produced products, no viable kind of British machine aesthetic had been formulated. The Deutscher Werkbund typified Germany's farsighted approach to the issue of the machine. Traditionally the response to the machine of the academically-trained architect or the designer, had been to ignore it. However, the Werkbund was to draw into its orbit the leading German architects.

The Deutscher Werkbund was founded in 1907 and represents the first large-scale attempt to reconcile the arts with industry. Membership of the Werkbund was by invitation and open to manufacturers, architects and industrial artists. Among distinguished Werkbund members were: Peter Behrens, who had been appointed design co-ordinator for the great electrical combine AEG in the same year that the Werkbund was founded; Walter Gropius, who was to be Director of the Bauhaus from 1919 to 1928; Richard Riemerschmid, who had planned the garden city – a British idea – at Hellerau, near Dresden; and Henry van de Velde who had been initially inspired by the Utopianism of Ruskin and Morris but who had come to the conclusion that the modern artist should collaborate with commerce and industry. Among Austrian members of the Werkbund were Josef Hoffmann, Otto Wagner and, somewhat unexpectedly, Gustav Klimt.

The Werkbund had been founded by Hermann Muthesius as the outcome of a furore after he had publicly condemned German manufacturers for their mindless filching of historic styles with which to clothe their products. Muthesius, a Prussian architect and civil servant, had already established a reputation with two immensely ambitious surveys of British Arts and Crafts and progressive architecture – W. R. Lethaby called him 'the historian of English free architecture'. (Muthesius' studies are – the four-volume *Das Englische Baukunst und Gedenwart*, completed in 1904, and the three-volume *Das Englische Haus* – the better known of the two works – completed in 1905.) During the six years, from 1896, that he spent in Britain, Muthesius became fully acquainted with the philosophy of the Arts and Crafts Movement. However, he saw that the Arts and Crafts Movement, with its emphasis on the revival of traditional craft values, was fostering an entirely negative attitude towards the machine.

The first yearbook of the Werkbund was published in 1912. It illustrates Behrens' powerfully monumental AEG factories as well as his light-fittings and ventilating fans for AEG. Worker's houses by Riemerschmid are also shown, as well as designs for wooden toys, tombs, ceramics and linoleum. Many of the Werkbund designs do not differ very greatly from contemporary Arts and

Opposite German industrial advertising, 1914; Germany was the first nation to apply industrial design on a large scale to manufactures, especially those of the automobile industry.

Crafts-inspired designs shown in contemporary publications like *The Studio*, the emphasis being upon simplicity and appropriateness of ornamentation.

A significant feature of the Werkbund yearbooks was the high standard of their theoretical debate. In his address at the Werkbund convention at Dresden in 1911, *Wo Stehen Wir?* (Where do we stand?), which was published in the 1912 yearbook, Muthesius indicated his own position. He stressed the importance of quality, form – in its pure and abstract sense – and standardization.

The interest in form seems peculiarly German and stems from the idea of the Platonic archetype, the governing form which transcends transitory forms, that had been so prevalent in the thinking of Goethe and his contemporaries. As a theorist Muthesius has an obvious importance, as a designer he lacked the inventiveness of Werkbund colleagues like Behrens or Hans Poelzig.

The 1913 Werkbund yearbook was in great part devoted to factory design. Behrens' famous turbine assembly building for AEG is illustrated. This building represented, in its classical refinement, the most potent Werkbund ideals. There are also factories by Hans Poelzig – romantic and almost Piranesi-like – as well as Walter Gropius'

Fagus shoe-last factory, a harbinger of Bauhaus architecture. Muthesius' factory is Neo-classical and altogether undistinguished. A number of North American factories are also shown, including the Ford factory at Detroit. A lesser portion of the yearbook is devoted to illustrations of shop fronts and window displays. Gropius, Muthesius and August Endell, a survivor from the Jugendstil era, contributed articles. No true Werkbund style – as there was a Bauhaus style – can be said to have emerged, although there seems to have been a distinct preference for monumentality.

One of the most interesting examples of collaboration between a Werkbund designer and the manufacturer is to be found in the work of Ernst Neumann illustrated in the 1914 Werkbund yearbook. Neumann designed elegant and functional limousines, while his commercial car body (for Bussing Braunschweig) is very sculptural. Other designs for vehicles, locomotives, ships and aircraft are anonymous. Among these are the Zeppelin *Sachsen* – the first airship to operate commercially and an advanced-looking monoplane by the Luftverkehrs Gesellschaft, Johannistal. The locomotives shown are light and compact and there is clear visual evidence of a concern for aerodynamic form in some of the designs –

Below Limousine coachwork designed by Ernst Neumann, 1914.

Bottom Commercial vehicle body designed by Ernst Neumann for Bussing Braunschweig, 1914.

Above The Ford factory at Detroit, illustrated in the 1913 Werkbund yearbook, one of the first factories specially built for production-line techniques.

Right Interior of the glass pavilion designed by Bruno Taut for the 1914 Werkbund Exhibition.

funnels, domes and cabs are unmistakably flared, if not streamlined.

In 1914 the Werkbund mounted a large-scale outdoor exhibition at Cologne. Unfortunately its full impact was to be greatly diminished by the outbreak of war. The Cologne exhibition is documented in the 1915 Werkbund yearbook. Among the buildings of note were Gropius' model factory and administration building in which the influence of Frank Lloyd Wright is very evident in the main façade. In the rear courtyard façade Gropius further developed the idea of the window-skin with which he had experimented in the Fagus factory. Bruno Taut designed an exquisite little proto-expressionist glass pavilion with an ingenious, almost geodesic, roof structure. Henry van de Velde's Werkbund Theatre has certain curvilinear features and decorative details that remind one of his affinities with Art Nouveau. Peter Behrens' conference hall is Neo-classical and confirms the impression of classicism latent in the work of many Werkbund designers. Josef Hoffmann's Austrian pavilion is also Neo-classical, but in a chic Viennese way. Apart from railway carriage design, and Hermann Muthesius' interiors for the Hamburg-Amerika Line steamship *Bismarck*, transport design was not represented at Cologne. Although the Werkbund continued in existence after the 1914–18 war, it was to be overtaken by the Bauhaus as an influence in the future direction of design.

Although there was a good deal of anti-German feeling in Britain after the outbreak of war on 4 August 1914 the lessons of the Werkbund were carefully studied. In May 1915, the Design and Industries Association was founded. 'Where an enemy has a noble lesson to teach', said Clutton Brock, one of the founders of the D.I.A., 'it can only be learned from him nobly'. The D.I.A. published a number of yearbooks, but at two-yearly intervals, in emulation of the Werkbund. The first of these came out in 1922, seven years after the D.I.A. had been founded.

C. H. Collins Barker, Keeper and Secretary of the National Gallery, in the 1922 yearbook's introduction asserted that the chief article of the creed of the D.I.A. founders was 'fitness for purpose'. If 'a thing were unaffectedly made to fulfil its purpose thoroughly, then it would be good art'. Collins Barker also remarked that 'the disease of modern design and industry was not due to machinery, but to the imperfect comprehension of its limitations and possibilities'. Apart from this introduction there is no theoretical content in the first D.I.A. yearbook. We must look at the illustrations if we are to understand the ideals of the D.I.A. in its early stages.

Work illustrated in the 1922 D.I.A. yearbook comes from Heal and Sons, good, sensible, 'cottage furniture'; Dryad Handicrafts, excellent cane furniture inspired by German models; Josiah Wedgwood and Sons, refined, traditional pottery; W. Foxton, bold fabrics designed by Lovat Fraser and Gregory Brown; Leslie Mansfield's house style for Macfisheries, restrained and purposeful – a series of designs that were outstanding for their day. Motor cars by Lanchester, Bentley and bodywork by Hooper are illustrated as examples of 'fitness for purpose'. London Underground

Above Leslie Mansfield's design for the shop fronts of the Macfisheries chain of shops, 1922.

Left Interior of a London Underground carriage, 1922.

rolling-stock and aircraft by Bristol and Vickers are also used to emphasise the same point, and an airman's costume is praised for its functional beauty. The contents of the D.I.A. yearbook for 1924–5 are similar to the first D.I.A. yearbook. The London Underground is featured again as well as a number of rather unadventurous stands at the British Empire Exhibition, 1924.

John Gloag in his introduction to the D.I.A. yearbook for 1924–5, is cautious in his prognosis of the role of the D.I.A., 'It is a great temptation to dream of imposing plans that will recast the world and destroy all the foolish legacies of bad custom from past generations, the cramping traditions and other obstacles that stand in the way of an orderly and beautiful civilization; but the improvement of even one section of industry is a much more serviceable contribution to general betterment than a thousand Utopias – on paper'.

The D.I.A., then, was modest in its aims and its early work was admittedly unexciting. However, in the spring of 1932 the D.I.A. was to publish a journal, *Design in Industry*, to be superseded by *Design for Today* in 1933. The specialist editor of the first issue of *Design in Industry* was a pioneer of the Modern Movement in Britain, E. Maxwell Fry, and from this time onwards the D.I.A. was to be associated with the burgeoning British Modern Movement. Typographically *Design in Industry* is somewhat uncomfortable, the typefaces are sans-serif but arranged without the Bauhaus aplomb, but the journal itself was by no means fusty. Lethaby is quoted on the cover: design did not 'involve some strange originality . . . . it should be just the appropriate shaping and finish for the thing required'. The D.I.A. in many ways spanned the gulf between the Arts and Crafts Movement and Modernism.

Le Corbusier's *Vers une Architecture*, published in Paris in 1923 and in London in 1927 as *Towards a New Architecture*, is a key work. Many of Le Corbusier's ideas were to penetrate to the very subconscious of a generation. As a polemicist he was quite the equal of predecessors like Pugin or Viollet-le-Duc. The Argument from *Towards a New Architecture* is justly famous. Here is the opening paragraph: 'The Engineer's Aesthetic, and Architecture, are two things that march together and follow one from the other; the one being now at its full height (the engineer's), the other (the architect's) in an unhappy state of retrogression'.

The argument based on the analogy of the aeroplane shows Le Corbusier as a machine age

Below Theatre project by Norman Bel Geddes, 1932.

Right Pierce-Arrow car exhibited outside the House of Tomorrow at the Century of Progress Exposition, Chicago World's Fair.

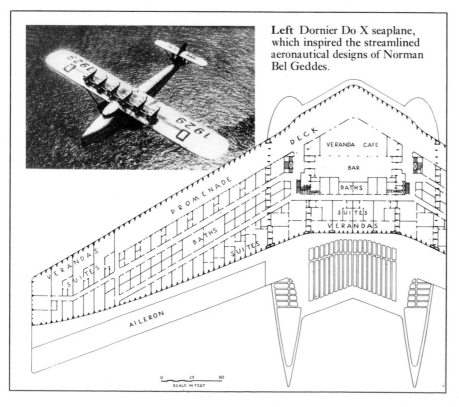

Left Dornier Do X seaplane, which inspired the streamlined aeronautical designs of Norman Bel Geddes.

romantic: 'The airplane is the product of close selection . . . . . . The lesson of the airplane lies in the logic which governed the statement of the problem and its realization. The problem of the house has not yet been stated. Nevertheless there do exist standards for the dwelling-house. Machinery contains in itself the factor of economy, which makes for selection. The house is a machine for living in.' Le Corbusier's ideas were demonstrated in his L'Esprit Nouveau pavilion at the Paris 1925 Exhibition. The L'Esprit Nouveau pavilion was merely a single apartment, taken like a drawer from a chest-of-drawers, from a large block of flats from his city of 3,000,000 inhabitants of 1922. The apartment, with its colour-washed walls, was furnished with cheap bentwood chairs and mass-produced equipment. A model monoplane was hung on a wall like a trophy.

Some of Le Corbusier's ideas, glossily packaged, appear in Norman Bel Geddes' *Horizons* which was published in 1932. Bel Geddes was a film and stage designer – he also wrote and directed for the film and stage – who, in the 1930s, had built up a successful industrial design practice. Bel Geddes tells us: 'We are entering a new era which, notably, shall be characterised by design in four specific phases: Design in social structure to insure the organization of people, work, wealth, leisure. Design in machines that shall improve working conditions by eliminating drudgery. Design in all objects of daily use that shall make them economical, durable, convenient, congenial to everyone. Design in the arts, painting, music, literature, and architecture, that shall inspire the new era.'

There was nothing really new in the principle of streamlining and in the First World War some of the later Zeppelins had comparatively sophisticated aerodynamic forms. Even before the war, some of the locomotives illustrated in the 1914 Werkbund yearbook approached the streamlined form.

Although there were other excellent designers in the streamlined idiom – Henry Dreyfuss, Otto Kohler and Raymond Loewy, for instance – Bel Geddes, in *Horizons*, did more than any one else to propagandise the streamlined form.

Bel Geddes said in *Horizons* that he had decided in 1927 to cease to work only for the theatre. Henceforward he would design for sources 'more vitally akin to life to-day'. He then worked on projects for streamlined ocean liners, motor cars, motor coaches and steam locomotives, most of which were never to exist even in prototype form. Bel Geddes' transatlantic airliner, inspired by Claude Dornier's giant Do X of 1929, had twelve engines and a cruising speed of 100 mph. There was to be luxurious accommodation in the wings and the twin hulls for 451 passengers and a crew of 155. Refuelling was to take place, in flight, over Newfoundland. The fact that Bel Geddes could jettison a respected 'high art' – the theatre – in order to embrace industrial design is highly significant. Since Behrens, the Werkbund, the Bauhaus or Le Corbusier industrial design had become an increasingly esteemed activity. The 1930s were the heroic age of industrial design. The outbreak of war in 1939 brought that age which had such faith in design to an end.

PART TWO

DESIGNS
AND
DESIGNERS

1890-1940

France

Furniture and Interior Design *by Philippe Garner*

THE 1890S SAW THE DEVELOPMENT in France of Art Nouveau, the fully evolved characteristics of which enjoyed their greatest success at the 1900 Exhibition, combining the threads of naturalism, abstraction from nature and Japanese-inspired refinement that had been at the roots of the style. From the various displays at the 1900 Exhibition the concept of Art Nouveau furnishing emerges as a total one – designers were seen as *ensembliers*, rather than as creators of individual pieces of furniture, and it is perhaps the overpowering effect of a complete French Art Nouveau interior that made the fashion fairly short-lived.

During the Art Nouveau period, France had two centres for furniture and interior design: Paris, naturally, as the capital, and also the town of Nancy, where Emile Gallé encouraged local artists to work in the more naturalistic version of Art Nouveau which he favoured. In Paris, one of the most significant names in the evolution and success of the Art Nouveau style interior was that of Samuel Bing.

Bing, dealer, patron and publisher, was an enthusiastic admirer of Japanese art through the last quarter of the nineteenth century. Much travelled, Bing had visited the Far East he so much admired; he also met Louis Comfort Tiffany in the United States and returned filled with Tiffany's ideals of allying industrial methods of production to high standards of artistic creativity. In 1888 Bing had launched a monthly magazine, *Le Japon Artistique*. At the Galeries de l'Art Nouveau which he opened at 22 Rue de Provence in December 1895 Bing exhibited the work of the artists he admired, including Tiffany, Aubrey Beardsley, René Lalique and Emile Gallé. During the late 1890s Bing sponsored the work of a number of artists whose potential he admired, notably Georges de Feure, Edward Colonna and Eugène Gaillard and it was with their contributions to his Pavillon de l'Art Nouveau at the Paris Exhibition of 1900 that he was to achieve his greatest success. By the time of Bing's death five years later in 1905 the style to which he gave a name had begun to decline. Colonna had ceased to work for Bing in 1903 and neither Gaillard nor de Feure was to create anything to equal their contributions of 1900.

The suite of rooms which constituted the Pavillon de l'Art Nouveau are amongst the most important interiors created in the style and deserve particular attention. The entrance itself was a seductive promise of the delights within, in the form of panels by the talented Dutch-Belgian Georges de Feure depicting life-size female figures in elaborate peacock-skirted dresses. De Feure had a distinctive graphic style, comparable in its colours, emphasis on outlines and elegant harmonies of women and flowers, to that of Alphonse Mucha, but with a more sophisticated flavour. His graphic talent found expression in the design of textiles, papers and stained glass, examples of which, together with his furniture, a Sitting Room and a Dressing Room, were to be found in Bing's Pavillon. The Sitting Room was certainly one of the most refined rooms created in the Art Nouveau style. With its use of embroidered silk upholsteries and gilt wood furniture delicately carved with stylised floral motifs the room achieved an aristocratic flavour in the best traditions of the French eighteenth century.

Eugène Gaillard exhibited two rooms, a Dining Room and a Bedroom. In the Dining Room, Gaillard contrived to use elegant whiplash motifs everywhere, on the tooled leather upholstery of chairs, on the carved panels of the cabinet that dominated the room, woven in the design of the carpet, in the metalwork ornamental frieze which adorned the *boiseries* beneath murals by José Maria Sert and in the carved limbs of the furniture. Gaillard's passion for the undulating line was given a free rein in the Bedroom where the lines of heavily figured wood panelling emphasised the fluid concept of the furniture. Edward Colonna's Drawing Room had more of the refinement of de Feure than the exuberance of Gaillard. Muted green plush walls set off the lines, elegantly abstracted from nature, of Colonna's furniture.

Julius Meier-Graefe played a role similar to that of Bing as entrepreneur and patron. His interest was in applying modern ideas in a cohesive way to every aspect of domestic design. Setting up workshops and commissioning work from a wide range of designers, both from France and abroad, Meier-Graefe opened La Maison Moderne in 1898 in the Rue des Petits Champs as a showcase and retail outlet. The shop-front was designed in his characteristic abstract dynamic style by the Belgian artist Henri van de Velde, whose work strongly influenced Abel Landry, head of the Maison Moderne furniture atelier. Paul Follot and Maurice Dufrêne both designed furniture and other items for Meier-Graefe. The success of La Maison Moderne was short-lived as was that of a group formed in 1898 and calling itself 'les Six.'

The six included three artists who achieved distinction as furniture designers, Alexandre Charpentier, Charles Plumet and Tony Selmersheim. Charpentier designed furniture with strong yet fluid lines and would incorporate the low-relief

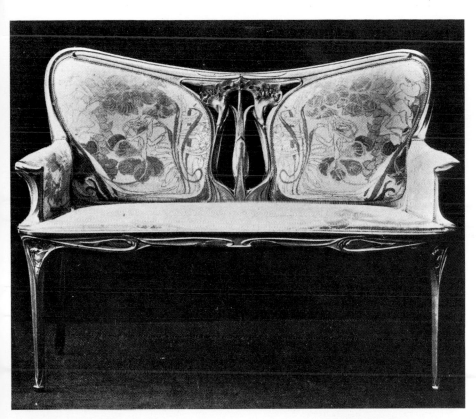

Left Giltwood and silk *canapé* designed by Georges de Feure for his sitting room in Bing's Pavillon de l'Art Nouveau in the 1900 Paris Exhibition.

Below Mahogany table designed by Edward Colonna for his drawing room in Bing's Pavillon de l'Art Nouveau.

Bottom Bedroom designed by Eugène Gaillard for Bing's Pavillon.

Pearwood cabinet designed
by Hector Guimard, *c.* 1900.

Carved wood chair by
Rupert Carabin, 1896.
Collection Mr. and Mrs.
Robert Walker, Paris.

carved panels at which he was so talented. Plumet and Selmersheim designed furniture on elegant abstract organic lines in the Paris mode and continued to work together on architectural and interior design schemes after the dissolution of the original group. Decorator Georges Hoentschel distinguished himself with his naturalistically carved furniture and *boiseries* in his *ensemble,* La Salle du Bois, at the Pavillon de l'Union Centrale des Arts Décoratifs in 1900.

Architect-designer Hector Guimard was one of the most important practitioners of the principle of total environment. Active as an architect from 1888, he evolved his Art Nouveau style towards the mid 1890s. Guimard's high Art Nouveau period lasted until about 1905 when his work mellowed into a more restrained, more elegant phase. He designed every detail of his interiors, plasterwork, stained glass, tiles and fireplaces, light fittings, woodwork, handles and lock-plates as well, of course, as the furniture. During his high Art Nouveau period, his furniture was truly eccentric, with energetic lines sweeping over fireplaces, and filling corners, echoing the relief of wall mouldings and fitted woodwork and emphasising the sense of unity. At a later date, between about 1905 and 1912, whilst still employing interplays of sculpted, abstract curvilinear forms, Guimard showed greater restraint in the more subdued carving of the steamed pearwood which he favoured.

An isolated but significant talent working in the 1890s was that of Rupert Carabin. He carved slightly bizarre pieces of furniture incorporating full-relief allegorical female nudes. Carabin was his own craftsman and a feature of his furniture is the rich patina achieved by soaking in linseed oil and long and patient rubbing.

The school of furniture design encouraged by Emile Gallé in Nancy had its origins in the 1880s, when Gallé first discovered the qualities of exotic woods and added furniture design to the crafts of glass and faïence which had been the mainstay of his family's business. Gallé spent the late 1880s in the preparation of his first major furniture exhibit, for the Paris Universal Exhibition of 1889. Although in these early years of furniture production the forms tended to be ponderous and uninspired, the details of his work were already full of invention. He revitalised the craft of marquetry, using a wide variety of fruitwoods and exotic woods in their natural hues, often with details carved in relief. Plant and animal life inspired this rich marquetry with which he filled flat areas and the shapes he gave to limbs and framework. Gallé's debt to Japanese art was evident in the elegant abstract designs which he created within the tenets of his naturalism. An example is to be found in his chair 'aux ombelles' the back of which represents the plant theme in the style of a Japanese *tsuba*.

Gallé's principles of furniture design were set out in an essay, 'Le Mobilier Contemporain orné d'après la Nature', published in the November/December 1900 issue of the *Revue des Arts Décoratifs*. Here he explained the logic of Nature as a source of inspiration and emphasised the importance of choosing a theme relevant to function. The dining table 'aux herbes potagères' of 1892 is a good illustration of Gallé's principles.

Below 'Les Fleurs du Mal', carved wood and fruitwood marquetry cabinet on a theme from Baudelaire, designed by Emile Gallé, 1896.

Below right Carved fruitwood *sellette*, designed by Emile Gallé, *c.* 1900.

Bottom Gallé carved wood and fruitwood marquetry tray, *c.* 1900.

Gallé's masterpiece is the magnificent bed, *Aube et Crépuscule*, made in the last year of his life, 1904, with its spectacular panels of marquetry work, carved in relief and incorporating glass and mother-of-pearl.

The most important cabinet-maker to come under Gallé's influence in the 1890s was Louis Majorelle, whose career would otherwise have been spent in the manufacture of the Louis-Quinze style pieces in which his family business specialised. Majorelle followed in Gallé's footsteps in the application of natural themes to furniture design and many of his naturalistically carved pieces with marquetry decoration on the panels bear a very strong affinity to Gallé's work. At his best, however, Majorelle showed a distinctive personal style, escaping from the often cloying naturalism preached by Gallé to a more plastic, more abstract style that is amongst the strongest, purest expressions of French Art Nouveau and somehow avoiding the provincialism of much Nancy furniture. Majorelle's major works were the suites 'aux nénuphars' and 'aux orchidées', created between 1900 and 1908, in which the undulations of the design, fluidly carved in rich mahogany, are emphasised by the sensual lines of stylised gilt-bronze orchids, lily-pads and stems.

Other Nancy furniture designers of note were Jacques Gruber, Eugène Vallin and Emile André, all of whom became members of the 'Ecole de Nancy, Alliance Provinciale des Industries d'Art' founded by Gallé in 1901. Gruber, during the late 1890s, showed an interest both in glass and in furniture, working for a few years for the Daum brothers and designing furniture for Majorelle. He ran his own cabinet-making business for ten years between 1900 and 1910, creating pieces which, at their best, exploited to the full the abstract sculptural possibilities of French Art Nouveau, but which, at their worse, mixed heavy sculptural themes with naturalistic motifs with an overpowering effect in a ponderously provincial style in certain complete room designs. Gruber's interest in glass can be seen in his use of cameo glass panels in his furniture. After 1910 he devoted all his energies to work in another favoured medium, stained glass.

Eugène Vallin was, like Majorelle and Gruber at their best, interested in the plastic possibilities of wood. His furniture seems to grow from the ground in liquid, unbroken lines. Abandoning furniture design, Vallin turned full-time to architecture and satisfied his sculptural interests in work in poured concrete. Emile André, architect and furniture designer, was a founder member of the Ecole de Nancy. Victor Prouvé, friend and associate of Gallé, and, after Gallé's death, artistic director of his factory, created designs for marquetry panels for Gallé and for Majorelle.

The reaction against Art Nouveau and the evolution towards the style and motifs of Art Deco can be traced back to the years between 1905 and 1908. The flowing lines of Art Nouveau were subdued into more sober forms whilst more disciplined bouquets of stylised flowers, garlands and ribbonwork replaced the lush and convoluted motifs of the Art Nouveau style in the carved or inlaid details of furniture. A number of Art Nouveau furniture designers and decorators were able to change with the times and evolve towards the emerging Art Deco style; others, such as Guimard, mellowed their Art Nouveau style or, indeed, seem to have completely abandoned their work, unable or unwilling to adapt. Gallé died in 1904, Bing in 1905, and two leaders of taste were lost. Majorelle had, by 1910, evolved the more sober style in which he worked until his death in 1926.

Maurice Dufrêne and Paul Follot, leading contributors to Meier-Graefe's La Maison Moderne, did some very notable work in this transitional phase and emerged as leading designers in the Art Deco style in the early 1920s when, in 1921, Dufrêne assumed responsibility of the La Maîtrise ateliers for the Galeries Lafayette and, two years later, Follot took charge of the Atelier Pomone at the Bon Marché. The first such atelier of Art Deco design concerned with every aspect of furniture and the interior was the Atelier Martine opened by Paul Poiret in 1911. Journals of the pre-war years show a confusion of styles in furniture, but the recurrent thread is the restraint and Neo-classicism of the emerging Art Deco style which found one of its most perfect expression in the years immediately after the war in the work of Louis Süe and André Mare, whose Compagnie des Arts Français was founded in 1919. Süe et Mare, as they became known, created furniture in rich, highly-polished woods, of simple, slightly bulbous form with conventionalised floral Art Deco motifs carved in low-relief or inlayed in mother-of-pearl. They also created textile and paper designs using similar motifs and enjoyed the opportunity to present their total style in various exhibits including their Musée d'Art Contemporain at the 1925 Exhibition.

Léon Jallot and François Jourdain were amongst the more successful designers of the transitional phase, the latter favouring a rather advanced angular style. Paul Iribe, better known as an illustrator, designed a few exceptional items of furniture in the Art Deco style for the couturier Jacques Doucet, notably a commode in mahogany, sharkskin and ebony of about 1912, carved with Neo-classical garlands and inlaid with a highly stylised spray of flowers, and a series of *fauteuils-gondole* of about the same date. Clément Mère made furniture in the Art Deco style, elaborately inlaid and incorporating panels of tooled leather in their design.

The greatest *ébéniste-décorateur*, however, working in the Art Deco style was undoubtedly Emile-Jacques Ruhlmann, probably the most important cabinet-maker of the twentieth century. Although Ruhlmann had exhibited at the Salon d'Automne in 1910, it was at the Salon of 1913 that his work attracted attention when he introduced the slender tapered leg which was to become his hallmark. His pre-war successes included the *meuble d'encoignure* of 1916 inlaid in ivory with an elaborate bouquet of flowers in pure Art Deco taste. Shortly after the war Ruhlmann launched his Etablissements Ruhlmann et Laurent which, in the years up to his death in 1933, became the most prestigious decorating firm in France. At the Salon of 1919 Ruhlmann showed a superb cabinet in dark, figured wood, raised on his now characteristic slender tapered legs and inlaid in ivory with a

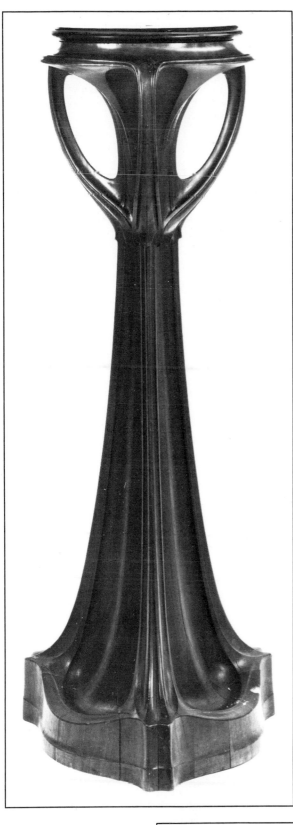

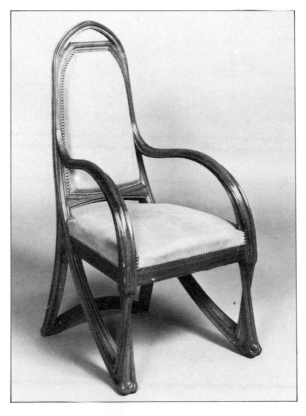

Above Mahogany desk and chair with gilt-bronze mounts 'aux orchidées', designed by Louis Majorelle, *c.* 1905.

Left Carved oak armchair, designed by Louis Majorelle, *c.* 1900.

Far left Carved mahogany *sellette*, designed by Jacques Gruber, *c.* 1900.

Pair of chairs and occasional table produced by the Compagnie des Arts Francais, Süe et Mare, early 1920s.

stylised motif of a classical god in a chariot. The Neo-classicism was evident the following year in his major work exhibited, a large cabinet in finely figured wood inlaid with overlapping circles of ivory and with a central panel of Neo-classical figures. Ruhlmann was gradually evolving the distinctive repertoire of forms and decorative motifs that were the elements of his personal style.

The obvious features of Ruhlmann's work, in addition of course to the prodigious labour required to achieve the perfection he demanded, were his simple, at times monumental shapes, perfectly proportioned and often raised on slender tapered legs, his use of rich exotic woods, notably *ébène de macassar* and amboyna, and the decorative use of rich materials, inlays of ebony or tortoise-shell and ivory used for key plates, *sabots* and plaques or inlaid in filets or rows of minute spots.

Ruhlmann's work was a central feature of the 1925 Exhibition where he decorated the Hôtel d'un Collectionneur and designed a Study in the Pavillon d'un Ambassadeur. In the creation of grand public rooms Ruhlmann was in his element, and here could be seen the full range of his skills. The grandiose schemes were judiciously enhanced by the heavy Neo-classical paintings of Jean Dupas and sculptures of Joseph Bernard.

In the last few years of his life Ruhlmann made

Opposite page Interior design by Emile-Jacques Ruhlmann, 1925.

Left *Meuble d'encoignure* in macassar ebony inlaid in ivory, designed by Emile-Jacques Ruhlmann, 1916.

Below left The Grand Salon d'un Collectionneur designed by Emile-Jacques Ruhlmann. The mural on the right is by Jean Dupas.

Below Cabinet covered in sharkskin with ivory lock plates, *sabots* and decorative details, designed by André Groult, and included in his Chambre de Madame in the Pavillon d'un Ambassadeur in the Paris 1925 Exhibition. Collection N. Manoukian, Paris.

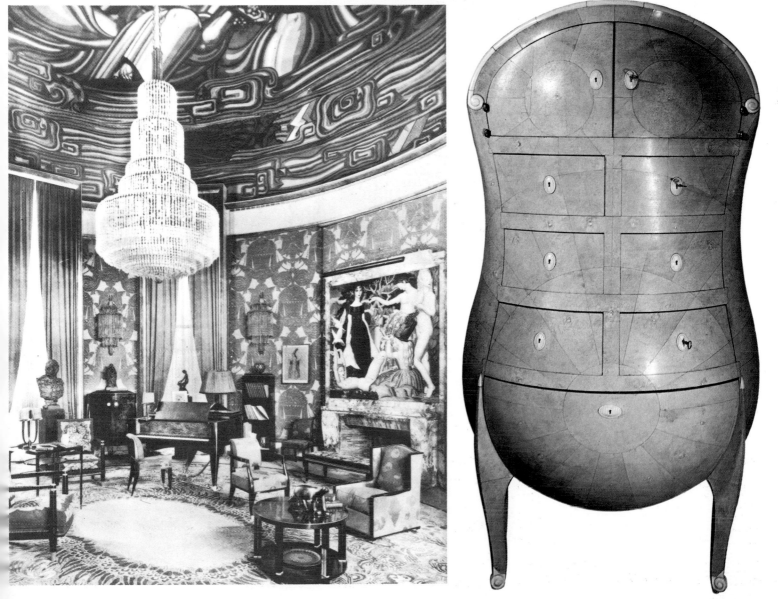

certain concessions to the taste for Modernism, designing a bar on chromium-plated metal skis, a kidney-shaped desk fitted with telephone, chromium-plated metal lamp, handles and foot-rest and, in the early thirties, a spectacular polished metal bed for the Maharajah of Indore in pure Modernist style.

After Ruhlmann's death his nephew Porteneuve took over his ateliers and worked from his designs for a limited period. From the early twenties, however, he had many imitators. These included Jules Leleu, who began to exhibit regularly at the Salon des Artistes Décorateurs after 1922 and who figured quite prominently in the 1925 Exhibition; the firm of Dominique, founded in 1922 by André Domin and Marcel Genevrière, which decorated the Salon in the Pavillon d'un Ambassadeur in 1925; the firm of Joubert et Petit and countless other Paris and provincial firms made a heavy-handed version of Ruhlmann's style, the ubiquitous bourgeois furniture of the late twenties and the thirties.

The twenties was a rich and varied decade in furniture and interior design and brought forth a number of talents too individual to be grouped under the blanket label of Art Deco. These included André Groult, Armand-Albert Rateau, Clément Rousseau and Eugène Printz. Groult, who had been exhibiting at the Salon des Artistes Décorateurs since 1910, worked at first in a style evocative of Louis-Seize and the Restauration, but is best remembered for his use of sharkskin. His most remarkable creation was the furnishing of the Chambre de Madame in the Pavillon d'un Ambassadeur, the swollen forms and softly curving lines of each piece completely covered in pale sharkskin. Groult incorporated wallpaper designs by Marie Laurencin into his decorative schemes.

Rateau's most interesting work is the furniture he designed in bronze, inspired from the antique. His work in the twenties included a series of commissions for Jeanne Lanvin, a highly individual bathroom for the Duchesse d'Albe's Madrid home, the home of the Baronne Eugène de Rothschild and various other commissions. He participated in the decoration of the Pavillon de · l'Elégance in 1925.

Clément Rousseau used rich materials, ivory, sharkskin, ebony and palm-wood in small pieces of furniture and decorative objects of considerable refinement and simplicity. His patrons included Jacques Doucet and Robert de Rothschild.

Eugène Printz specialised in the use of metal, not in the functionalist style of the Modernist movement, but richly oxydised, or burnished and contrasted with panels of rich lacquer.

The design of textiles and wallpapers enjoyed very specific attention during the Art Deco period, before the austerity that characterised the Modernist movement ousted exotic patterning in avant-garde circles in favour of the purity of unadorned surfaces. Raoul Dufy designed fabrics and papers for Paul Poiret before going under contract in 1912 to the textile firm of Bianchini et Ferier, a contract which lasted until 1930 and was responsible, especially in the early years, for a series of delightful designs. After 1912 André Groult supervised the manufacture of textiles and papers to his own designs and to those of various

other artists including Laurencin and Iribe. Paul Véra and André Mare designed fabrics for the Compagnie des Arts Français. The published folios of designs by Edouard Benedictus for the firms of Tassinari & Châtel, Brunet and Meunié & Cie. bear witness to his considerable talent. The Lyons silk works of François Ducharne, founded in 1920, produced rich fabrics under the artistic direction of Michel Dubost.

The revival of the craft of lacquer in the 1920s can be credited almost exclusively to the craftsmanship of one man, the Swiss-born Jean Dunand whose first encounter with lacquer was in 1912. He first used it to patinate the metal vases he was then making. By 1920 he had extended its use to furniture and this became his major area of work. During the 1920s he expanded his Rue Hallé ateliers as demand for his work increased until he occupied almost an entire block. Although Dunand lacquered furniture for other designers or cabinet-makers, including Printz, Ruhlmann and Pierre Legrain, he did not rely on outside cabinet-makers for his own creations, as furniture had to meet specific requirements of construction if it was to be successfully lacquered. Dunand designed many pieces himself but he also enlisted the help of artists who contributed their own designs and this accounts for the very wide range of motifs with which he is associated.

Dunand's most exciting works exploit the richness of large expanses of undecorated lacquer, relieved perhaps by painted or incised angular motifs or the inlaid particles of crushed eggshell, clustered like a miniature crazy paving or scattered like a snowstorm, which became his speciality. His stark black and silver lacquer Smoking Room in the Pavillon d'un Ambassadeur was amongst the highlights and surprises of the 1925 Exhibition. In 1929 he executed furniture and wall decorations for an extraordinary apartment in San Francisco for a Mr. Templeton-Crocker. In the twenties he had created furniture for Madeleine Vionnet, in the early thirties he worked on giant panels for the *Normandie* and was active until the closure of his workshops at the outbreak of war in 1939.

Amidst the diversity of furniture and interior design in the 1920s there emerged a distinct trend among a small but important group of artists towards a style which found its main inspiration in Cubism and primitive African art. The most distinguished and successful exponents of this style were Pierre Legrain, Marcel Coard and Eileen Gray and its most significant and enlightened patron was *couturier* and *mécène* Jacques Doucet.

Doucet's story is fascinating and remarkable. One of the foremost talents in the profession of *couture*, a profession only recently made socially acceptable, he emerged as one of the most perceptive art collectors and connoisseurs of his generation, amongst the first to appreciate the revolutionary work of Cubists, Picasso and Braque, of Modigliani, Ernst, Miro, de Chirico. After years spent collecting the finest works of the French eighteenth century, he sent the entire collection for sale at auction in 1912 to devote himself to forming a collection of contemporary works. Paul Iribe was commissioned to redecorate Doucet's apartment and he, in turn, enlisted the

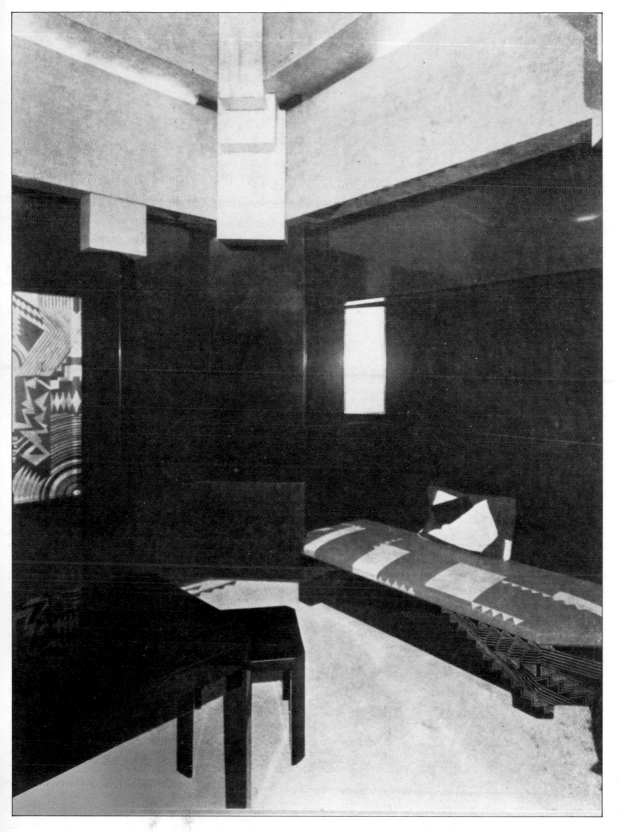

Smoking room, lacquered
walls, ceiling and fittings,
by Jean Dunand, for the
Pavillon d'un Ambassadeur.

Opposite page Lacquer screen by Jean Dunand, *c.* 1925.

Left and below Lacquer screen and *meuble d'appui* designed by Léon and Maurice Jallot, 1929. Collection Hervé Poulain, Paris.

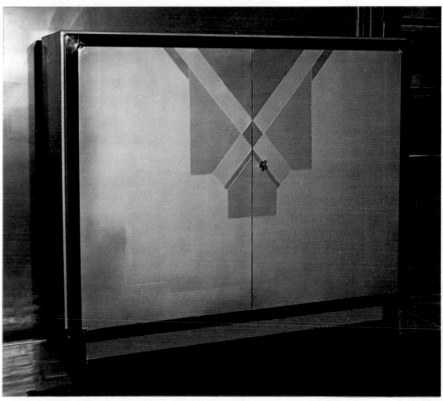

help of Pierre Legrain. In 1914 Iribe left for America and thus ended his work for Doucet. The next ten years or so were spent by Doucet in commissioning and acquiring works of art and furnishings that he found exciting and it seems likely that his own passion for Cubism and African art encouraged his protégés to follow the new source of inspiration.

Doucet's energy was extraordinary. Already into his seventies, he decided in the late 1920s to create a spectacular setting for his collection and entrusted Pierre Legrain with the *aménagement* of a villa at Neuilly that was to be a shrine to contemporary artistic achievement. Doucet died in 1929, the villa barely completed.

Entering one room through massive cast glass doors by René Lalique one sees, beneath Douanier Rousseau's *Snake Charmer*, a remarkable sofa, banded in ivory, by Marcel Coard, beside it a lacquer table of primitive inspiration by Eileen Gray, behind the table a gold lacquered ornamental cube by Pierre Legrain supporting a stone sculpture by Joseph Czaky, to the right a small table by André Groult, the sharkskin top supporting a primitive sculpture, and a sharkskin and lacquered wood stool by Pierre Legrain, its form inspired by the ceremonial stools of the Ashanti

people of Central Africa. Other artists whose furniture and furnishings filled the villa included Rose Adler, Clément Rousseau, Paul-Louis Mergier, Gustave Miklos and Etienne Cournault. Doucet was an exception and as a rule such highly individual designers as Gray, Legrain and Coard found relatively limited success, requiring from their patrons a rare combination of wealth and discernment, and it is therefore not surprising that their clients should often be creative artists themselves, including several *couturiers*, or from artistic or intellectually strong backgrounds.

Eileen Gray's work in lacquer was noticed as early as 1913 by Doucet, who bought the screen *Le Destin* from her in that year. This Irish-born designer who had studied at the Slade before settling in Paris in 1907 created several pieces for Doucet, including a beautiful lacquered table, the legs conceived as giant lilies on stems. However, her most important interior was created in 1924 for Mme. Mathieu Lévy, known professionally in the fashion world as Suzanne Talbot. Here Miss Gray combined the luxury of her lacquer with certain elements that reflected the influence of Doucet and other, purer, more sculptural elements derived from her interest in the ideas of the Dutch De Stijl group. Among the remarkable features of this elegant apartment were the screens and panels of articulated rectangles of lacquered wood. The sophisticated lines of the furniture were contrasted with genuine African stools and objects and wild animal skins. In the late twenties, Miss Gray abandoned lacquer and worked in collaboration with architect Jean Badovici creating furniture that was at once functionalist and eccentric, using such materials as tubular and sheet metal and cork in its manufacture.

Pierre Legrain's patrons included Maurice Martin du Gard, Pierre Meyer, the Vicomte de Noailles and Mme Jeanne Tachard, a milliner friend of Doucet. Legrain was the designer most directly influenced by African art and the strong and aggressive styles of central African furniture and carving are a prominent feature of his work. He also loved to use and to mix unusual textures and materials: open-grained palmwood or limed oak were used with areas of gilt or coloured lacquer, polished chromed metal, parchment, etched glass and ivory. Legrain's career was cut short by his death in 1929 at the age of forty.

Marcel Coard had trained as an architect at the Ecole des Beaux Arts, but found his vocation as a decorator and designer. Like Legrain, he loved and exploited rich materials, rich woods, mother-of-pearl, and lapis lazuli and was one of the first to cover furniture in parchment and leather. His forms were bold and inventive and his feeling for African art is often reflected in the concept or carved details of his furniture.

The late twenties saw the pendulum swing against the highly decorative aspects of Art Deco, against the rich patterns and the multiplicity of opulent woods and materials. The growing taste for simplicity could be seen even in the work of expensive decorators. Jean-Michel Frank was foremost amongst Parisian decorators to abandon pattern, relying on the more subtle luxury of fine materials and plain forms in mellow, neutral tones of cream, ivory and beige. The relative austerity of Pierre Chareau's Bureau Bibliothèque in the Pavillon d'un Ambassadeur of 1925 foreshadowed the tastes of a few years later, by which time Chareau was deeply involved in the design of functional iron-framed furniture and sculptural light fittings.

The principles and achievements of the Bauhaus school were a significant formative influence on French designers, notably in the field of tubular metal furniture. The chairs of Le Corbusier, notably his *chaise longue* of 1928, have become accepted as classics of design and are still in production. The changes that were in the air

Opposite page and above Salon for Mme. J.–Suzanne Talbot, designed by Paul Ruaud, using glass and white cellulose paint to create a Modernist setting for furniture by Eileen Gray, certain elements of which were included in the original Eileen Gray design for the Suzanne Talbot apartment in 1924. *L'Illustration*, May 1933.

Left Chromed tubular-metal and sheet-metal adjustable table, designed by Eileen Gray.

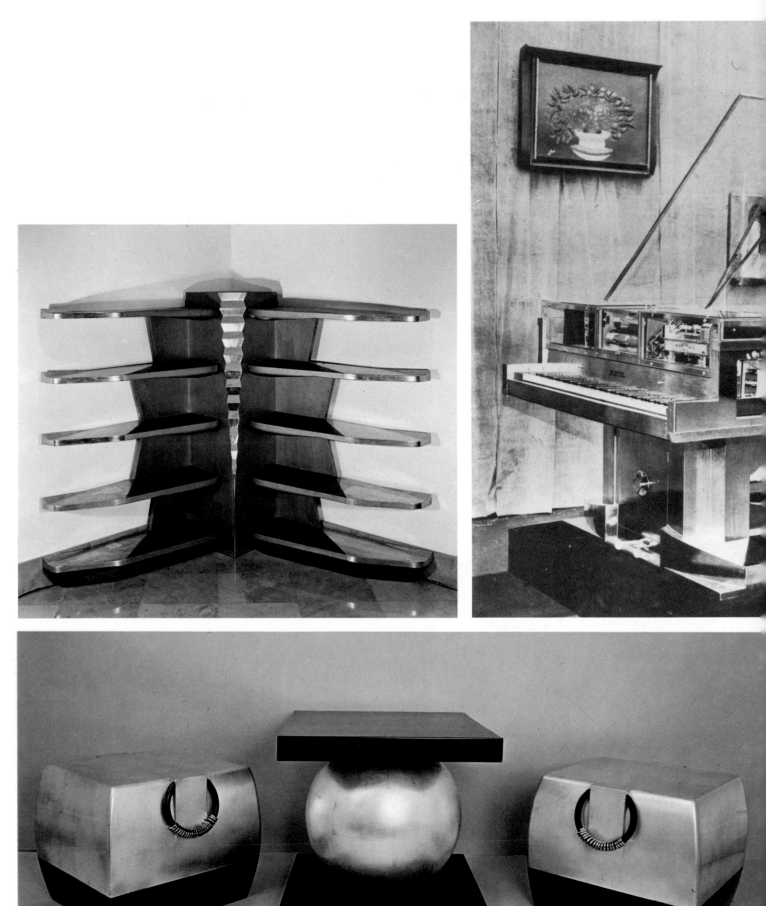

Above Metal and glass piano designed by Pierre Legrain for Pleyel. *Mobilier et Décoration*, April 1929.

Above left Gilt and lacquered wood corner *bibliothèque*, designed by Pierre Legrain.

Left Pair of stools and table designed by Pierre Legrain for Mme. Tachard. Made of silvered and lacquered wood. Collection Mr. and Mrs. Robert Walker, Paris.

Above right *Bureau-bibliothèque* in a modern apartment designed by P. Chareau for Jacques Doucet. The desk, desk stool, table and chairs are by Pierre Legrain, *c.* 1923. *Art et Décoration*, 1924.

Right An interior view of the Doucet villa at Neuilly, 1929.

affected every aspect of domestic design. Modernist rugs by artists such as Jean Lurçat, Eileen Gray or Bruno da Silva Bruhns replaced the florid rugs and carpets associated with the Art Deco style; wall decorations were virtually eliminated. The designers and decorators working in this new style saw themselves as purists, as rationalists, though their brand of functionalism by no means precluded a sense of style. On the contrary, the best Modernist interiors were totally chic, though their icy perfection and often clinical appearance suggest that their designers have somehow overlooked their ultimate function as living spaces for imperfect humans. The welcome virtues of Modernist interiors were in their sense of space and their emphasis on light and cleanliness.

The rallying point for French Modernism was the Union des Artistes Modernes founded in 1930 with, as *Comité Directeur*, Hélène Henry, René Herbst, François Jourdain, Robert Mallet-Stevens and Raymond Templier. The Union was a high-principled organisation whose fecund membership came to include some of the foremost designers in France, several of whom had now outgrown the more decorative style in which they had previously worked. The 1934 list of active members included Rose Adler, Pierre Chareau, Paul Colin, Etienne Cournault, Joseph Czaky, Jean Lambert-Rucki, Jacques Le Chevalier, Le Corbusier, Pierre Jeanneret, Jean Lurçat, Jan and Joël Martel, Gustave Miklos, Charles Moreaux, Charlotte Perriand, Jean Puiforcat and Gérard Sandoz.

There is a law of physics which states that to every action there is an equal and opposite reaction. This law might well be said to apply also to tastes in decorating, and the reaction against Modernism in the mid and late 1930s was as strong as the ideals that had originally fostered the U.A.M. Although the principles of functionalism by no means died a complete death, and, indeed, the U.A.M. enjoyed a renewed lease of life after the Second World War, fashionable decorators reacted against the bareness of interiors. The desire for *fantaisie* allied to the Surrealist taste for the *imprévu*, the *objet trouvé* was responsible for some very remarkable interiors. One of the best known is that of Carlos de Bestigui, particularly interesting because Bestigui had commissioned Le Corbusier to design the structure as the height of the fashion for Modernist simplicity. De Bestigui, a leader of fashion, reacted immediately against the austerity of Le Corbusier's concept by filling the rooms with Baroque furniture and ornaments, blackamoors, elaborately carved mirror frames and fireplaces, dripping chandeliers and well-rounded deep-upholstered seats.

The neo-Baroque taste was also perfectly represented in the apartment decorated in the late thirties for Mme. Helena Rubinstein. In the bedroom, walls, doors and the bed itself were covered in quilted satins, the furniture heavily inlaid with mother-of-pearl. In the salon was a bizarre mixture, carved Indian furniture, a suite of Venetian eighteenth-century shell seat furniture, the inevitable blackamoors. On the walls were paintings by Dali and other Surrealists. including an extraordinary sequin-spangled study of Mme. Rubinstein herself by Pavel Tchelitchew.

Above Coco Chanel photographed by Cecil Beaton with fashionable blackamoor props, 1937.

Right Detail of the apartment of Mme. Helena Rubinstein, late 1930s.

Glass *by Philippe Garner*

FRENCH LUXURY GLASS PRODUCTION had, by the 1890s, reached a remarkably high standard of technical and creative inspiration. This achievement can be traced back to the innovations of a small but significant number of talented artists, notably Philippe-Joseph Brocard, Auguste Jean, Ernest Léveillé and Eugène Rousseau, but above all the genius of one man, Emile Gallé, who inspired a whole generation of artisans and made the Paris Universal Exhibition of 1900 the showcase for creations in glass of an unprecedented technical virtuosity.

If the 1900 Exhibition was a high point for glass elaborately wrought into works of art, it was also the occasion for the prediction by Eugène Houtart that, 'Steel and glass are without doubt the two elements which will characterize the twentieth century and will give their name to it.' The prediction seemed to find its fulfilment after the First World War, when glass became the chosen material for designs of every scale, from the mass-produced luxury of René Lalique's scent bottles to Pierre Chareau's Maison de Verre, undertaken in the late 1920s and completed in 1931. After the First World War, whilst a few artists such as Maurice Marinot continued the tradition of glass object as work of art, established by Emile Gallé, though in a quite different stylistic vein, glass found wide favour with designers and decorators. Madame Lipska created an eccentric home for Antoine, the hairdresser, in which virtually every feature was of glass; Pierre Legrain designed a piano where glass replaced wood, laying bare the internal mechanism.

Léon Rosenthal, writing in 1927 in *La Verrerie Française depuis Cinquante Ans*, pinpointed the Paris Universal Exhibition of 1878 as the dawn of a revival in glass production. Here, beside the grandiose but predictable displays from such large and well-established glassworks as Baccarat and Saint-Louis, were fascinating and innovative exhibits. Brocard showed the fresh and colourful results of his experiments in enamelling, though his debt to Islamic models was still very evident. Jean showed enamelled pieces, but his most notable innovation was in his free-form applications of glass and in his vases of free-blown organic form. Gallé enjoyed his first major opportunity to exhibit. It was Rousseau, however, who attracted most praise and attention for vases of Japanese inspiration, both in their form and in their decoration, but more especially for his glass decorated in the mass, glass imitating agates, jades and other semi-precious stones and often enhanced with internal *craquelé* effects.

Emile Gallé took over the family glass and faïence works in 1874. He had enjoyed the benefit of an extensive education, including a technical apprenticeship in glassworks at Meisenthal and was eager, on taking over the family business, to experiment and extend the range of production. During the late 1870s he built new workshops and experimented with techniques. His exhibit of 1878 was predominantly of enamelled wares in styles of historical inspiration. In 1884 he sent an exhibit to Paris that included his first significant experiments with the internal chemistry of glass itself. His *notice* of exhibits itemises examples of 'Colorations nouvelles du verre, doublés, triplés, verres marbrés, imitation de pierres précieuses, emploi de feuilles métalliques, bulles d'air.'

The sources of Gallé's inspiration were rich and varied. As with so many of the avant-garde of his generation, Gallé's introduction to Japanese art was an important step in creating a new visual language. The ability to create elegant, often almost abstract graphic designs from the plant and insect life that were his most constant fund of motifs, owes a strong debt to Japanese art. Many creations bear witness to this source of inspiration, a taste that Gallé's acquaintance with Count Robert de Montesquiou no doubt did a great deal to foster. Nature was Gallé's great source of

Cameo glass vase by Eugène Rousseau, 1880s.

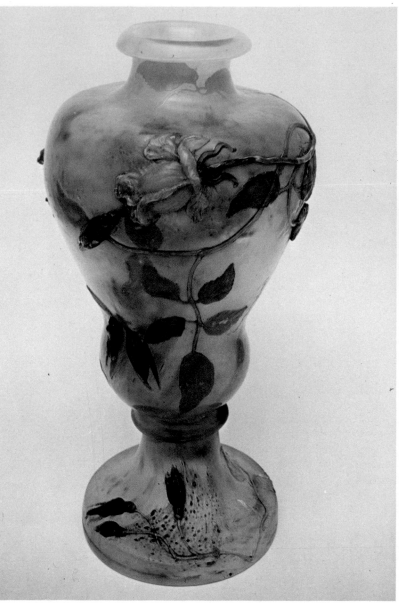

Top Glass vase by Emile Gallé, the decoration in *marqueterie-sur-verre c.* 1900.

Top right 'Rose de France' glass vase by Emile Gallé, *c.* 1900.

Above Emile Gallé in 1889.

Right Enamelled glass bottle by Emile Gallé, 1880s.

Far right 'Onion' vase by Emile Gallé, 1900.

inspiration as the enthusiasm aroused by the botanical studies of his school days hardened into an aesthetic discipline.

Gallé's more personal creations also reflect his poetic ideas, often culled from his extensive reading of contemporary French poets. His *vases parlants* were inscribed with extracts from the verses which had inspired the decoration, verses from Hugo, Baudclaire, Maeterlinck, Gautier, Rimbaud and others, or lines from sources as far apart as Shakespeare and the Bible, the latter in response to Gallé's urge to imbue many of his works with a quasi-religious mysticism.

Triumph at the Paris Exhibition of 1889, where Gallé won a gold medal and the Grand Prix, crowned the growing success of the 1880s. His major innovation in 1889 was his cameo glass, glass of two or more layers carved or etched back, leaving the design in relief in one or more colours against a contrasting ground. The technique was copied from that of Chinese Chien Lung cased glass studied by Gallé in the South Kensington Museum. It was on a debased, mass-production, acid-etched version of his cameo technique that Gallé was to base the prosperity of his business, expanding during the 1890s to the point where, around 1900, he employed some three hundred people with retail outlets as far afield as Frankfurt and London (opened 1904). Gallé's status as an artist of national importance was confirmed by the award in 1889 of the Légion d'Honneur and by major public commissions such as the vases presented by the nation in 1896 to the Tsar and Tsarina of Russia.

The year 1897 saw the introduction by Gallé of a new technique, *marqueterie-sur-verre*, which involved inlaying semi-molten glass details of decoration into the semi-molten body of the piece being worked on. The 1900 Paris Exhibition was perhaps Gallé's finest hour, his last major showing before his death from leukaemia in 1904. He at last escaped from his tendency to make vases fascinating in the detail, but pedestrian in form. In 1900 he showed more sculptural freedom with pieces of completely organic form or worked in high relief with fluid applications of glass. Two of his greatest masterpieces date from his post-1900 Exhibition period, the *Main aux Algues* and the extraordinary lamp, *Les Coprins*, of 1904.

Gallé's influence on contemporary glassmakers was considerable, as indeed was his influence on craftsmen in other media in his home town of Nancy. A group of artists allied themselves in 1901 as the 'Ecole de Nancy, Alliance Provinciale des Industries d'Art'. Gallé, naturally, was their president and guiding light; Louis Majorelle, Eugène Vallin and the Daum brothers were vice-presidents. The Ecole de Nancy style of glass became prevalent in France, produced by local firms, such as that of the brothers Désiré and Eugène Muller and the Verrerie de Nancy of the Daum brothers, and by other firms such as that of Auguste Legras who had taken over the Cristalleries of Saint Denis and of Pantin. The Muller brothers had started as craftsmen working in the Gallé ateliers before setting up their own business in the late 1890s, a business that was to prosper through a succession of styles until finally closing down in 1936.

Carved cameo and applied glass vase from the Daum workshops, with gilt-bronze base, *c.* 1900.

Above Daum glass bowl, overlaid and etched, 1920s.
Above right *Pâte-de-verre* medallions by Henri Cros, 1880s. Collection of Roger Marx.

Right *Pâte-de-verre* bowl by François-Emile Décorchemont, 1920s.

Alphonse-Georges Reyen, after an apprenticeship, first with Gallé in the 1870s and then with Rousseau, produced cameo vases of fine quality in the Nancy idiom around 1900. Eugène Michel, who had worked with Rousseau and subsequently with his associate and successor Ernest Léveillé, produced a few exceptional cameo vases worked in high relief. The Frères Pannier created a series of fine carved cameo vases for the Escalier de Cristal in Paris, again showing a strong debt to Gallé.

Though the largest glassworks operating in the shadow of Emile Gallé was that of Legras, employing at the turn of the century some fifteen hundred people, the most notable rivals to Gallé were the Daum brothers, Auguste and Antonin, who, by the 1890s, shared the responsibility of the family business. They were more dependent than Gallé on the creativity of their employees and this was to their advantage. When Gallé died there began a steady decline in his factory's production until its final closure in 1935. The broader creative basis of the Daum works, however, ensured their success through several generations, with the result that Daum is still today an important name in French glass production.

Though the Daum works were never able to produce *tours de force* as extraordinary as the best of Gallé's creations, they were capable of a very high technical and artistic standard. They made their own a particular style of broad surface faceting, an effect described as *martelé*. They counted amongst their collaborators Jacques Gruber, who worked with them between 1894 and 1897 before turning his interest to cabinet-making, Eugène Goll, their most talented glassworker, responsible for some of the most sculptural and inventive pieces that bear the Daum mark, and Walter who had his own atelier within the Daum works between about 1906 and the First World War for the creation of *pâte-de-verre*, a process which the Daum brothers were the first to exploit commercially.

After the hiatus of the war the Daum works went back into production and worked through the twenties and thirties in a new decorative idiom. Natural motifs fell out of favour, to be replaced by abstract geometric designs. Amongst the factory's most impressive creations during this period were the deep-etched angular table lamps in colourless glass that marked so strong a contrast with the warmth and femininity of the cameo glass table lamps of the early years of the century.

The *pâte-de-verre* process used by Walter *chez* Daum involved the firing of a body built up in a mould from a paste of powdered glass and metallic oxides to give colour. The technique was first revived in the nineteenth century by artist-sculptor Henri Cros. The classical themes he favoured reflected his original source of inspiration, ancient glass paste creations exhibited in Paris in 1878. Cros' work, characterised by a rough, pitted surface, weak, pastel colours and a total opacity, became more ambitious after 1892, when the Manufacture de Sèvres put a workshop at his disposal, and included such projects as the mural fountain of 1893 for the Musée du Luxembourg. His son Jean continued in his father's footsteps and produced similar work.

Two other artists of note worked independently through the 1890s to perfect their own *pâte-de-verre* techniques. Albert Dammouse, working at Sèvres, turned his attention from porcelain to glass, exhibiting his first fragile, brittle and opaque *pâte-de-verre* bowls and vases in 1898. The next few years saw the perfection of his skills as his glass achieved a more translucent quality and he undertook daring works combining motifs of translucent *pâte-d'émail* within an opaque tracery of *pâte-de-verre*. Dammouse worked in *pâte-de-verre* until his death in 1926. Georges Despret achieved his first successes around 1900. His hallmark was work in relief, *pâte-de-verre* fish, masks or figures, vases modelled with scarabs or seahorses. He worked through the 1920s and 1930s, changing his style to suit the times and collaborating with sculptors, such as Pierre Le Faguays, on the creation of fashionable themes.

Walter similarly employed sculptors to design subjects for execution in *pâte-de-verre* in the new workshops he set up in 1919. His collaborators included Henri Bergé, whose taste was still unfashionably confined to the stylised motifs from nature of Nancy Art Nouveau, and the sculptor J. Descomps. This same lingering-on of Art Nouveau motifs was evident in the post-war output of the most commercial of *pâte-de-verre* artists, Gabriel Argy-Rousseau, though he proved himself equally capable of interpreting current tastes, including the mid and late twenties taste for Egyptian motifs.

The major talent to work in *pâte-de-verre* was perhaps François-Emile Décorchemont, whose first pieces date from 1903. His earliest pieces were evocative of Dammouse with their mat, thin and brittle bodies and trailing Art Nouveau motifs, but after 1908 he found a more personal style when he started to cast his vases by the *cire perdue* process. Between 1908 and 1914 Décorchemont produced a series of semi-translucent, heavy-bodied vases cast with scarabs or natural motifs such as seaweed. The chunky self-confidence of these vases was much admired as was the quality of the more sober forms, sometimes enhanced with geometric decorations, which he created after the war. During the 1930s his work became more ponderous, more mechanical and less inspired.

The Art Deco style found expression in the feminine and decorative glass designs of a number of artists and was most successfully captured in the enamelled glassware very much in evidence in contemporary illustrated folios on the French decorative arts during the early and mid twenties. The names that recur are those of Marcel Goupy, Decuper-Delvaux, Quenvit, Jean Luce, Georges Chevalier working for the Cristalleries de Baccarat and Mme Cless-Brothier for Louis Vuitton; the most usual motifs were sprays of blossom, highly formalised flowers, figure or animal subjects in a restrained Neo-classical taste.

The trade marks Le Verre Français, Déguy and Schneider, the latter representing the Cristalleries de Schneider founded by Charles Schneider, an old pupil of Emile Gallé's, became known during the twenties and into the thirties for etched glass, usually in harsh colours, and decorated with rigidly stylised flowers, insects, or the geometric motifs that were becoming increasingly popular. The names of Déguy and Schneider also became

Left *Pâte-de-verre* dish by Gabriel Argy-Rousseau, 1920s.

Right 'L'Oiseau de Feu', Lalique glass and bronze lamp, 1920s.

Below left *Pâte-de-verre* vase by Gabriel Argy-Rousseau, 1920s.

Below Lalique glass 'Serpent' vase, 1920s.

Below right *Cire perdue* glass vase by René Lalique, *c.* 1905–10.

Below far right Perfume bottles, powder boxes and an eagle's head seal, from Lalique's and other factories, 1920s.

Deep etched glass vase by
Maurice Marinot, 1920s.

associated with the mottled glass regularly used for shades in ornamental lamps, often in elaborate mounts by *ferronniers* such as Edgar Brandt.

French art glass production between the wars was dominated, however, by two strong yet contrasting talents, René Lalique and Maurice Marinot, the former responsible for combining modern techniques of mass-production with a consistently high level of artistic involvement, the latter for raising glasswork to the level of a fine art in an idiom as appropriate to the twentieth century as that of Gallé had been to the *fin-de-siècle*.

René Lalique's interest in glass dated back to the 1890s and his use of cast glass in multi-media works of art; around 1900 he first began to use glass in his exquisite jewellery, caring nothing for its lack of intrinsic worth if its qualities were appropriate to the design. It is from about this time that date his earliest experiments in the creation of all-glass *cire perdue* pieces, including vases and panels such as those used by Lalique in the decoration of his 40 Cours de la Reine home.

In 1902 he set up a small glassworks, employing four workers, at Clairfontaine. Lalique's first commission for commercial glass was from the parfumeur Coty who approached him to design scent bottles. Between 1907–8 these were

made for Lalique by the firm of Legras

Lalique's growing interest in glass encouraged the opening of his own glassworks at Combs-la-Ville in 1909. By 1912 his career as a jeweller was over and a new career lay open to him. Between 1918 and 1922 he supervised the construction of enlarged works, the Verrerie d'Art – René Lalique & Cie., at Wingen-sur-Moder. Through the 1920s and until the final close of production in 1939 the Lalique factory produced an extensive range of vases, glasses and other tableware, clocks, lamps, scent bottles, brooches, pendants, dressing table sets, even motor car mascots and items of furniture. Produced in very large quantities in clear, opalescent or, more rarely, coloured glass, the Lalique output was of good but not remarkable quality; its greatest distinction was in the stylish repertoire of designs, ranging from elegant evocations of Lalique's Art Nouveau phase, through pretty renderings of all the typical Art Deco themes to more aggressively modern motifs, most of them Lalique's own creation.

Lalique triumphed at the Paris Exhibition of 1925 with examples of his factory's work in many of the French pavilions, notably glass beams, panels and furniture for the Pavillon de la Manufacture Nationale de Sèvres. Amongst his most

Enamelled glass *coupe* by
Maurice Marinot, *c.* 1920.

prestigious commissions was the decoration of the grand dining saloon of the *Normandie*, launched in 1932. Lalique's success inevitably spawned imitators at various levels of the market, from Sabino, whose creations could on occasion rival those of Lalique, to Hunebelle, Verlys and others.

Maurice Marinot ranks in a category of his own. A painter working in the *fauve* style, he first became intrigued by the possibilities of glass during a visit to the Bar-sur-Seine glassworks of his friends the Viard brothers in 1911. Nineteen-thirteen marked the beginning of his serious concentration on glass as he decorated in brilliant enamels glass bodies made up to his designs by the Viard's gaffers. Writing in 1920 in *L'Amour de l'Art* on 'Le Métier du Verre Soufflé' Marinot expressed his feeling, in strong contrast to the ideas of Art Nouveau glassworkers, that 'the two essential qualities of glass are its translucence and its brilliance.' His interest in enamelled decoration waned with the growth of his passion for the intrinsic qualities of glass.

By 1922 he had abandoned enamelling and started to learn the skills of glass-blowing at a furnace put at his disposal by the Viard brothers. He blew heavy-bodied clear glass vases and flasks, often enhanced by internal flights of minute air bubbles, which he would then decorate, cold, with strong angular motifs achieved by deep and rough etching and wheel carving. In his pursuit of the ultimate purity in glass creation Marinot, about 1927, showed greater interest than before in what he called 'modelage à chaud'; all the creative work was done at the furnace on semi-molten glass. Internal effects were achieved by metallic oxides on the surface which would then be sheathed in a gather of clear glass; heavy applications were worked deftly around the semi-molten glass with rudimentary but effective tools.

The film made in 1933 by Jean Benoît Lévy of Marinot at work well conveys the magic and confidence of his sculpting the liquid metal in this method of 'modelage à chaud' that characterised his mature phase. He abandoned glass in 1937 to revert to painting, but it is on his glass and not his canvases that his reputation rests.

Marinot's strong personal style found considerable success with contemporary critics and bred the inevitable crop of imitators. The Daum works produced a series of deep-etched vases in a more decorative version of the Marinot style; Henri Navarre and André Thuret were perhaps his most gifted imitators, though, even at their best, their work lacked the brilliance of Marinot's.

Ceramics *by Lynne Thornton*

THE CERAMISTS OF THE LATE NINETEENTH CENTURY remained, to a certain extent, outside the mainstream of the applied arts of the time, for temperamental, stylistic and geographical reasons. The two main centres of Art Nouveau, except for ceramics, were Paris and Nancy. The designers, who did not carry out the work with their own hands, were generally part of artistic, literary or fashionable circles, or closely connected with them. The members of the circles not only bought the objects, but also helped the designers to be better known through their social connections.

The ceramists, on the other hand, although they participated in international exhibitions and Paris salons, were scattered around France, using local clays and, for the most part, themselves throwing, turning, glazing and firing, selling only to close friends or personal customers. They were passionately involved with the fusion of earth and fire, going through poverty or ill-health with a dogged determination. There was none of the *fin-de-siècle* intellectualism of the other branches of Art Nouveau, but a profound love of the craft, a sensual contact with the grain of a glaze or the form of a vase, which had taken shape through the potter's skill and artistic impulsion, which came from the heart rather than from the brain.

By the twentieth century, there were many more retail outlets. There was also a closer collaboration between the large manufacturers and ceramic designers. By the late twenties and thirties, things had gone to the extreme; many ceramists believed that there was no longer place for unique pieces, but that ceramics should be made to be distributed on a wide scale. The split became so great between the ideals of the artist-potter of the late nineteenth century and the ceramic industrialisation of the twentieth, that nowadays in France there are very few studio potters; on the one side there are the factories, and on the other, artisans working in a traditional manner in the provinces.

The first stirrings of the modern art pottery movement began in France in the 1830s, with Avisseau, Pull, Barbizet and Sergent, who were inspired by the naturalism of the sixteenth-century potter, Palissy. At the same time, Ziegler was making heavy saltglazed stoneware in archaic forms. We then come to Théodore Deck, a remarkable technician who made brightly-coloured faïence with motifs drawn from Japan, Turkey, Egypt and China. The 1870s were notable for the Haviland workshops in Auteuil, directed by Ernest Chaplet. Although this short-lived enterprise was not a great success financially, the red earth vases decorated in coloured liquid clay (*barbotine*) were an important stand against the ostentation and impersonality of factory-produced ceramics.

In 1881 the Haviland workshops moved to Rue Blomet in Paris, where Chaplet, together with Edouard and Albert Dammouse, Ringel d'Illzach, Hexamer and others, made dark-brown stoneware with incised decoration, the coloured glazes encircled with gold in the manner of *cloisonné* enamels. It was at this time that Paul Gauguin started making ceramics, fired by Chaplet, who had bought the business from Haviland's in 1885. Two years later, Chaplet sold it to Auguste

Left Stoneware vase by
Albert Dammouse, *c*. 1900.

Right Stoneware dish by
Ernest Chaplet, *c*. 1900.

Auguste Delaherche
drawing his ceramics from
the kiln. Illustrated in *Les
Arts*, Paris 1920.

Delaherche and it was with Delaherche that Gauguin continued to work on his return from Martinique in 1887.

The main purpose of Chaplet's decision to move from Paris to Choisy-le-Roi was to continue his research into *flambé* glazes on porcelain. The remarkable results ranged from shiny *sang-de-boeuf* to veined, spotted and jaspered turquoise and white. He also made vases and dishes with thick glazes whose granular surfaces resembled pitted orange peel. Although porcelain became his great passion, he went on making stoneware, some in collaboration with the sculptor Jules Dalou. Chaplet went blind in 1904 and left the direction of the studio to his grandson, Emile Lenoble.

Auguste Delaherche was more prolific than Chaplet, and it is perhaps because his work is to be found in relatively large quantities, that his masterpieces are overshadowed by the earlier rustic work. He came from the Beauvaisis, a traditional ceramic making area. Between 1883 and 1886 he worked in saltglaze stoneware, but his aim to sell art ceramics at low prices met with little success. In Paris, he began to use drip glazes which he had seen on Japanese stoneware, with engraved or raised floral decoration, eventually winning a gold medal at the 1889 Universal Exhibition. In 1894, Delaherche moved to Armentières, in the Beauvaisis, and in the following ten years he relied for effect on deep, pure monochrome glazes on simple forms. After 1904, he made unique pieces, only keeping those which were perfect, refusing to accept any result, however beautiful, if it was by accident and not entirely controlled by himself. At the age of sixty-eight, Delaherche began to make delicate white porcelain vases with a pierced decoration of stylised flowers, now very rare.

Of Chaplet's collaborators, Albert Dammouse is of particular interest. Son of a Sèvres sculptor, he began his career by decorating in *pâte-sur-pâte*. After having worked with Chaplet, he set up his own studios in the village of Sèvres in 1892, where he made stoneware, faïence and porcelain ornamented with flowers, leaves or seaweed. Dammouse then turned to making vases and bowls in translucid paste, which he first exhibited in 1898.

François-Emile Décorchemont, painter and later famous glass-maker, also made fragile objects in *pâte-d'émail* and *pâte-de-verre* around 1900. His first experiments, however, were in stoneware, which he fired in his own room. A more professional ceramist was Adrien-Pierre Dalpayrat. As a Master Potter, he travelled all over France, settling in 1889 in Bourg-la-Reine, where he worked with his wife and three sons. Although he made some porcelain and faïence, Dalpayrat is best known for his stoneware vases, sculpted either in strange twisted shapes or in the form of animals, fruit or vegetables. He perfected a *sang-de-boeuf* glaze called 'rouge Dalpayrat', which he mixed with spinach green, lapis blue, purple and white. Together with Adèle Lesbros and Voisin, Dalpayrat made ceramics for wide distribution at a low cost, but he also created unique pieces, sometimes mounted in ormolu. Many of his best pieces were bought by European museums.

Edmond Lachenal was a painter, sculptor and decorator. After having worked with Théodore Deck for ten years, he set up his own ceramic workshops at the age of twenty-five, at Châtillon-sous-Bagneux. He first of all made faïence decorated in the Isnik taste, then, perfecting a technique of metallo-ceramics by electrolysis and using hydrofluoric acid to obtain matt *velouté* glazes. Lachenal's faïence and stoneware vases ornamented with flowers or animals had a certain success, but he became particularly known for his stoneware editions of sculptures by Rodin, de Frumerie, Dejean, Fix-Masseau and Saint-Marceaux. Lachenal, in the first years of the twentieth century, abandoned ceramics for the theatre, leaving his workshops to his wife and son Raoul. In 1911, Raoul set up on his own in Boulogne, where he made ceramics, either in series or unique pieces, with geometric or stylised floral designs in chestnut, red, black, green and white.

This editing of sculptures in ceramics and the application of stoneware to architecture was an important feature of Art Nouveau. Besides Dalpayrat, Lachenal and Jeanneney, the two leading figures in this field were Bigot and Muller. Alexandre Bigot, inspired by the Japanese ceramics at the 1889 Universal Exhibition, set up a kiln at Mer in the Loire-et-Cher. From 1894 on, he showed his plates with newts, frogs and mermaids in low relief swimming among deep translucid glazes. After 1900, he turned towards making stoneware for both inside and outside buildings (including Guimard's Castel Béranger), and editing sculpture. He got into financial difficulties and his workshops closed in 1914.

Emile Muller's factory at Ivry was more commercial in every sense. In his published catalogue there were lists of all the stoneware sculpture available, including the well-known portrait of Yvette Guilbert by Toulouse-Lautrec. Muller, together with the firms Gentil et Bourdet and Hyppolyte Boulanger, made much of the architectural ceramics of the time.

Japan can be said to have been one of the major influences in Art Nouveau ceramics, but there were in fact two streams of influence. Firstly, there was the Japan of blue and white porcelain, fans, kimonos and woodcuts enjoyed by the Goncourts, Bing, Whistler, Vever and the Impressionists. Among the ceramists who used these superficial motifs of the Orient were Deck, the Cazin family, Moreau-Nelaton and Gallé. Jean-Charles Cazin, who had been employed on a freelance basis by the Fulham Factory in England in 1872, decorated his stoneware with incised branches of flowers and leaves in the Japanese manner. His son Michel, painter, engraver, sculptor, medal-maker and ceramist, worked with his wife Berthe in his father's studios. His squat vases in monochrome glazes have leaves and shells in low relief, sometimes mounted in bronze.

Etienne Moreau-Nelaton was a well-known writer, painter and collector. While his first pieces were of rustic simplicity in grey-yellow and blue, his later work, vases and bottles in faïence and stoneware, were decorated with flowers. This observation of nature in close-up, learnt from the Japanese, was particularly marked in the work of Emile Gallé. During the 1890s, he covered faïence with insects and flowers on gold grounds. His earlier ceramics, though, had shown none of this realism, being at first closely based on eighteenth-century models and then decorated with historical subjects or Egyptian motifs.

The other aspect of the Japanese influence, the rough stoneware, the impurities of natural ingredients, the drip glazes and, indeed, the Oriental philosophy, touched many Art Nouveau ceramists, but most notably the School of Saint-Amand. The leader was Jean Carriès, a man of humble origins, who had painfully made a career for himself sculpting in a realist manner quite opposed to the current academic style. Although he had been impressed by the Oriental ceramics at the 1878 Universal Exhibition, it was those pieces in the collection of his friend, Paul Jeanneney, which struck him like a divine revelation. Carriès settled in Saint-Amand-en-Puisaye in the Nièvre where he learned the rudiments of ceramic making from the local potters. He worked like a man inspired, strenuously fighting against technical and financial difficulties making vases with *gris*, *cendré* and *ciré* glazes over which he poured pink or gold enamels. Out of his hands grew grotesque masks, hare-eared toads, squat grinning goblins, like malevolent manifestations of the devil driving

Grotesque mask in stoneware by Jean Carriès, *c.* 1890.

Right Stoneware vase with ormolu mounts by Georges Hoentschel, *c.* 1900.

Below Stoneware vases and pears by Georges Hoentschel, Emile Grittel and Henri de Vallombreuse, *c.* 1900.

Opposite page Stoneware bust, *Flore*, by Louis Chalon and Emile Muller, *c.* 1900.

him on. In 1889 the Princess of Scey-Montbéliard commissioned from him a doorway for a library containing the partition of Wagner's *Parsifal*, but Carriès, tubercular from an early age, exhausted by the demands of his chosen craft and harrassed by his patron's demands, died before it could be finished.

All Carriès' work was left to his great friend, Georges Hoentschel, a celebrated interior decorator, collector and man of the world. Hoentschel bought Carriès' house, the Château de Montriveau, and began to make stoneware himself. His work is closer to the Japanese originals than to Carriès; the vases, in sober blue, green, grey and beige, were sometimes finished with ivory stoppers, sometimes mounted in ormolu, revealing his taste for the Orient and the eighteenth century. In the last few years of his life, he worked mostly in the studio in Clichy belonging to Emile Grittel.

Grittel, who had worked for Hoentschel's large decorating company, had joined him at Saint-Amand and probably himself executed much of the ceramics signed with Hoentschel's monogram. Grittel made vases, pears and gourds with coloured or gold drip glazes on coral, olive-green and deep brown grounds. His name was scarcely mentioned in the art press of the time and his work has only recently been rediscovered. Carriès' great passion for ceramics inspired others to go to Saint-Amand after his death, including Paul Jeanneney, who made stoneware with bamboo shapes, cut-out bodies and dripped or 'curdled' glazes. He was followed by William Lee, Henri de Vallombreuse and Count Nils de Bark, who were little more than dilettantes.

Lustreware is another piece in the jig-saw of nineteenth-century ceramics. Less important than in England (Maws, Pilkingtons, De Morgan), there was nonetheless a most interesting production made at Golfe-Juan by the Massier family, Clément, Delphin and Jérôme. Some of the best stoneware with shimmering blue, violet, mauve, silver and green lustre glazes was signed by Lucien Lévy-Dhurmer, famous pastellist, who was at one time the artistic director of the works.

The making of French Art Nouveau porcelain remained almost exclusively in the hands of the Manufacture Nationale de Sèvres and Limoges. Sèvres, having reached the peak of technical perfection, had been trying for some years to shake the state-supported artists out of their torpor. Experiments were made with new pastes and glazes and models were provided by Frémiet, Chéret, Léonard, Guimard, and others. With an administrative and artistic shake-up in preparation for the 1900 Universal Exhibition, Sèvres began to come into line with the Modern Movement.

One of the most interesting Sèvres ceramists was Taxile Doat who, besides his work for the factory, fired in his own kiln in Paris and, after 1898, in the village of Sèvres. Internationally famous for his *pâte-sur-pâte* medallions applied to porcelain bodies, Doat published a technical treatise on high-fire ceramics in the United States and in 1909 taught at the St. Louis University City. With the opening of hostilities, he returned to France, where he continued to work until the early 1930s. As for the Limoges porcelain, this was designed by Georges de Feure and Edward Col-

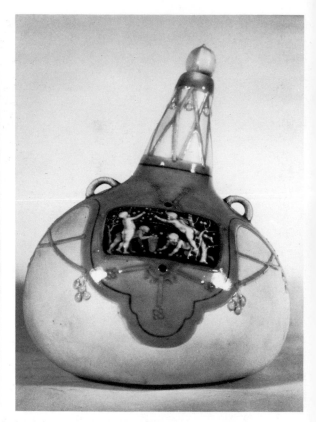

Right and far right
Porcelain gourds decorated in *pâte-sur-pâte* by Taxile Doat, *c*. 1902.

onna for Samuel Bing's shop, L'Art Nouveau, the delicate white bodies painted with sophisticated designs in pink, powder-blue and green, which are typically Parisian in feeling. Both Bing and Meier-Graefe, owner of La Maison Moderne, were helpful in bringing Art Nouveau ceramics to the public's notice.

If the late nineteenth century was marked by the influence of Japan and the revival of stoneware, then the early twentieth century was notable for the interest in Chinese and Islamic ceramics, and the importance of brightly-coloured painted faïence. Emile Decoeur was perhaps the greatest purist of the 'Chinese' ceramists. At the age of fourteen he was employed by Edmond Lachenal with whom he worked for ten years; many pieces of faïence are marked with both their monograms or names. Decoeur eventually left Lachenal's workshops and, after a brief collaboration with Rumèbe, set up on his own. A great admirer of Carriès, he began to work exclusively in stoneware but was later to consider the Art Nouveau decoration on these early vases as 'youthful mistakes'.

In 1907, Decoeur settled at Fontenay-les-Roses. The thin or 'clotted' glazes on his stoneware and later porcelain vases and bowls became completely monochrome, in pink, pale green, yellow, white and black. His pure Oriental forms and the perfection of his glazes made Decoeur the best known ceramist in France of the 1920s and 1930s.

Another notable ceramist of the twenties was Emile Lenoble. After seven years in an industrial ceramic factory, in 1903 Lenoble went back to the home of his grandfather, Ernest Chaplet, in Choisy-le-Roi. Around 1910 he began to paint his stoneware, something usually done only to porcelain or faïence. His vases were later overlaid with slip engraved with friezes of chevrons, spirals, zigzags, arabesques and stylised leaves and flowers in broken white, bronze-brown and black. Lenoble

had been inspired by Japanese and Korean ceramics seen in the collection of the engraver Henri Rivière, but after the war, he became attracted to China. Between 1919 and 1930, he widened his palette, using wallflower-yellows and browns, celadon-green and lapis-blue, azure and turquoise, the *sgraffito* decoration becoming secondary to the depth and quality of the glaze.

Henri Simmen studied ceramic techniques with Lachenal. His first personal pieces of stoneware were with black and brown abstract motifs on salt-glazed grounds, with occasional touches of gold enamelling. On his return from the Far East after the war, he modelled his stoneware by hand and used only natural ingredients to make his remarkable glazes in *aventurine*, imperial yellow, celadon, white and brilliant red. His Japanese wife, Madame O'Kin Simmen, sculpted stoppers, bases or handles in ivory and horn.

Séraphin Soudbinine, a Russian from Novgorod, had become one of Rodin's favourite assistants. However, after seeing the Far Eastern ceramics in the Metropolitan Museum in New York, he began to create archaic-looking vases sculpted with grotesque monsters in matt stoneware on brown shiny grounds, and animals and dishes in retractory, 'wickerwork' or 'curdled' glazes. He kept only the perfect pieces and struggled for three years to obtain a black glaze. A bomb destroyed Soudbinine's studio during the war; ill and ruined, he died in 1944, leaving only a few pieces, all of exceptional quality.

Georges Serré was an apprentice at the Sèvres factory from 1902 until the beginning of the First World War. During the war, he was sent to Saigon, where he taught ceramics in the native art schools. He participated at the Colonial Exhibition of Marseilles, (1922) and Paris (1931), remaining attached to Chinese and Khmer art all his life. He engraved geometric patterns on the half-dried grounds of his unique pieces, fired in his studio in

Left Stoneware bowl by Georges Serré, *c.* 1934.

Below left Faïence vase by Edouard Cazaux, *c.* 1930–5.

Below Stoneware pot and cover by Séraphin Soudbinine, *c.* 1930–5.

A group of stoneware
vessels; behind: plate
(*c*. 1914) and vase
(*c*. 1925) by Raoul
Lachenal; front (l. to r.):
two vases (*c*. 1930) by
Emile Decoeur; vase by
Emile Lenoble (*c*. 1913).

the village of Sèvres. His talent was recognised at an exhibition at Rouard's (Rouard had replaced Bing and Meier-Graefe as patron and dealer of contemporary applied arts). Sculptors such as Dejean, Gimond, Niclausse, Comtesse, asked him to edit their works in brown granular stoneware.

Paul Beyer was very much involved in the revival of stoneware in France during the twenties and thirties, but his stylistic sources were very different from those of Serré. Working in Lyons, Beyer made objects for everyday use with salt-glazes, in the manner of the traditional country potters. Besides these pieces, often with zoomorphic forms and concentric engraved surfaces, he sculpted hierarchic statues of saints with their attributes. In the mid-1930s, Beyer was lent a mill by Sèvres where he went on experimenting, moving even further towards simplification. In 1942, he settled at La Borne, near Bourges, and gave a new lease of life to this village of potters.

One of the most marked features of early twentieth-century ceramics was the taste for decorated faïence. The leading exponents were Fernand Rumèbe, Edouard Cazaux, Jean Mayodon, René Buthaud and André Metthey. While Rumèbe was influenced by Middle Eastern ceramics and Khmer art, the others ornamented their work

with figures and animals in a Neo-classical style. Metthey had become renowned for his ceramics decorated by the Fauve artists; this lasted only a few years, and he began himself to paint, using thick polychrome glazes with a crackled gold finish, which were especially popular at the time. While Metthey, in chronic ill-health, died in 1920, Mayodon was to continue decorating pools, fountains and transatlantic liners, while Buthaud, from 1939 to 1955, made statues in stanniferous glazed faïence.

During the 1920s and 1930s, many ceramists and decorators were employed by manufacturers or received commissions from them, while those working individually were no longer willing to make rare and unique pieces at the price of continual effort and sacrifices of time, money and health. They preferred to make or design ceramics which, through casting or other methods, could be made on a large scale. Sèvres, now financially independent, could no longer impose its taste on the public, but had to join the Modern Movement in order to survive commercially: they opened a faïence section under Etienne Avenard, experimented in new pastes, asked well-known painters for models to decorate services and edited sculpture by popular artists.

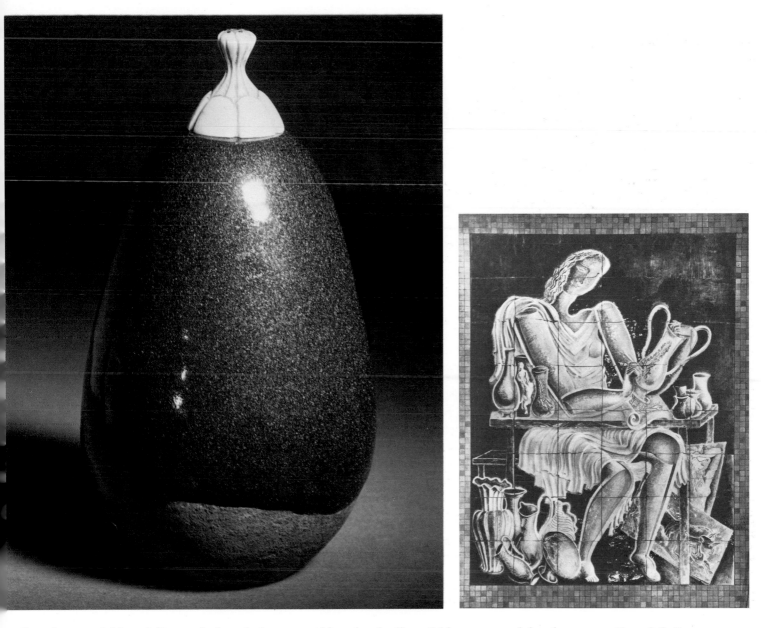

Jean Luce and Marcel Goupy designed elegant and useful tableware, and Maurice Gensoli made pieces with zoomorphic finials sculpted in porcelain paste and covered with crystalline glazes of great purity. Sèvres participated in the decoration of the *Normandie* launched in 1932, and exhibited giant ceramic murals designed by Zadkine, de Chirico, Gromaire, and others, at the 1937 Paris Exhibition. Limoges too, commissioned independent artists, including Luce and Goupy. Nearly all the large Parisian department stores and decorators had their own ceramic section; Louis Süe and André Mare (La Compagnie des Arts Français) sold Baroque faïence with thick white slip glaze; Claude Lévy, Colette Guéden and Jean and Jacques Adnet designed for Primavera (Printemps). The Adnet brothers also supplied models to La Maîtrise (Galeries Lafayette).

Among the ceramists working on their own were Jean Besnard, who began by making robust primitive pottery with moulded or incised geometric decoration. During the 1930s, he made vases with lacy surfaces (*dentellés*) and humorous figures with retracted glazes (*crispés*). Jacques Lenoble, son of Emile Lenoble and great-grandson of Ernest Chaplet, worked with his wife, Hélène, daughter of the painter Henri Lebasque. The

white clay bodies of his vases and bowls were covered with creamy slip in turquoise, white, black, coral, burnt ochre; all surprise results of firing or glazing were to be eliminated. Lenoble, like so many others during the 1930s, turned towards the decoration in ceramics of transatlantic liners, swimming pools and buildings. André Fau, who had worked in the faïence section of Sèvres, became an 'industrial art ceramist', believing in 'selection and diffusion'; Pierre Lebasque, brother of Hélène Lenoble, modelled fish; Henri Chaumeil made moulded and pierced faïence in crackled glazes; Luc Lanel and his wife Marjolaine, whose first pieces were fired by Chaumeil, made stanniferous faïence fountains, light fittings, radiator covers and panels to be applied to furniture; Guidette Carbonnel tiles with flowers, animals and figures in low relief; and Georges Jouve, vases with gun-metal glazes and ceramic panels for interior decoration.

Of course a new generation of ceramists with different aesthetics and priorities of production began to work after the Second World War, but never again were French ceramics to reach the heights and magnificence of its Art Nouveau and Art Deco artists. The exhibition of 1925 had heralded a decline in the French applied arts.

Above left Stoneware vase with an *aventurine* glaze by Henri Simmen. Ivory stopper carved by Mme. O'Kin Simmen, *c.* 1925–30.

Above Low-relief panel in Sèvres stanniferous faïence after a drawing by Ossip Zadkine. Executed for the 1937 Paris International Exhibition.

Silver, Jewellery and Metalwork *by Philippe Garner*

THE CRAFTS OF SILVER, jewellery, metalwork and small-scale sculpture and the allied skills of enamelling and, of course, design, make a rich and significant study in the period from 1890 to 1940. The standards of French craftsmanship within these areas were very high indeed, unrivalled in any other country, and the period was rich in its constant variety of invention. Tastes in jewellery most notably, so susceptible to the vagaries and whims of fashion, serve as an expressive mirror of the period, reflecting in turn the hot-house decadence of the *fin-de-siècle*, the world of Boldini's frothy aristocrats, and the brittle austerity of Modernism.

The Art Nouveau period was a truly great one for French jewellery, and there was no greater single talent than René Lalique. At the age of sixteen, on the death of his father, Lalique was apprenticed to the celebrated goldsmith Louis Aucoc, whilst simultaneously pursuing his studies at the Paris Ecole des Arts Décoratifs. A period of study in England in the late 1870s completed his education. On his return to France he worked freelance for the prestigious houses of Cartier, Boucheron, Renn, Gariod, Hamelin, and Destape, the latter becoming his full-time employer. By 1885 Lalique was in charge of the Destape workshops and in 1886 Destape handed over the atelier to his talented protégé.

Lalique's success dates from his first major exhibition, at the Paris Salon of 1894. He had, by that time, already designed jewels for Sarah Bernhardt and was evolving his distinctive style. His considerable success earned him the Légion d'Honneur in 1897 and brought forward such significant but diverse patrons as Calouste Gulbenkian and Count Robert de Montesquiou. The former became enamoured of Lalique's artistry and offered him a virtual carte-blanche commission, while at the same time buying many fine examples of his work from exhibitions.

The resulting collection of over one hundred and forty works, displayed in the Gulbenkian foundation in Lisbon, is undoubtedly the finest in the world and includes such major pieces as the oft-illustrated *parure de corsage* of a giant *plique-à-jour* enamelled, grotesque dragonfly with the carved chrysoprase body and head of a woman. Montesquiou, in an essay 'Orfèvre et Verrier' (the *verrier* being Gallé) from the *recueil* of 1897, *Les Roseaux Pensants*, wrote with rapture of a visit to Lalique's shop and of the fantastic treasures to be found within. His career as a jeweller lasted until about 1910 by which date Art Nouveau was démodé and Lalique's passion was for glass.

A daring innovator with a total disdain for traditional ideas on the concept and substance of jewellery, Lalique extended the palette available to jewellers through his passion for semi-precious stones and non-precious materials. He would devote to work in carved horn, mother-of-pearl and enamels the care that others might reserve exclusively for gold, platinum and diamonds. He incorporated his first nude figure in a jewel in 1895 and first used carved horn in 1896. His skill with enamels, and, most notably translucent, *plique-à-jour* enamels, was remarkable.

But what was perhaps most striking about Lalique's jewellery, and, indeed, the multi-media works of art which he also created, was the fertility of their graphic invention. Lalique's motifs reflected perfectly the often morbid aspects of *fin-de-siècle* taste; he devised refined, graphic designs from the Medusas, the Ophelias, the drugged, poppy-wreathed maidens, the grotesque creatures, half-animal, half-human of Symbolist literature and painting; he froze into exquisite and precious works of art the literary world of a Des Esseintes, the visual world of Khnopff, Delville or Schwabe. And, always, whatever the motif, Lalique's graphic ability created distinctively personal linear patterns that could be visualised as an abstract art in themselves. Critic Roger Marx writing in *Les Modes* in 1901 noted, 'Lalique has laid open new and unknown possibilities for jewellery – the evolution of jewellery design today owes its sole debt to him.'

The brothers Paul and Henri Vever and Lucien Gaillard were the most gifted of the jewellers influenced by Lalique. The Vever brothers were the inheritors of a family business, as indeed was Gaillard, and first attracted attention at the 1900 Exhibition. They exploited the style and the techniques made fashionable by Lalique and their workshops became particularly adept at the *plique-à-jour* and other enamel work so much in favour. The brothers acted as entrepreneurs and many of their designs were commissioned from artists such as Edward Colonna, whose jewellery designs were also sold in Bing's Maison de l'Art Nouveau, and Eugène Grasset. Lucien Gautrait, who had worked for the Maison Vever, was one more talented jeweller in the Lalique tradition. Henri Vever also wrote a major documentary work, *La Bijouterie Française au XIXe Siècle*.

Lucien Gaillard became director of his family's firm in 1892, and his primary interest was in metalwork until, around 1900, Lalique encouraged him to design jewellery. Despite the evident Lalique influence, Gaillard's jewellery was

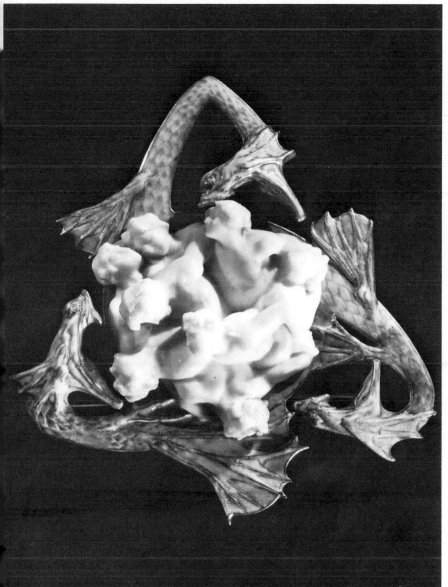

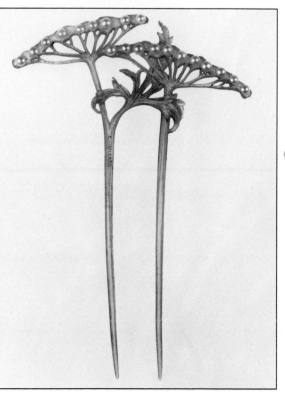

Above Gold enamel and carved ivory brooch by René Lalique, *c.* 1900.

Right Hair ornament, carved horn and seed pearls, by Lucien Gaillard, *c.* 1900.

Far right Chalice in silver and blown opalescent glass by René Lalique, *c.* 1900.

Belt buckle by René
Lalique, enamel on copper,
gold clasp, *c.* 1900.

very successful, winning him first prize at the Société des Artistes Français in 1904. He made a distinctive series of carved horn hair combs as stylised sprays of honesty, ombellifers or mistletoe, often set with small Baroque pearls as flowerheads or berries.

Georges Fouquet, who took over the family firm in 1895 and was anxious to express himself in the fashionable Art Nouveau style, found an ideal collaborator in Alphonse Mucha, the graphic artist whom he commissioned in 1901 to design his new Rue Royale shop. This combination of Mucha's luscious and refined graphic sense with Fouquet's ability to translate the artist's designs into exquisite works of art was responsible for only a limited number of jewels, but they are amongst the most extraordinary works created in the Art Nouveau period. The major known examples of this collaboration are works of pure fantasy, jewels of theatrical proportions. These include a bizarre bracelet conceived for Sarah Bernhardt, a grotesque enamelled and articulated gold griffin encircling the forearm and hand and incorporating a ring; a giant *parure de corsage* incorporating a carved ivory face surrounded by carved ivory and gold arabesques of hair, an enamelled halo, pendant Baroque stones and a pendant painted panel, watercolour on ivory within a gold border, and a recently rediscovered *devant de corsage*, the centrepiece of a concoction that included decorated chains and shoulder pieces, incorporating a similar but larger painted ivory panel within an exquisite, part-*plique-à-jour* enamelled, openwork border. Alphonse Mucha's published folio, *Documents Décoratifs*, includes delightful designs for jewels that were never executed.

La Maison Moderne retailed jewellery in high Art Nouveau taste by Paul Follot, Maurice Dufrène and Manuel Orazi. More traditional firms such as that founded by Frédéric Boucheron in 1858 made certain concessions to the fashions of 1900 as can be seen for example from the designs of L. Hirtz for Boucheron, published in the winter 1901 *Studio* special number on jewellery and fans.

Eugène Feuillâtre left the Lalique workshop in 1899, having mastered the skills of enamelling. Though he designed and exhibited jewellery, examples of which are illustrated by Vever, his forte was in large-scale *tours de force* of enamelling including *plique-à-jour* creations of unprecedented daring. The 29 cm. diameter dish from the Charles Handley-Read collection with its vigorous design of a grotesque fish in polychrome enamels in a silver framework, is perhaps the finest surviving example. He joined the Société des Artistes Français and exhibited with them until 1910.

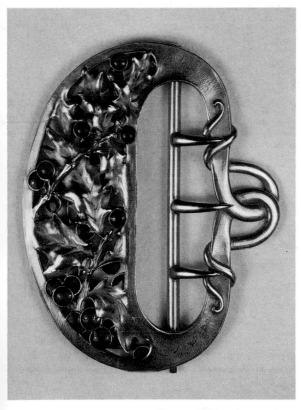

Above Gold and enamel belt buckle, *c.* 1900.

Right Enamelled bottle and stopper by Eugène Feuillâtre, *c.* 1900.

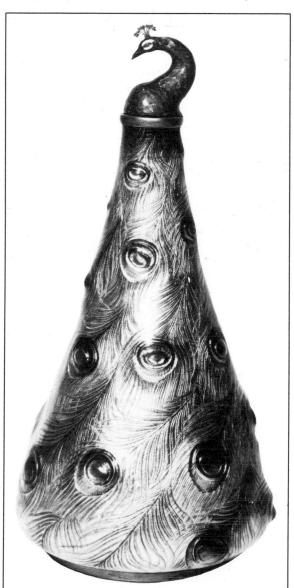

Chocolatière in silver-gilt by
Cardeilhac, *c.* 1900.

The firm of Cardeilhac produced a number of exciting designs in the Art Nouveau taste. The firm's involvement in fine *orfèvrerie* dates back to the late 1880s and stems from the enthusiasm of Ernest Cardeilhac, grandson of the founder. His entries won a silver medal in 1889 and he distinguished himself in 1900 with objects executed by his firm to the designs of Lucien Bonvallet. Cardeilhac created a series of attractive mounts for vases by leading glass-makers and potters. The most characteristic Cardeilhac pieces were those in silver or silver-gilt decorated with stylised yet restrained plant motifs and with details such as handles and finials in carved wood or tinted ivory.

The firm of Falize, directed after 1897 by André Falize, grandson of the founder, was another of the major *orfèvres* active at the turn of the century and its diverse output included works in the Art Nouveau taste made up to the designs of various artists including Lucien Lévy-Dhurmer.

Lucien Gaillard's output was by no means restricted to jewellery. He studied in depth the various aspects of metalwork, patination, plating, alloying as well as Japanese techniques of decoration and produced a variety of objects from parasol handles to hairpins which combined fine and unusual workmanship with a strong sense of design, using precious and non-precious materials with equal respect.

Dinanderie, work in non-precious metals, came into its own in the early years of the twentieth century, partly perhaps as a result of exposure to Japanese works of art. Bonvallet exhibited vases in 1902 in *repoussé* copper. Two years later the Swiss-born craftsman Jean Dunand exhibited his first examples of *dinanderie*. Dunand, who was to achieve considerable renown between the wars as a lacquer artist first came to the notice of critics with a series of vases of organic form, gourds, marrow forms, and other semi-naturalistic shapes meticulously hammered from flat sheets of metal. Gradually Dunand abandoned these forms in favour of vases of simple silhouette with decoration achieved by inlays or contrasting patinations; although the forms of this period immediately preceding the First World War were no longer naturalistic, the decorations often were, with Dunand recreating the appearance of snake-skin or inlaying the elegant lines of peacock feathers.

A branch of the decorative arts which enjoyed a particular vogue around 1900 and subsequently, in different styles, in the twenties and thirties, was decorative sculpture. Small, domestic-scale sculptures were to be found serving a variety of functions, from vide-poches to table lamps, as well as being created in a purely ornamental capacity. The main source of inspiration to Art Nouveau sculptors was undoubtedly Loïe Fuller. This American dancer who first appeared at the Folies Bergère in 1893 and triumphed at the Paris Exhibition of 1900 was hailed as the living embodiment of the Art Nouveau style. The greatest sculptural tributes are probably the two versions of her in the full flight of her dance by Raoul Larche, cast in bronze by Siot-Decauville. Pierre Roche, Théodore Rivière and Rupert Carabin were among the sculptors who attempted to

Bronze table lamp modelled as the dancer Loïe Fuller by Raoul Larche, *c*. 1900.

Above *Parure de corsage*, designed by Alphonse Mucha and executed by Georges Fouquet, in gold, enamels, emeralds, watercolour and metallic paint on ivory, and hung with a Baroque pearl, *c*. 1900.

Opposite page Gilt-bronze bust by Maurice Bouval, *c*. 1900.

capture in bronze the fluid magic of her dance movements.

Maurice Bouval modelled some of the most sensual decorative Art Nouveau sculptures. His works, which were conceived as paper knives, dishes, door-handles, appliques or purely decorative objects, were usually in gilt-bronze and always on the theme of the dream-maiden or *femme-fleur* so dear to French Art Nouveau. Leo Laporte-Blairsy designed a clever series of lamps as female figures holding giant pierced flowers or carved glass shades that concealed light fittings. Louis Chalon, Charles Korschann, G. Flamand, Max Blondat, Agathon Leonard and Villanis were amongst the more gifted of the decorative sculptors to work in the Art Nouveau style.

Alphonse Mucha designed only a few decorative sculptures but they are amongst the most impressive of the Art Nouveau period. Although dependent for the translation of his ideas into bronze on the help of the sculptor Auguste Seysses, his few ventures into three-dimensional work bear his own unmistakable hallmark. Mucha's interest in sculpture covered the period 1899 to 1903 and at least two of his sculptures were conceived for the Paris Exhibition of 1900. One, for the Houbigant stand, he describes as '... a bust of a woman, gilded and crowned with a diadem', and another was a symbolic sculpture for the Bosnia-Herzegovina pavilion. From 1900 also dates the large bust of a woman, her hair swirling to form the stylised base in typical Mucha graphic style, of which four casts are now known; from 1901 dates a softer interpretation of the same concept cast as part of the furnishings of the Fouquet shop. From about 1900 dates the beautiful wall-applique preserved in a private Brussels collection. Representing the part-veiled head of a young woman, it is hung with amethysts, malachite and enamelled details. The bare light bulbs at the centre of giant flowerheads either side of the face harmonise in a way that could only have been possible in 1900, contemporary taste finding an acceptable harmony between the magic of electric lighting and the mysticism of the subject.

A remarkable but somehow isolated talent in the realm of Art Nouveau metalwork was Paris architect-designer Hector Guimard, perhaps best known for his inventively organic cast-iron entrances to the Paris underground, designed in 1900, which have been described as '... gateways to a subterranean Venusburg such as Beardsley described so vividly in his story *Under the Hill*.' Between 1907 and 1910, Guimard designed small objects, vases, frames, a cane handle to be cast in bronze or silver, giving rein on a reduced scale to his characteristic abstract organic motifs. His most important metalwork venture, however, were his cast-iron architectural details, the designs for which were published in 1907 under the title *Fontes Artistiques pour Constructions, Fumisterie, Articles de Jardins et Sepultures, Style Guimard* by the Fonderies de Saint-Dizier.

Sculptor and decorator Alexandre Charpentier modelled low-relief, sensitive allegorical nude figures for door handles and lock plates and was regarded as one of the best medallists during his active period at the turn of the century.

After the interruption brought about by the First World War, altogether new styles and techniques of metalwork came into prominence. Lush and extravagant examples of Art Nouveau had seemed *passé* as early as 1905, though more restrained versions, such as the taut elegance of Guimard's metalwork, were still in evidence up to just a few years before the war. For certain artists the transition into Art Deco was a natural and easy one. The close of the war, however heralded the emergence of a host of new talents.

Not least among them was Edgar Brandt, master *ferronnier* and largely responsible for the sudden and tremendous popularity after 1920 of wrought iron work. René d'Avril, writing in 1925, recorded the claim that Brandt was already a competent iron worker at the age of fifteen. He was in his late thirties, however, when, in 1919, after the war, he finally set up his own atelier. His success in the early 1920s was immediate as he forged his metal into the stylised motifs, the scrolls, ribbonwork, Neo-classical figures and formalised flowers of Art Deco. By 1925 and the International Paris Exhibition, Brandt, working in collaboration with his partner, designer-architect Louis Favier, emerged as one of the major contributors, to whom was entrusted the creation of the Porte d'Honneur to the Exhibition. The

major work on show in 1925 was the magnificent five-fold screen, *L'Oasis*, which summarised the motifs that Brandt helped popularise. The central panel represented a stylised fountain, whilst the remaining area was filled with stylised leaves and the repeated flower-like scroll that became a leitmotif of French Art Deco. *L'Oasis*, like many of Brandt's larger-scale works, was enlivened with a warm-coloured patination, thus avoiding the sombre effect of large areas of blackened metal.

The Brandt workshops made decorative radiator covers, jardinières, floor, wall and table lamps, the glass shades usually from the Daum factory, firescreens, mirror frames, console tables, indeed any item of furnishing that could successfully be wrought in iron. Brandt also, on occasion, worked in bronze as was the case for his serpent lamps.

Brandt's style and techniques were adopted by a number of imitators including Charles Piguet in Lyons, Paul Kiss, Edouard, Marcel and Charles Schenck, Nics Frères and Raymond Subes. Emile Robert has been given credit for teaching the skills of ironwork; it was undoubtedly Brandt's talent, however, that led and encouraged French Art Deco metalwork.

When Jean Dunand resumed his activity in 1919, he had already evolved a new personal style in his *dinanderie*. By its quasi-oriental simplicity and dependence on totally abstract geometric design it placed him apart from and chronologically in advance of artists such as Brandt. Dunand, having perfected the techniques of inlaying and patinating his metal, had now introduced the use of lacquer in his metalwork, either providing a rich even surface or crisp contrasts of red and black in strong geometric designs. Although his growing interest was in the use of lacquer on wood, metalwork, now usually lacquered, remained a constant area of his output through the 1920s and 1930s. Amongst his most successful vases were those with free-standing lacquered fins. Dunand's workshops in the Rue Hallé also produced a variety of small-scale lacquered metalwork items such as cigarette cases, and jewellery.

Claudius Linossier, a former apprentice with Dunand, set up an atelier in Lyons and his hammered, patinated and inlaid metal dishes and vases, evocative of the work of Dunand, earned regular mention in contemporary surveys of the decorative arts in the twenties. Jean Serrière worked in a similar vein.

Decorative sculptures in the styles of the twenties and thirties enjoyed the popular success that Art Nouveau sculptures had enjoyed at the turn of

Above *L'Oasis*, an elaborate wrought metal screen by Edgar Brandt, 1925.

Right The *porte d'honneur* to the 1925 Exhibition, wrought iron, by Edgar Brandt and Louis Favier.

the century. They ranged from top quality artifacts in bronze and carved ivory to stylish but cheaply-made figures that must have been manufactured in substantial numbers. Sculptors whose work has strong claims to be categorised as fine rather than decorative art include Gustave Miklos, Joseph Czaky and Joseph Bernard, though each of these artists collaborated with leading decorators. Miklos created models to be decorated in lacquer by Dunand; for Doucet he made a remarkable pair of andirons in gilt and enamelled bronze, and the bronze mounts and sabots of a pair of *tabourets*; he designed a piece of jewellery executed in gold in 1927 by Raymond Templier. Czaky incorporated one of his sculptures into a cabinet designed for Doucet by Marcel Coard; he also designed the sculptural stair-rail for Doucet's new Neuilly home. Bernard's Neo-classical sculptures, in stone or cast in bronze, provided a decorative counterpoint to Ruhlmann's rich but austere furniture in his room schemes at the 1925 Paris Exhibition.

Edouard Marcel Sandoz and François Pompon modelled heavily stylised animals in stone or to be cast in bronze. The twin brothers Joël and Jan Martel, working as one, abandoned their early monumental style and evolved a more fashionable style in the twenties, as they translated the visual language of Cubism into a decorative idiom. Their work was well represented at the Paris 1925 Exhibition where they designed bas-reliefs for the Pavillon du Tourisme and the Porte Concorde and sculpted details in the bathroom for the Pavillon de la Manufacture de Sèvres. The brothers Jean and Jacques Adnet created decorative bas-reliefs and sculptures in a style similar to that of the Martels.

Purely ornamental figures as domestic decoration enjoyed considerable popularity and the genre was successfully exploited by a wide range of artists. The Rumanian-born sculptor Demetre Chiparus, working in Paris, proved his pre-eminence in the creation of figures in painted bronze and carved ivory. The complete absence of reference to his work in contemporary folios on the decorative arts, however, seems to suggest that he was considered somewhat bad taste by more serious critics. He created totally lifelike figures of exotic dancers, often in brief, jewelled costumes that revealed large areas of ivory flesh, or in more elaborate costumes that reflected such fashionable fads as the quasi-oriental exoticism of the Ballets Russes or the taste for all things Egyptian which followed the discovery of Tutankhamen's tomb. J. Descomps and R. Philippe created figures in

Below left Josephine Baker wearing lacquered bracelets by Jean Dunand; photograph taken in 1926 when Josephine was nineteen.

Below Decorative sculpture, signed 'J. Martel', in polished metal, 1920s.

Below Wrought and inlaid metal vase by Jean Dunand, *c.* 1920.

Below right Eggshell lacquer vase by Jean Dunand, 1929. Formerly in the collection of Edgar Brandt.

bronze and ivory, though less extravagant than those of Chiparus. Pierre Le Faguays and Bouraine also mixed bronze and ivory, but are better known for works fully cast in bronze; typical of their work are their stylised semi-naked female figures with formalised, almost two-dimensional draperies. Bouraine sculpted memorable Amazon warriors and a group of Leda and the swan. The mark Le Verrier appears on stylish figures cast in spelter.

The inter-war years provided an equally varied range of jewellery, from the ostentatious creations of the great traditional jewellery houses, through the more intellectual and artistic creations of a small group of designers who treated jewels as miniature sculptures, to the vast range of cheaply-produced costume jewellery, designed to be briefly worn, and as rapidly discarded as fashion dictated, the popularisation of which is generally credited to Coco Chanel in the late 1920s.

The Establishment of the jewellery world was represented in Paris by the *grandes maisons* such as Boucheron, Cartier, Van Cleef and Arpels, and Lacloche Frères. In the 1920s these firms found a style that combined elements of Art Deco, the vibrant colours and Orientalism of the Ballets Russes and a love of chinoiserie motifs. They used

Above left Patinated
bronze figure, marked
'Fringue', 1920s.

Above Silvered metal
figure, modelled by Fayral
and cast by Max le Verrier,
1920s.

Left Silvered and
patinated bronze figure of a
female javelin thrower by
A. M. Bouraine, 1920s.

Below Bracelet by Raymond Templier in platinum, white gold, onyx and diamonds, late 1920s.

Right Pendant in platinum, coral, jet and brilliants by Jean Fouquet, late 1920s.

Tea service in silver and wood by Jean Puiforcat, late 1920s.

onyx, carved coral and jade, frosted crystal and brilliants. Typical of their creations are cigarette or vanity cases mixing exotic materials, elaborate diamond-studded brooches, tassels of seed pearls or brilliants. Cartier also produced remarkable clocks, including their celebrated 'mystery' clocks. The 1920s was a very successful time for such firms. The Crash of 1929 and the depression that followed, however, had an inevitable effect on such a high-luxury industry, as, of course, did the social acceptance of costume jewellery. During the 1930s the most ubiquitous jewel, exquisitely created in diamonds by Cartier or mass-produced in paste, was the double dress clip. The Surrealist fashions of the late 1930s inspired a series of *fantaisie* brooches, typical of which were the carved ebony negro heads or coral hands holding gold flowers made by Cartier.

Perhaps the most exciting phase in jewellery design between the wars, however, is to be found in the late 1920s work of a select group of artists, notably Raymond Templier, Gérard Sandoz, Jean Fouquet and Paul Brandt. Templier, Sandoz and Fouquet were second generation jewellers, the sons of Paul Templier, Gustave Sandoz and the George Fouquet who had enjoyed such success around 1900. They each combined a background

Cigarette case by Paul
Brandt, eggshell lacquer on
silver, late 1920s.

of technical involvement with an acute sensitivity to the emerging aesthetic of Modernism. The most important document on their work is the folio *Bijoux et Orfèvrerie* published *c.* 1930 by Charles Moreau in the series 'L'Art International d'Aujourd'hui.' Here can be found the motifs and materials which these artists employed. The motifs are almost invariably abstract, tough geometric forms that evoke the dynamism of machinery, a sophistication of Futurism. The materials are cold and the works are finished with the perfection of precision-engineering. Platinum, silver and white gold are allied with black areas of onyx, jet or enamel. Black, red or other brilliant lacquers emphasise the graphic elements of designs, sometimes incorporating areas of crushed eggshell to provide a counterpoint to the otherwise total austerity. The Moreau folio illustrates Templier's extraordinary *parure* created for Brigitte Helm's role in *L'Argent* of 1927, Fouquet's split bullet-form frosted crystal pendant, a display of Brandt's dynamic eggshell lacquer cigarette cases in a setting by René Herbst.

The silversmith Jean Puiforcat adapted the abstract, geometric elements of Modernism to the creation of fine quality work in which he would contrast the texture of the silver with emphatic handles, finials and details of dark rich woods or rock crystal. His best pieces date from the mid and late twenties. Sandoz designed silverware along similar lines in addition to creating decorative costume jewellery.

The Modernist style was adapted to work in non-precious metals, perhaps more appropriately since an important element of Modernism was the tradition of functionalism which somehow seemed at odds with work in precious materials. The Union des Artistes Modernes, established in 1930, led the field in France in the design of Modernist metalwork. Members such as René Herbst and Jacques Le Chevallier worked on new ideas for light fittings, those of Le Chevallier often with self-consciously exposed screwheads in the functionalist tradition.

In the early 1920s, designer Jean Perzel specialised in the creation of light fittings. He won first prize in the lighting section at the 1928 Salon des Artistes-Décorateurs and perfectly reflected the ideals of Modernism in his elegant, discreet designs for floor, wall and table lights in chromed metal and glass. Desny used the geometric language of Modernism in clever metalwork designs such as his double cone drinking vessels, and in a series of glass and metal table lamps.

Graphic Art *by Martin Battersby*

FROM THE CLOSING YEARS of the nineteenth century, the graphic arts in France showed a steadily improving standard in design and production. As a result of this new excellence, there arose a corresponding enthusiasm on the part of bibliophiles for collecting limited editions of contemporary illustrated books, thus giving a greatly increased field of work for artists, typographers, makers of fine papers and bookbinders. In 1820 the Société des Bibliophiles Français had been founded, and for the next fifty years informed its members about the comparatively small number of *éditions-de-luxe* being produced, as well as of antiquarian books. Developments in technical processes and a consequent increase in the number of volumes published gave rise to the founding of the Société des Livres in 1874, the Société des Cent Bibliophiles in 1895, the Société des XX two years later and the Société du Livre Contemporain in 1904. In the 1920s, the number of these associations increased still further both in Paris and the provinces as edition after edition of classics and modern works were produced for this exclusive market.

Right Poster by Eugène Grasset for Sarah Bernhardt as Jeanne d'Arc.

Opposite page *Le Retour*, lithograph by Georges de Feure, *c.* 1900.

These associations of book lovers and, more especially, those formed in the latter years of the century were also concerned with raising the standard of book production and of the graphic arts, which with few exceptions had degenerated below the standards set during previous centuries. Encased in bindings which, like the furniture and architecture of the mid 1800s, were timid pastiches of past historical styles, the texts, often difficult to read, were set in badly-designed types and printed on paper of indifferent quality. The illustrations were reproduced from pen and ink drawings transferred to boxwood blocks and subsequently engraved by skilled technicians, upon whose dexterity artists unversed in the actual techniques of wood engraving imposed almost impossible demands. It was surprising that so much of the character of the original drawings survived, but this was only due to the craftsmanship of the engravers who painstakingly reproduced the slightest nuances of line of the originals. One of the best examples of this translation of one medium into another were the engravings of Gustave Doré's drawings by Sotain and Pisan.

Other methods of reproduction, such as steel-engraving, *eau-forte* or lithography in the main failed to satisfy the high standards of book production demanded by collectors aware of the excellence of the eighteenth century. It was William Morris as the producer of the volumes from his Kelmscott Press, founded in 1891, who proved influential in restoring the essential features of a well-produced book – a perfect balance and harmony between the text and the illustrations, the text being well-designed and sympathetic to the spirit of the words.

Even before the appearance of the Kelmscott Press, the teachings of Morris and of Walter Crane had considerable influence in France. The designer Eugène Grasset with his specially designed type and illustrations for *Les Quatre Fils Aymon*, published in 1883, had shown the way to a renaissance in book production after overcoming a lack of enthusiasm from critics and public. Grasset continued his pioneering efforts in designing new original and legible types – his 'Grasset' fount appeared in 1898 and was widely used – and his example was followed by George Auriol, Bellery-Desfontaines and Naudin. The illustrator Bracquemond, already well-known as a water-colourist, agreed with William Morris in advocating the use of original woodcuts to achieve, as he wrote in his *Etude sur la Gravure sur Bois*, published in 1897, 'the unity of the elements on a printed page'. The woodcut should, he main-

Numéro 1   Mai 1897

L'ESTAMPE
Moderne

Directeurs :

CH. MASSON & H. PIAZZA

✶

Publication Mensuelle

Contenant

Quatre estampes originales inédites

en Couleurs et en Noir

des

principaux Artistes Modernes

Français et Étrangers

éditée par

L'IMPRIMERIE CHAMPENOIS

ABONNEMENTS D'UN AN :	LE NUMÉRO :
Paris 40 frs.	Paris 3 frs. 50
Départ^{ts} et Etranger 43 frs.	Départ^{ts} et Etranger 4 frs.

SOMMAIRE

Femme du Riff.
     L. A. GIRARDOT

Marchande de Lacets.
     L. MALTESTE

Automne.
     R. MÉNARD

Corinne.
     M. REALIER-DUMAS

Direction et Administration : 66, Boulevard Saint-Michel, Paris.

Cover to the first issue of *L'Estampe Moderne*, incorporating a design by Alphonse Mucha, May 1897.

tained, be true to itself and should not be forced into a facsimile of a steel engraving, a pen drawing or even a photograph. From a practical viewpoint the woodcut had an advantage in that it could be printed simultaneously with the type on a wider choice of paper, thus obviating the use of the coated papers needed for half-tone or process blocks. The editor, Bracquemond considered, should be 'the architect of the book', choosing a type which suited the feeling of the author's intention, the paper upon which it was printed, the binding and even the design of the endpapers – all refinements which had been too often disregarded for decades.

The editor who first realised these aims to the fullest was Pellatan who achieved European renown from 1896. For each of his publications, which included titles from authors as diverse as Alfred de Musset, Theocritus, Jean Lorrain, François Villon and Molière, a different type was used – many being designed by Grasset – while illustrations were commissioned from Grasset, Daniel Vierge, Bellery-Desfontaines, Jeanniot and Bellenger.

Grasset, Bracquemond and Pellatan were later realised to have been the pioneers whose creative efforts had a profound influence on the graphic arts in France. The standards they set gave encouragement to others to follow their example, giving hitherto unrealised opportunities to young and promising painters to extend their talents to book illustration. As the critic Raymond Cogniat commented in 1929 when the fashion for collecting illustrated éditions-de-luxe was at its height, 'the modern book offers an amateur of the arts unlimited scope for possessing works by artists which no collector of paintings could own even if he were endowed with an enormous fortune. Who could unite in one gallery hundreds of canvases or drawings signed by Matisse, Picasso, Rouault, Laboureur, Maurice Denis, Chagall and Dufy? The book allows the greatest eclecticism of taste and the right to indulge contrary tendencies in art. Realism and Surrealism, abstract and concrete, can be juxtaposed in a collector's library'.

The number of illustrated éditions-de-luxe produced in the 1920s was so large that several periodicals devoted a regular monthly feature to new publications, but paradoxically, while giving so many opportunities to graphic artists, their work in these volumes was little known to the general public. For an explanation of this it is necessary to describe the system by which the books were distributed. Each volume was produced in an edition limited to anything between one hundred and fifteen hundred copies – generally the more lavish the presentation, the smaller the edition, as only the highest standard could justify the extremely high prices. While the text and the illustrations were constant there were different categories. A small number would be printed on an extremely costly hand-made paper of which there were many kinds both made in France and imported from Holland, China and Japan. The cost of this paper could account for as much as a fifth of that of the book. Extra loose plates of illustrations signed by the artist and in some cases one or more of the original drawings were included. In all likelihood this edition would be rebound by a leading artist bookbinder, thereby increasing its artistic and financial value.

A rather larger number would be printed on less costly paper with fewer loose plates, while the bulk of the edition would be on still less expensive fine quality paper, the entire edition being signed and numbered. This last category could be priced at a fifth of that of the first, while being exactly the same in appearance and quality of printing. Very often the entire edition was sold as soon as an advance notice was given, and without even being examined by the purchaser.

The entire edition was frequently distributed solely through the bibliophile societies to their members, and thus the general public had no opportunity of buying or even seeing a copy. They were regarded more as works of art with a possibly increasing financial value than as books to be read for enjoyment.

In many cases éditions-de-luxe were left with the sections unsewn with a protective covering of card necessitating rebinding to ensure their preservation. Private collectors would commission artist-binders to provide this protection for their libraries, generally with uninspired versions of eighteenth century bindings. It was Henri Marius-Michel who, in his La Reliure Française published in 1880, advocated that the binding should echo the feeling of the text rather than conform to conventions of traditional bindings with their tooled and gilded ornaments.

Woodcut by Mariano Andrieu for *Amphitryon 38* by Giraudoux.

Right Eggshell lacquer and mother-of-pearl binding by Jean Dunand, late 1920s.

Below right Binding designed by Pierre Legrain and executed by René Kieffer, 1920s.

The work of William Morris and Walter Crane in this field played a considerable part in this revolutionary concept and the break with conventional ideas gave limitless opportunities for decorative bindings to designers working in the Art Nouveau manner, whether using expensive leathers for single copies or cloth ornaments with stamped or printed designs for large editions.

About 1920 a further innovation was introduced by Pierre Legrain already well-known as a designer of interiors and furniture inspired by African primitive art. Hitherto the front and back covers and the spine of the book had been treated as separate entities, but Legrain spread his design over the entire cover so that when the book was fully opened a complete composition was revealed. In addition to the usual coloured leathers – and in the 1920s a range of brilliantly hued skins were utilised – he incorporated wood, ivory, mother-of-pearl and shagreen as decorative elements. Legrain's influence can be seen in the work of Rose Adler who, with René Kieffer, Robert Bonfils, Georges Cretté, Gruel, Louis Creuzevault, Paul Bonet and even Jean Dunand, raised bookbinding in France to new heights of originality of design combined with consummate technical excellence in its execution.

Left Binding by Rose Adler for *Chéri* by Colette, late 1920s.

Below left Binding by Greuzevault, late 1920s.

An indication of the demand for the *éditions-de-luxe* can be gauged from the fact that, while in 1905 there were fifteen publishers specialising solely in this type of book, the number in 1920 was estimated to be well over sixty. Inevitably this led to a scarcity of books suitable for presentation in an illustrated version and a consequent duplication, particularly of the classics. This particularly happened in the case of *Les Fables de la Fontaine*. Illustrated in the eighteenth century by Jean Baptiste Oudry, in 1802 by Percier the official architect to Napoleon I, in 1833 by Gouget in the romantic Gothic revival manner, no less than three versions were planned during the 1920s in as many years. The magnificent version with decorations by Paul Jouve appeared in 1929.

Jouve had first attracted attention when at the age of sixteen he had sculpted an important frieze of animals for the 1900 Exhibition. Specializing in the portraiture of animals and particularly the larger wild fauna of the jungle he was an obvious choice to illustrate *Le Livre du Jungle* by Rudyard Kipling in 1919. Kipling, indeed, enjoyed considerable popularity in France, more perhaps than any other English contemporary author – his original drawings being interpreted in wood engravings by François-Louis Schmied. Jouve was not interested in depicting humans, so Schmied was commissioned to illustrate *Kim* in the following year. In 1930, Jouve and Schmied again collaborated on *Le Pélerin d'Angkor* by Pierre Loti. In the same year Jouve decorated *La Chasse de Kâa*, an episode from *Le Livre du Jungle*, and in 1932 *Paradis Terrestres* by Colette.

Another edition of La Fontaine's *Fables* was that of Joseph Hemard, but this seems to have aroused little enthusiasm. The third version was the cause of a remarkable scandal, when in 1927 Ambroise Vollard commissioned illustrations from Marc Chagall. The choice of an artist so closely identified with mystical Russian folklore caused a furore of protest in the press and the general indignation was so intense that it caused a special debate in the Chambre des Députés. Unperturbed, Chagall produced a hundred drawings over the next four years, but the delays which seemed to be a matter of course with Vollard's publications put off publication when the latter died in 1939. *Les Fables*, together with another project for Chagall, *Les Cinq Livres du Bible*, had to wait until after the war, when they were published by Tériade.

Two versions of *Les Contes de Perrault* appeared, the first in 1922 with magnificent etchings by Etienne Drian, and the second in 1929, illustrated by no less than thirty-three artists including Marie Laurencin, Alexeieff (who was much in demand for translations of Russian classics), Pierre Pinsard, Hermine David, Dignimont, Laboureur and Laborde. It was commended more as a compendium of the leading artists of the book than as an integrated work of art.

Kees van Dongen, whose *fauve* portraits of society beauties convey so much of the spirit of the 1920s was an appropriate choice to illustrate *Deauville*, written by Paul Poiret, and *La Garçonne* by Victor Margueritte, a novel which had been a *succès de scandale* in 1923 with its frank treatment of drugs and lesbianism. Van Dongen's travels in

Right Illustration by Paul Jouve to *Le Livre du Jungle* (The Jungle Book) by Rudyard Kipling, 1919.

Below right Illustration by Etienne Drian to *Les Contes de Perrault*, 1923.

the Near East resulted in a series of colourful drawings for *Les Contes des Mille et une Nuits* and for another Kipling book, *Les plus beaux Contes*.

Georges Rouault undertook the illustrations for *Réincarnation du Père Ubu* written by Ambroise Vollard in 1918, but again this too had to wait until 1932 for publication. Rouault's own book *Cirque de l'Etoile Filante* with characteristic drawings of tragic clowns was published by Vollard in 1936.

The Symbolist painter Maurice Denis had a similar experience with Vollard and his illustrations for Verlaine's *Sagesse*, for although Denis started work in 1889, twenty-two years elapsed before publication. In the meantime Denis had created 216 illustrations for *L'Imitation de Jésus Christ*, which were engraved by Tony Beltrand and published in 1903. One of the great masterpieces of French graphic art and book production was *Les Eclogues de Virgile*, edited by Count Kessler (who did so much to raise the standards of typography), and illustrated with woodcuts by Aristide Maillol. Started in 1912, the project was abandoned for some years and was finally published in 1926.

These excessive delays were obviously exceptional in view of the constantly increasing demand, and some artists like Charles Laboureur turned out no less than thirty books between 1917 and 1929, a prolific output which gave rise to the criticism that his illustrations were so alike as to be interchangeable.

A complete catalogue of the graphic artists working in the field of book illustration would need several volumes and would include much work that was negligible by deservedly forgotten artists. The most talented were recorded in a series of booklets *Les Artistes du Livre* produced in the 1920s, each volume being devoted to the work of a single artist. Carlègle, Charles Martin, Hemard, Laboureur, Herman Paul were some of the more notable names celebrated. The work of Pablo Picasso for *Les Métamorphoses d'Ovide* and Balzac's *Le Chef d'œuvre Inconnu*, of Raoul Dufy for *Le Bestiaire* and *Le Poète Assassiné*, both by Guillaume Apollinaire, of Sylvain Sauvage for *Contes Antiques* by Pierre Louÿs, of Maxime Dethomas, Alexeieff, Dunoyer de Segonzac and Daragnès are among those who in their different ways made important contributions to the renaissance of book production in France.

On a far more modest scale the collection *Le Livre de Demain* with its distinctive orange and black covers produced well-printed books, with woodcuts by notable artists, within the reach of a wider public. Issued at an extremely low price, printed on inexpensive paper, with the woodcuts reproduced mechanically, the monthly volumes by well-known authors first appeared in 1921 and continued until well after the war.

The woodcut, whether an original by an artist or a rendering by another hand, was not of course the only method of reproducing graphics. A photographic copy of an original drawing in colour or black and white could be made by a process invented in 1886 by Gillot, but the generally poor quality of photography, particularly in colour, together with the necessity of printing on a paper heavily coated with kaolin, which was liable to stick together and deteriorate in damp conditions,

Illustration by Silvain Sauvage to the *Contes Antiques* by Pierre Louÿs, 1929.

rendered this method unsatisfactory. Techniques of drypoint, acquatint, steel engraving, mezzotint and lithography were often used, but had the disadvantage of needing a separate printing from the text and were generally used for *hors-texte* illustrations.

For the connoisseur the ideal method of reproduction was the *pochoir* process by which the colour was stencilled by hand. Early playing cards and the popular prints of the eighteenth century were crude examples of this, but by the first decade of the century the technique had become more sophisticated, enabling the printers to reproduce drawings with great accuracy. By the 1920s the process had become mechanised, but the hand method was still being used for the best of the *éditions-de-luxe*.

Prior to 1908, information about the latest fashions was communicated either by photographs or by conventionalised pen drawings characterised by elongated doll-like figures with vapid expressions. Of a low standard of draughtsmanship and amateurish in execution, these drawings showed a sad degeneration from the charming fashion plates of the nineteenth century.

This was abruptly changed in that year by the appearance of a slim booklet *Les Robes de Paul Poiret* issued in a limited edition of 250 copies which were sent to Poiret's clients as an advertisement for his new and revolutionary ideas of fashion, and the drawings in black-and-white with added colour by the *pochoir* process had a far-

Poster by Jules Chéret for
Loïe Fuller at the Folies
Bergère, 1893.

reaching effect which neither Poiret nor the young artist could have foreseen.

Iribe, then twenty-five-years-old, interpreted Poiret's ideas rather than actual dresses, and his lifelike animated models, which even betrayed private amusement, were as much of an innovation as the uncorseted bodies advocated by Poiret.

The small number of copies of the album, which included no text, were more than enough to spread the idea that a serious artist could, without demeaning his art, depict the latest fashions to the advantage of himself as well as the couturier. No longer were the insipid drawings acceptable in the better periodicals. Coincidentally, the influence of the Ballets Russes and of Bakst confirmed the changes Poiret was effecting in *haute couture*: women were wearing the new high-waisted line or Oriental tunics and draped dresses in brilliant colours, reminiscent of odalisques from an Arabian Night's harem.

There also emerged a new generation of young and extremely talented artists eager to record the new feelings permeating both fashion and the decorative arts in general. Advertisers and, in particular, the makers of the new exotic scents created to enhance the Oriental mood were among the first to employ Iribe to represent their products with evocative drawings, and soon the editorial pages were enlivened with similar drawings.

Even before the appearance of a second album, *Les Choses de Paul Poiret*, in 1911, this new trend was firmly established. This time the illustrations were by Georges Lepape; again, there was no text, but the treatment was more sumptuous with drawings reproduced in colour by the *pochoir* method and heightened with gold and silver to accentuate the more pronounced Oriental flavour of the drawings and the fashions, while the debt to Japanese prints, discernible in the Iribe drawings, was more noticeable. Lepape's drawings are the embodiment of the craze for Oriental luxury and colour pervading fashion and interior decoration in the years immediately before the First World War.

His contemporary Georges Barbier was equally obsessed with this overcharged atmosphere of a legendary Orient and many drawings of the Ballets Russes dancers in their roles bear witness to the fascination the world of ballet had for him. After the war Barbier was more attracted by the eighteenth century and his designs for Maurice Rostand's play *Casanova* were published by Lucien Vogel.

Not enough credit has been given in the past to Vogel, through whose taste and judgment so many of the graphic artists of the time are indebted in the exquisitely produced volumes he published. His most notable achievement was undoubtedly *La Gazette du Bon Ton*, issued between 1912 and 1925, which remains the most beautifully produced periodical ever concerned primarily with fashion, although it also dealt with the decorative arts, music, ballet and the theatre. In 1925 it was acquired by Condé Nast and incorporated into *Vogue*. The colour plates and the decorations interspersed through the text gave full rein to the individual treatment of fashion by the many contributing artists. Of these the most notable were Lepape, Charles Martin, Pierre Brissaud and André Marty, whose work could also be found in *Vogue*, *Fémina*, *House and Garden*, *Le Jardin des Modes* and *Comoedia Illustré*. Occasional contributors included Benito, Guy Arnoux, Drian, Valentine Gross, and Brunelleschi.

After 1925, with the decline of Art Deco and with radical changes in fashion, many of these artists gave up this work. Photography began to occupy more space and the number of drawings decreased. However, to bring variety to the layouts, fashion editors still used artists for the more dramatic creations of important couturiers, and during the thirties Erik, Willaumez, Jean Cocteau, Jean Hugo, Reynaldo Luza and particularly Christian Bérard conveyed the feeling of the latest collections. Mention should be made of two albums designed for a Parisian furrier as examples of the best of graphic work. *La Dernière Lettre Persane* was issued by Fourrures Max about 1923 with striking drawings by Benito and an equally distinguished work for the same firm, *Toi*, featured drawings by Jean Dupas of nude female statues draped with extravagant furs as an accompaniment to poems by Colette.

Lithography was a medium ideally suited for printing posters, whether from an original drawing on the stone by the artist himself and printed under his close supervision, as Toulouse-Lautrec often did, or whether reproduced by a mechanical process involving light sheets of metal which replaced the cumbersome blocks of lithographic stone. The effervescent Watteau-style fantasies of Jules Chéret, the richly patterned intricacies of Alphonse Mucha with the use of gold and silver to enhance the luminous colouring, the mordant line of Steinlen, the Japanese inspired exoticism of Orazi and the sedate elegance of Grasset enlivened the walls of Paris and were seriously discussed and collected by enthusiasts. Among the best examples of Art Nouveau as interpreted by different artists, they gradually disappeared from the hoardings of

Illustration by Jean Cocteau to *Opium*, 1930.

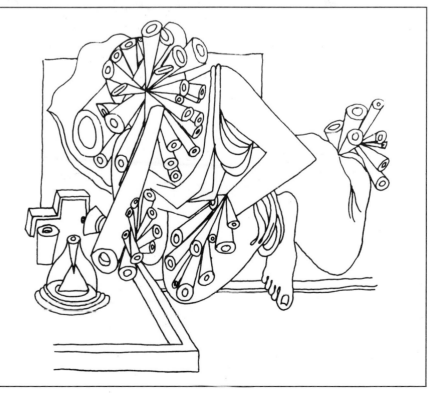

Poster by Cassandre
for the French Line
c. 1930.

Below Painting by Paul Colin of Josephine Baker, 1926.

Right Poster by Zig for Mistinguett at the Casino de Paris, 1931.

Paris with the decline of that effervescent style.

After this short period of brilliance, poster art reverted to a mediocrity which with few exceptions was general through the twenties and thirties. The explosion of graphic talent which marked the early years of Art Deco seemed not to have extended to posters, although exception must be made for those advertising the Ballets Russes. André Marty designed the first for the company, while Cocteau's portraits of Karsavina and of Nijinsky in *Spectre de la Rose* and that of Anna Pavlova by Valentin Serov were brilliant by any standards. George Barbier, Drian, Benedictus, Bonfils and Jean Dupas, all so active in other branches of graphic art, designed occasional posters for art exhibitions, for charity balls and similar occasions with an appeal to a more sophisticated public, but were rarely, if ever, commissioned by manufacturers. Jean Dupas's work was in fact more popular in England and the United States than in his own country.

In the late twenties and the thirties the pace of life in Paris, as in every capital, increased and, with the growing use of motor cars, the function of a poster became increasingly that of a *télégraphiste*, as a contemporary writer commented. The bold Cubist-inspired styles of Cassandre – one of the great masters of the poster – Coulon, Loupot, and Gio Ponti were ideally suited to convey the advertiser's message at a glance. Paul Colin, influenced by Negro art, and Gesmar were particularly successful in their posters for the theatre and music hall.

Theatre and Ballet *by Martin Battersby*

THE STANDARD OF DESIGN in the French theatre during the closing years of the nineteenth century was extremely low, partly from indifference on the part of theatrical directors, but mostly because there were few if any designers willing to submit to the megalomania of most of the leading actors of the time. It had become the custom to order scenery from firms of scene painters who were often talented painters in a debased *trompe l'oeil* manner but were lacking in design sense or a feeling for historical accuracy.

Costumes were ordered in a similar fashion from theatrical dressmakers, especially made for the leading characters and hired from stock for minor parts. In historical dramas the leading actresses made no concessions to period feeling and their clothes were modern in line with applied details of dubious authenticity. For modern plays the stars would be dressed *gratis* by a well-known couturier, regardless of the character played, on the understanding that she would be photographed for the fashion journals.

In the small experimental theatres, however, new seeds of theatrical presentation were germinating. In 1887 Antoine founded the Théâtre Libre on the principles of historical accuracy, combined with an overall unity of design. Wherever possible he used the real thing, substituting for papier-mâché imitations real joints of meat in a butcher's shop, a real fountain in a woodland scene and even real cobwebs in a dungeon setting. Lugné Poé took a diametrically opposite attitude at his Théâtre de l'Oeuvre, reducing the décor to the minimum of a few draperies arranged in an empty space and having the costumes designed to express the character portrayed and to harmonise with each other. He commissioned designs from painters, including Pierre Bonnard, Odilon Redon, Edouard Vuillard and Paul Serusier, and among his innovations were a sloping stage for Ibsen's *Solness* and a projected production of a Shakespearian play set in a circus. In parenthesis it should be noted that Loïe Fuller, the American dancer who caused a furore on her debut at the Folies Bergère in 1893, invented a glass stage lit from below and a setting of large sheets of mirrors which reflected multiple images of her as she danced.

The literal realism of Antoine and the poetic realism of Poé influenced innovators outside France: Stanislavsky and Meyerhold in Russia, and Max Reinhardt in Germany. It was from Russia that there emerged a company destined to revolutionise theatrical design in France and subsequently most other countries, besides contribut-ing an important element to the new style of Art Deco which made its appearance about 1910.

The unique personality and talents of Serge Diaghilev found expression in the founding of the Ballets Russes with the help of two of the greatest painter-designers of the time, Alexandre Benois and Léon Bakst. The Ballets Russes were able to propagate new concepts in theatrical design to a greater extent than the small experimental theatres which were often little known outside a small circle of admirers and were financially handicapped. The technical demands of ballet – the need for an uncluttered stage and the use of little more than a painted backcloth and wings – gave the designer greater scope for unity of concept. In addition, ballet has no language barrier but uses a universal language of movement and thus can be shown with equal effect in many different countries. In the case of the Ballets Russes there was a shrewdly organised publicity campaign before the first night.

It is difficult to imagine the impact upon Parisian audiences of the Ballets Russes, for later generations have become almost over-familiar with reproductions of the original designs and with generally mediocre revivals. Accustomed to insipid and third-rate performances at the Paris Opéra the new company overwhelmed audiences by the dazzling artistry of the dancers, the originality of the staging and, above all, the masterly designs.

In particular, the visions of a legendary Orient depicted by Bakst in *Schéhérazade* and *Thamar*, with their sumptuous settings and brilliant costumes, had an immediate effect upon every branch of the decorative arts besides theatrical design, as contemporary writers on the arts testify, justifying the comment that life could be divided into two parts – before and after seeing the Ballets Russes.

Paul Poiret, then the rising couturier, his collaborators Paul Iribe and Georges Lepape, Georges Barbier and André Marty all added to their reputations as painters by embarking upon stage design. Poiret's elaborate Oriental masquerades were in the nature of theatrical presentations, with costumes designed for each guest. In his memoirs, he describes his collaboration as dress designer with the painter Ronsin for the production of an Oriental fantasy *Le Minaret* at the Théâtre de la Renaissance. The first act was in tones of blue and green, the second in red and violet, the only note of colour in the black and white third act being a vivid apple-green costume. Barbier's most notable production was *Casanova* by Maurice Rostand in 1919 the success of which led to his being asked to design the costumes for

A drawing by
Georges Barbier of
Nijinsky in
Schéhérazade.

Above Design for setting by André Derain for *La Boutique Fantasque*, 1919.

Right 'La chambre à coucher d'un libertin': design for setting by Georges Barbier for *Casanova*, 1919.

Previous page Design by Leon Bakst for the décor of *Schéhérazade*, probably executed after the first Paris production of 1910.

Rudolph Valentino's film *Monsieur Beaucaire*. Iribe went to Hollywood in 1914 and worked extensively for Cecil B. de Mille while Lepape and Marty had extensive careers designing for plays and revues in Paris. It is likely that none of these careers would have been so successful had not the Ballets Russes shown the way.

In 1912, Diaghilev established his company in Monte Carlo and increasingly engaged the services of young French painters and of foreigners based in Paris. Picasso, Braque, Rouault and Derain were employed in preference to his original Russian collaborators, though Bakst was recalled to design the superb settings and costumes for *La Belle au Bois Dormant* in 1921, unfortunately a financial failure.

The success of the Ballets Russes forced the authorities at the Paris Opéra to bring their productions up to date, and in 1914 a new director, Jacques Rouché, was appointed. He was thus enabled to realise on a wider scale the ideas formulated by his previous experience as manager since 1910 of the Théâtre des Arts where he had worked with Dunoyer de Segonzac, Edouard Vuillard, Poiret and Dresa as designers. 'It is necessary', he had written in 1910, 'that a painter should advise the producer, designing costumes, settings and properties, sitting in at rehearsals with the author and indicating in agreement with him the gestures and movements of the actors'. Although this function is taken for granted today, the need for such a statement is an indication of the lack of cohesion prevalent in the theatre in the early years of the century.

Rouche's first task was to jettison the old-fashioned and shabby décors, and to commission designs for the classics and for new productions from painters including Maxime Dethomas, Drésa, René Piot, Derain, de Chirico, Pruna, Brianchon and Cassandre. Similar reforms took place at the Théâtre Chatelet under the direction of Ida Rubinstein, the creator of the leading role,

Zobëide in *Schéhérazade* and now, with the help of a large personal fortune, in management in her own right. The founding of the Théâtre du Vieux Colombier by Jacques Copeau in 1913, with a repertory which included Shakespeare and other Elizabethan playwrights, brought an English influence by Copeau's admiration of the work of William Poel and Granville Barker, and led to his asking Duncan Grant to design the clothes for *Twelfth Night* against a setting by François Jourdain.

In post-war years, a short-lived rival to the Ballets Russes was the Ballets Suèdois company, started in 1920. The standard of design in the productions was higher than that of the dancing. Bonnard devised a new version of Debussy's *Jeux*, Jean Hugo returned to the fashions of 1900 for *Les Mariés de la Tour Eiffel* and Picabia designed the avant-garde *Relâche* with its interpolated film extracts by René Clair. Most notably Fernand Léger made use of Negro art as an inspiration in *La Création du Monde* to a score by Darius Milhaud. Negro artifacts from the French colonies in Africa had been exhibited the previous year, and this ballet had a considerable influence on the decorative arts, reinforced later by the presentation of the Revue Nègre, starring Josephine Baker, by Rolf de Maré in 1925 after the failure of his Ballets Suèdois.

During the 1920s the Ballets Russes spread its influence even more widely by its extensive tours and its repertoire demonstrated Diaghilev's search for greater novelties as diverse as the witty and elegant *Les Biches*, with the Marie Laurencin designs perfectly complementing the music of François Poulenc and *La Chatte* in a Constructivist setting with costumes of talc and black American cloth.

The 1920s gave opportunities to two remarkably talented young men who played a decisive part in both French theatre and ballet. Jean Cocteau had provided the scenarios for ballets for

Design for setting by A.–M. Cassandre for the Ballet Russe production of *Aubade*, 1936.

'Arlequin': costume design
by Georges Lepape, 1915.

Diaghilev's company, including the unsuccessful *Le Dieu Bleu* in 1912, the scandal-provoking *Parade*, with its designs by Picasso in 1919, and *Train Bleu* costumed by Chanel in 1924. In 1922 he turned his attention to the theatre with an adaptation of Sophocles' drama *Antigone* presented at the Théâtre de l'Atelier, again with costumes designed by Chanel. This production began his long preoccupation with the themes of classical mythology, which was carried further in 1926 in his original play *Orphée*, designed by Jean Hugo and Chapel.

Christian Bérard first attracted attention as a painter in 1925 when he exhibited as a member of the short-lived 'neo-romantic' group, which included Pavel Tchelitchew and Eugene Berman, both destined to make notable contributions to theatre design. In 1930 Cocteau and Bérard collaborated for the first time on the former's one-act play *La Voix Humaine* to be followed in 1934 by *La Machine Infernale*. Tentative plans for a ballet by Bérard had been made by Diaghilev before his death in 1929 but it was not until 1933 that the unforgettable *Cotillon* – in the opinion of many one of the most perfect ballets – was first performed by the Ballets de Monte Carlo.

Diaghilev's death threw the world of ballet into confusion and it seemed as though an era of

Left 'Romeo': costume design by Jean Hugo.

Below Design for setting by Lanvin for the Theatre Daunou.

Above Design for setting by Christian Bérard for the Ballet Russe production of *The Seventh Symphony*, 1938.

Right Design for setting by Eugène Berman for *Devil's Holiday*, 1939.

greatness had come to an end. The Ballets 1933 lasted only some six weeks as a company, but during its brief career approximated the panache of the Diaghilev company with a brilliant assemblage of talent, much of it in fact drawn from the Ballets Russes. With Balanchine as choreographer, Bérard as designer for *Mozartiana*, Tchelitchew for *Errante*, Derain for *Fastes* and *Songes* and Tilly Losch, Tamara Toumanova, Roman Jasinsky among the dancers, not to mention Lotte Lenya in a speaking role, success should have been assured had not difficulties intervened.

A reassembly of many of the former Diaghilev company with a repertoire of revivals and new productions started in 1932 and under different names due to internal shifts of power toured extensively until the outbreak of war. Apart from revivals of Diaghilev's creations, and particularly the early ballets with their predominantly Russian feeling, the considerable number of new productions had an entirely French influence and reflected the current trends of the artistic world of Paris. Surrealism was represented by André Masson's designs for the first symphonic ballet of Léonide Massine, *Les Présages*, and those of Miro for *Jeux d'Enfants*. Bérard, already recognised as an arbiter of taste in Paris, combined masterly economy of means and a sure sense of colour in the neo-romantic ballets *Cotillon*, *Symphonie Fantastique* and *Seventh Symphony*, the two last-named to symphonies by Berlioz and Beethoven respectively. Raoul Dufy also designed the enchanting *Beach*.

In addition to his settings for Cocteau plays, Bérard designed in 1935 *La Reine Margot* by Bourdet, Jouvet's production of Molière's *L'Ecole des Femmes* in 1936, another Jouvet production of Corneille's *L'Illusion Comique* in 1937, and in the following year *Cyrano de Bergerac* and *Le Corsair*.

One of the main tourist attractions since the 1900s has been the French music hall which presented spectacles devoted mainly to a glorification of the female form, either over-dressed in feathers and diamanté-embroidered chiffon, or the opposite – a nude Marie Antoinette and Empress Theodora being particularly memorable.

With minimal differences, the style of presentation remained unchanged, with the main attractions of 'historical tableaux' designed to include as many female nudes as possible, interspersed with conventional music hall acts. A specialised genre of design, it attracted a host of imitators of Gesmar and Erté, the two most celebrated exponents. Gesmar designed almost exclusively for the shows featuring Mistinguett and her celebrated legs. The talents of Erté (Romain de Tirtoff), a much better designer than Gesmar, were ideally suited to this type of design where he could give full rein to his ingenuity and taste for elaborate ornament. On the whole the world of the music hall was an enclosed one and few if any of the designers working for the straight theatre or for ballet entered it.

It will be seen that between 1900 and 1940 there were radical changes in theatrical production in France and that the painter as designer played an increasingly important part, adding crucial elements to the magic and fantasy which is an essential part of any theatre.

Below Design for setting by Christian Bérard for Molière's *L'Ecole des Femmes*, 1936.

Bottom Design for a theatrical curtain by Erté, c.1920s.

Fashion *by Philippe Garner*

THE FASHION INDUSTRY is a twentieth-century phenomenon. The growth of the industry, the commercial necessity for a fairly rapid turnover, helped along greatly by the profusion of rival fashion magazines, have had the snowball effect of accelerating the evolution of fashion and encouraging a fertile and rapid turnover of ideas.

The *fin-de-siècle* styles involved only small variations on a mode of dress that had, in its essentials, dominated female fashion for several decades, a mode that combined the stiffness of a tight-fitted boned bodice with the impracticality of a full, floor-length skirt. Woman's role as object in a male-dominated world was reflected in the restrictions imposed by the fashionable trussing of the bodice and the cumbersome fullness of skirts. Georges de Feure's illustrations of fashionably dressed ladies of the turn of the century reflect clearly that the decorative element predominated to the virtual exclusion of any sense of practicality.

A significant aspect of the fashion history of the period was the evolution of the creative *couturier*. It was Charles Frederick Worth who, in the last quarter of the nineteenth century, had given the role of the *couturier* social acceptability; no longer was he merely regarded as a tradesman not to be invited to one's home other than on business. The second generation of *couturiers*, after Worth, be-

came a new aristocracy of taste and included important patrons of the arts such as Jacques Doucet. The best known amongst the talented designers of this generation were the Callot sisters, Chéruit, Dœuillet, Drecoll, Paquin and Doucet.

The most exciting talent to emerge in the early years of the century, as a liberating force, and one of the major influences in contemporary fashions and tastes was Paul Poiret. After starting his career in the house of his great hero, Doucet, Poiret set up his own *maison de couture* in 1903. He was far more than a dress designer. The fastidious concern he showed for costume extended to every aspect of his lifestyle, his Atelier Martine had a strong influence on interior design, whilst Poiret's lavish entertaining and the exotic fancy-dress soirées in his garden-club, L'Oasis, became legendary. His publications of 1908 and 1911, *Les Robes de Paul Poiret racontées par Paul Iribe* and *Les Choses de Paul Poiret vues par Georges Lepape*, revitalised the art of fashion illustration.

In his role as *couturier*, Poiret's major influence was in liberating women from the stiff and restricting corsetry in which they had been trapped for so long. In 1906 he introduced his distinctive loose coats, often fur-trimmed, the sleeves lost in the amorphous gathers of cloth. Iribe's drawings of 1908, however, show the more revolutionary idea of looseness in day and evening dresses. The new fashion launched by Poiret was evocative of the Empire period with the softness of its lines and the *style Empire* high waist. In 1910, as if from a perverse desire to assert his total control over fashion, Poiret launched the hobble skirt, restricting, in a new way, the women he had sought to liberate. The fashion enjoyed only a brief success.

Poiret's major fashion success was in launching his own orientalised designs at the time of the dazzling Paris stage success of the Ballets Russes in 1909. Poiret's turbans, aigrettes, harem pants and skirts were an immediate and total success with a public delighted and inspired by Bakst's designs for *Schéhérazade*.

Despite the brave front maintained by fashion writers, the First World War was a lean time for Paris *couture*. Many houses, including that of Poiret, were forced to close their doors. The period immediately after the war was one of confusion in fashion. Women were reluctant to sacrifice the ease of the mid-calf length which had become popular during the war years; designers were uncertain whether to revert to the luxurious Oriental pre-war styles for afternoon or evening wear. Dipping hems provided a compromise. A

Right French gown *c.* 1907.

Opposite page A drawing by Georges Lepape of Paul Poiret's design, 'Au Clair de la Lune', 1913.

drawing of 1919, *Au Thé Dansant, Schéhérazade*, by Marthe Romme, well illustrates the lingering taste for Poiret's Orientalism, together with the new use of draped cloth and full wings over the hips. Amongst the most exquisite drawings of the Paris fashions of this period are those of Russian émigré Erté who, since 1914, had been supplying the American *Harper's Bazaar* with refined, meticulously drawn ink and gouache illustrations of the latest Paris trends in fashion. Amongst the most delightful creations of this period were the tightly-pleated, clinging velvet dresses of Mariano Fortuny, introduced before the war and still in evidence in virtually the same, classic styles through the twenties.

It was about 1922 that there emerged the silhouette popularly associated with the 1920s; the bust was eliminated and dresses fell in a straight line past a waistline that had dropped to the hips. Spanish-born illustrator Benito, in his 1922 drawing 'Florentin' for Poiret, shows his female subject as virtually rectangular. About a year later other fashions emerged which are so closely linked with the accepted image of the 1920s, the 'Cloche' hat, the shingle and the short-lived cropped hairstyle that became known in England as the 'Eton' crop.

By 1925, skirts were being worn a little higher, but it was only for a brief season in 1926 that hems reached a record height, stopping just below the knee. Gabrielle 'Coco' Chanel was the rising star of Paris *couture* with her timely, and commercially successful, emphasis on easy pleated skirts and soft jackets and 'sports' clothes. By 1927 Chanel's casual, lean, tanned look for daytime was law and Jean Patou, Lucien Lelong and Madeleine Vionnet successfully followed her lead. A softer, more feminine element, however, was ousting the short straight dress for evening wear.

After a brief spell of uncertainty between the shorter or longer dresses for evening wear, an uncertainty which certain designers tried to resolve with the somewhat unsatisfactory compromise of handkerchief skirts with irregular hems, the late twenties and early thirties emerged as a period of almost unequalled elegance in evening wear.

The new full-length line was smooth, sleek and figure-hugging, the cleverly-cut dresses, often deceptively simple sheaths of cloth without fastening, simply fitted where they fell and required a flawless slender body if they were to look as stunning as they did in the photographs of Edward Steichen or George Hoyningen-Huené. Two designers excelled in the creation of evening dresses in a fashion conceived in perfect harmony with the streamlined chic of the Modernist interiors so much in vogue. Foremost was Madeleine Vionnet who is acknowledged as the originator of the bias cut so essential for the clinging effect she now achieved with consummate mastery. Vionnet created her designs and worked out their complex cutting directly in cloth on a half-life-size dummy.

The other great specialist of the new sleek silhouette was Alix, later known as Madame Grès, who opened her *maison de couture* in 1933 and enjoyed an immediate success with her distinctively personal interpretation of the fashion. Alix specialised in clinging evening dresses with tightly tucked drapes of cloth, seemingly inspired by

Above Erté in fancy dress in Monte Carlo, 1922.

Opposite page Mme. Poiret wearing a dress designed by her husband.

Right Schiaparelli quilted jacket from the 'Circus' collection, 1938.

Below right 'Florentin', drawing for Poiret by Edouard Garcia Benito, 1922.

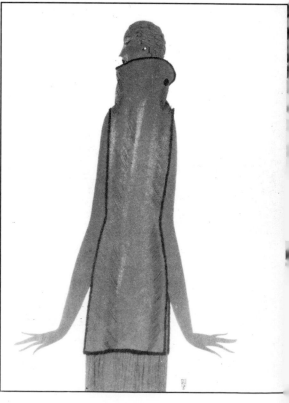

Hellenistic sculpture. The fashionable fabrics were shiny and clinging, satins, silk jersey and *crêpe*. In 1934 Alix created a sleek cellophane evening dress described in *Vogue* as 'glistening like a magnificent black scarab.'

Just as the clean, uncluttered lines of Modernism were ousted in the mid thirties by a phase of revivalism tinged with a taste for Surrealism, so there was a movement in fashion away from the sleek glamour of the Vionnet style towards a more romantic phase. Spanish-born Cristobal Balenciaga scored an immediate success on opening in Paris in 1937 with a collection of neo-Victorian dresses. The trend was towards a more elaborate style, full-skirted and wide-shouldered, which found its most delightful graphic expression in the drawings of Christian 'Bébé' Bérard. Some of the wittiest *Vogue* covers and illustrations of the late thirties bear Bérard's signature and often light-heartedly caricature the imagery of fashionable Surrealist painters.

The most exciting talent to emerge in the thirties was the unpredictable Italian Elsa Schiaparelli who had opened in Paris in 1928 and won immediate acclaim for her imaginative knit-wear and 'sports' clothes. Typical of her inventive-ness was the 1928 knitted jumper with a *trompe*

Left Knitted jumper with *trompe l'oeil* cravat by Elsa Schiaparelli, 1928.

Below left The sleek lines of the mid 1930s.

l'oeil knotted cravat incorporated into the pattern of the knit. The element of surprise was ever-present in 'Schiap's' work. She made 'Shocking' pink her colour, launched her 'Shocking' perfume and ultimately wrote her autobiography, *Shocking Life*. After 1935 and the opening of her Place Vendôme Boutique the name of Schiaparelli became synonymous with amusing ideas in fashion. Her collections followed a succession of novel themes and she had particular success with her 'Circus Parade' of 1938. She popularised the short, box-shouldered jacket, quilted or encrusted with mirror, sequin or embroidered designs. Her most memorable clothes, however, are those which bear witness to her collaboration with Salvador Dali and Jean Cocteau.

Cocteau made witty drawings of faces and hands to be applied to evening dresses. Dali inspired such designs as the dress printed with *trompe l'oeil* rips and tears or yet another dress printed with a life-size lobster and salad over which he was persuaded with some difficulty to restrain from splashing mayonnaise.

The highly individual fabrics and luxurious silks and satins created by artists and manufacturers of the early years of the fashion industry contrast sharply with today's man-made fibres.

United Kingdom

British Design 1890–1940 *by Isabelle Anscombe*

The Arts and Crafts Movement

FROM THE 1860s ONWARDS Britain rose to a prominent position in European decorative arts. The founding of Morris, Marshall, Faulkner & Co. in 1861 had been the beginning of a new movement in reaction to the allegorical flourishes of design in the 1851 Great Exhibition. The Arts and Crafts Movement, absorbing the tenets of the Gothic Revival, was committed to honest and simple design for domestic use. Inspired by the teachings of John Ruskin and Pre-Raphaelite art, it was an intellectual movement, the majority of the designers being professional architects, which captured the imagination of its time. Arts and Crafts furniture and artifacts laid stress on the honest presentation of materials, structure and production, taking as its highest principle Ruskin's and William Morris's belief that only the highest good could come from man transforming his own environment by the work of his own hands. The machine was despised, as was any decorative idiom which slavishly copied past styles. Handicrafts flourished, especially in the fields of embroidery, metalwork, stained glass and art pottery.

All over the country handicraft guilds were founded to involve both the working man and the hitherto unemployable young lady in the practical creation of their own environment. The most influential of these guilds were the Century Guild, founded in 1882 by Arthur Heygate Mackmurdo, the Art-Workers' Guild founded in 1884, Charles Robert Ashbee's Guild of Handicraft formed in 1888, the same year as the Arts and Crafts Exhibition Society, and, in 1900, the Birmingham Guild of Handicraft.

The original impetus of the Arts and Crafts ideals gave rise to considerable activity which was chronicled in the pages of *The Studio*.

Below Sideboard and furniture designed by Snell & Co. and exhibited at the Great Exhibition of 1851.

Below right Earthenware vases showing the over-elaborateness of design typical of many exhibits at the Great Exhibition of 1851.

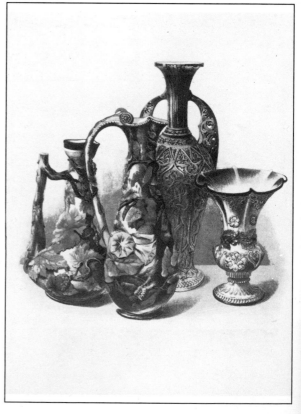

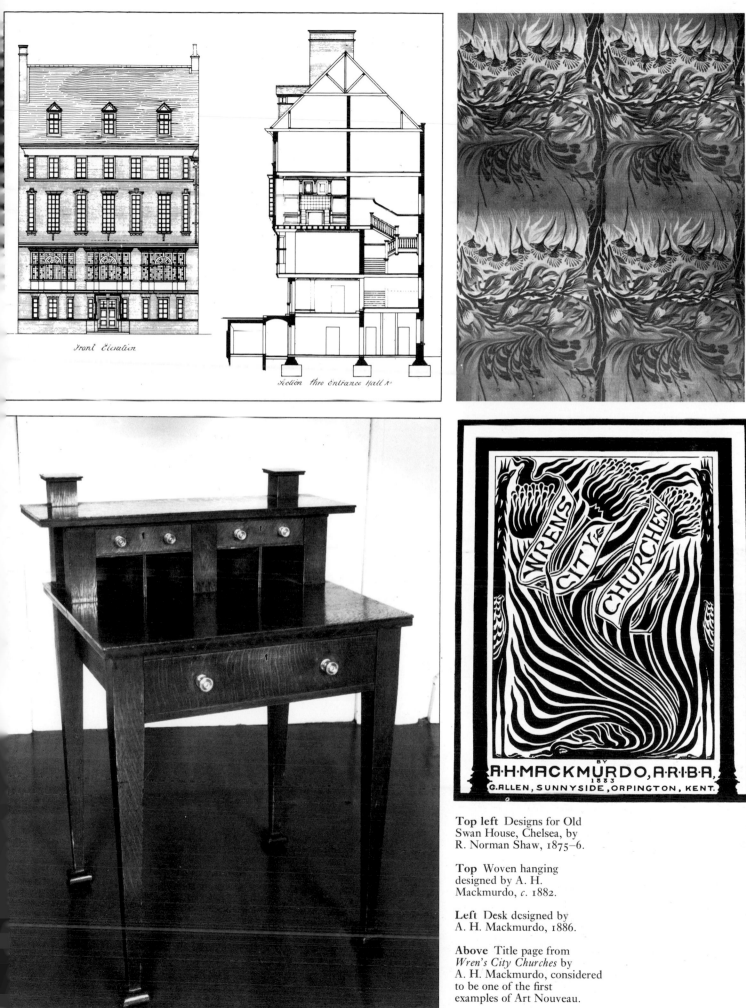

Top left Designs for Old
Swan House, Chelsea, by
R. Norman Shaw, 1875–6.

Top Woven hanging
designed by A. H.
Mackmurdo, *c.* 1882.

Left Desk designed by
A. H. Mackmurdo, 1886.

Above Title page from
Wren's City Churches by
A. H. Mackmurdo, considered
to be one of the first
examples of Art Nouveau.

The magazine was frankly propagandist for the movement and through its pages the inspiration of British design was made known in Europe and America. Another outcome of the reaction to the Great Exhibition was that some industrial design almost underwent a revolution, notably in the work of Dr. Christopher Dresser or William Arthur Smith Benson, who became the director of Morris & Co. after Morris's death in 1896. The Arts and Crafts Movement was the start of an entirely contemporary design idiom.

The Arts and Crafts home was eclectic. Houses built by Philip Webb, Norman Shaw or Charles Francis Annesley Voysey stressed the architectural qualities of wood and stone. Morris & Co. wallpapers or woven hangings presented a backdrop for Gothic-inspired, sturdy oak furniture. Every detail, from light fittings to carpets, was chosen to reflect an internal coherence which was as much intellectual as aesthetic. As Walter Crane wrote: 'The great charm of the Morrisian method is that it lends itself to either simplicity or splendour. You might be almost as plain as Thoreau, with a rush-bottomed chair, piece of matting, and oaken trestle table; or you might have gold and lustre (the choice ware of William de Morgan) gleaming from the sideboard, and jewel-

Portrait of William Morris, attributed to C. Fairfax-Murray.

led light in the windows, and walls hung with arras tapestry.'

The Aesthetic Movement

The 1890s in Europe reflect an almost conscious sense of *fin-de-siècle* decadence. In England the writings of Swinburne, Wilde or Beardsley mirrored the preoccupations of the French poets who wrote of the inexorable birth of the modern city at the zenith of capitalism, and the legal feuds between Whistler and Ruskin or Buchanan and D. G. Rossetti accentuated the fact that feelings were running high.

The decorative arts entered this arena under the

banner of the Aesthetic Movement, with Osca Wilde in the front line. The Aesthetic Movemen depended, in the eyes of a public educated by th lampooning it received in the press, on a handful o beings who declared themselves for Art, an nothing but Art. Wilde summed up this popula image in a lecture given on his American tou when he said, tacitly referring to Du Maurier' *Punch* cartoons, that his audience no doubt re garded him as 'a young man . . . whose greate difficulty in life was the difficulty of living up to th level of his blue china – a paradox,' he added 'from which England has not yet recovered.'

The Aesthetic Movement had successfully ass

milated the Japanese taste which had been seized upon after the first Japanese artifacts had been displayed at the 1862 International Exhibition. Japanese motifs, asymmetry and delicacy were absorbed into the Arts and Crafts ideals in the work of Edward William Godwin, Bruce J. Talbert or Thomas Jeckyll, the Art Pottery of Minton & Co. under the direction of William Stephen Coleman, or the fabrics and wallpapers by Walter Crane or Lewis F. Day. In the 1860s and 1870s Godwin and Norman Shaw had introduced an architectural style known as Queen Anne, using red brick in a form of domestic, secular architecture removed from the earlier Gothic, in their

houses at Bedford Park, the first garden suburb begun in 1876, and Tite Street, Chelsea.

Into houses such as these came the blue and white china, the emblems of the peacock, lily or sunflower which were to symbolise the Aesthetic Movement. Art had reached the middle class home with new fabrics for women's dresses and new books, such as those by Kate Greenaway, to entertain in the nursery. This movement only had credence in England and America and was made much fun of within the context of a final flourish before the new century was ushered in. Yet even those who set out to ridicule it gave it respect; for example, the costumes for *Patience, or Bunthorne's*

The William Morris Room at the Victoria and Albert Museum, London.

Above Two illustrations by Kate Greenaway, 1914.

Right Carpet, 'Green Pastures', designed by C. F. A. Voysey, 1896.

Bride: An Aesthetic Opera were designed by W. S. Gilbert using 'authentic' Liberty & Co. fabrics.

In 1890 William Morris began his last great enterprise, the Kelmscott Press, which was to lead to British domination in the art of fine printing and typography for many years to come. In 1894 *The Yellow Book* was published with illustrations by Aubrey Beardsley. In 1897 Pilkington's established their pottery with designs by Walter Crane, Voysey and Lewis F. Day. Also in 1894 the Belgian Henry van de Velde designed four rooms for Samuel Bing's new shop, La Maison de l'Art Nouveau in Paris, influenced by his visit to Liberty & Co. in 1891. In 1898 the Grand Duke of Hesse commissioned designs from C. R. Ashbee and Mackay Hugh Baillie Scott for furniture, made by the Guild of Handicraft, for the artists' colony set up at Darmstadt. Britain's lead was beginning to have its effects abroad.

The 1890s in Great Britain

In 1894 Liberty & Co., which had opened in 1875 selling Japanese and Oriental goods, went public and the new shares were eagerly bought. In 1890 Liberty's had an entire section in the Paris Exhibition, where Arthur Liberty was himself a juror. He had always been aware of the importance of remaining slightly ahead of changes in taste and during the 1890s began new ventures, ably supported by the Welshman John Llewellyn, who had been appointed to the board in 1898 after his success in the fabrics department where he had commissioned designs by Voysey, Jessie M. King and Arthur Silver, founder of the Silver Studio. In 1899 a new silver range, Cymric, was introduced with designs by Bernard Cuzner, Rex Silver (Arthur's eldest son) and Jessie M. King. It is probable that the name itself was bestowed on the range by Llewellyn.

In 1901 a new company, Liberty & Co. (Cymric) Ltd., was formed in conjunction with the Birmingham silver firm W. H. Haseler, and around the same time the Manxman Archibald Knox, probably introduced to Liberty by his friend Christopher Dresser, began his work in the Cymric range and quickly came to dominate the design of the silver.

From 1900 Liberty's had stocked German Kayser-Zinn pewter, but from 1903 their own Tudric range, with designs by Knox, was introduced, probably on the suggestion of William Haseler of the Birmingham firm. Liberty's fabrics and wallpapers and especially Knox's metalwork designs give the most coherent suggestion in England of the Art Nouveau forms which were beginning to appear in Europe. However, British designers always remained adamantly opposed to Art Nouveau and although Arthur Liberty had welcomed a new style, he would have agreed with Lewis F. Day that the Continental work showed 'symptoms . . . of pronounced disease.'

After Britain's lead in the decorative arts it seems strange that from this time on she was to strongly oppose any new influences, from Art Nouveau to the Bauhaus and the Modern Movement, and to remain firm in her adherence to the simple functional lines and country morals of the Arts and Crafts Movement. Within her own boundaries artists such as the Glasgow Four, who

Above Interior of Hill House, Dunbartonshire, Scotland, designed by C. R. Mackintosh, 1904.

Far left Charles Rennie Mackintosh as a young man.

Left Margaret Mackintosh photographed in the Mackintosh's flat in Mains Street, Glasgow.

Woven silk designed by Arthur Silver for Liberty & Co., *c*. 1895.

were acclaimed abroad, were to be virtually ignored by critics and public alike.

The Glasgow Four were Charles Rennie Mackintosh, Herbert McNair and Margaret and Frances Macdonald, all of whom studied at the Glasgow School of Art in the early 1890s. Mackintosh, an architect, had produced his first furniture designs in the early 1890s and this early work already shows an avoidance of reference to period design and a sparseness in the absence of applied ornament. His designs were dictated by the problems of the arrangement of interior space and he laid stress on vertical elements, his high-backed chairs giving a variety of height within a room, despite the acknowledged criticism of their impracticality. When the Macdonald sisters (Margaret married Mackintosh and Frances married McNair) left the Glasgow School of Art they opened their own studio for embroidery, gesso, leaded glass, *repoussé* metalwork and book illustration, which quickly became a meeting place for other Glasgow designers, such as Jessie M. King, Ernest Archibald Taylor and Talwin Morris.

In 1896 the Four were invited to send furniture, craftwork and posters to the Arts and Crafts Exhibition Society show where their work, especially the posters, met with a puzzled and shocked reaction. However, the editor of the *Studio* made a visit to Glasgow and in 1897 published two appreciative articles on their work. This was quickly picked up in Europe and the following year the Darmstadt magazine *Dekorative Kunst* contained an article on the Glasgow School.

Earlier, in 1895, work from Glasgow Art School had been sent to the Liège Exhibition where it was received enthusiastically, although Mackintosh himself never favoured the Belgian and French excesses of Art Nouveau. It was in Vienna that he found like minds. In 1900 he visited the 8th Vienna Secessionist Exhibition, which was devoted to the work of foreign designers, including Mackintosh and his wife, C. R. Ashbee and Van de Velde. There he met Josef Hoffmann with whom he was to remain in contact for many years, warmly supporting the decision to found the Wiener Werkstätte. Mackintosh received two commissions in Vienna, including the design of a music room for a house for the banker Fritz Waerndorfer, who was to finance the Werkstätte, where a dining room was commissioned from Hoffmann. Mackintosh also exhibited successfully at the Turin Exhibition of 1902. It must have been a sore disappointment to Mackintosh to find his work received so sympathetically abroad while being almost ignored in England.

His most important commissions in and around Glasgow were for the Glasgow School of Art (1896), the series of tea rooms designed for Miss Cranston, on which he at first collaborated with George Walton, and a few private houses, notably Hill House, Helensburgh (1902). These projects where he designed almost every element, from cutlery for the tea rooms to rugs for Hill House, demonstrate his remarkable creation of a distinctive style totally removed from the influences of the preceding century.

Further south another geographical area was to give its name to a style of craftsmanship which owed its being more directly to the Arts and Crafts Movement: the Cotswold School. In 1890 Kenton & Co. was formed by Ernest Gimson, Sidney Barnsley, Alfred Powell, Mervyn Macartney, Reginald Blomfield and W. R. Lethaby. In 1891 the company held an exhibition at Barnard's Inn.

The company gave these architects a taste for furniture design, and in 1893 Gimson and Barnsley moved out of London to Ewen, near Cirencester, to look for a suitable place to found a workshop. Ernest Barnsley left his Birmingham architectural practice to join them. In 1901 they employed Peter Waals, an experienced Dutch cabinet-maker. They began a workshop at Pinbury and in March 1902 settled permanently in workshops of their own building at Sapperton. *The*

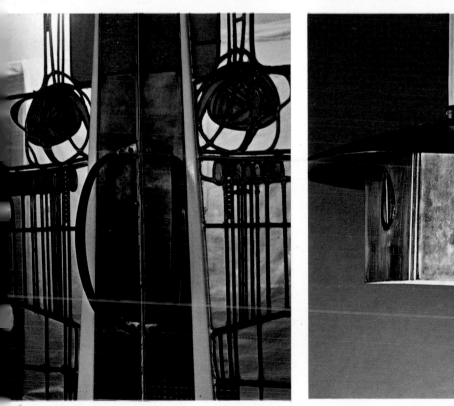

Above Wall panels and mirrors for the Willow Tea Rooms, Glasgow, by C. R. Mackintosh, 1904.

Far left Detail of the doors for the Willow Tea Rooms, designed by C. R. Mackintosh.

Left Metal lampshade designed by C. R. Mackintosh, *c*. 1900.

Studio naturally warmly supported the work they produced, although other critics condemned their use of dovetail joints which could be felt when one sat down upon a chair, or, as in a review in *The Builder* of a bow-fronted oak dresser exhibited by Sidney Barnsley in 1899: '. . . the turn-buttons to the small top cupboards look like the work of a savage; the wooden handles to the lower doors . . . are actually nailed on at one end, the rough nail head showing at the top. This is not only not artistic, it is not even good taste.'

However, they would have defended their work by reference to the Arts and Crafts ideals of

The work of the Cotswold School, which influenced Ambrose Heal and Gordon Russell, demonstrates the continuance of the Arts and Crafts antipathy to the machine. As Gordon Russell noted in his autobiography, when considering art education, no schools existed which recognized the need for particular training for machine production. It was this legacy of the Arts and Crafts Movement which led to the culpable ignorance in England of the co-ordination, as at the Bauhaus, of technical and art trainings. As late as 1927 Harry Peach, who started the Dryad Workshops and was a militant member of the

The Pinbury workshop shared by Ernest Gimson and Sidney and Ernest Barnsley, *c.* 1895.

honesty of materials and production and their solid wardrobes and dressers all show beautiful workmanship in the treatment of the wood, allowing the material to stand alone, or in contrast with different inlaid woods. Gimson himself never executed his designs, except some turned ash chairs; the work was carried out by the various craftsmen they employed and the metalwork – handles and the like – were made by the local blacksmith, Alfred Bucknell, to Gimson's designs. Gimson died in 1919 and the Barnsleys in 1926, but Waals continued until 1937, moving to his own workshops at Chalford in 1920, still using some of Gimson's designs.

Design and Industries Association, could organise the D.I.A. display for the Leipzig Exhibition as show of country crafts. From the First World War England began to lose her place among the leaders of European design.

The Design and Industries Association
In many ways the period under discussion, 1890–1940, is divided by the founding, in 1915, of the Design and Industries Association. The foundation of the D.I.A. followed a visit to the Werkbund Exhibition in Cologne in 1914 by Harold Stabler, Harry Peach, Ambrose Heal and other founder members of the D.I.A. who had fo

ong been concerned about the lack of good design for ordinary manufactured household items. The Arts and Crafts Movement had treated manufacturers with disdain and the manufacturers unsurprisingly reacted by ignoring any overtures made in their direction. Despite the enthusiasm of the original 199 members of the D.I.A., this antipathy to the machine remained, hidden in their Ruskinian approach to design.

William Richard Lethaby, for example, who had founded the Central School of Art in 1896, for long regarded as the most progressive school in Europe, still championed the idea that the idioms of craftwork should inspire the machine and that

design should be for people and not for the sake of theoretical concepts such as those held at the Bauhaus or in the French review, *L'Esprit Nouveau*. In 1913 he had written: 'Although a machine-made thing can never be a work of art in the proper sense, there is no reason why it should not be good in a secondary order . . . Machinework should show quite frankly that it is the child of the machine; it is the pretence and subterfuge of most machine-made things which make them disgusting.'

His definition is of art and not of design in the modern sense and it is hardly surprising that the D.I.A. was never to champion an attitude to the

Top left Unpolished oak furniture designed by Ambrose Heal for houses in Letchworth, the first English garden city, *c.* 1901.

Top Steel firedogs designed by Ernest Gimson, *c.* 1910.

Above Extendable oak dining table by Peter Waals, *c.* 1924.

Right Dresser designed by Ambrose Heal and exhibited at the Royal Academy, London, 1935.

Below Table and chairs designed by Ambrose Heal, c. 1920.

machine which would allow it an order of its own. The new reformers were not only designers, but manufacturers and retailers as well, such as Ambrose Heal, Gordon Russell or James Morton, of Morton Sundour textiles, who advocated plain, sturdy 'cottage' furniture.

The Omega Workshops

Just before the First World War a group of artists, under the leadership of Roger Fry, came together who combined the Arts and Crafts ethic with the impetus of Post-Impressionist art. On 8 July 1913 the Omega Workshops opened at 33 Fitzroy Square. The artists involved, Duncan Grant, Vanessa Bell, Wyndham Lewis, Frederick

Letterhead for the Omega Workshops, probably designed by Wyndham Lewis.

Etchells, Cuthbert Hamilton and Edward Wadsworth, produced painted screens and furniture, hand-dyed textiles, pottery, designs for murals and a miscellany of smaller items. The Omega was shortlived, mainly due to the war, which removed

Grant and Bell from London, the walk-out over a disagreement on a commission for a Post-Impressionist room at the Ideal Home Exhibition of Lewis, Etchells, Wadsworth and Hamilton, and competition from Heal's. The Omega closed in 1919.

From the beginning it had been clear that Wyndham Lewis found it hard to suppress his love of machinery and aggressive attitude to art within the rule of anonymity which ensured the domination of the more temperate Bloomsbury charm, but his artistic preoccupations did lead the others into conveying non-representational abstract designs into their fabrics and screens. His mural designs for Lady Drogheda's Futurist dining room, 1913–14, showed how different were his aspirations from the pastel colours, dancing figures and vases of flowers of Grant and Bell, who also absorbed the influence of Bakst into their interiors. Duncan Grant and Vanessa Bell were in the forefront of mural design, which flourished with artists such as Douglas Davidson, Eric Ravilious, Rex Whistler's murals for the Tate's tea room or Mary Adshead's designs for Bank Underground station, John Banting who painted a wall in Fortnum & Mason's new decoration department and Boris Anrep who produced mosaic pavements.

Modernism in Britain

The 1920s were the years of the interior, whether the very English intellectuality of Grant and Bell or Francis Bacon's 'constructivist room', with white walls, circular glass tables and mirrors and neutral coloured rugs woven in 'thought patterns'. In 1927 Syrie Maugham uncovered her 'all-white room' in her seventeenth-century Chelsea house, decorated with white flowers according to the season; some said she had originated the all-white idiom, others claimed it was Arundell Clarke, while yet more have it as Da Silva Bruhns; whatever the truth, the scheme was widely adopted, as in Claridges all-white restaurant.

The turning-point for interior design had come with the 1925 Paris Exhibition. Germany, and therefore the Bauhaus, had been excluded from exhibiting and it was not until 1930–1 that the Salon des Artistes-Décorateurs included a Bauhaus section.

The 1925 Exhibition was dominated by the work of Ruhlmann, Süe et Mare and Lalique, but England's reaction was summed up by the *Architectural Review* of that year: 'Unquestionably every Englishman who visits the pavilions and stands of the modern French *ensembliers* will ask himself whether he would care to live among such impeccable surroundings from which cosiness is markedly absent. . . . But little doubt that our Englishman, mindful of fireside joys, of capacious easy chairs, will, perhaps, admire, then turn aside and leave such artificialities to the exhibition and to France.'

The exhibition did influence one important aspect of British design, the Modernist rug. The American poster designer Edward McKnight Kauffer, encouraged by Marion Dorn, first used Cubist abstract designs in rugs and from 1928 their work was hand-woven at the Wilton Royal Carpet Factory, which also commissioned Marian Pepler, John Tandy and Ronald Grierson. Also in

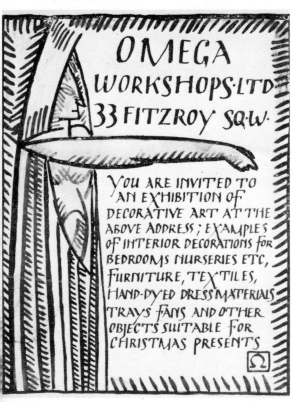

1928 James Morton started the Edinburgh Weavers as a specialist branch of Morton Sundour
Fabrics Ltd.

Gradually the new ideas did begin to find
expression in England. The influence of modern
Scandinavian design reached the British public;
Fortnum & Mason's held an exhibition of the
furniture of Alvar Aalto. In 1928 Shoolbred's, the
decorating firm, held an exhibition of work by the
French Décoration Intérieure Moderne which had
exhibited in the 1925 Paris Exhibition. Steel frame
furniture by PEL was exhibited at the Ideal Home
Exhibition, although it was criticised in com-
parison to the work of Marcel Breuer, and in 1933
Gordon Russell began making steel frame chairs.
In 1933 the Dorland Hall Exhibition was organised by the architects Oliver Hill, Wells Coates,
Serge Chermayeff and Raymond McGrath. In
1931 Jack Pritchard of Isokon had visited the
Bauhaus and in 1934, under his aegis, Walter
Gropius came to England. However, like Breuer,
Chermayeff and Moholy-Nagy, he did not stay for
long before departing for America. Although
Britain no longer rejected Modernism out of hand,
it was still a minority taste, held by many to belong
only to left-wing intellectuals. As Herbert Read
wrote in 1934, in *Art and Industry*: '. . . the real

Above Interior designed
by Serge Chermayeff,
c. 1930.

Left Advertisement for an
exhibition at the Omega
Workshops.

problem is not to adapt machine production to the aesthetic standards of handicraft, but to think out new aesthetic standards for new methods of production.' This the English were loathe to do.

The design of the late 1920s and 1930s divides itself between the architects who had to depend mainly upon state commissions, such as the excellent work done by Frank Pick for London Transport or Raymond McGrath's work as Decoration Consultant to the BBC, and the design shops which owed their custom mainly to educated Mayfair or, as with Duncan Miller, to the financial support of film companies. Architects such as Chermayeff, Max Fry or Wells Coates found their work in short demand, although Brian O'Rorke's designs for the R.M.S. *Orion* stood in obvious contrast to the Edwardian excesses lauded in the *Architectural Review* of 1914 for the Cunard liners which included 'genuine antiques and replicas of Old Masters as part of the decoration'.

The real discipline of the Bauhaus furniture, founded upon geometry, was scarce, but modern design, square furniture or the later rounded curves in plain veneer, were to be found at Curtis Moffat's Fitzroy Square galleries, at Betty Joel Ltd. at 25 Knightsbridge, at Arundell Clarke's in Bruton Street or at Heal's.

Opposite Interior at Claridge's Hotel, London, showing rugs designed by Marion Dorn, *c.* 1935.

Left and below Modernist interiors by Serge Chermayeff, *c.* 1930.

Furniture *by Isabelle Anscombe*

Glasgow cabinet designed
by E. A. Taylor, *c*. 1900.

IN 1859 PHILIP WEBB had designed and built the Red House for William Morris at Upton in Kent. Together with Dante Gabriel Rossetti and Edward Burne-Jones they also designed and painted the furniture; solidly constructed in native woods, according to Morris's tastes, panels were painted with medieval scenes not unlike Morris's own romances. On the founding of Morris, Marshall, Faulkner & Co., Webb became chief designer, continuing to produce solid oak trestle tables and other furniture in the sturdy British tradition. His most successful houses, Clouds, at East Knoyle in Wiltshire, furnished by Morris & Co., and Standen, at East Grinstead, both reflect a new awareness of elegance without grandeur, using wood panelling as interior decoration.

Morris & Co. was capable of producing decorative schemes for houses such as these, or for Stanmore Hall, where furniture by W. R. Lethaby was commissioned from Kenton & Co., and also items such as the simple rushed Sussex chairs based on traditional designs. Mervyn Macartney, W. A. S. Benson and Frank Brangwyn also designed furniture for Morris & Co., the latter two also working for J. S. Henry & Co. who specialised in simple inlaid furniture based on Art Nouveau lines. Benson also designed silver mounts and hinges for Morris & Co. Brangwyn continued to produce inlaid furniture with simple lines, such as his decorated screens for the Rowley Gallery. In 1890 George Jack became the chief designer for Morris & Co. and he introduced a quasi-eighteenth-century style with large cabinets with intricate inlaid decoration, mainly in mahogany.

In 1882 A. H. Mackmurdo founded the first of the influential guilds, the Century Guild. Using mahogany, oak and satinwood, Mackmurdo's designs are true precursors of Art Nouveau with asymmetrical patterns of vigorous stems, leaves and flowers running aslant his pieces giving an almost harsh impression of growth. His proportions were carefully and simply planned for a severe impression relieved by painted panels, fretwork or brass detailing. His idioms dominated the work of the Century Guild. Another designer who developed an idiosyncratic style approaching Art Nouveau was C. F. A. Voysey. His own house, The Orchard, built at Chorley Wood, Hertfordshire, in 1900, showed a more restrained style with little surface decoration, relying mainly on a juxtaposition of lines and the qualities of wood. In 1931 an exhibition of Voysey's work was held at the Batsford Gallery where even the retrospective pieces compared favourably with the best contemporary design.

In 1897 M. H. Baillie Scott was commissioned to design the dining room and drawing room for the Grand Duke of Hesse's Palace at Darmstadt. He collaborated with C. R. Ashbee, whose Guild of Handicraft carried out their designs for furniture and metalwork. This commission, along with the British exhibits at foreign exhibitions, did much to make known the work of English Arts and Crafts designers in Europe and was to inspire many European designers.

Baillie Scott's elaborate inlays and Ashbee's enamels enhanced the almost eccentric shapes of some of the designs and created a rich and luxurious interior, demonstrating, as did Ashbee's silver designs, that the Arts and Crafts Movement was not dedicated solely to the revival of 'cottage' crafts. Ashbee's house, Magpie and Stump, in Cheyne Walk, Chelsea, had been completed by the Guild of Handicraft in 1895; a true demonstration of their many accomplishments with tooled leatherwork, metalwork and carving. From 1898 Baillie Scott designed furniture for John White of Bedford which was sold to Liberty & Co.

The work of Norman Shaw, who had introduced the Queen Anne style at Bedford Park, shows the link between the Gothicism of early Morris or William Burges and the craftsman tradition of Ernest Gimson. Gimson used simply proportioned structures to show his mastery of geometric pattern and delicate inlay, using different woods, metals or mother-of-pearl. An architect by training, Gimson's first craft work was with plasterwork and gesso, which he continued to use in his houses and also as a decorative feature on his woodwork, using simple motifs such as the English rose.

Gimson's designs were produced by his workmen at Sapperton but his intricate designs for inlaid patterns, beading or stringing show an intimate understanding of his materials. His particular idiom has remained unsurpassed, but the work of his colleagues at Sapperton, Ernest and Sidney Barnsley, influenced the later work of Ambrose Heal and Gordon Russell. His own designs were still produced after his death by Peter Waals, although Waals adopted the larger sense of geometry rather than Gimson's smaller intricate designs. The work of the Barnsleys was in the tradition of British woodwork, giving attention to the effects of handwork in total opposition to the possibilities of machine finishes. A border decorated with gouging shows the man at work, although their work was sometimes criticised for a roughness of finish.

In Glasgow George Walton had his own firm of

Above left Rosewood
cabinet inlaid with
purplewood, tulipwood and
ebony, designed by W. A. S.
Benson and made by
Morris & Co., *c.* 1899.

Above Table and chair
with stencilled canvas back
by C. R. Mackintosh, *c.* 1901.

Left Dining room of the
Red House, built by Philip
Webb for William Morris,
1859.

decorators and George Logan and E. A. Taylor designed for Wylie & Lockhead. Walton left Glasgow for London in 1897, where he designed for Liberty & Co. and E. A. Taylor went to Manchester in 1908, where he designed for George Wragge Ltd. All three were inevitably influenced by the work of the Glasgow Four although, because they were designing for commercial production, their designs necessarily are more conventional than the elongated shapes of Mackintosh's furniture. Mackintosh's interiors show a concern for an integral whole, as for example in the furniture for the Willow Tea Rooms, designed for Miss Cranston in 1903, where the high-backed chairs were for look rather than comfort or practicality. They were designed to solve a specific artistic problem within the conception of filling the interior space in the best possible manner and the high, spindly backs suggest the young trees after which the rooms were named.

For the Ingram Street Tea Rooms Mackintosh designed the screens, murals, lampshades and even the cutlery to fulfil his overall design. He never used veneers for his furniture, preferring a black, dark or light green stain or the use of a white enamel-like surface obtained by a coach-painting technique, which he first used for his own flat in Mains Street in 1900. Where the designs of the contemporary Cotswold School could be used in almost any setting, fitting into the long tradition of English woodwork design, Mackintosh's work required the total interior, devoid of any reference to past traditions, perhaps the reason why his work was opposed in England. Mackintosh left Glasgow in 1914 but completed little work after that date.

For the first quarter of the twentieth century the idioms essential to the Arts and Crafts Movement declined in favour either of reproduction furniture and the eighteenth-century models such as those produced by George Jack or of the craftsman tradition maintained by Heal's and Gordon Russell, supported by the doctrines of the Design and Industries Association. Dunbar-Hay (and to some extent the Dryad Workshops which sold caneware) continued to market solidly made pieces which relied on the qualities of the wood with little ornamentation.

Following the vogue for mural decoration, the Omega Workshops produced painted furniture; mainly using second-hand furniture, Roger Fry prided himself on incorporating any original pattern within the applied design, with the result, however, that the Omega furniture was not destined for survival. The historical models admitted by designers changed from Gothic and medieval to the more classical lines of the Adam Brothers, praised in the *Architectural Review* by Paul Nash. The rich decoration of the French exhibits at the 1925 Paris Exhibition was ignored in England in favour of the 'cottage' tradition, as was the use of new materials introduced by Le Corbusier and the Modernist design ethic promoted by the masters of the Bauhaus.

In 1925 Marcel Breuer designed his first steel chair but it was not accepted in England until PEL introduced a steel chair at the Ideal Home Exhibition, which even then failed to comprehend the true theory of the structure. Designers such as John Tandy or Eileen Gray sought more congenial surroundings in Paris. As Herbert Read wrote in 1934 in *Art and Industry*: '. . . in many cases when a good design is discovered in this country, it can be traced to a foreign prototype.'

The most serious of the new designers and architects realised that they owed their new aesthetic to the machine, and in so doing turned their attention to machine design. Both Heal's and Gordon Russell introduced steel and laminated wood furniture and in 1931 Russell designed his first Murphy Radio cabinet. Serge Chermayeff also designed a wireless cabinet, Jack Gold electric

Below Fruitwood armchair designed by Ernest Gimson, *c.* 1900.

Below right Single door oak wardrobe with three rows of bevelled panels *c.* 1930, and oak chest of drawers with walnut handles, *c.* 1930, designed by Gordon Russell.

Top Oak dresser designed by Ambrose Heal, *c.* 1910.

Above left Altar chair from Queen's Cross Church, Glasgow, in oak and horsehair, designed by C. R. Mackintosh, 1897.

Above High chair of stained wood, exhibited by C. R. Mackintosh at the Secessionist Exhibition in Vienna, 1900.

Left Piano designed by M. H. Baillie Scott, *c.* 1898.

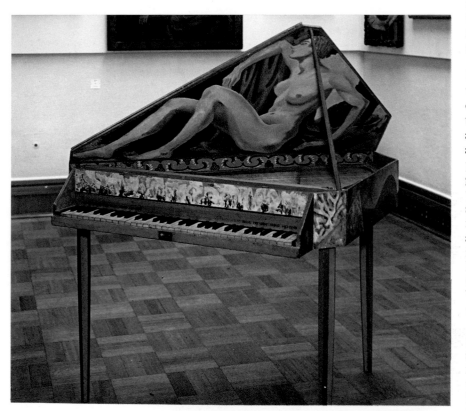

Above Painted virginals by Roger Fry for the Omega Workshops.

Right Silvered wood cabinet designed by Serge Chermayeff, *c.* 1930.

light fittings, Wells Coates an electric radiator, Raymond McGrath was commissioned to design for the BBC and designed not only studios and sets but also microphone stands and other equipment and a Nobel prizewinner, Dr. Dalen designed the Aga cooker. Equally, modern architecture was largely limited to G.L.C. housing and other official commissions; there are very few Modernist houses built for private use in the English countryside. Herbert Read went on to say that: 'If we decide that the product of the machine can be a work of art, then what is to become of the artist who is displaced by the machine? Has he any function in a machine-age society, or must he reconcile himself to a purely dilettante role – must he become, as most contemporary artists have become, merely a social entertainer?'

Apart from Roger Fry's 'little group of Post-Impressionists', few artists concerned themselves with furniture design, although Edward James commissioned work from Salvador Dali, such as the famous lobster telephone receivers. As abstract art rose in importance above the applied arts, the artists themselves saw their importance as being political, especially as Fascist régimes in Europe gradually gained a stranglehold on art. In many ways, in the field of the decorative arts, Read's statement bore more than a grain of truth. When, in 1936, the first ten Designers for Industry were appointed by the Royal Society of Arts, they included new designers such as Eric Gill and Keith Murray, but also such central Arts and Crafts figures as Harold Stabler and C. F. A. Voysey. The majority of new furniture designers worked out of exclusive shops.

Betty Joel Ltd. at 25 Knightsbridge was perhaps the most exclusive new designer, selling signed rugs and expensive furniture, far from functional, with large rounded curves and patterned veneers. As the *Architectural Review* noted in 1935: 'Laminated wood frees the cabinet maker (perhaps to his regret) from the tyranny of frame and panel. Doors can be cut out like so much cardboard. Ornament is sought in the grain of veneer, the direction of which need no longer bear any relation to the construction.'

Betty Joel's work is a perfect example of this freedom. More simple, functional lines were achieved by Arundell Clarke who, it is reputed, was the first to introduce the large square armchair. His furniture fitted into a plain decorative scheme with pattern employed only on the floor with commissioned signed rugs, the big upholstered armchairs and curved veneered furniture. The use of veneers on the walls was also popular. Curtis Moffat, who opened in 1929, followed much the same style as Arundell Clarke, while J. Duncan Miller used more dramatic effects.

All these decorators catered very much for an élite; cheaper furniture was available from Plan Ltd., who produced basic units for built-in furniture, which became more and more of a necessity as people moved into smaller houses and flats, or PEL Ltd., who produced steel frame chairs and steel and glass furniture, or The Makers of Simple Furniture who produced items in plywood. A friend of Walter Gropius, Jack Pritchard of Isokon, produced steel frame furniture which was probably the best available in England.

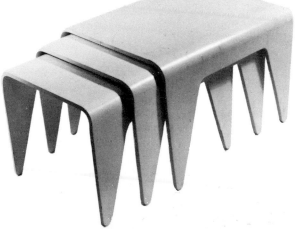

Top left Cocktail cabinet in coromandel ebony and walnut on a mahogany frame, designed by Serge Chermayeff, *c.* 1930.

Above left Plywood chair designed by Gerald Summers, *c.* 1930.

Top Nest of tables designed by Marcel Breuer and made by Isokon of London, *c.* 1936.

Above Painted table from the Omega Workshops.

Left *Chaise longue* by Betty Joel, *c.* 1930.

Ceramics *by Ian Bennett*

THE SECOND HALF of the nineteenth century was an age of stylistic eclecticism in the arts. The expansion of empires, combined with a conscious historicism, created an amazing variety of influences. In the applied arts, Gothicism, *japonisme* and Islamic art were the three principal influences. The ceramics of the late nineteenth century show these three very strongly. The willowy 'whiplash' style of French Art Nouveau had a very minor effect, and when its presence is seen in English applied art, it is usually in a somewhat debased and commercialised form, as in certain of the Moorcroft Florian and Flammarian wares and Minton's Secessionist wares.

The influence of Japan on late nineteenth-century European applied art is of the utmost importance. Indeed, it is questionable whether the Aesthetic Movement in English decorative arts or French Art Nouveau could have existed without it. The French artist and designer Félix Bracquemond is credited with being the agent behind the spread of Japanese motifs in European art. In 1856, Bracquemond had discovered a volume of Hokusai's *Manga* in the studio of the Paris printer Auguste Delâtre, a volume which he purchased subsequently and showed to a number of his friends, including Manet, Degas, Fantin-Latour, Whistler and the Goncourts.

As a direct result of this discovery, Bracquemond himself, in collaboration with the designer and retailer Eugène Rousseau, designed a famous dinner service, known as the Bracquemond-Rousseau service. Individual images of birds, flowers and insects were transfer-printed asymmetrically on to plain white blanks, these blanks being in an eighteenth-century revival style.

Despite the incongruity of image and ceramic shape, an incongruity pointed out by several contemporary critics, this service was to have a profound influence both in France and the rest of the Western world. Similar wares were produced by Maria Longworth Nichols at her newly founded Rookwood Pottery in Cincinnati in 1881. In England, W. S. Coleman designed a transfer-printed service for Milton's in 1870 and five years later, the same factory registered its Bamboo and Fan service. Worcester also began marketing similar wares including a service decorated with scenes after Ando Hiroshige's *Fifty-three Stages of the Tokaido Road* in 1873 and the Sparrow and Bamboo pattern in 1879.

Such wares represented one aspect of the Japanese influence, the transference of what were originally woodcut images to ceramic surfaces.

There was also much porcelain made in styles simulating Japanese metalwork and ivory, including Minton pieces based on enamel, and the Worcester Factory's sculptural pieces, many of which were modelled by the extremely gifted James Hadley.

The 1860s and 1870s also saw the founding of a number of art potteries which attempted to produce ceramics based upon new ideas in design and individual inspiration within a more intimate atmosphere than that found in the large industrial factories. Of these, the most important were: Milton's Art Pottery Studio, founded in 1871 in Kensington Gore, London, under the directorship of William Coleman; the De Morgan Pottery, which began producing ceramics on a commercial scale around 1872; the Linthorpe Pottery of Middlesbrough, Yorkshire, founded in 1879 by John Harrison and Christopher Dresser, and the Doulton Factory of Lambeth, London, which was originally founded in 1815, but only began making artistic stoneware in the 1860s.

The work of Doulton's and C. J. C. Bailey's Fulham Pottery was concerned principally with the revival of medieval saltglaze stoneware (*grès de Flandres*). Doulton's also produced painted wares called Faïence and Impasto, and it was this type of painted pottery which was also the main product of the Minton Art Pottery Studio, which lasted for only four years.

The saltglaze revival took place largely as the result of the presence in England of the French painter-potter Jean-Charles Cazin, who had arrived in 1871 to take up the Directorship of the South Kensington Art School in succession to Alphonse Legros; he was also employed on a freelance basis as a ceramic designer by the Fulham Pottery and taught drawing and ceramics at the Lambeth School of Art. The head of the Lambeth School, John Sparkes, had been the man principally responsible for persuading Henry Doulton to employ ex-students in his factory, and among those taught by Cazin were Walter and Edwin Martin. Their elder brother Robert Wallace joined the Fulham Pottery in 1872 as a modeller, and he too was influenced by Cazin.

Cazin had been a teacher at Tours in France, and was thus in touch with the Palissy revival of the French potter Charles Avisseau. Certainly the medievalism of the Fulham Pottery's wares, as well as that of Doulton and early Martin ware, combined with a strong element of Renaissance decoration, point to Cazin's influence, and the realism of much of the modelling at Doulton and Fulham has faint echoes of Avisseau.

Left Vase by Mark V. Marshall, made at Doulton's in 1904.

Right Isnik ware vase by William de Morgan and painted by Fred Passenger, *c.* 1906.

Bottom left Collection of painted underglaze earthenware tiles by William de Morgan, late nineteenth century.

Bottom Plaque designed by W. S. Coleman for Minton's, 1872.

An example of the grotesque birds made by Robert Wallace Martin in the 1890s.

By 1890, the first major phase of the English art pottery movement was over. Doulton had produced much of its best work, although fine things were still being done by Mark Marshall and Frank Butler, the most successful of only a very few English artists who made use of the French 'whiplash' style of Art Nouveau. Painted Doulton faïence was also produced in a style apparently based on Alphonse Mucha's poster art.

William de Morgan, who had begun producing pottery on a commercial scale in about 1872, had fully developed his range of Isnik inspired designs and colours and his range of metallic lustres based on Hispano-Moresque prototypes. He had moved to Merton Abbey in 1882, and then to Sand's End in Fulham in 1888. He took as a partner the architect Halsey Ricardo. During this period, all the hollow wares were thrown by De Morgan's workmen (previously he had purchased blanks from industrial factories) and the production of the lustres, although improved technically, was reduced to a quarter of the firm's output.

During the 1890s De Morgan spent six months of every year in Florence; while there, he made contact with the Cantagalli Factory, at which some of the first nineteenth-century revivals of lustre had been made under the directorship of Ulisse

Cantagalli. De Morgan designed several pieces which were fired by the factory, and recent evidence suggests that these continued to be made bearing only the factory mark, long after the designer's death in 1917. In 1898, De Morgan entered into a new partnership at the Sand's End factory with three of his long-serving workmen, the thrower Frank Iles and the brothers Charles and Fred Passenger who were decorators. This partnership, during which some splendid work was produced, lasted until 1907 and is known generally as the Late Fulham Period. The Passengers and Iles carried on making pottery at Sand's End until 1911. From 1923 to 1931, Fred Passenger was employed by Ida Perrins at the Bushey Heath Pottery, making ceramics in a debased De Morgan style.

In 1873, Robert Wallace Martin and his brothers Walter and Edwin had established the firm of R. W. Martin at Pomona House, Fulham. They were joined later in the same year by the fourth brother, Charles Douglas, who remained essentially a somewhat inefficient business manager although occasionally turning his hand to designing or even modelling. In 1877, the brothers set up a workshop at Southall and a shop in Brownlow Street, London, as an outlet for their wares.

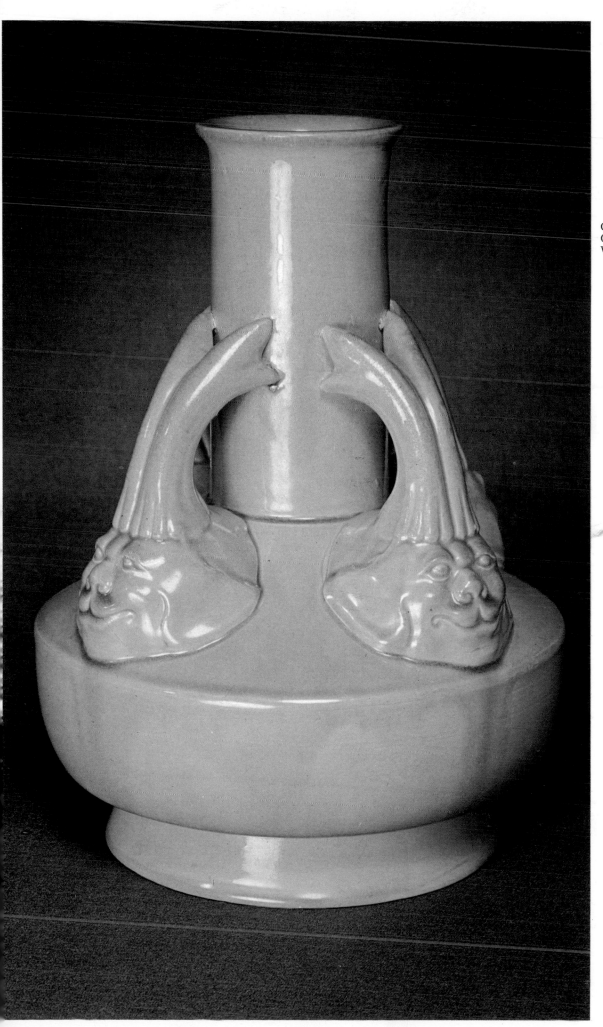

Grotesque vase designed by
Christopher Dresser for
William Ault, *c.* 1892.

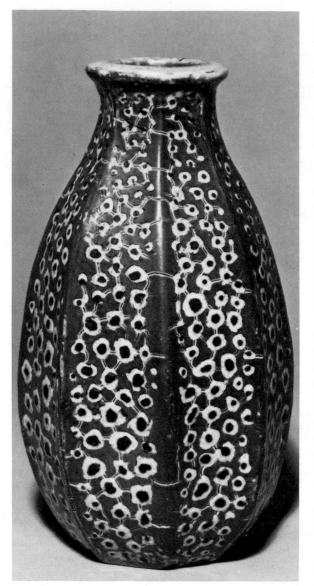

Saltglaze stoneware gourd
vase designed by Edwin
Martin, 1906.

The Martin Brothers produced a wide variety of
ceramics. The grotesque animals and birds are
mainly the work of Robert Wallace. In the early
years Gothic and Renaissance themes predo-
minate, but in the 1880s and 1890s, first natural
history, insects and marine life, and then mytho-
logical beasts such as dragons and animals and
fishes with strange gargoyle faces, began to appear
either incised or in low relief on vases, jugs and
other ware. Much of the inspiration for such
themes came from Japanese woodcuts and illustrated books, examples of which were in the
brothers' possession. From 1880 until 1895, the
brothers employed Edward Willey as an assistant,
and it is obvious from his surviving sketchbooks
that he was responsible for much of the designing
during this period.

In the late 1890s, following Willey's departure,
Edwin Martin began producing gourd vases,
usually very small, based on vegetable forms and
certain types of marine life. The surfaces of these
pieces are inspired by the various natural sub-
stances – tortoise-shell, sea-shells, mother-of-
pearl, dried sea-urchins – which the brothers are
known to have collected. It is probable that the
sudden appearance of this type of decoration was
hastened by Willey's departure and arose out of
the detailed decorative work on which Edwin had
been engaged during the time Willey was at the

pottery. In 1900, Edwin and his brother Walter, in
company with the collector S. K. Greenslade, who
had been enthusiastic about the new abstract
glazed pieces, visited the Paris International Exhibition. Many of Edwin's subsequent pieces, which
continued to be made well into the twentieth
century, were obviously influenced by the techniques of the Japanese folk pottery which he saw
there, but there is evidence that the brothers were
unimpressed by the French studio pottery.

After two years of severe mental illness, Charles
Douglas Martin died in 1910. In 1912, Walter died
of thrombosis, which virtually ended the active life
of the pottery since he had been the only one of the
brothers with a technical knowledge of glazing and
firing. Edwin lived until 1915 and the elder
brother Robert Wallace until 1923. After 1923,
Robert Wallace's son Clement, with a Captain
Butterfield as partner, glazed and fired the surviving biscuit pieces, and also produced pieces from
the surviving moulds.

One of the most important industrial designers
in the second half of the nineteenth century was
Christopher Dresser. Born in 1834, Dresser began
his career as a botanist. In the 1860s, he began
designing metalwork for some of the leading firms
of Sheffield and Birmingham, and also designed
ceramics for Minton's in the 1870s. It is probable
that he designed for several other industrial and art
potteries (his connection with some of the Devon
potteries has not yet been documented), as well as
designing glass, metalwork, furniture, wallpapers
and fabrics for many different companies.

He visited Japan in 1876, one of the first
European designers to make this trip, and in 1879
he started the Linthorpe Pottery at Linthorpe
Village, near Middlesbrough, Yorkshire, with
John Harrison, a wealthy local landowner. The
motivation for this venture was partly philan-
thropic and partly artistic, this area of Yorkshire
being then, as now, economically very depressed.

The Linthorpe Factory lasted until 1889, when
Harrison became bankrupt. Dresser's association,
however, is thought to have ceased in about 1883.
In the Dresser period, most of the pieces were
designed by him and bear his facsimile signature.
The dark green-brown streaky abstract glazes,
which largely characterised the firm's wares, were
influenced by Dresser's knowledge of Japanese
pottery, as some of the monochrome green, blue or
yellow wares were influenced by Chinese ceramics. Recent evidence suggests that much of the
glaze palette of Linthorpe Pottery was developed
by the factory's brilliant manager Henry Tooth.

Tooth left Linthorpe in 1882 and in the same
year opened a pottery with William Ault at
Woodville, near Burton-on-Trent. This was called
the Bretby Art Pottery. Ault severed his connections with Tooth in 1887 and opened his own
pottery at Swadlincote, not far from Woodville.
This factory was known as Ault Potteries Ltd.
until 1922 when the Ashby Potter's Guild of
Pascoe Tunnicliffe was absorbed; from 1923 until
it ceased production in 1947, the firm was known
as Ault and Tunnicliffe Ltd.

The pottery produced in both the Bretby and
Ault factories were obviously closely influenced by
that of Linthorpe. Dresser himself designed a
range of pieces for Ault in the 1890s; some of these

CHEVALIER SANS PEUR ET SANS REPROCHE UN

Lancastrian Ware wall plaque painted in silver lustre by Richard Joyce after a design by Walter Crane for Pilkingtons, 1907.

are almost indistinguishable from Linthorpe, although a few outrageous, grotesque, Gothic pieces are immediately recognisable as Ault, and remain among Dresser's most famous ceramic designs. Also in the north, a Leeds firm, Wilcox and Company, opened an art pottery studio called Burmantofts Faience in 1880. Some of the Linthorpe decorating staff moved there and influenced some of the factory's products. However, Burmantofts also produced a range of pieces painted in the Isnik palette, often of very high quality, which were obviously inspired by the work of William de Morgan.

Although the connection has never been clearly documented, it is certain that De Morgan's revival of lustre also influenced the products of the Pilkington Factory. The latter came into existence as the result of the discovery of clay by the Clifton

and Kersley Coal Company in 1889 while sinking mine shafts at Clifton in Lancashire. The owners of the company, four brothers called Pilkington, consulted an expert chemist at Wedgwood's, William Burton, and in 1891 the Pilkington Tile and Pottery Company was formed under the management of William and his brother Joseph. It was not, however, until after 1903, when the art pottery was called Lancastrian Ware (Royal Lancastrian after 1913) that the famous lustre was produced.

Although Lancastrian lustre reached a very high technical standard, the designs and colours are frequently vulgar and garish, and suffer generally from too mechanical a handling. In the early years of the twentieth century, a number of talented decorators were recruited, including Richard Joyce, who had worked at Bretby, in 1905,

Top Linthorpe bowl
designed by Christopher
Dresser, *c.* 1880.

Above Bowl designed
by William Moorcroft.

Above right Pot with lid
made by Charles Cox at the
Mortlake Pottery, 1912.

Gordon Forsyth, who became art director of the factory, in 1906, and William S. Mycock, Charles Cundall and Gladwys Rogers in 1907. Designs were also commissioned from three of the leading Arts and Crafts designers and artists: Charles Voysey (tiles only), Lewis F. Day and Walter Crane. Both Day and Crane had previously designed ceramics for a number of different factories, including Maw and Company, a Shropshire firm which began producing art pottery in the 1870s; they made about six pieces to Crane's designs, these usually being decorated with copper lustre.

The Pilkington Factory continued the production of art pottery until 1957, except for a break between 1938 and 1948. In the early years of the factory, the production of wares with streaked and monochrome glazes: Ultramarine Blue (later renamed Kingfisher Blue), Uranium Orange, Orange Vermilion, as well as pieces with crystalline glazes, equalled or outnumbered those pieces with the more expensive and hazardous lustre glazes. In 1928, Joseph Burton developed Lapis ware, a process for abstract or pictorial decoration in soft muted colours. Some of these latter pieces are of good quality.

In the last decade of the nineteeth century and the first decade of the twentieth, the obsession with various high temperature metallic-oxide glazes which had been a feature of the French, German and Danish industrial factories and some studio potteries in those countries since the 1870s, spread to England.

Considerable controversy exists over the chronology of European and American high-temperature transmutation glazes. The German glaze chemist and potter Hermann Seger began experimenting in the early 1870s and developed fine *flambé* glazes while technical director of the Royal Porcelain Factory, Berlin, from 1878 to 1890. In France, Théodore Deck at Sèvres and the studio potter Ernest Chaplet each had produced

successful copper red glazes by the early 1880s, although the Sèvres factory had produced isolated examples as early as the 1830s, and more pieces under the supervision of the glaze chemist Ebelman in the 1850s. In 1884, several soft-paste porcelain pieces with copper red (*sang-de-boeuf*) glazes made by Lauth and Vogt at Sèvres were exhibited at the Exposition de l'Union Centrale in Paris, an exhibition which also contained the first successful examples of Seger's Berlin *sang-de-boeuf* seen in public. By an extraordinary coincidence, 1884 is also the year in which Ernest Chaplet in France and Hugh C. Robertson at the Chelsea Keramic Works in the United States produced their first successful stoneware decorated with high temperature *flambé* glazes.

In England, the earliest experiments seem to have taken place in the 1890s, although, typically, not by any of the major industrial factories. It seems probable that the first English ceramist so engaged was Bernard Moore. Moore's family firm was disbanded in 1905, and from 1906 to 1915, he headed his own small art pottery at Wolfe Street, Stoke-on-Trent. The majority of Moore's pieces are low-temperature, red *soufflé* glazes (as are those by Doulton, Howson and many other factories, both large and small, which produced such work in the early years of the twentieth century). However, a few genuine high-temperature glazed pieces were produced by Moore, although these were probably not made until the last years of his factory's existence.

For the production of high-temperature glazes based principally on Chinese porcelains of the Ch'ing dynasty, the most important English potter must be William Howson Taylor, who founded his Ruskin Pottery at West Smethwick, near Birmingham, in 1898. The Ruskin Factory, which lasted until 1935 (although it closed its doors officially in 1933) produced a wide range of glazed wares – low temperature *soufflé*, monochrome lustres, some with simple painted decoration, crystalline glazes

and some unpleasant matt glazes made in the late 1920s and early 1930s, these last being the factory's only concession to the prevailing English version of sub-Art Deco taste.

However, the factory is best remembered for its high-temperature *flambé* glazes, which achieved a range of colour and brilliance unknown in the work of any other Western potter or factory. Many such pieces are gaudy and violent in their effects; at their best, however, they are of an extraordinarily high quality.

As in the nineteenth century, the major industrial factories in the present century have shown little interest in new approaches to ceramics. One notable exception were Wedgwood's pieces commissioned from the New Zealand architect Keith Murray in the 1930s, which compensate for the artistically cheap Fairyland Lustre produced by Daisy Makeig-Jones at the factory in the previous two decades. The latter wares inspired a somewhat tasteless movement in English ceramic decoration which could be described as 'Twenties Chinoiserie'. Murray's designs, in contrast, are a genuine attempt to interpret in ceramics the spare, clean lines of the new Functionalist architecture; combined with the high quality of Wedgwood's glazes and bodies, they are particularly handsome and their true importance has not yet been fully recognised nor reflected in saleroom prices.

Other attempts by Staffordshire factories to produce work in a new idiom were generally lamentable. The Newport Factory of A. J. Wilkinson Ltd. in Burslem, under the influence of Clarice Cliff, produced pottery painted with designs by many leading British artists, including Laura Knight, Duncan Grant, Vanessa Bell, John Armstrong, Frank Brangwyn (who had also designed a range of wares for Doulton), Barbara Hepworth, Paul Nash, Ben Nicholson and Graham Sutherland. Their work, although cheaply produced, is a relief from the aptly named Bizarre designs of Cliff

Above Pots designed at the Omega Workshops, *c.* 1917.

Left Earthenware vase with matt green glaze by Keith Murray for Wedgwood, *c.* 1933.

Far left Earthenware coffee set with Moonstone glaze by Keith Murray for Wedgwood, *c.* 1934.

Below left Example of early twentieth-century glazed ware from the Ruskin Factory, Birmingham.

Above Stoneware vase made by Shoji Hamada at the St. Ives Pottery, *c.* 1922.

Right Guru stoneware vase made by W. Staite-Murray, *c.* 1935.

herself, which have, unfortunately, come to be considered a major British contribution to Art Deco; they were not, at the time, held in much esteem, nor should we afford them much today. Cliff also designed vases and jars painted in strident colours, involving gold.

In England, the predominant influence in the history of twentieth-century ceramics has been the work of Bernard Leach. Leach, however, was not the first English studio potter nor was he the first to seek inspiration from Japan and, more importantly, from Chinese ceramics of the T'ang and Sung dynasties. The Martin Brothers might be considered the first English studio potters and in the first decades of the twentieth century, several individuals, notably George Cox and Reginald Wells, and one or two small potteries, of which the most important was Upchurch, began making earthenware and stoneware with thick monochromatic glazes based on early Chinese models.

Leach made his first pots in Tokyo in 1911. By the time he returned to England to found his own pottery in 1920, he had come into contact with Soetsu Yanagi, the brilliant Japanese scholar who was instrumental in founding the Japanese Folk Craft movement. Leach's ideas from then on were based on a notion of anonymous craft combined with the Zen discipline of repetition.

His work, which spans the years from 1911 to 1972, when increasingly poor eyesight forced him to give up pottery, was an attempt to synthesise Oriental ideas and techniques with English traditional ceramics. Certainly the work most admired by Japanese connoisseurs is that in which the English influence is predominant. Ironically, such connoisseurs find little to admire in Leach's work when it is most self-consciously Oriental in flavour.

In the early years of the 1920s, the St. Ives Pottery took on a number of pupils. Shoji Hamada had come to England with Leach as a budding potter and spent three years at St. Ives. He returned to Japan to become perhaps the most distinguished exponent of the *Mingei* (folk) school of ceramics. The first English pupils included Michael Cardew, Katherine Pleydell Bouverie and Norah Braden. Cardew's work from the beginning was rooted in the English slipware tradition and has always been less 'Japanese' than that of Leach himself. In the late nineteenth century, several small art potteries had started in Devon and Cornwall making earthenware and slipware (Charles Brannum's Barum Ware being the most accomplished) and it was these and such surviving country potteries as that of Edwin Beer Fishley at Fremington, which may be said to have guided Cardew as a potter.

The main alternative to the Leach tradition in English ceramics in the late 1920s and 1930s was the work of William Staite-Murray. Murray had collaborated with the Vorticist painter Cuthbert Hamilton at the Yeoman Pottery during the First World War and was throughout his comparatively short career (he emigrated to Rhodesia in 1939 and gave up potting thereafter) concerned with relating his pottery to current developments in painting and sculpture. He thought of himself primarily as an artist and it is this aspect of his philosophy, quite apart from the magnificent body of work he produced, which has caused the great revival of interest in his career in recent years. As head of the ceramics department of the Royal College of Art from 1925, Murray taught many gifted students, including Thomas Haile, Henry Hammond, Reginald Marlow, Heber Matthews and Helen Pinkham, all of whom subsequently became distinguished studio potters.

English studio pottery in the two decades preceding the Second World War was dominated by two great potters, Bernard Leach and William Staite-Murray, although there were other brilliant individuals. The work of Charles and Nell Vyse, for instance, can be divided into three main groups – figure subjects, which were executed from 1919 onwards, pots closely influenced by T'ang and Sung ceramics (in many cases such pieces were actual copies of known Chinese pieces), and wares painted either with figure subjects or with an abstract decoration based on Cubist-Vorticist painting. The earliest examples of the 'Chinese' wares seem to have been executed in the late 1920s. In terms of the techniques of Oriental glazes – *chun, celadon, tenmoku,* etc. – the Vyses were supreme among English studio potters, although much of their work in these idioms lacks individuality.

The coming to power of Hitler in 1933 caused the migration of many artists from Europe. Among those who came to England were Lucie Rie and Hans Coper, the former from Austria and the latter from Germany. Rie had attended Polowny's ceramic classes at the Vienna Kunstgewerbeschule and was before the war an accomplished potter who had been represented in many exhibitions. She taught Coper ceramics in England and their real significance lies in the work they have produced, and the extraordinary influence they have had, during the past twenty-five years on many studio and art potters in the United Kingdom.

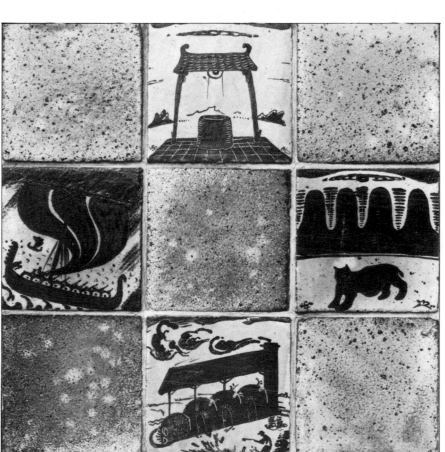

Top left Chelsea stoneware vase made by Charles Vyse, *c.* 1934.

Top right Tobacco jar made by Michael Cardew, *c.* 1923.

Above Tile panel in stoneware by Bernard Leach, *c.* 1938.

Glass *by Isabelle Anscombe*

A single light stained glass window designed by Henry Holiday for James Powell, *c.* 1875.

WITHIN THE ARTS AND CRAFTS Movement the two most renowned firms making decorative glass were Powell's of Whitefriars and James Couper & Sons of Glasgow. From 1890 to 1900, under the influence of Harry J. Powell, the Whitefriars firm had pioneered forms of glass which relied more upon firing techniques and upon the form itself rather than decoration. The firm had earlier produced stained glass for Morris & Co. and simple uncut table glass for Philip Webb, and were happy to absorb the ideas of beauty lying in shape and method of production rather than applied decoration. Frank Brangwyn also designed glassware for the firm.

The Glasgow firm produced a range called Clutha glass and although George Walton designed for them from 1896–8, the true spirit of the Clutha glass was developed by Christopher Dresser from the mid 1890s. Freed by the nature of the material from his adherence to strict utility or scientific principle, Dresser shows a rare sensuousness in his glassware which reflects a profound reaction to the force and beauty of natural forms. His forms are irregular, following the sinuousness and rhythm of organic growth which was to become the central motif of Art Nouveau, and lack the aggression of some of his silver designs, although one still sees the influence of his botanical studies. The blown Clutha glass uses opaque green glass, often shot with translucent streaks of gold or cream, perhaps the result of Dresser's interest in Roman or Middle-Eastern ancient glass. The Art Nouveau forms were also utilised by Stuart & Sons of Stourbridge with furnace decoration and Stevens & Williams, also of Stourbridge, experimented with crackled glass or silver-deposit decoration and were known for their Japanese-style work in which the glass was cased and decorated.

In its early years the firm of Morris & Co. had depended financially on their stained glass, meeting the demand for ecclesiastical glass created by the Gothic Revival. D. G. Rossetti, Henry Holiday and William Morris designed stained glass, but the firm's most notable designer was Edward Burne-Jones who used the same delicate figures and pensive faces with borders of acanthus leaves or flowers not unlike Morris's designs. Morris himself was concerned with the qualities of colour in the glass. Holiday's glass is much stronger in its design, often using two layers of glass to give the required texture of a more painterly conception. There were many firms making stained glass, such as Hardman's, Powell's or Heaton, Butler & Bayne, who also made glass mosaics.

Gradually the conception of stained glass changed, as the designs in the *Studio Yearbooks* testify. Stained glass was used to add an element of depth and fantasy to a room and the designs became simpler, less pictorial and more true to the medium. The work of the Glasgow designers Oscar Paterson and E. A. Taylor shows a greater use of the lead lines to delineate figures or landscapes of imaginative style: fewer colours were used to greater effect.

E. A. Taylor began designing stained glass around 1900 when he began work for the Glasgow furniture-makers Wylie & Lochhead and he and designers such as Walter J. Pearce, Alex Gascoyne or Selwyn Image firmly established the fashion for plain leaded glass begun by the Arts and Crafts designer Christopher Whall. Frank Brangwyn was commissioned by Samuel Bing to design windows for the opening of his shop, L'Art Nouveau, in Paris, as was L. C. Tiffany. Stained glass became a major feature of the Art Nouveau home.

In the 1920s and 1930s the lack of good table glass was criticised. In 1933 John Gloag, while praising the architectural adaptations of glass, wrote: 'Glass which is often beautiful in shape is tortured with ornament: its merit as a design dies the death of a thousand cuts. . . . The cocktail has much to answer for . . .'

Most glass of good design, and reasonable price, sold in England in the thirties was Czechoslovakian, such as that sold at the newly opened Primavera. Keith Murray designed plain glass in simple shapes for Stevens & Williams of Stourbridge and Arundell Clarke stocked some interesting designs, but there seemed to be little else available apart from the classic cut glass.

As a building material glass now found a new importance as the technology of modern architecture allowed for walls to be filled in free from the dictates of structural necessity: plate glass and glass bricks were used and the *Daily Express* building was the first to be faced entirely on the exterior with glass panels. In 1933 Oliver Hill designed the Pilkington Brothers' stand at the Dorland Hall Exhibition, showing glass floor tiles, mosaics, mirrors and engraved panels and even glass furniture. In the same year Paul Nash designed a bathroom for Mrs. Edward James using panels of different coloured and textured glass and mirrors in an abstract design. Lawrence Whistler and Eric Gill also used glass decoratively and it was most popular for modern cocktail bars and lounges. Raymond McGrath designed the interiors of Fischer's restaurant in New Bond Street and of the Embassy Club.

Right and below Clutha vases designed by Christopher Dresser for James Couper & Sons, 1890s.

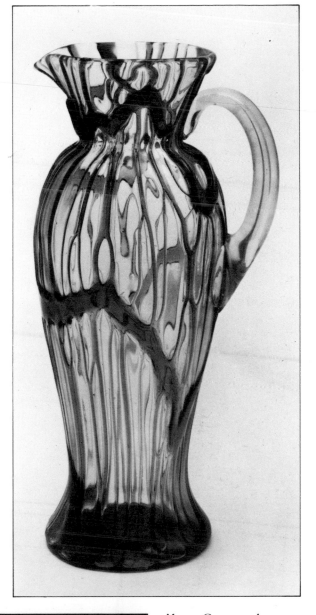

At Fischer's the space was divided by white circular pillars with the floor patterned with abstract squares of different coloured rubber reminiscent of Marion Dorn rugs. The furniture picked up the circular lines as did circular pieces of glass set into the counter. The walls were mirrored. The Embassy Club was decorated with panels of cut and polished glass. McGrath also used engraved glass which was made by Pugh Brothers.

Glass-topped tables and mirrors were an asset in renovating old London houses, enlarging small flats and enabling the occupiers to create modern surroundings. *The Studio* of 1930 commented that: 'Instead of sitting in dignified but disconsolate fashion on chairs designed apparently for the mortification of the flesh we sprawl at full length at so low an elevation that it has become necessary to introduce special low tables so that we can reach our cocktails or cigarettes without any serious physical exertion. . . . Here may be noted a significant change in our social habits affecting the character of our furnishing.'

The lightness and luminosity of glass in the home reflected the change from the 'horrors' of Victorian clutter and stuffiness.

Above Green on clear glass jug by Harry Powell, *c.* 1905.

Left Design for a stained glass window by E. A. Taylor, *c.* 1900.

Silver, Jewellery and Metalwork *by Isabelle Anscombe*

SILVER AND JEWELLERY were two of the media which received renewed attention due to the Arts and Crafts Movement. Silver design was taken out of the hands of the established manufacturers, whose productions at this time were of a deplorably low standard, as artists and architects turned their hand to silversmithing. One group of designers emerged who were to meet at the premises of Montague Fordham, House Furnisher, Jeweller and Metalworker at 9 Maddox Street in London. Fordham was a solicitor and successful businessman who had been the first director of the Birmingham Guild of Handicraft, founded in 1890. He left Birmingham in 1896 and opened his showrooms in 1898–9, acquiring also the Artificers' Guild in 1903, when Edward Spencer succeeded Nelson Dawson as artistic director.

The work of John Paul Cooper and Henry Wilson was sold through Montague Fordham and the Artificers' Guild, 1902–10 being J. P. Cooper's most intense period of activity. Both men were articled to the architect J. D. Sedding, and occasionally their work can be almost indistinguishable. It shows the influence of Sedding's Gothic designs in the combination of ivory and crystal with gold and silver and in certain motifs. Cooper's first departure into craftwork, en-

couraged by Wilson, was a number of gesso boxes of various shapes and similar boxes covered in shagreen with silver mounts which were to remain popular until the 1930s. Spencer's work was also influenced by Cooper. These designers all incorporated fine gems, mother-of-pearl, ivory and other materials into their intricate settings and employed the various motifs of the Arts and Crafts Movement.

Arthur Dixon, who had been a director of the Birmingham Guild, and Arthur Gaskin and his wife, Georgina Cave France of the Birmingham Group of painters, must also have been known to Fordham. Mrs. Gaskin had designed silverwork while still a student at Birmingham School of Art and from 1899 she collaborated with her husband, marking their pieces with a capital 'G'. Arthur Gaskin became head of the Vittoria Street School for jewellers and silversmiths in Birmingham.

The craft of enamelling was propagated by the work of Alexander Fisher, who had studied the technique in France and opened his own school in 1904. In 1901 he had worked briefly with Nelson Dawson, who was then to teach his wife Edith the art and she carried out most of the enamelling on their silver and jewellery. Other designers at this time were Harold Stabler, a founder member of the Design and Industries Association, who had

Silver cup with wirework handles by C. R. Ashbee at the Guild of Handicraft, *c.* 1900.

been a director at the Keswick School of Industrial Art from 1884 until 1902, when he left to join Richard Llewellyn Rathbone, a relative of W. A. S. Benson, in Liverpool. Omar Ramsden and Alwyn Carr worked together from 1898 until the outbreak of the First World War, although their partnership was not formally dissolved until 1919; Carr continued to work until the 1920s and Ramsden until 1939.

All these designers worked recognizably within the Arts and Crafts idiom, although each had an individual attitude towards his treatment of the medium. During the 1890s the Japanese taste was absorbed, most markedly by the Birmingham firm, Elkingtons, who were the first to adapt Japanese designs, such as Komai. The most idiosyncratic of the Aesthetic Movement designs were in cast-iron, made by Barnard, Bishop and Barnard to Thomas Jeckyll's designs.

Perhaps the best known of the Arts and Crafts metalwork designers was C. R. Ashbee. He had founded the Guild of Handicraft in 1888 and John Pearson was their first metalwork instructor. Himself self-taught, probably through the manuals of the American Charles G. Leland, the Guild began by producing simple embossed platters of brass and copper. John Pearson also supplied Morris & Co. with his embossed metal dishes, which was probably a contributing factor in his resignation from the Guild in 1892. In his last years he ran his own workshop.

The Guild of Handicraft first began working in silver and electroplate in 1889, although Ashbee did not register a mark until 1896. The first work, in keeping with the aspirations of the Guild, shows that the craftsmen – John Williams, W. A. White and William Hardiman – were self-taught, although Ashbee hated the mechanical finish of commercial silverwork and encouraged his silversmiths to leave the impression of hammer marks on the surface of their work. From 1890 they began using gems and enamelling, mainly done by Arthur Cameron who worked on Ashbee's Chelsea house, Magpie and Stump, and their best work was done while the Guild was at Essex House between 1890 and 1902. Ashbee's own work is most recognizable from his wirework, which he perfected around 1897, and the delicacy of his designs, often using green glass and silver together.

The work of Dr. Christopher Dresser represents the highest achievement in design for industrial manufacture. A doctor in botany, he based his design ethic upon the principles of Owen Jones and upon a scientific elegance for 'fitness for purpose' more akin to the design of the Modern Movement than to the Victorian 1880s. Most of his designs were executed in electroplate, due as much to his concern for an economic use of materials as to the manufacturers' financial preference. He designed for Elkington & Co. from 1875 to 1888, for Hukin & Heath from 1878 and for James Dixon & Co. from 1879. Although one of the few designers of his time to have visited Japan, his metalwork designs show a sparseness and complete absence of decoration in total opposition to the eclectic leanings of other designers. He wrote: 'In order to justify its existence a vessel must be constructed, but when formed it need not of

Left Pendant designed by C. R. Ashbee, 1903.

Below Electroplated soup tureen, cover and ladle with ebony handles and knop, designed by Christopher Dresser for Hukin & Heath, 1880.

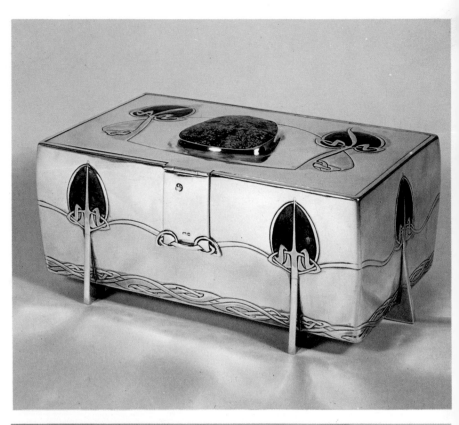

Top left Guild of
Handicraft silver
christening mug made for
Lord David Cecil, 1902.
Top right Liberty & Co.
silver and enamel casket
designed by Archibald
Knox, 1903.
Above Candlestick in
painted copper, brass and
wood by Christopher
Dresser made by Perry &
Co., 1883.
Right Enamelled triptych
by Alexander Fisher,
c. 1900.

necessity be ornamented; ornamentation must ever be regarded as separate from construction.' This was a revolutionary view at the time. Other designers for industrial production were rare, although the work of W. A. S. Benson, who set up his own workshop in 1880, was for mass production. His metal lamps, firescreens and light fittings, in brass and copper, have a starkness unusual in Arts and Crafts designs, although his kettles and teapots are nearer in their shape to that ethic. C. F. A. Voysey also designed metal light fittings for machine production.

The designs for silver, jewellery and metalwork for Liberty & Co. were commissioned from various designers, including Rex Silver, Oliver Baker, Bernard Cuzner, Arthur Gaskin and Jessie M. King.

The most outstanding of Liberty's designers was Archibald Knox, who was to determine the Liberty style. Knox had studied Celtic design at Douglas School of Art on the Isle of Man and applied the Runic interlacing of forms in his designs for silver and pewter. There is an affinity between the Celtic forms used by Alexander Fisher and those by Knox, but where Fisher used the style by way of decoration, Knox employed the form in a more integral, structural manner. The use of gems or enamel was often dependent on the commission of the purchaser and the price rose accordingly.

After the flourish of activity in this field of the Arts and Crafts Movement, interest in silver and jewellery design seems to have declined, leaving the field once again to the established manufacturers who continued to produce reproduction styles. Apart from the work of Keith Murray, perhaps the first freelance designer for industry since Dresser, for Mappin & Webb there is a sad lack of notable designers, most modern design being carried out in stainless steel.

Above left Silver-mounted jug by C. R. Ashbee at the Guild of Handicraft, *c.* 1900; green glass by Powell's of Whitefriars.

Above Liberty & Co. Cymric silver and enamel covered box, 1900.

Left Brooch-pendant, enamelled and set with a moonstone with three pendants of crystal, enamel and moonstone, by Henry Wilson, *c.* 1913.

Textiles and Graphic Art *by Isabelle Anscombe*

THE GOTHIC REVIVAL had inspired the increasing use of Gothic patterns and motifs in textiles, hangings and tiles, but the formation in 1861 of Morris, Marshall, Faulkner & Co. caused an enormous change in taste towards a new use of such items in the home. William Morris produced his first hand-blocked wallpaper designs in 1862 and in 1875 branched out into experiments with dyeing fabrics with Thomas Wardle in Leek. There are many stories of Morris with permanently blue hands from the indigo vats and he spent much of his time perfecting the use of natural dyes in his private war against the use of commercial chemical colours.

In 1883 he moved his fabric works to Merton Abbey where he had already set up looms for weaving his 'Hammersmith' rugs and carpets. The entwining floral designs of Morris's wallpapers and chintzes are too well known to require description, but it is interesting to note that despite his mastery of conveying the sense of growth in his designs he never mastered the art of drawing animals and birds, which were usually executed by Edward Burne-Jones. John Henry Dearle, who worked with Morris at Merton Abbey, also designed some wallpapers, fabrics and tapestries.

Above Tile by Pilkington, 1902.

Right Fabric design by Morris & Co.

Carpet designed by E. McKnight Kauffer, c. 1934.

Morris encouraged all forms of workmanship and his daughter May became known for her embroideries; she took over the embroidery section of the firm in 1885. William de Morgan had met Morris at Red Lion Square in the early days of the firm and in 1869 started his kiln in the basement of 40 Fitzroy Square, coming closer to Morris in 1874 when the firm was reorganised as Morris & Co. Between 1882 and 1888 he worked at Merton Abbey, producing tiles which were mainly for interior use, adapting Morris's favoured Persian models and echoing Morris in his use of floral forms. The colours of his birds, animals, ships and grotesques show the same concern for purity and brightness which all but obsessed Morris.

Following the example of Morris & Co. and in line with the Arts and Crafts ethic, many designers whose primary interests perhaps lay elsewhere also worked on flat designs. In 1870 Lewis F. Day began his own business making stained glass, embroidery, textiles, wallpapers and carpets; A. H. Mackmurdo, whose work was to influence C. F. A. Voysey, produced fabrics and rugs through his Century Guild; Christopher Dresser, although few of his flat designs have survived, filled *Studies in Design* (1875) and *Modern Ornamentation* (1886) with wallpaper designs, friezes and dadoes and his studio was mainly concerned with textile design during the 1890s. Many firms commissioned Arts and Crafts designers: Jeffrey & Co. (wallpapers) employed Walter Crane, Lewis F. Day, E. W. Godwin, Mackmurdo and George Walton. Both Maw & Co. and Pilkingtons (tiles) commissioned Lewis F. Day and Walter Crane, who also designed for Mintons and Wedgwood. Alexander Morton – later Morton Sundour – produced designs by Voysey and George Walton for fabrics, hangings and carpets. Voysey designed hand-printed wallpapers for Essex & Co. and fabrics for many companies, including the Glasgow firm Wylie & Lochhead.

Liberty & Co. naturally kept pace with their competitors and sold designs by Crane, Day, Voysey, Arthur Silver and Jessie M. King. In comparison to the fulsome naturalistic patterns which had predominated at the 1851 Exhibition, the smaller, neater repeating motifs of these fabrics and papers and more restrained designs for carpets, all executed in subtler colours, must have been a welcome relief to the woman of taste. It proved also that the leading designers of the time could, when they chose, co-operate quite happily with large manufacturers, thus realizing one of the principal ambitions of the later Modern Movement: bringing good design to industry.

Embroidery enjoyed a new vogue at this time, encouraged by the newly founded ladies' guilds and stimulated by the example set by Morris & Co. The Glasgow School of Art also gave rise to a local community of embroiderers, led by Jessie R. Newberry, the wife of the Principal. She taught embroidery at the School from 1894 to 1908, as did Ann Macbeth. Their two most famous pupils were Frances and Margaret Macdonald.

At this time *The Studio* magazine contained models for needlework and held competitions for designs and work; what had been revived as an interest in craft became an art. The interest was continued into the wave of Post-Impressionism by the needlepoint designs of the Omega Workshops, especially in the work of Vanessa Bell and Duncan Grant, whose designs were executed by his mother. They used needlepoint, in vivid colours and bold patterns not only for chair seats, but for mirror frames and screens.

Another successful offshoot of the Arts and Crafts Movement was the art of fine printing. The first achievement was *The Hobby Horse*, a quarterly magazine of A. H. Mackmurdo's Century Guild, which was printed on hand-made paper and supervised by Emery Walker. It first appeared in 1884 and was followed in 1890 by Morris's

'The Angel of Night', gesso
and mother-of-pearl panel
by Frederick Marriott, 1904.

Kelmscott Press. He had earlier planned, with Burne-Jones, to issue an edition of *The Earthly Paradise*, so the idea of following the model of medieval illuminated manuscripts was already in his mind by the time he came to his Kelmscott *Chaucer*, for which he designed his own type and decorated the pages. Lewis F. Day, in *The Easter Art Journal* of 1899 criticised Morris's typefaces as being too heavy and bemoaned the fact that, for a socialist, the books immediately became collectors' items.

Lewis F. Day himself, in company with the artists Walter Crane, Jessie M. King and Kate Greenaway, instituted a new style of illustration for children's books. Kate Greenaway especially adopted many of the colours and motifs of the Aesthetic Movement, while Jessie M. King, with the stylisation of line peculiar to the Glasgow School, portrayed the classic fairy stories in fine detail with attention to trees and landscapes and the differing textures of an Art interior. Colour and an element of fantasy opened new realms of nursery reading.

A rather more sinister fantasy element dominated the work of Aubrey Beardsley which appeared in *The Yellow Book*, running for thirteen volumes before disappearing in the midst of the Wilde scandal. It had done much, however, to introduce the French decadents to England. Fine printing was again encouraged in 1912, the year in which *Imprint* appeared, owing much in its typography to the work of Edward Johnston.

'Long Live the Vortex!' was the next cry to be heard, in total opposition to the gentle art that typography had been until April 1914 when *Blast No. 1* was issued under the editorship of Wyndham Lewis. The anarchic presentation of the Vorticist manifesto, containing work by the artists of the Rebel Art Centre, destroyed any hope for an apolitical art and made other efforts at private presses, such as Bloomsbury's Hogarth Press, seem all too unrealistically gentle. The excesses of this review foresaw the future of poster design and is reminiscent, in its violence on contemporary taste, of the posters produced by the Glasgow Four.

Meanwhile the gentler arts still continued. Frank Brangwyn, who combined nineteenth-century elements with a more modern taste, designed carpets, fabrics and pottery. Charming tiles were designed by Bernard Leach, Edward Bawden and Vanessa Bell and Duncan Grant, who continued to work on their almost Italianate interiors and artifacts. Their fabrics were used successfully for costumes when Grant designed the set for Jacques Copeau's production of *Twelfth Night*.

While the fortunes of British design tended to decline from the twenties into the thirties, England led in one important aspect of the complete interior, in the field of textile and rug design. During this time women began to enter the scene as designers in their own right, conscious of their recent emancipation and eager to be regarded as professional in their chosen spheres. Among the new designers, many of whom worked for Allan Walton Fabrics Ltd., were Elspeth Little, Dorothy Larcher, Phyllis Barron, Enid Marx, Sonia Delaunay, Margaret Stanfield and Riette Moore.

Top Tapestry by William
Morris and Edward Burne-
Jones, *Love Leading the Pilgrim*.

Left Poster for the London
Underground by Frank
Pick, 1930s.

Above Illustration by
Kate Greenaway.

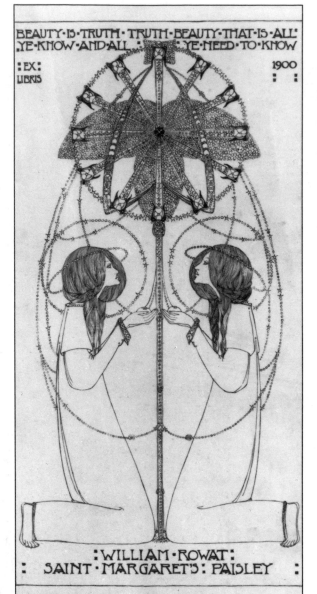

BEAUTY·IS·TRUTH·TRUTH·BEAUTY·THAT·IS·ALL·
YE·KNOW·AND·ALL :   : YE·NEED·TO·KNOW

:EX:
LIBRIS   1900

:WILLIAM·ROWAT:
:SAINT·MARGARET'S·PAISLEY:

Right *Ex libris* design by Jessie M. King, 1900.

Below Music room designed by Vanessa Bell and Duncan Grant, 1933.

In *The New Interior Decoration* (1929) by Dorothy Todd and Raymond Mortimer, the authors wrote that: 'Roughly speaking, there are two schools of modern textile design: that which employs purely geometric patterns, and that which is generally more free and fanciful, in which trees, horses, the human figure, and so on, are freely and often amusingly introduced.' Raymond Mortimer's tastes lay more with the latter style, but it was the geometric patterns which were probably the more popular at the time, reflecting the absorption of Cubist art. During the late twenties strong colours and a mass of detailed decoration were considered inadmissible in the interior and it was often curtains or rugs alone which introduced an element of movement into the otherwise calm environment. Allan Walton, Tamessa Fabrics Ltd. or Arundell Clarke all sold the new fabrics and artists and architects also either designed their own fabrics or commissioned them especially for their interiors. Other designers were Edward Bawden, Marion Dorn, McKnight Kauffer, Paul Nash, Bernard Adeney, Raymond McGrath, Evelyn Wyld, Ashley Havinden or Serge Chermayeff.

The most revolutionary change in design came in the area of rugs. James Morton of Morton Sundour and Edinburgh Weavers expressly wanted a new form of decorative textile to complement modern architecture and both his company and the Wilton Royal Carpet Factory led the field in rug design. Some artists employed the Irish designer Jean Orage, based in Chelsea, to weave their designs. Others sent their designs out to India or China to be made up and Ronald Grierson even taught himself the technique. Duncan Miller Ltd. sold rugs made by the Edinburgh Weavers to designs by John Tandy, Ashley Havinden, Terence Prentis, Jean Varda and Marion Dorn; Gordon Russell Ltd. sold rugs by Marian Pepler, who was married to Richard Russell, Gordon's brother; in 1934 Simpsons held an exhibition of Ashley Havinden's rugs, a departure from their usual style perhaps due to his directorship of Crawford's, Simpsons advertising agency; Fortnum & Mason also held a show of Modernist rugs; Betty Joel sold her rugs exclusively through her own showrooms.

While McKnight Kauffer and Marion Dorn had instituted the plain background, often in neutral shades, and lack of border, their strong abstract designs differ from the more fanciful designs of Ronald Grierson or John Tandy. There is a distinction to be made between those rugs designed by interior designers as a part of a decorative whole and those designed by artists whose true interests lay elsewhere.

The alternative to the sparseness of the modern home was the mural, although most artists worked mainly in the houses of friends for special commissions. In 1933 Duncan Grant and Vanessa Bell painted a music room, featured in the *Architectural Review*, where the walls were painted with panels of flowers and even the piano was decorated with abstract shapes. However, in 1935 Grant was commissioned to decorate a lounge in the new Cunard liner RMS *Queen Mary*, but when the painted panels were erected they were vetoed by the company director.

MAY 31
COLLECT FOR
THE FEAST OF S. ANGELA MERICI

DEUS, QUI NOVUM PER BEATAM
ANGELAM SACRARUM VIRGINUM
COLLEGIUM IN ECCLESIA TUA FLOR-
ESCERE VOLUISTI: DA NOBIS, EIUS
INTERCESSIONE, ANGELICIS MORI-
BUS VIVERE; UT, TERRENIS OMNIBUS
ABDICATIS, GAUDIIS PERFRUI MERE
AMUR AETERNIS · PER DOMINUM NOSTRUM
IESUM CHRISTUM FILIUM TUUM QUI TECUM
VIVIT ET REGNAT IN UNITATE SPIRITUS SANCTI
DEUS PER OMNIA SAECULA SAECULORUM

ABCDEFGHIJJKLMN
OPQQRRSTUV
WXYZ

Raymond Mortimer commented that such a decorative scheme would have been out of place within so lavish a setting which catered for people perhaps more at home with the luxurious Art Deco or Hollywood style. Other murals depicted more modern themes, such as John Armstrong's gesso panels for the restaurant of Shellmex House which showed cars, horses and aeroplanes symbolising the speed of modern life, John Banting's Surrealist interiors with huge abstractions of the human figure, or Ben Nicholson's decorative carved reliefs.

Industry benefited from the new designers in the fields of advertising and typography. In 1925 Eric Gill was drawing alphabets for Stanley Morison, the director of the Monotype Corporation's typography section, which were then adapted as the Perpetua typeface. Gill had trained as an architect and then studied typography under Edward Johnston. Johnston had been influenced by W. R. Lethaby, who supported craft above art, the commonplace above genius, and Gill also retained a sense of the importance of commonplaceness and normality in his work.

He and Johnston also refined a second type for the Monotype Corporation, the Sans Serif alphabet, which was widely used for lettering in public notices. Johnston was commissioned by Frank Pick to design the lettering for London Transport, where McKnight Kauffer was also employed to design posters. Disregarding Gill's masonry sculpture, for which he is now justly better known, his work in typography almost revolutionised the art. The work of Frank Pick for the London Underground and of Jack Beddington for Shellmex, equally, is now daily taken for granted, but at the time was a vital innovation. Many leading artists of the time were concerned with poster design and new ways of presentation, each bringing their own 'ism' to bear upon their work; most notable are Rex Whistler, Eric Ravilious, John Piper and Graham Sutherland.

Top An example of text set in the Sans Serif face designed by Eric Gill.

Above 'The Peacock Skirt', illustration by Aubrey Beardsley for Oscar Wilde's *Salome*, 1894.

Right Poster for *The Scottish Musical Review* by C. R. Mackintosh, 1896.

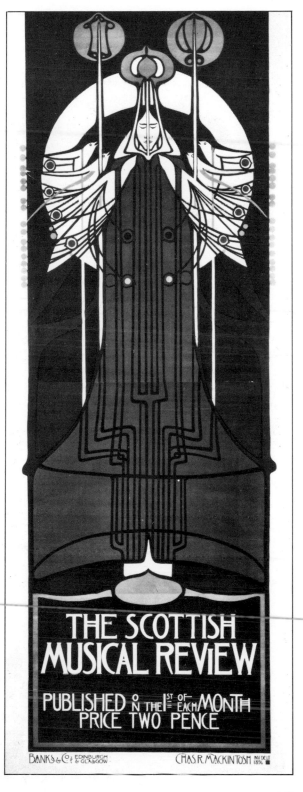

THE SCOTTISH MUSICAL REVIEW
PUBLISHED ON THE 1ST OF EACH MONTH
PRICE TWO PENCE

BANKS & CO EDINBURGH & GLASGOW   CHAS R. MACKINTOSH INV DEL T 1896

United States

by Isabelle Anscombe

American Design 1890–1940

IN THE MAIN, the decorative arts in America in the nineteenth century took their lead from Europe, whether from Greek classicism or Louis-Quinze, and these revivalist tendencies were adopted also in architecture. The United States, however, led in technical virtuosity, as in various types of spring revolving chairs or John H. Belter's bentwood chairs, or in the far-sightedness of some individuals to collect the best of ancient cultures. Louis Comfort Tiffany collected ancient glass and his father commissioned Christopher Dresser to collect Japanese objects for Tiffany & Co. while in Japan in 1877. The American Institute of Ar-

Cover of *The Craftsman* magazine.

chitects was founded in New York in 1857 and gradually a more coherent American style was evolved by men such as Frank Furness in Philadelphia or Henry H. Richardson in Boston. The development of the shingle style is even thought to have influenced the work of C. F. A. Voysey in England.

However, contemporary movements in Europe tended to reach the United States somewhat anachronistically and haphazardly. The Gothic Revival of Pugin and Ruskin reached America merely as a style adopted by a few designers, such as Isaac Scott, and lacked both the emotional and nationalistic impact of the English movement. Although the Eastlake style swept the East Coast it was misinterpreted because Eastlake's book was taken out of context and the work of similar designers, Bruce Talbert or Norman Shaw, was little known.

The opening up of Japan, however, and the resultant Aesthetic Movement, did catch the American imagination, perhaps not least because it had an able and flamboyant preacher in the figure of Oscar Wilde who lectured throughout the United States in 1882–3. Japanese ceramics were shown at the 1876 Philadelphia Centennial Exposition and influenced the course of art pottery and also book design and graphics. Indeed, the Aesthetic Movement was an English-speaking phenomenon.

By 1890 the most important foreign importation of style was the Arts and Crafts Movement of Morris and Ruskin. Many Americans visited England and even met Morris personally and returned fired with his ideals, dedicated to handicrafts and the rejection of the machine in art. Publications such as *International Studio, House Beautiful, The Ladies Home Journal* or *The Craftsman* spread the word to a wider audience. What was largely lost in translation across the Atlantic was the political background to the movement. When Walter Crane, a member of the Socialist League, spoke in Boston in 1891 in support of the Chicago Anarchists, he was banned from several clubs and a dinner in his honour was cancelled. A kind Bostonian lady warned him that if he persisted in such views his whole trip – and he depended on American commissions to finance himself – would be ruined.

The vast continent of America was not so concerned with problems of labour or class; the 'land of opportunity' offered different solutions to such problems in concepts of the frontier and freedom. Gustav Stickley began publication of *The Craftsman* in 1901 and for the first few years

Top 'When Hearts are Trumps' by Will H. Bradley, 1895.

Above left A library bookcase from *Hints on Household Taste* by Charles L. Eastlake, 1868.

Above A Craftsman living room illustrated in *The Craftsman*.

Left Poster by Maxfield Parrish.

Below left Sullivan's Guaranty Building in Buffalo (1894–5). **Below right** The Bayard Building, probably the last building by Sullivan still in existence in New York State, dating from 1897–8.

Bottom Interior of the Darwin Martin house, Buffalo, by Frank Lloyd Wright, 1904.

invited socialist guest writers to contribute. He upheld the doctrine of a truly democratic art in rejection of past styles of extinct civilisations. By 1906 his views were changing; his bankruptcy in 1916 was hastened by his earlier admission that he had never built the 'Craftsman' houses whose plans he published and that he knew their cost to be higher than stated.

The Arts and Crafts Movement was important in America not only for the fine workmanship it encouraged from individuals, but also for the growing awareness it developed among Americans that they should also find a truly national art. It should be noted, however, that the concepts of a national art differed across the country. On the East Coast Morrisian communities were founded and furniture and other decorative items made which have a direct resemblance to the British movement. In California, however, the climate and landscape and also the impact of the destruction of San Francisco in 1906 led to different interpretations. Morris's romantic return to the medieval European past was supplanted by the recognition of California's own past in Spanish-Mexican culture and Indian culture, as in Charles F. Lummis's publication *Land of Sunshine*.

Chicago was perhaps the most important centre of Arts and Crafts activity but was also an area most affected by frontier concepts. A style had to be evolved which no longer took its lead from the commercial and organisational centres of the East Coast, rooted as they were in European traditions. The high office buildings of Louis Sullivan almost foretold the future of the machine age of the automobile centre of the world which was to grow in Detroit. The mid-west relied on modern machines and means of communication for its survival and could, even in the 1890s, ill afford to espouse the microcosmic ideals of the Arts and Crafts Movement. The movement did, however, supply the impetus for a freedom of style.

As in England, the movement broke the barriers of traditional imitation in commercial areas such as wallpaper and fabric design and graphics. The adoption of Art Nouveau styles by firms such as the York Wallpaper Co. or M. H. Birge & Sons allowed people to see for the first time that contemporary design was available. Similarly, the art of the book was transformed by the output of Morris's Kelmscott Press. (Roberts Brothers of Boston were Morris's American publishers.) Dard

Hunter at Roycroft produced books on handmade paper, hand-bound in leather, which proved immensely popular. And the practice of illuminated lettering, floral borders and Gothic typefaces was adopted by many publishers. Will H. Bradley had adopted Beardsley's influence by the 1890s and went on to form his own idiosyncratic style, using Art Nouveau and Aesthetic motifs. Where Maxfield Parrish also reflects the self-conscious poses and dreamy light of Art Nouveau, his young ladies look out over landscapes of truly American proportions.

Despite the flourish of individual design brought about by the spread of Arts and Crafts ideals, by 1925 the United States found that it could not contribute to the Paris Exhibition where the rules of admission stipulated that work had to be both original and modern. Although in 1876 American exhibits at Philadelphia had relied on over-adorned copies of past styles, by 1893 at the Chicago World's Fair there was much new and original work to admire and American potters especially had won prizes at foreign international exhibitions.

The lesson of the 1925 Paris Exhibition flooded the American market with 'Art Moderne', reflecting the lavish decoration of the French exhibits. The United States led the world in architecture with the development of the skyscraper, and the ornamentation of buildings appeared to take precedence over domestic decoration. Not only skyscrapers but theatres, factories, churches, the Bay bridges or the Hoover Dam became the showpieces of American design. Geometric motifs replaced the sinuous curves of Art Nouveau; the zig-zag, sun-ray, bolt of lightning, waterfall or Aztec motifs and the stylised human figure, birds or leaping deer signified the 'speed' of Futurism as America began to 'go somewhere'. Steel grid buildings, reinforced concrete and the first working elevator, developed by Otis in 1889, all contributed to the new style.

Every aspect of a building was decorated, from the façade to the elevators, the ceiling to the mail boxes, the floors and doors to the radiator grilles. Coloured marbles, bronze, glass and many reflective surfaces were used to augment the powerful image of the skyscraper. In New York the Chanin Building, Radio City, the Chrysler Building, with an automobile motif picked out in brick on the exterior walls and repeated in Van Alen's interiors, or Donald Deskey's interior decoration for the Rockefeller Center are all examples of a style which glorified economic growth and technological advance. The Niagara Mohawk's office building in Syracuse was given a façade of stainless steel with horizontal strips of frosted glass; above the main entrance is a helmeted, winged figure in stainless steel, 'The Spirit of Power', and in the main entrance are four glass wall panels depicting 'Gas', 'Generation', 'Transmission' and 'Illumination'. Diego Rivera's murals in the RCA Building depicted the decadence of capitalism and included portraits of Communist leaders: they were replaced. In Michigan Eliel Saarinen (Eero's father) employed his wife to design the upholstery and rugs for his interiors.

By 1930 the American economy was in deep depression. The lavish scale of decoration which signified the glories of the capitalist system at its zenith had to give way to a vocabulary which expressed the utilisation of that technological knowledge and gave the consumer not just abundant ornamentation but also value for money. Industrial designers were recruited from the realms of theatrical design and advertising; new products had to show evidence of the benefits of science. Luxury could still be had, but under the banner of scientific economy and reductivism.

Designers such as Norman Bel Geddes, Henry Dreyfuss, Raymond Loewy and Walter Dorwin Teague introduced streamlined forms into automobile, ship, railroad and aeroplane design. Exterior styling was gone, integral design became the rule. On the surface, the new science of design was comparable to the theories of the Bauhaus which defined the house as a machine for living, but the decorative idiom of streamlining was misapplied and became a symbol of scientific progress rather than a true theory, the expression of an attitude rather than an understanding.

Walter Dorwin Teague designed Kodak cameras, again employing the horizontal parallel, and showed a plain interior, again using curves, in his lounge for the Ford Exposition at the 1939 New York World's Fair. Raymond Loewy turned from graphics for *Harper's Bazaar* and *Vogue* to designing refrigerators and trains and Henry Dreyfuss worked on objects as disparate as perfume bottles and telephones.

By 1940 the style had been discredited. The Depression had heightened commercial competition and style became an element of obsolescence. The mythologies of Hollywood sets encouraged the idea of streamlining as an element of decoration rather than a scientific principle. In England in 1935 the *Architectural Review* had

Below Modernist interior by A. L. Kocher and G. Ziegler, New York, *c.* 1930.

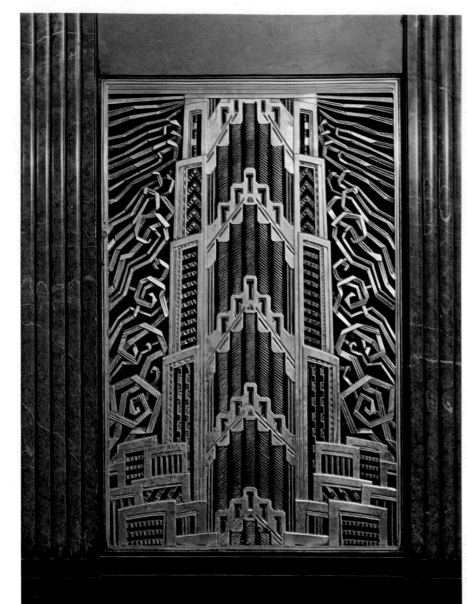

described the importation of American 'Plaza' architecture in cinemas by saying: 'They are around us on every side like a nightmare of pale, expressionless film faces fringed with impossible Garbo eyelashes.'

But whatever the criticisms, both social and aesthetic, of the American style, the idioms of power, the United States had shown that it could develop a national style, in the automobile and the skyscraper façade as much as in the home, and could stand apart from European historicism.

Above Radiator grill by Jacques Delamarre in the foyer of the Chanin Building, New York, 1929.

Above right Elevator door by William van Alen in the Chrysler Building, New York, 1930.

Right S. L. Rothafel's private suite by Donald Deskey in Radio City Music Hall, 1933.

Furniture

DURING THE 1850s and 1860s American furniture design was dominated by historical revivals, culminating in an excess of eclecticism in the exhibits at the Chicago World's Fair in 1893. In the 1850s the most popular cabinet maker in New York was John Henry Belter, a German, who worked in the Rococo style and also Louis Seize. By the 1860s a French Renaissance style was a favourite, although some makers, such as Isaac Scott, did absorb the Gothic idiom from England, as shown in the work of Daniel Pabst, the leading Philadelphia cabinet maker, also German-born. The influence of Christopher Dresser, who lectured in Philadelphia in 1876, is clear in Pabst's work after that date. Most American furniture therefore, although perhaps dignified, was rather heavy and imposing, with an excess of carving and added ornamentation, or was admirable by virtue of its technical inventiveness, as in the work of the American Chair Company of New York.

A more sobering and elegant influence was the work of the Shakers who had first settled in America at the end of the eighteenth century. In 1852 they had founded a chair factory to produce their craftsmanship for outside sale and by 1860 the simple designs and materials of the Shaker philosophy had become fashionable on the East coast. Another element of simplicity was added in the 1860s with the publication in America of Charles Eastlake's *Hints on Household Taste*, which was extremely successful and gave rise to a so-called 'Eastlake style' which the author himself was forced to disavow in the fourth edition of the book. Eastlake advocated Gothic ornamentation, although with restrained, conventionalised motifs and an absence of clutter in the decoration of the home. However misinterpreted, the book led the way to an alternative to the earlier heaviness of mahogany and relief carving.

In 1882 Oscar Wilde lectured in America, accompanying Gilbert and Sullivan's 'aesthetic opera' *Patience* and preaching not only the aesthetic ideals for which he was lampooned but also a healthy attitude for a relatively new country, that America should find the inspiration for her art in her own lands and not attempt to copy past or dissimilar civilisations. Both Wilde and the styles of the Aesthetic Movement were clearly heard and even the established New York firm of Herter Brothers, who had been making furniture in light walnut in the Rococo manner, now designed Japanese-inspired furniture in ebonised wood with delicate inlays. However, the 1890s vogue for Orientalism led away from the delicacy of Japanese designs and also introduced Turkish

Left An illustration from *Hints on Household Taste* by Charles Eastlake, 1868.

Below Bed, bureau and mirror, and night table by Daniel Pabst *c*. 1876.

Interior of Frank Lloyd
Wright's house, Taliesin,
built in 1911.

or 'Moorish' themes with upholstered divans
generously tufted, tasselled and fringed; a style
especially popular for the smoking room. It is
interesting to note that an early photograph of a
room in Frank Lloyd Wright's house depicts just
this Victorian clutter of the Aesthetic Movement
influence.

Towards the end of the nineteenth century
many contacts were made across the Atlantic in the
field of the decorative arts. In the same year that
Oscar Wilde toured America, the Boston architect
Henry H. Richardson visited England and met
William Morris and Burne-Jones; in 1889 an
exhibition of American arts, including Rookwood
faïence and designs by John La Farge, was held in
London; the following year Walter Crane visited
the States, lecturing and designing and in 1891 an
exhibition of C. F. A. Voysey's work was held in
Boston.

In 1893 Samuel Bing visited America and two
years later published *La Culture Artistique en
Amérique*. In 1896 C. R. Ashbee made his first visit
to America and in 1901 met Frank Lloyd Wright,
forming a friendship which was to last for many
years. Both Gustav Stickley and Elbert Hubbard,
perhaps the foremost Arts and Crafts designers,
visited Europe and England and returned inspired
by the ideals they had met with. Gradually Arts
and Crafts and handicraft societies were founded
across America and magazines such as *House
Beautiful* and the *International Studio* promoted
Arts and Crafts aims and designs.

One of the first to assimilate European trends in
design was Charles Rohlfs. Rohlfs was originally
an actor, a profession disliked by his wife and,
encouraged by her, he opened a small workshop in
Buffalo in 1890. He worked independently on
commission, never employing more than eight

craftsmen. His woodwork reflects both the Mission style of California and Art Nouveau in
elaborate carving and detailing, mainly in oak, the
most delicate work carried out by George Thiele.
In the Arts and Crafts tradition joints or pegging
are included as features of the overall design. He
exhibited at Turin in 1902, was elected a member
of the Royal Society of Arts in London and even
commissioned to design furniture for Buckingham
Palace. He retired in 1920.

Charles Rohlfs often lectured at the Roycroft
community at East Aurora which had been started
by Elbert Hubbard in 1895, following a visit to
Morris's Kelmscott Press in Hammersmith. Previously Hubbard had been a successful soap
salesman and Roycroft was run along good business lines, beginning with a press and book
bindery and gradually incorporating other crafts;
the furniture shop was started around 1901. Janet
Ashbee, when she visited East Aurora in that year,
criticised the work there for a lack of organic unity
and although the Roycroft furniture is solidly and
honestly made, generally in oak or mahogany, it
does lack the presence of a true designer's form.
Some of the first productions were slightly heavier
versions of Morris & Co. chairs and later pieces
bear a resemblance to the Craftsman style of
Gustav Stickley.

Stickley had trained as a stonemason and then
been apprenticed to relatives who were furniture
makers within the general style of the period.
However, in 1898 he visited France and England
and returned full of the desire to create a new
American style, totally divorced from European
traditions and, following his debt to Ruskin,
absorbing the principles of architecture. In 1901
he founded *The Craftsman* magazine in which he
upheld the social aims of the British Arts and
Crafts designers and called for a truly democratic
national art. He held a quasi-psychological view
that simpler surroundings would lead to a spiritual
regeneration, especially in the industrial cities, and
his solid, severe furniture would seem to reflect his
social aims more than any artistic genius.

In 1900 the company was enlarged and changed
its title from the Gustav Stickley Company to the
Craftsman Workshops and also acquired a timber
mill in the Adirondacks to supply the oak which
was most generally used. From 1903-4 Harvey
Ellis worked for the company, ornamenting the
furniture with inlaid metals, the only decoration
ever employed. In 1915 the company was declared
bankrupt and taken over by his two brothers as the
Stickley Manufacturing Company, which still
exists today, but 'craftsman' had already become
synonymous with a certain style of furniture.

Other communities were founded with the same
aims as Roycroft, one by an Englishman who had
been a pupil of Ruskin's at Oxford and one
inspired by the ideals of Morris's *News From
Nowhere* and modelled on Ashbee's Guild of
Handicraft. Ralf Ratcliffe Whitehead's colony,
Byrdcliffe, at Woodstock was founded in 1902
which produced some furniture; the Elverhoj
Colony near Washington was started by a Dane
named Anderson and the Rose Valley Community
was founded in 1901 by the Philadelphia architect
William L. Price. Price, like Stickley, was concerned with the morality of the honesty of

Left Morris chair by Gustav Stickley, *c.* 1905.

Centre Teak storage bench designed by Charles and Henry Greene for the Blacker House, Pasadena, 1906.

Below Maple cabinet with silver inlay made for the Gamble House, California, by Charles Sumner Greene, 1908.

Below Oak chair by Charles Rohlfs, 1898.

Bottom left The Craftsman Workshops illustrated in *The Craftsman* magazine, 1904.

Far left Side chair by Frank Lloyd Wright for the Aline Barnsdell House, Los Angeles, 1920.

Below left Redwood side chair by Frank Lloyd Wright for the Paul R. Hanna House, Palo Alto, California, 1937.

Centre left Armchair by Frank Lloyd Wright for the B. Harley Bradley House, Kankaki, Illinois, 1900.

Centre right Oak armchair by Frank Lloyd Wright for the Darwin T. Martin House, Buffalo, 1904.

Left Carved and painted wood hexagonal box by Lucia K. Mathews c. 1910.

Below Interior of the Kaufmann House by Frank Lloyd Wright, 1936.

Right An arrangement of objects by The Furniture Shop (1906–20), now in the Oakland Museum, California: pair of carved and painted cylindrical candlesticks by Arthur F. and Lucia K. Mathews; gold-leafed and painted wooden jar with lid by Lucia K. Mathews; portrait of Lucia Mathews, *c.* 1899, oil on canvas, by Arthur F. Mathews; carved and painted chest by Arthur F. and Lucia K. Mathews.

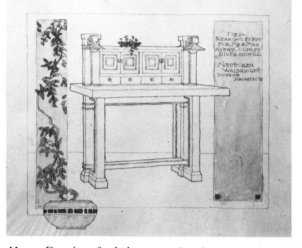

Above Drawing of a desk by Frank Lloyd Wright for the rear guest room in the Avery Coonily House, Riverside, Illinois, 1908.

production, an echo of the Shakers, and sold the furniture made in the community's workshops through an outlet in Philadelphia where it was hoped that the simply constructed and decorated pieces would influence contemporary taste.

In California the Arts and Crafts ideals were interpreted with new emphases. The work of Charles Sumner Greene and his brother Henry absorbed the local Mission style and also a Japanese influence. All their furniture (mostly designed by Charles) was commissioned, generally for the interiors of the houses they built around Pasadena in 1907–9. Ashbee visited them in 1909 and admired their work above everything he had seen in America, but noticed with regret that the craftsmen who executed their furniture designs were mostly elderly men who had been trained in the tradition of hand craftsmanship, before the generalised use of machines. Their work, often inlaid with fine metals or carved panels with Japanese motifs, although inspired by a visit to England in 1901 shows an elegance and eclecticism lacking in the work of the East Coast designers.

The work of The Furniture Shop (1906–20) reflects a truly Californian style. It was founded in 1906 after the Great Fire in San Francisco by Arthur F. Mathews, the Director of the Art Institute of California, and his wife (and one-time pupil) Lucia. *Philoplis* magazine was founded at the same time, dedicated to the formulation of a new style, influenced by A. F. Mathews's Beaux-Arts training as a painter in Paris, for the rebuilding of the city. Thirty to forty craftsmen were employed and the furniture reflects A. F. Mathews's own work as a muralist and decorator rather than the preoccupations of a craftsman-designer. The carved inlay and painting work was carried out by Lucia using the bright colours – orange, yellow and green – of the California landscape to depict local flowers, plants and trees.

The arrival of European influences in America tended to be anachronistic and the Arts and Crafts, or Craftsman, idiom was scarcely established before a genuine American style was forged through the work of Louis Sullivan and Frank Lloyd Wright in Chicago. Sullivan had introduced Art Nouveau forms in a system of architectural ornament, holding that the outward form of a building should express its function. His best work was for office buildings, but his ideas were taken and expanded in residential buildings by the younger architects who worked in his offices.

Frank Lloyd Wright worked as a draughtsman in the offices of Adler & Sullivan from 1888–93, leaving to join D. H. Perkins, Myron Hunt and R. C. Spencer at Steinway Hall. His first independent commission was the Winslow residence in 1893 and his style reached its peak during his period of work at his own Oak Park studio. Wright believed in integral design for his houses and his furniture was designed to solve specific problems within a particular interior, as in the Hanna house where the polygonal furniture reflects the hexagonal design of the house. Each house also had a particular ornamental theme and any added decoration was to echo that chosen motif; decoration generally relied on positioning geometric shapes.

Chicago had been quick to absorb the influences of the Arts and Crafts Movement – the Chicago Arts and Crafts Society was founded in 1897 and

Left Modernist furniture and interior by Jean-Michel Frank for the Templeton-Crocker apartment in San Francisco.

an Englishman, Joseph Twyman, did much to publicise Morris & Co. goods – but although Wright was involved with the movement through his friendship with C. R. Ashbee he held that it was the machine that was to determine a truly American art for the future. While Sullivan wrote for *The Craftsman* from 1905 onwards, and although Wright knew designers such as Elbert Hubbard his style moved forward on into the twentieth century and away from his original influences.

At the Paris Exhibition of 1925 there was no American work shown; it was suggested that the only representative object of American decorative arts would be the skyscraper. It is true that the major innovations in America at this time were in architecture, although changes obviously brought with them alterations in decorative styles.

In 1923 the Austrian Richard Neutra came to America to join his old associate Rudolph Schindler, who had worked with Frank Lloyd Wright. Neutra had studied under Adolf Loos who had seen Sullivan's buildings in Chicago in the early 1890s. His pupil Neutra went on to California where in 1928 he build the Health House, experimenting with new building techniques and technologies. Influenced by a visit to the Bauhaus in 1930 he returned to experiment with prefabricated housing and, in 1936, a model house using plywood. This influence took Wright's principles one step further and created plain interiors using much glass, uniform surfaces or exposed interior brick.

Until the 1925 Exhibition the main decorative styles were again historical revivals and the econ-

omic stringencies of the 1929 Wall Street Crash doomed any real expansion of the new 'Art Moderne' influence, although geometric forms in exotic woods or new materials were introduced. In 1931 the American Institute of Interior Designers was founded and women enjoyed a heyday of importance in this profession. The best-known New York designer was Elsie de Wolfe, an actress turned designer, whose style based on eighteenth-century furniture and floral chintzes was extremely popular in the twenties and early thirties. Her dining room at the Colony Club introduced lattices as an indoor device which, combined with floral fabrics, produced a garden-like interior. Rose Cummings also used clear colours.

The all-white idiom, known as the 'White Look' also had its vogue, especially in Hollywood which also favoured the jazzy zigzags and black outlines of the modernistic idiom. Streamlining, motifs from Hollywood film sets, Art Deco, 'Cunard' lines all found some expression in both domestic and commercial interiors.

In the 1930s Swedish Modern became popular, with functional forms in blond woods. Knoll International made furniture in this style designed by Florence Knoll, Mies van der Rohe and Eero Saarinen. This style also absorbed the tenets of the Bauhaus and Charles Eames and Saarinen experimented with new materials; in 1939 they won first prize in an International Furniture Design Competition for a moulded plywood chair with a light metal frame, based on Marcel Breuer's prototype. As Frank Lloyd Wright had predicted, the machine and scientific theory had come to stay in furniture design.

Ceramics

ART POTTERY was perhaps the area of design where Arts and Crafts ideals were most widespread in America. Practically and financially it was, and is, a form where the artist-designer and craftsman could be one and, it is interesting to note, potteries in America were often set up either for therapeutic reasons or to provide some useful, but ladylike, occupation for women. The initial stimulus for American pottery came with the Philadelphia Centennial Exposition of 1876 where the first Oriental exhibits were seen as well as work from Doulton and examples of Ernest Chaplet's barbotine slip-painted technique. Both the Robertsons and Mary Louise McLaughlin visited the exhibition of ceramics and returned to their native states of Massachusetts and Ohio to put what they had seen into practice.

From the 1870s art pottery was dominated by the method of underglaze decoration. In 1872 the Chelsea Keramic Art Works was formed by James Robertson and his three sons, George, Alexander and Hugh. Specialising first in Greek terra cotta forms, in 1877 Chelsea faïence was introduced using simple shapes and glazes in soft colours. The process known as barbotine, similar to Haviland faïence, – painting with coloured slips, generally on a blue or green ground – was introduced; about the same time Mary Louise McLaughlin produced her first slip-decorated ware, also inspired by the Philadelphia exhibits.

In 1884 Hugh C. Robertson, then the only member of his family remaining at the Chelsea Works, achieved his first oxblood glaze. He had been experimenting with various Oriental glazes, including a mustard yellow, sea and apple greens and turquoise, all used with no ornamentation on simple stoneware shapes. His experiments however almost led him to bankruptcy and he closed the pottery in 1889. It was reopened in 1891 with support from Boston businessmen along more commercial lines and in 1895, upon the move to a new site, became the Dedham Pottery, best known for Robertson's crackleware, the blue in-glaze borders decorated with a variety of flora and fauna, the most popular being the rabbit.

The other exponent of the underglaze technique, Mary Louise McLaughlin, developed her Limoges glaze – to become known as 'Cincinnati Limoges' – in 1877. She had herself exhibited some china painting in 1876 and in 1879 she formed the Cincinnati Pottery Club to follow her faïence experiments and encourage other women, firing the work at the Coultry Pottery. From 1881 the Club used the facilities at Rookwood, but in 1882 these were refused and Miss McLaughlin had to cease work on her underglaze decoration. In 1895 she resumed work using inlaid clays, but abandoned this in 1898 in favour of hard-paste decorative porcelain. In 1901 the best results were achieved with her high-fired translucent creamy-white Losanti ware, on which she herself prided her reputation. She abandoned ceramics completely in 1906, but remains the most important of all the Cincinnati ceramists.

There were over thirty potteries in the state of Ohio after the initial impetus of the Philadelphia Exposition, the most famous being the Rookwood Pottery in Cincinnati. Rookwood was started by Maria Longworth Nichols Storer with financial help from her father and support from some of the ladies from the Cincinnati Pottery Club. Mrs. Nichols had already accomplished some china painting before she tried her first experiments in ceramics.

From 1880 to 1884 the work at Rookwood was mainly the ladies' experiments, with heavy relief or incised decoration and much gilding, but from 1884 due to Laura Fry's work with underglaze decoration the 'Standard' Rookwood ware became the best known feature of the firm, with brown, red, yellow or orange slips under a yellow-tinted high glaze. In 1883 William Watts Taylor had been employed as manager of the firm to establish Rookwood on a more commercial footing, but the pottery always retained its philosophy of allowing

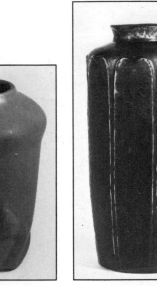

Above Rookwood earthenware vase by Albert R. Valentien, 1890.

Centre left Vase by S. A. Weller, *c.* 1905.

Centre right Earthenware vase by the Grueby Faience Co. of Boston, *c.* 1899.

Above right Vase by George E. Ohr made at the Biloxi Art Pottery, *c.* 1900.

individual artists a free hand in their designs. Several designers later left Rookwood to found their own potteries, such as Albert Valentien and Artus Van Briggle. Rookwood was also the first pottery in America to have a chemist on the staff, Karl Langenbeck, who joined them in 1885.

In 1886–7 Rookwood carried out the first experiments with a matt glaze but, due to concentration on the development of the elusive Tiger Eye glaze, it was not until the St. Louis Exposition in 1904 that the first Vellum matt glazes were seen, to be followed in 1910 with a second grey or brown matt glaze known as Ombroso. Also in the early 1900s unsigned ornamental wares were produced, cast in moulds, and in 1915 a range of soft porcelain. Rookwood, unlike so many other potteries, survived both the Depression and the Second World War.

The first serious rival to the domination of underglaze decoration came with the introduction of the matt glaze, which was most fully developed in the work of William H. Grueby of Boston. The Grueby Faience & Tile Company had been incorporated in 1891, but it was the work of Delaherche exhibited at the Chicago World's Fair of 1893 which probably inspired the forms of Grueby's work. Grueby vases are distinguished not only for the quality of the glaze but also for the simplicity of the shapes, decorated with incised relief motifs, usually of leaves.

Artus Van Briggle, who had worked with Karl Langenbeck at the Avon Pottery, was sent by Rookwood to France where he too studied the use of a matt glaze. In 1899, forced by tuberculosis to move to Colorado Springs, although he himself only survived until 1904, he set up his own pottery, where he perfected his glaze, using Art Nouveau motifs. Most of the work which employs matt glazes shows an austerity of form, in contrast to the reliance on ornamentation of the technique of

underglaze painting. Van Briggle fused the arts of sculpture and ceramics, as in his famous Lorelei vase, in a manner reminiscent of the work of Emile Gallé. Charles Volkmar, of the Volkmar Kilns, New Jersey, also experimented with matt glazes.

In 1902 an Englishman Frederick H. Rhead began work with William P. Jervis at the Vance/Avon Faience in Ohio, then moving to the Weller Pottery in Zanesville. There he introduced a technique (which he called Jap Birdimal) of using a squeeze-bag to pipe the outline of a decoration in white slip, generally on a grey or blue ground, and then filling in the design with a contrasting colour. From 1904–8 Rhead worked at the Roseville Pottery in Zanesville where he added the Della Robbia line – using a *sgraffito* process – to their line of underglaze decorated ware known as Rozane, comparable to Standard Rookwood, Lonhuda Pottery or Weller's Louwelsa range. Rhead himself considered the process of inlaid decoration the most effective as it gave the potter the most control over his design, and he produced some beautiful work at the Arequipa Pottery in California – set up, as was Marblehead in Boston, as a therapeutic centre for tuberculosis patients – between 1911 and 1913, when he left to found his own pottery. He left his own company in 1917, abandoning also his newly founded journal, *The Potter*, and returned to Zanesville. Rhead was also obsessed with finding the technique for the Chinese mirror or reflecting black glaze and as late as 1934 he was honoured for his experimentation and success.

Perhaps the most distinctive style using the inlaid process was achieved at the Newcomb College Pottery. Newcomb College was the women's college of Tulane University in New Orleans and the pottery was set up by Ellsworth Woodward to provide both a technical and artistic training for women. A succession of potters were

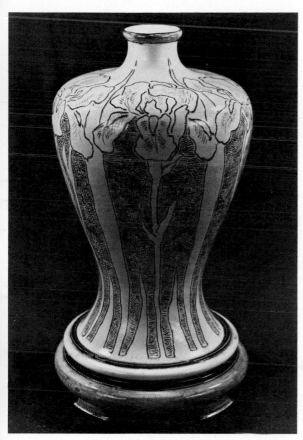

employed to throw the ware, the most notable being Joseph F. Meyer and Paul E. Cox, and the women undergraduates then decorated the blanks. The distinctive colouring – blue, green, black and yellow were most often used – and conventionalised floral motifs of the Newcomb vases seem evocative of the American South. In 1918 the direction of the school changed when a new educational laboratory was taken over in the Art Building and the graduate students could not only study their medium more deeply but also now work through the complete process of ceramics. Woodward retired in 1931 and Newcomb ceased producing art pottery.

One of the most remarkable examples of the ascendancy of American art pottery in the eyes of the world is the University City Pottery in Missouri. The pottery belonged to the Art Institute of the People's University started by the opportunist entrepreneur, Edward Gardner Lewis, who had launched the American Women's League in 1907. Lewis himself was interested in ceramics, self-taught using Samuel Robineau's translation of Taxile Doat's *Grand Feu Ceramics*, and in 1903 an extremely fine porcelain clay had been found in the area, fine enough to tempt Taxile Doat to leave his native Sèvres, with his ceramic collection, for University City in 1909. There he was joined by Samuel Robineau and his wife Adelaide, who had in 1899 published the *Keramic Studio*, Frederick H. Rhead and Kathryn E. Cherry. The school specialised in correspondence courses.

The first kiln was fired under Doat's supervision in April 1910 and many different glazes were used, most notably high-fired porcelain with *flambé* and crystalline glazes. The pottery won many prizes, the greatest being the Grand Prize awarded to Mrs. Robineau's scarab vase at the Turin International Exhibition in 1911.

Louis Comfort Tiffany first began experimenting with pottery in 1898 at his Corona works, New York, although the pottery bases for his lamps and other items were purchased from the Grueby Pottery. Tiffany exhibited his Old Ivory ware in 1904 and again the following year, but no ceramics were offered to the public until 1905. The majority of the work was moulded using a high-fired white clay which gave a light yellow-green glaze from which the name 'old ivory' was derived. He also experimented with mat, crystalline and iridescent glazes and from 1911 he introduced Bronze Pottery, probably influenced by the work of Clewell Metal Art which had opened in 1906 and by 1909 was producing ceramics with a metal coating of copper or silver. Tiffany's pottery was, from its inception, overshadowed by his Favrile glass and shows the same concern for flowing Art Nouveau lines and idioms. Production ceased between 1917 and 1920.

The many other potteries of this period are too numerous to name, although worth mentioning are the Paul Revere Pottery in Boston, Pewabic in Detroit, in New York the Volkmar Pottery, Buffalo Pottery and Fulper Pottery, which introduced its Vasekraft art pottery in 1909 with a multitude of glazes on stoneware bases which continued until 1930, Kenton Hills in Kentucky, Cowan Pottery in Ohio which from 1920 to 1931 produced limited edition moulded porcelain figures in addition to their art pottery, which proved extremely popular. In contrast was the Biloxi Art Pottery where George E. Ohr produced individual pieces, some paper thin in tortured shapes.

Art pottery was the area where, perhaps more than any other, America demonstrated that she could learn from the examples provided at the 1876 Philadelphia Centennial and create an American art by the time of the Chicago World's Fair seventeen years later.

Above left Vase from the Newcomb College Pottery, New Orleans, late 19th century.

Top centre Vase from the Fulper Pottery Company, *c.* 1910.

Top right Cast ceramic tile by Ernest Batchelder, *c.* 1910.

Centre Four vases from the University City Pottery characteristic of the work of Taxile Doat, *c.* 1912.

Above Art Nouveau vase by Artus Van Briggle, 1902.

Glass

THE MIDDLE OF the nineteenth century in England had seen a considerable revival in the art of stained glass. America had not had a Gothic Revival, bringing with it the re-emergence of ecclesiastical art, and it was not until later in the century that stained glass was seen as a promising art form. In 1872–3 the illustrator and watercolourist, John La Farge, visited France and England where he not only admired medieval glass, but also met some of the Pre-Raphaelites and saw the work of Morris & Co. He produced his first stained glass in New York in 1876 and worked with the Boston architect Henry H. Richardson and also Stanford White; he designed the panels for Richardson's Holy Trinity church in Boston, perhaps the finest example of 'Richardson Romanesque'. Around 1887 he began experimenting with different techniques and developed an opalescent glass which lent itself to Art Nouveau forms, no longer requiring etching or painting for effect. La Farge died in 1906, by which time his work had been widely copied.

It is interesting to note that even by the 1890s there was a 'revival' of the old technique of

The John Harvard Memorial Window by John La Farge in St. John's Chapel, Southwark Cathedral, London, c. 1905.

colouring pot-metal glass. Otto Heinigke formed a partnership with Owen J. Bowen, who had previously worked with both La Farge and Tiffany, and they produced church glass using painted leaded glass, influenced by Heinigke's visit to Europe in 1896. In 1913 they were joined by Oliver Phelps Smith and in 1915 he and Heinigke's son formed a new partnership, Heinigke & Smith, continuing to produce church glass for several years. Charles J. Connick of Boston also produced church glass in the traditional style.

The undoubted leader of the medium, however, was Louis Comfort Tiffany. He was the son of the founder of Tiffany & Co. and had studied painting under George Innes and travelled in Europe before he set up L. C. Tiffany and the Associated Artists in 1879 with the help of Candace Wheeler. By the early 1880s they were the most successful New York decorating firm and were commissioned in 1882 to decorate President Arthur's White House. By 1885 however the association had come to an end and the independent Tiffany Glass Company was founded. At the same time Tiffany moved into the top floor of his father's mansion where he created his own studio.

In 1892 Tiffany acquired his own glass furnaces at Corona and in 1895 the first Tiffany lamps were offered to the public. On bronze stands, the shades were leaded with varying qualities of glass, usually in floral designs. Amongst the successful designs were Clara Driscoll's dragonfly lamp and Mrs. Curtis Freschel's wisteria lamp, both produced around 1900. The lamps incorporated the best elements from Tiffany's glass which, with mosaics, he had begun to produce as early as 1876. Tiffany himself saw a social need for decorative stained glass to create interiors full of warmth and light, where perhaps otherwise a window might have looked out only on to a brick wall. It did not take long for every artistic household to own a lamp or window.

The first Favrile (meaning hand-made) glass was offered for sale from the Corona works in 1896. The first year's production had gone straight to museums. Tiffany owned an extensive collection of ancient glass which provided him with his fascination for texture and integral decoration. The workshops first produced plain gold lustre ware, followed by peacock blue and then other colours. This work was commercial in comparison to Tiffany's own experiments in achieving iridescent finishes or the Paperweight decorated glass, the Cypriote or Lava glass. From 1900 until his retirement from the firm in 1919 Tiffany Studios were best known for their art glass.

The popularity of Tiffany glass obviously led many other manufacturers to follow his lead. The Quezal Art Glass and Decorating Co. of Brooklyn was started in 1901 by two former employees of the Tiffany Studio and in 1893 Handel & Co. of Connecticut began producing cheaper versions of the Tiffany lamps. In 1904 the New York Steuben Glass Works first produced their Aurene glass which was based on the Favrile glass, in Art Nouveau forms. Other companies were the Fostoria Glass Speciality Co. and Imperial Glass Co. of Ohio, Fenton Art Glass Co. of Virginia, Lustre Art Glass Co. of New York or Vineland Flint Glassworks of New Jersey.

Frank Lloyd Wright used leaded glass in his decorative schemes, using plain glass in totally geometric designs which picked up the central motifs used within a specific house. As skyscraper design took over from the more sinuous forms of Art Nouveau, glass was used as much in a structural capacity as in a decorative manner. As in England in the twenties and thirties, glass was used, etched, plain or mirrored, in interiors for bars and theatres; it was used in the home, especially in bathrooms.

Top right A collection of Tiffany iridescent glass vases, *c.* 1900.

Top centre Tiffany 'Jack-in-the-pulpit' glass vase, *c.* 1900.

Far right Tiffany miniature wisteria lamp, *c.* 1900.

Right Tiffany poppy lamp, *c.* 1900.

Right Tiffany acorn lamp, *c.* 1900.

Far right Hanging lamp in leaded glass by Frank Lloyd Wright for the Susan Lawrence Darner House, Springfield, Illinois, 1903.

Bottom right Leaded art glass ceiling lamp by Charles Sumner Greene, 1907.

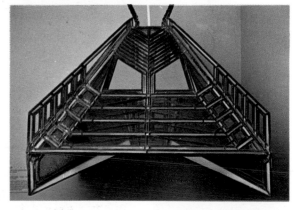

Silver, Jewellery and Metalwork

Silver and jewellery in the United States tended to be dominated by the work of old, established firms such as the Gorham Manufacturing Co. or Tiffany & Co. Jabez Gorham founded his firm in Rhode Island around 1815 and Charles L. Tiffany's company took the name Tiffany & Co. in 1853, forming a silver department in 1868. Both firms were influenced by the changes in style of the craft revival and Art Nouveau, but on the whole their stock was conservative in design.

The director of Gorham, Edward Holbrook, organised a group of silversmiths with high technical skill to carry out the designs of William C. Codman, an Englishman who came to Providence in 1891. The silver and jewellery produced was sold under the name of Martele from about 1900 and embraced the new styles. The jewellery was mainly in silver, with some copper, set with pearls, quartz or mother-of-pearl. In other fields, the company was known for being the first to introduce mass production of silver items.

Tiffany & Co. was known for its wealth of precious stones and gems and when L. C. Tiffany, the founder's son, began to design jewellery he was able to use materials not generally found in designs stemming from the craft ethic. Tiffany silver derived its designs from Japanese art, following the ideals of the Aesthetic Movement; L. C. Tiffany sent silver from the company as a wedding gift to Mucha in Paris in 1906. When L. C. Tiffany became vice-president of the firm a separate department was set up under Julia Munson to make artistic jewellery, often following his own designs, which tended to be only a rough sketch, a model from his own extensive collection of Eastern and European objects, or just the suggestion of a

flower or other natural form which could be adapted. Few pieces were made and production ceased in 1916.

L. C. Tiffany also worked with Julia Munson at his own Tiffany Studios where, in the late 1890s, experiments began with enamels, often used on *repoussé* copper bowls or vases. Opaque and translucent layers were used, fired separately, and often finished with a final iridescent coat, leaving an effect similar to his glassware.

As in England the Arts and Crafts Movement inspired many individuals to turn to the professional practice of their particular craft. In Boston, where Arts and Crafts first took hold in America, Elizabeth E. Copeland, after studying in England, combined silverwork and enamelling, her work showing clearly the handicraft of the maker. Following Miss Copeland, Edward Everette Oakes designed jewellery in Boston and showed at the Arts and Crafts Society Exhibition in 1923.

In Chicago also several individuals set up shop. There the work was more elegant in design, inspired by the powerful influence of the Prairie School architects. Around 1910 Florence Koehler made jewellery in the Art Nouveau style, owing more to France than to England for her designs. Her work was extremely popular in Chicago intellectual circles. The Kalo Shops were opened

Right Copper lamp by Dirk van Erp, *c.* 1911.

Below and centre Two examples of Gorham silverware illustrated in *The Craftsman* of 1904.

by Clara Barck Welles and sold extremely simple and elegant silverware; they continued until 1970, although Mrs. Welles retired in 1940. Robert R. Jarvie was listed as a silversmith in Chicago from 1893 until 1917 and was principally known for his simple copper candlesticks, but from 1912 he also designed commissioned trophies for cattle shows in Chicago and the surrounding area. His work was also known on the Eastern seaboard.

The style in jewellery between 1895 and 1910 was predominantly Art Nouveau, which combined either a form of stylised sculpture, as in some of Tiffany's work, or the mixture of precious metals and perhaps worthless stones, where the overall design becomes of more importance than the value of the piece. The Art Nouveau influence was to give way to a far more geometric style with patterns of small dots, circles and triangles, rather after the fashion of Josef Hoffmann.

Margaret de Patta, a painter and sculptress, began jewellery design in 1929, originating a structural style and introducing cuts which widened the visual scope of transparent gems. Paul Flato designed jewellery in Hollywood in the thirties with pieces such as 'shooting stars', a brooch made up of a spray of diamante stars. After 1930 the sculptor Alexander Calder designed some jewellery using hammered or twisted silver and brass wire. Man Ray also designed some jewels.

The Arts and Crafts communities fostered a revival in metalwork. The Roycrofters made wrought iron and the Roycroft Copper Shop was headed by Karl Kipp, from Vienna, helped by Dard Hunter who was primarily concerned with the book bindery. Kipp designed bookends, candlesticks, trays, vases and other household items which were then made by the other members of the Shop. The hammered copper was decorated with stylised designs, usually of flowers or trees. The work sold well, advertised through the Roycroft catalogues. Up to thirty-five men were employed in the Copper Shop. Kipp left Roycroft for a short period around 1912 when he founded his own Tookay Shop in East Aurora, although he continued many of the Roycroft designs.

In California Dirk van Erp opened the Copper Shop in Oakland in 1908, moving in 1910 to San Francisco. He had begun by making vases out of brass shell casings which he sold to a San Francisco gallery in 1906. At the Copper Shop he produced a range of copper lamps with mica shades as well as vases, trays and other items. His work was simple and he left the hammer marks to demonstrate the handmade qualities of his work. He retired in 1929 although he still continued to design some pieces until his death in 1933.

Top left 'American Beauty' vase in hand-hammered copper, made by the Roycroft Copper Shop, c. 1912.

Top right Inkpot, c. 1926, in hand-wrought copper with sprayed-on lacquer finish, made by the Roycroft Copper Shop.

Left Desk lamp in hand-hammered copper with mica shades made by the Roycroft Copper Shop, c. 1908.

Below Tiffany & Co. inkwell in carved ivory with crocidolite eyes, gilded leaves and enamelled top, c.1900.

Germany and Austria

by Ian Bennett

Movements and Influences 1890–1940

OF ALL THE MAJOR MANUFACTURING countries, it was Germany which made the most serious attempt before the First World War to resolve the problems of designing machine-made products. Although the machine-versus-craftsman debate was carried on as vociferously as elsewhere, the solution was realised to lie not in the 'either-or' framework created by Morris in England or even the somewhat vague compromise of the Wiener Werkstätte in Austria, but in a realistic attempt at synthesis.

Art historically, the Germans were better prepared for such a synthesis than were the English or Austrians (the debate hardly touching the mainstream of French applied art at this time). A typical German interpretation of the English Arts and Crafts Movement can be found in the writings of Hermann Muthesius, one of the most influential architects and designers in the pre-Bauhaus era. Muthesius had spent seven years in England between 1896 and 1903 with the official task of observing and reporting on the developments in English architecture and design.

As a result of his English sojourn, Muthesius published *Das Englische Haus* between 1904 and 1905, in which he analyzed the architectural achievements of Richard Norman Shaw, William Godwin and others, architects who, in the 1890s, had already influenced many of the younger generation of Germans, including Spalding, Grenander, Hans Poelzig, Ernst Eber and Muthesius himself.

The concept of the *Gesamtkunstwerk* is strong in Muthesius' book, in which he devotes as much space to the integral fitments of buildings – lights, door handles, heating, plumbing, furniture – as he does to the architecture itself. However, in one crucial respect, he differed from the attitude expressed by the Arts and Crafts Movement: 'Let the human mind think of shapes the machine can produce. Such shapes, once they are logically developed in accordance with what machines can do, we may certainly call artistic. They will satisfy because they will no longer be imitation handicrafts but typical machine-made shapes.'

In *Das Englische Haus* and other works, such as the essay 'Kunst und Maschine' which appeared in *Dekorative Kunst* in 1902, Muthesius was the first and most important spokesman for the industrialization of design at the beginning of the century. There was, however, one very significant precursor of his arguments; this was the book entitled *Wissenschaft, Industrie und Kunst* published in Braunschweig in 1852 by the architect and critic Gottfried Semper. Like his English contemporaries, Semper was dismayed by the quality of work shown at the Great Exhibition of 1851 and believed that design would not flourish again on a worthwhile aesthetic level until the machine was used to its full potential.

The two magazines primarily responsible for the propagation of the Art Nouveau concept of design were *Pan*, founded by Julius Meier-Graefe in 1895, and *Jugend*, which began publication the following year, and gave its name to the stylistic movement in Germany. In Darmstadt, two was published *Deutsche Kunst und Dekoration*. In 1897, there appeared not only the three Darmstadt journals mentioned previously, but two others also, *Kunst und Handwerk* and *Dekorative Kunst*, both of which were published in Munich, the latter by Meier-Graefe again.

The Munich group designed metalwork, furniture and graphics. Paul and Pankok collaborated on interior schemes for the German Pavilions in the Paris 1900 and Turin 1902 International Exhibitions; Riemerschmid exhibited a room in Paris on the ubiquitous theme of a 'Room for an Art Lover', and at Turin Behrens exhibited the living-room interior he had designed for the home of Ludwig Alter. Members also worked on architectural commissions, the most important of which, with regard to Art Nouveau, was the Atelier Elvira, a photographic studio in Munich, the façade of which was decorated by August Endell between 1897 and 1898 with dramatic, swirling forms obviously influenced by Obrist. Two commissions won by Endell in 1901, the Sanatorium at Föhr and the Bunder Theatre, Berlin, both of which are of a more restrained appearance than the Atelier Elvira.

Most modern authors hold the view that the 'whiplash' Art Nouveau style all but disappeared from the work of the Munich group after about 1902–3. Pankok left for Stuttgart in the former year, while Behrens had settled at the Mathildenhöhe colony in 1899.

At Darmstadt in 1901, Behrens designed his own house, including every detail of the interior fitments down to the domestic crockery. Although possibly less organic than, for instance, Mackintosh's designs, there is an obvious curvilinearity about the interior and some of its appointments.

Another important influence on the curvilinear style of German Jugendstil was the Belgian-born architect, painter, designer and teacher Henry van de Velde. He had studied painting at the Antwerp Academy between 1880 and 1884, and in the latter year went to Paris, where he remained for a year.

Cover for *Deutsche Kunst und Dekoration* designed by Margaret Macdonald Mackintosh.

He made some personal contact with the Impressionists and Symbolists. He was invited to join Les Vingt, a Brussels Secessionist group, in 1889, at which time he began to paint in a Divisionist style. Four years later, however, encouraged by his fellow Belgian Willy Finch, he abandoned painting to devote himself to designing for the applied arts, to architecture and to codifying his theories of design.

In 1894–5, he moved to Uccle, near Brussels, designing both the architecture and interior furnishings of his house Bloemenwerf; into the façade of the building, he incorporated ceramics made by local craftsman under his supervision to the designs of Willy Finch; his fiancée, Maria Sethe, who had visited England, where she had interviewed William Morris, purchased English Arts and Crafts furniture and wallpapers for the interior, which blended well with the pieces designed by Van de Velde himself.

At this time, Van de Velde met both Bing and Meier-Graefe, the two most important entrepreneurs of Art Nouveau design; he exhibited work in Dresden in 1897 and decorated the Paris offices of *Dekorative Kunst* in the Rue Pergolese in 1898. In the latter year he also established his own decorating firm in Brussels with financial help from Count Harry Kessler. Largely through the

efforts of Meier-Graefe, his work and ideas became widely known in Germany.

In 1899, Van de Velde moved to Berlin, exhibiting at the salons of Keller and Reiner. He lectured extensively in Germany and Austria between 1900 and 1901 and in the latter year published *Die Renaissance im Modernen Kunstgewerbe*. In 1902, he published a collection of his lectures under the title *Prinzipielle Erklärungen*; it was in these lectures that he expressed one of the principles of his aesthetic philosophy: 'Ornament and its shape should express – symbolise – the object's function and nothing more. Through its shape it should clarify the aim of the object and allude to its function – always based on reason'.

In 1900, he collaborated with Willem Hirschwald, owner of the Hohenzollern Kunstgewerbehaus, on designs and in 1901 he was employed by the Grand Duke Wilhelm Ernst of Sachsen-Weimar 'to raise the artistic level of design' and to establish workshops in Weimar in which to train artisans. Work was successfully exhibited at the Leipzig annual fair and the Weimar Kunstgewerbeschule created a new approach to teaching and design – the artisans were encouraged not to produce 'one-off' pieces but to develop a new concept of design for mass-production.

Until 1907, the Weimar venture had been

The Atelier Elvira, Munich, by August Endell, 1897–8.

private, but in that year the school became state-run and collaborated with commercial firms in the dukedom. Wilhelm Ernst did not, however, approve of the way in which the school was run and Van de Velde, as an alien, was forced to resign on the outbreak of war in 1914.

Throughout his career at Weimar, Van de Velde's work showed the influence of some of the leading German and Austrian designers, including Behrens, Olbrich and Hoffmann. Also, in the Villa Hohenhof, which he designed for the industrialist Karl-Ernst Osthaus in 1908, he showed that he was influenced by the English designers such as Baillie Scott and Mackintosh, the Villa itself being clearly based (as were many German houses at this time) on Baillie Scott's 'House of an Art Lover' scheme of 1900–1. On his resignation from Weimar, Van de Velde moved to Switzerland for the duration of the war. His recommendations for a successor included the young Walter Gropius, and it was Gropius who was given the appointment in 1919, the name of the institution changing its name officially on April 11 of that year to the Staatliches Bauhaus in Weimar.

The Deutscher Werkbund
In 1906–7, most of the Secessionist groups formed themselves into a single design association which

Left Bloemenwerf, Van de Velde's residence in Uccle, Brussels, 1895–6.

Bottom Project for Restaurant Webicht, Weimar, by Henry van de Velde, 1904.

Above The Tietz store in Dusseldorf, designed by Josef Olbrich, 1907–9.

Right Airship passenger saloon designed by Bernhard Pankok and illustrated in the Deutscher Werkbund yearbook of 1914.

Below Richard Riemerschmid's furniture workshop of the Deutscher Werkbund at Hellerau.

called itself the Deutscher Werkbund (DWB). The instigator of this amalgamation was Karl Schmidt, who in 1898, had formed the Dresdener Werkstätte für Handwerkkunst, a workshop with a markedly commercial outlook, and one which was concerned primarily with designing for industry. Schmidt was a cabinet-maker by profession and furniture was the principal product of the workshop; he was also the brother-in-law of Richard Riemerschmid, who began designing standardized furniture units for the Werkstätte in 1905, units which were machine-made and designed for easy assembly.

The majority of leading designers in Germany, including Behrens, Riemerschmid, Pankok, Paul, Gropius and Van de Velde worked for the Werkbund and outside contributors showed at the great exhibition of 1914 in Cologne, including Hoffmann, who produced a somewhat decadent pavilion in a style reminiscent of nothing so much as Regency, which appeared a little strange in such surroundings. By 1909, the Werkbund could claim 731 members, including 360 artists and 267 manufacturers and retailers.

The DWB established itself at Hellerau, a garden suburb near Dresden. The idea of the garden city itself was the product of that peculiar mixture of nationalism, sociology and arts and crafts which runs through much German architecture and design at this time.

It was also the theme of numerous books, including the Austrian Camillo Sitte's *Der Städtebau nach seinen Kunstlerischen Grundsätzen* of 1889, one of the first and most important, and Muthesius' *Landhaus und Garten* of 1907. The nationalistic element was to be found most strongly expressed in the influential book by Julius Langbehn published anonymously in 1890 under the title *Rembrandt als Erzieher*, in which the blatant historicism of German nineteenth-century art and architecture was attacked, especially as the majority of historical models were not German but French and English.

At the same time, many of the leading young German designers were influenced by a series of books by Friedrich Ostendorf, in which the importance of geometry in architecture was stressed, and by a work published in 1907 by A. G. Meyer, *Eisenbauten; ihre Geschichte und Aesthetik*. Meyer's book was symptomatic of a move towards industrial processes in architecture first made truly apparent in Adolf Messel's Wertheim Department Store in Berlin, which was built between 1897 and 1904.

In the early part of the century, a number of architects, including Adolf Messel, Frans Schwechten and Otto Eckmann, were employed by Emil Rathenau, head of AEG, to design his company's buildings and some of its products. In 1907, however, Paul Jordan, technical director of the company, asked Peter Behrens to take on overall responsibility for design, and to bring a sense of corporate identity to AEG's products. At the same time, he was asked to design the company's new Turbine factory building on the Huttenstrasse in Berlin in collaboration with the engineer Karl Bernhardt, and to design and coordinate AEG's new factory complex on the Brunnenstrasse site in the suburbs of Berlin.

Working in Behrens's office as an assistant on the AEG projects was Walter Gropius; encouraged by the critical success enjoyed by the AEG buildings, Gropius contacted Karl Benscheidt, founder of the Fagus Shoe firm in Berlin. Benscheidt had commissioned a new factory building from Eduard Werner in 1909 but was known not to be satisfied with the proposed exterior. Gropius submitted a series of plans which was eventually accepted, and the building was erected between 1911 and 1914; Gropius worked in collaboration with A. G. Meyer to achieve this new advance in industrial architecture.

Nevertheless, at the Werkbund Exhibition in Cologne in 1914, in which over 100 members of the group and invited guests showed work, the strong hint of a compromise was to be seen. The exhibition included a model factory, with seventy working machines, designed by Gropius and a pavilion in glass and steel by Bruno Taut. Behrens's pavilion, however, was in a strongly Neo-classical style and Van de Velde's theatre remained in the 'organic' style associated with almost all his work. Even Gropius's furniture was of a sort one would not associate readily with his name – lush, veneered pieces in a style somewhat similar to French Art Deco.

Above The Wertheim Department Store in Berlin, designed by Adolf Messel and built between 1897 and 1904.

Left The administrative buildings (rear elevation) of the 1914 Werkbund exhibition, designed by Walter Gropius.

Below left Model factory designed by Walter Gropius for the 1914 Werkbund exhibition.

Bottom left Theatre designed by Henry van de Velde for the Werkbund exhibition of 1914.

Right Electric kettle designed by Peter Behrens for AEG, c. 1908.

Bottom The Fagus factory, built between 1911 and 1914, designed by Walter Gropius.

The Wiener Werkstätte

In 1897, Josef Hoffmann, Koloman ('Kolo') Moser and Josef Maria Olbrich were the protagonists in the founding of the Vienna Secession; its motto was *Der Zeit ihre Kunst – der Kunst ihre Freiheit* (Art for the times – Art must be Free). All three had studied under the Austrian architect and designer Otto Wagner who, from 1894, had been a professor at the Academy of Arts in Vienna and was regarded by the Secession as a father-figure.

Hoffmann's first attempts at furniture design for the Secession building in 1898 were simple, plain pieces with lattice decoration, which owed much to English Arts and Crafts woodwork. Only in the Paris 1900 Exhibition did he begin to produce pieces in a geometric style combined with rich materials. In 1898, Wagner himself designed the Majolika Haus, with its ceramic decoration in a curvilinear Art Nouveau style which owed much to French and Belgian precedents; in the same year, the Secession held its first group show and also launched yet another *The Studio*-type publication, *Ver Sacrum*. This was followed in 1900 by *Das Interieur*.

In 1903, with the backing of a young banker, Fritz Warndorfer, the Wiener Werkstätte-Produktiv-Gemeinschaft von Kunsthandwerkern in Wien was founded, with Hoffmann and Moser as artistic directors (Moser resigned in 1906). At one time, the Werkstätte employed 100 workers, among them being thirty-seven masters who signed their work. Joseph Eduard Wimmer joined in 1912 and Dagobert Peche in 1915.

In the early years, all the designing was carried out by the two artistic directors, including bookbinding, leatherwork, gold and silver, lacquer, furniture, enamels, jewellery and, of course, the complete designing of buildings. By the end of the decade, however, other artists and architects were regularly submitting designs for a wide range of objects; they included Gustav Klimt, Adolf Loos, Otto Wagner, Carl Otto Czeschka, Otto Prutscher, Michael Powolny and Berthold Löffler.

Adolf Loos, mentioned above, was one of the most important and accomplished architects of his day. From 1893 to 1896, he was resident in Chicago and thus had first-hand experience of Sullivan's architecture and teaching. He was one of the initial members of the Secession but after 1898, when he had a disagreement with Hoffmann, who refused to allow to exhibit a complete room in the Secession's exhibition, he ceased to be an official member of the group, although he continued his association with it and subsequently exhibited with the Werkstätte.

He published important books in the 1900s,

The exhibition hall of 1898 designed by Josef Olbrich for the Secession in Vienna. The dome is made of wrought iron in the form of intertwined laurel branches.

including *Ornament und Verbrechen* (1908) and *Architektur* (1910). He became one of the few Austrian supporters of Muthesius' ideas.

In 1904, the Wiener Werkstätte received its most important commission, which was possibly the most significant awarded to any of the European Secessionist groups before the First World War: the Brussels house of Adolphe Stoclet. This was for the building and interior.

The interior of the Palais Stoclet is almost a vocabulary of the early Wiener Werkstätte; all the leading designers worked on every aspect, from Klimt's mosaic frieze in the dining room, entitled 'Expectation' and 'Fulfilment' to the light fittings and door handles. The Werkstätte was given absolute freedom to choose the richest materials, and the house was filled with marble, glass and highly polished hardwoods. Apart from Hoffmann, Moser and Klimt, others who designed work for the interior included Carl Otto Czeschka, the ceramists Michael Powolny and Berthold Löffler, the sculptors Richard Luksch and Franz Metzner and the painters Leopold Forstner and Ludwig Heinrich Jungnickel.

Klimt's mosaic frieze, perhaps his most famous single work, was executed in materials which are ample testimony to the almost Byzantine extravagance of the interior – enamel, coral, semi-precious stones, gold and silver.

Poster advertising one of the annual exhibitions held by the Vienna Secession.

Above Silver tea service designed by Josef Wimmer, 1912.

Left Lamp designed by Josef Hoffmann, *c.* 1905.

Above Metal baskets
designed by Josef
Hoffmann, founder of the
Wiener Werkstätte and a
member of the Secession,
c. 1905.

Right Box in various
woods, designed by Kolo
Moser, co-founder with
Hoffmann of the Wiener
Werkstätte, *c.* 1905.

Below Sitting room of the
Palais Stoclet, designed by
Hoffmann, rising through
two storeys of the house.

Right Exterior view of the Palais Stoclet, Brussels, designed by Josef Hoffmann and begun in 1905.

Below Dining room of the Palais Stoclet, designed by Hoffmann, incorporating marble veneers and mosaics by Klimt.

The Weimar Bauhaus 1919–24

In 1915, Henry van de Velde recommended a number of successors to his post as director of the Weimar Kunstgewerbeschule, including Walter Gropius. Gropius had already formulated his theory of the unity of art and technology, and the unification of all the arts and crafts within an architectural whole – again the *Gesamtkunstwerk*. In 1916, he submitted a report to the Grand-Ducal State Ministry on his proposals for the school.

Gropius' appointment to the directorship was confirmed in 1919, and on 11 April the school officially changed its name to the Staatliches Bauhaus im Weimar. In the same year, Gropius published his *Programm*, in which he stated most clearly the principal of the *Gesamtkunstwerk* which was to be the Bauhaus goal: 'The ultimate aim of all visual arts is the complete building! . . . Architects, painters and sculptors must recognise anew and learn to grasp the composite character of a building both as an entity and its separate parts.'

The teaching programme at the Bauhaus included 'all practical and scientific areas of creative work'. The three principal areas were architecture, painting and sculpture, to which all other branches of the crafts were considered adjuncts. The various crafts taught at Weimar included stonemasonry, stucco and plaster, woodcarving, ceramics, all forms of metalwork, including blacksmithing and locksmithing, cabinet-making, stained glass, enamels, mosaics, etching, wood engraving, lithography, chasing, weaving, typography, interior and exterior design, stage design and landscape gardening.

In addition, students were expected to take courses in art history, the science of materials, anatomy and 'the physical and chemical theory of colour'. There was even a course on 'basic concepts of book-keeping, contract negotiations, personnel'.

It was realised immediately that there was a

Left Vases made in the ceramics workshop of the Bauhaus by Gerhard Marcks, *c.* 1922.

Below Silver tea service, made by Christian Dell in the metal workshop of the Bauhaus, 1925.

conflict between the attempts of the craft workshops to teach students how to make things and the fact that the Bauhaus masters (this term being adopted in preference to the more academically formal professor) had no personal experience of manufacturing. Thus, in each workshop, there was a master of form, who was responsible for aesthetic and functional theory and for designing, and one or two masters of craft, who could actually work with their hands.

At the Weimar Bauhaus, Gropius was the master of form in the cabinet-making workshop, Georg Muche and Oskar Schlemmer in the woodworking workshop and Johannes Itten from 1919 to 1923 in the metal workshop, being succeeded by László Moholy-Nagy from 1923 to 1927. Georg Muche was master of form in the weaving workshop from the founding of the Bauhaus, and he was one of the few masters to continue in the same position after the move to Dessau, remaining in charge of weaving until 1927.

In the sculpture workshop, Ittens was master of form until 1922, in which year he was succeeded by Schlemmer; the stage workshop, begun in 1921, was run by Lothar Schreyer until 1923, when Schlemmer took over. The mural workshop was run at Weimar by Ittens initially, who was succeeded in 1923 by Schlemmer and Kandinsky. Book-binding was run as an independent workshop for Bauhaus students by Otto Dorfner, while the printing workshop was run by Feininger, although the prime influence after 1923 was Moholy-Nagy.

The architecture classes at the Weimar Bauhaus were, ironically, the least practical. Gropius himself had his own practice, which he continued to run; occasional theoretical lectures were given by Adolf Meyer, while after 1923, some classes were taught by Muche and Marcel Breuer.

Students at the Bauhaus were first required to attend the basic course, of which the most important parts were the *Vorkurs*, the classes taught initially by Itten on the characteristics of materials and the processes of arts and crafts. After completing this basic course, they could then join the craft workshop of their choice, first as 'apprentices', then as 'journeymen' and finally, after having taken examinations, they were awarded the title 'master'.

From the beginning, the products of the Bauhaus workshops were well received by art critics. In 1923, the Bauhaus held an exhibition of its products, which Walter Passarge, in *Das Kunstblatt*, described favourably: 'Very beautiful textiles, ceramics, and metalwork . . . in all these works, one perceives the thorough training in craftsmanship.' However, it was not art critics which the Bauhaus had to attract, but the leaders of industry.

The Dessau Bauhaus 1925–32

In 1924, when it became apparent that the days of the Bauhaus at Weimar were numbered, the council for the school began discussions with the local government of Dessau, a heavily industrialised town. The response was encouraging and it was agreed that the school could be moved there, new buildings would be financed and the school would be given a generous annual subsidy. Many of the leading German art critics, museum directors and art historians came forward in support of the Bauhaus, but the Dessau city council instituted its own investigation of the school as it had existed at Weimar.

The investigators were greeted by a slide lecture given by Gropius. One of the team, Master Carpenter Wagner, Chairman of the Guild Committee of Dessau, wrote a detailed report of what he had seen and heard; perhaps unconsciously, he discerned that the flaw in the Bauhaus argument was exactly the same flaw as had undermined the high ideals of Morris and Co. in England. The public was not interested in art, a fact presumably well-known to commercial manufacturers; as a result, any commercially made piece of 'artistic' design was not likely to sell and therefore had to be marketed in small numbers at high prices. Most crucially, the products of the Bauhaus workshops were essentially individualistic, hand-made crafts not suitable for mass production.

On the move to Dessau, many of the criticisms voiced by Wagner and others were heeded, even if Gropius did not openly admit to have considered them. There is, for instance, a new air of reality about his *Principles of Bauhaus Production* published in 1926: 'The products reproduced from prototypes that have been developed by the Bauhaus can be offered at a reasonable price only by utilization of all the modern, economical methods of standardization (mass production by industry) and by large scale sales.'

At Dessau, the workshops were subjected to a thorough reorganisation. Ceramics, which at Weimar, had been taught in a separate building in Dornburg, with Gerhard Marcks as master of form, were dropped, as were woodwork, stained glass and bookbinding. After 1928, the cabinet-making and metal workshops were amalgamated into the new Department of Interior Design under Josef Albers and Alfred Arndt (the distinction

between master of form and master of craft was also abandoned). The weaving workshop, which had been one of the few commercially successful departments at Weimar, continued at Dessau with the same staff, Gunta Stölzl succeeding Georg Muche in 1927; Stölzl was succeeded as head of department by Anni Albers in 1931, who was herself succeeded by Lilly Reich in 1932. The sculpture workshop was renamed the plastic workshop, in charge of which was Joost Schmidt. The printing workshop was renamed the printing and advertising department and was under the joint directorship of Schmidt and Herbert Bayer, although the latter resigned in 1928. The mural department was run by Hinnerk Scheper, although from 1928 to 1931 when he was in Moscow, Arndt deputised.

Architecture remained on a somewhat insubstantial footing. The Dutch architect and town planner Mart Stam was invited to lecture between 1928 and 1929, and in the last year of the Dessau Bauhaus, Marcel Breuer was in charge of the department. A new workshop at Dessau was photography, started by Walter Peterhans in 1929. The stage workshop ceased to exist officially in 1929 after Schlemmer resigned.

Although the emphasis on art remained strong at Dessau, the teaching staff made a great effort to make the much-needed breakthrough into industry. Although the Weimar Bauhaus had had some successes, notably with furniture, typography and textiles, the Dessau Bauhaus proved far more commercially minded and enjoyed a greater success.

Its most notable achievements were the designing of a wide range of light fixtures, including the Kandem range of desk lamps, and also textiles, both woven and printed, and wallpapers. The first wallpapers were not produced commercially until 1929, but thereafter proved one of the Bauhaus' main sources of income.

Magazine storage shelves in cherrywood and mirror plate, designed by Walter Gropius at the Bauhaus, 1923.

Despite these commercial successes, the history of the Bauhaus after 1928 was not a happy one. The Dessau Government, like that at Weimar, was becoming strongly loaded with right-wing political groups, of whom the most powerful were the National Socialists. The old accusations of socialist leanings were hurled against the school, and more specifically at Gropius, at every discussion of the Bauhaus' budget, and Gropius took the view that his position as head of the school had become untenable.

His eventual resignation also prompted the resignation of Breuer, Moholy-Nagy and Bayer, followed by Schlemmer in 1929. His place was taken by Hannes Meyer, who has been described as having a 'fanatical commitment to a functionalist view of architecture'.

Meyer was sacked in 1930 by Fritz Hesse, Mayor of Dessau, who had always been the staunchest supporter of the Bauhaus, and who believed that only by taking such a drastic measure could he save the school from closing under fascist pressure.

On the recommendation of Gropius (an unconstitutional move – directors were supposed to be appointed only by a full council of the Bauhaus masters), Hesse appointed Ludwig Mies van der Rohe as the new director. Mies had first met Gropius when they were assistants in Behrens' office (a third assistant was Le Corbusier) and since 1926, he had been vice-president of the Deutscher Werkbund, with which organisation the Bauhaus had always maintained close links.

Throughout the 1920s, Mies had proved himself one of the foremost German architects; he had undertaken numerous important commissions, including the Weissenhof housing development in 1927 (for which he had designed the famous Weissenhof cantilever chair) and the German Pavilion in the Barcelona World's Fair of 1929 (for which he had designed the Barcelona chair).

Under Mies, architecture flourished at the Bauhaus, and the various departments which had proven to be of financial worth continued to be successful. However, by 1932, the position of the Dessau Bauhaus was untenable and the school was forced to close. In October, Mies managed to reopen what remained of it as a private institution in a disused telephone factory in Berlin. However, it still did not escape the attentions of the National Socialists and on 10 August 1933 Mies announced the final dissolution of the Bauhaus. It had existed a mere fourteen years, but despite its economic success between 1928 and 1930, it never had the same impetus after Gropius' departure. He had conceived it and perhaps no one else properly understood it.

Expressionist Design in Germany

Although the interwar years in Germany were naturally dominated by the Bauhaus, the Deutscher Werkbund continued to exist as a strong influence, and there were other important, although perhaps less permanent, movements. The most significant was Expressionism, the major impact of which was upon painting, but which also influenced music, architecture and films.

Gropius and Bruno Taut had been under the spell of Expressionist ideas before the First World War (and to a certain extent remained so afterwards), as can be seen from Gropius' design for a diesel locomotive in 1913. Hans Poelzig, an influential industrial architect, designed a chemical factory at Luban in 1911 which, like his watertower executed at Posen in the same year, is one of the few realised Expressionist architectural projects.

The most bizarre and extraordinary, however, was Rudolf Steiner's Goetheaneum 11, built of concrete in 1925–8 at Dornach to replace an identical wooden building erected in 1913 but destroyed by fire in 1925.

Below Adjustable ceiling lamp designed by Marianna Brandt and Hans Przyrembel at the Bauhaus, 1926.

Below right Chemical factory at Luban, designed by Hans Poelzig, 1911.

Opposite Slit gobelin with linen warp and cotton woof, woven in the weaving workshop of the Dessau Bauhaus by Gunta Stölzl, 1927–8.

Furniture

IN GERMANY, there was little furniture made in a purely Art Nouveau idiom. Van de Velde had designed a number of chairs and desks between 1897 and 1898 before moving permanently to Germany. These are curvilinear and organic, with a frequent use in the large pieces of inset stained glass. Although more restrained than the majority of French Art Nouveau furniture, it is arguable that Van de Velde's designs owe at least as much to the less florid pieces by designers such as Majorelle as they do to Mackintosh. Van de Velde's influence can be seen in the work of several German designers in the early part of the present century, especially that of Bruno Schmitz of Berlin.

In Germany itself, as we have mentioned before, a certain amount of commercial Art Nouveau furniture was produced, particularly by the Möbelfabrik Olbernau in Saxony, for whom Otto Weinhold worked as a designer. Heinrich Vogeler of Worpswede also designed interesting pieces but, with their obvious rusticity, they are closer to the 'nationalistic', 'peasant' furniture associated with many Eastern European designers.

The most important German designer of furniture in the early years of the twentieth century was probably Richard Riemerschmid. Like the work of other designers associated with the Werkbund – Karl Bertsch, Bruno Paul, Adolf Schneck and Paul Schmitthenner, for instance – Riemerschmid's furniture as a whole represents a strange stylistic mixture which it is difficult to categorise.

Some of his earliest pieces are in a plain English Arts and Crafts idiom, while others may be compared to the early furniture of the Prairie School architects.

Riemerschmid's associate in the Munich Secession, Bruno Paul, was capable of even greater variety, although it has to be said that there was always an element of richness in his work which is absent from Riemerschmid's most characteristic Typenmöbel designed for the Werkbund. In 1914, for instance, Paul designed a bizarre blue lacquer commode in an elongated version of German Baroque, and even as late as the 1930s, he was designing pieces for the Werkbund with thick, glossy veneers, although the forms were decidedly uninspired.

August Endell produced interesting furniture in traditional materials such as elm, but mixed with modern elements such as forged steel. Bernhard Pankok designed furniture which, of all that produced by Munich designers, was perhaps the closest to the more outrageous products of the Nancy and Paris Art Nouveau schools.

Although the emphasis at Hellerau was on simplicity, some designers, such as Karl Bertsch produced pieces that could be described as late Biedermeier. Adolf Schneck was responsible for the simplest, most carpenter-like, pieces, although the most characteristic early Werkbund designs are those associated with Riemerschmid. All of his furniture was designed to be made by machine, the joints overlapping and held together by screws. There were three price ranges, depending on the quality of the wood used, the cheapest being pine. Domestic furniture, especially fitted elements, were designed in such a way that the shape could be altered or expanded by the addition or subtraction of separate elements.

Karl Schmidt, who was responsible for marketing these and other products of the Werkbund, would market a design for only a year, thus avoiding the sense of *déjà vu* usually associated with mass-produced objects. By 1909, Riemerschmid and Bertsch between them had produced a vast quantity of designs, including over 800 varieties of chair. Many of the same architects and artists also produced designs for carpets, curtains and other domestic textiles; these included several of the designers connected with the Werkbund including Bruno Paul, Van de Velde, R. Grimm, A. Grenander, and Gropius, while E. Seyfried specialised in wall-papers. Peter Behrens was employed by the Anker Linoleum Company as a designer and several of the Darmstadt group also designed wallpapers for Alexander Koch.

The early furniture of the Wiener Werkstätte, despite its frequent use of expensive woods and various inlaid materials, was comparatively simple, Hoffmann's designs in particular owing much to Mackintosh and the more restrained elements of English Arts and Crafts. Later pieces, however, while still remaining angular, tend to become richer and several writers have commented on the fact that the Werkstätte furniture of the period between about 1908 and 1915, with its rich veneers, inlays and lacquers, foreshadows French Art Deco furniture of the 1920s. Even Otto Wagner's furniture is suprisingly rich in taste.

Almost all the Werkstätte furniture was made by outside Viennese firms, including the Kunstmöbelfabrik August Ungethium, the Werkstätten für Wohnungseinrichtung, M. Niedermoser und Söhne (with upholstery by Wilhelm Niedermoser) and Porteis und Fix. In the 1920s, some weird carved and painted pieces were designed by Dagobert Peche, although the majority of Werkstätte furniture of this late period, notably that designed by Hoffmann for his Austrian Pavilion at the Paris 1925 Exhibition, did not differ

Left Longcase clock designed by Richard Riemerschmid, 1902 3.

Far left Cabinet designed by Otto Weinhold, *c.* 1900.

Below Round veneered table designed by Bruno Paul, 1935.

Left Dining chair designed by Richard Reimerschmid, *c.* 1900.

Far left Blue lacquered commode designed by Bruno Paul, 1914.

Above Armchair veneered in amboyna wood, designed by Koloman Moser, 1904.

Left Desk and chair designed by Josef Hoffmann, 1905, showing the influence of Charles Rennie Mackintosh and the English Arts and Crafts Movement.

much from pre-First World War examples; if anything it was richer and more ornate.

Following the war, the major impetus in furniture design in Germany came from the Werkbund and the Bauhaus. In the late nineteenth century, the Thonet factory, which had been producing elegant bentwood furniture for several decades, had farmed out its patents to some sixty factories all over Europe, employed a total workforce of around 35,000. Thonet continued to bring out new designs in the 1920s and 1930s, including examples designed by Ferdinand Kramer and Josef Frank. In 1927 Thonet marketed the chairs designed for the Weissenhof housing project by Mies van der Rohe in cantilevered tubular steel, with cane-work designed by Lilly Reich, the latter subsequently head of the Bauhaus weaving workshop.

The Weissenhoff development itself was probably the most architecturally prestigious enterprise of the twentieth century; the seventeen architects who each designed buildings included Behrens, Le Corbusier, Poelzig, Taut and Oud.

The major development in furniture design, and specifically of chairs, was the use of steel and other metals. In 1921, Adolf Schneck of the Werkbund, who worked in Stuttgart, and who was also involved on the Weissenhof project, designed a desk with chromium-plated legs. Schneck was also a pioneer in the use of inexpensive laminates, plywood and fibre-board, later used to good effect by the firm of Heinz and Bode Rasch, Josef Albers and Alvar Aalto.

The most influential period for Bauhaus furniture was the period immediately after the move from Weimar until 1928, during which time Marcel Breuer was in charge. Breuer's earliest furniture of 1922–3 was obviously inspired by Gerrit Rietveld and De Stijl – the famous Rietveld Berlin chair was first produced in 1917. By 1924–5, Breuer was using tubular steel for furniture and in 1925–6, as a private commission, produced in tubular steel and leather one of the most famous twentieth-century furniture designs, the Wassily chair. This was manufactured commercially by Standard-Möbel from 1926.

In 1926–7, Mart Stam and Mies van der Rohe both designed, apparently, cantilevered tubular steel chairs; evidence as to which came first is controversial, but there is some evidence that it may have been that of Stam. Mies' chair, the MR, was the first version of the Weissenhof chair and was manufactured by Berliner Metallgewerbe. The Weissenhof chair itself was marketed by Thonet, while Stam's design was manufactured by L. & C. Arnold. Breuer's tubular steel furniture designed for the Bauhaus Refectory was manufactured by Standard-Möbel from 1927, followed by the dining chair designed for the Bauhaus masters' private apartments and the chairs for the Bauhaus auditorium. Other Breuer designs were produced by Thonet.

In 1929, Mies van der Rohe designed what many would consider the single most brilliant piece of industrial furniture of the twentieth-century, the forged steel-strip and leather Barcelona chair which, despite its apparent simplicity, is a design which requires complicated and careful production techniques; it is extraordinarily luxurious in effect and has always been very expensive. Other, almost equally well-known Mies chairs are the cantilevered Brno and Tugendhat of 1930, both of which were designed for the Tugendhat house in Brno, Czechoslovakia; the former was produced in either steel-strip or tube, the latter in tube.

In the late 1920s, several other designers were working in tubular steel in Germany, including Mart Stam, Adolf Schneck, the firm of Heinz and Bode Rasch, Heinrich Bredendieck, Per Bücking, Heinrich Lauterbach (ex-Bauhaus students) and Walter Gropius.

Below The Wassily arm-chair in tubular steel and leather, designed by Marcel Breuer, 1925.

Below left The Barcelona chair in forged steel-strip and leather, designed by Mies van der Rohe, 1929.

Ceramics

GERMAN CERAMICS of the period 1890 to 1940 followed much the same pattern as in most other European countries. There were a few studio potters experimenting with new techniques, many small art potteries and some fine work done by some of the large established firms: in the case of Germany, by Meissen and Berlin.

Several individuals established themselves as potters in Germany in the 1880s and 1890s. The Von Heider family, Max and his three sons, Hans, Fritz and Rudolf, experimented with lustres at a kiln in Schongau, Bavaria. Max had established himself as a potter in Munich before moving to Schongau and his three sons were successful painters. Like many European potters, the Von Heiders were influenced indirectly by Hispano-Moresque lustres but it seems likely that their main source of inspiration was the work of Clement Massier in France and possibly Zsolnay in Hungary. Rudolf began working as an independent potter sometime after 1905, while his two brothers taught ceramics at the Magdeburg Kunstgewerbeschule.

Another German potter working in lustre was Franz Anton Mehlem of Bonn, who was given a special room in the German Pavilion at the Paris 1900 Exhibition; many of his pieces were painted by Frilling, and included panels composed of earthenware tiles.

Probably the most important German potter working towards the end of the nineteenth century was Hermann Mutz who had established his own factory at Altona on the Elbe in 1871. He was joined by his son Richard, who was also to become a distinguished potter, in 1893. Hermann's early pieces in earthenware have a rustic flavour but also show the influence of Japanese folk pottery, examples of which had been collected by Mutz's friend, Justus Brinkmann, first director of the Kunstgewerbe Museum in Hamburg. The Mutzes were also influenced by the stoneware of the French potter Jean Carriès and the lustreware by the Danish potter, Herman Kahler. The first stoneware was fired in about 1902, with abstract drip glazes in browns, blues and greens.

In 1904, Richard Mutz set up an independent workshop in Berlin. At this time, he began to collaborate on stoneware sculpture with his friends Ernst Barlach, their first commission being a portrait plaque of Brinkmann to celebrate the twenty-fifth anniversary of the Hamburg Museum in 1902. Barlach designed a number of pieces which were fired by Mutz, including a vase with grotesque handles which bears a remarkable resemblance to Christopher Dresser's designs for the Ault factory in the 1890s.

Barlach, although one of the great German sculptors of the twentieth century, also had a great influence on the development of ceramics in that country. In 1904, he had been appointed a Professor at the Staatliche Fachschule für Keramik at Höhr-Grenzhausen, Westerwald, and in 1908 wrote *Keramic, Stoff und Form* which was widely read. Apart from his work with Mutz, some of his sculptures of peasants and beggars were cast in white porcelain by the Schwarzburger Werkstatten für Porzellankunst. In the 1920s and 1930s, others were cast by Meissen, some in white porcelain and others in red Böttger stoneware.

In 1899, the painters Wilhelm Sus and Hans Thoma founded the Grossherzogliche Majolika Manufaktur at Karlsruhe in the Black Forest on the orders of the Grand Duke Friedrich I of Baden. The artistic director was one of Germany's best-known potters, Max Laeuger, who had studied painting in Paris at the Académie Julien in the early 1890s. Other ceramic designers working under him at Karlsruhe included Franz Blazek, who specialised in animal sculptures, Emil Pottner, a painter and printmaker from Berlin, and Fritz Behn, a Munich sculptor. Laeuger himself became an important member of the Darmstadt group, designing furniture, silver, carpets and posters in addition to ceramics. He also cast sculpture in stoneware for other artists.

Two other important German potters were Elizabeth Schmidt-Pecht and Julius Diez. The former was interested in neo-Rococo based on Dutch Delft. At the La Libre Esthétique Exhibition in Brussels in 1900, she showed vases in earthenware decorated in polychrome slip and with *sgraffito* decoration of flowers in an Art Nouveau style. Diez, known primarily as a book illustrator and poster artist, produced ceramics in much the same style as Schmidt-Pecht.

Many of the artists and designers connected with the Munich Secession and the Darmstadt group were involved with ceramics, either as makers or designers. Of these, the most important was Johann Julius Scharvogel, who had begun his career as a ceramist with the firm of Villeroy and Boch in the Saar in 1883, a firm which marketed its products, usually medieval and Renaissance inspired salt-glazed wares under the name Mettlach after the factory in the Rhineland originally owned by Jean-François Boch and which was one of the three factories which merged in 1839 to form Villeroy and Boch. Scharvogel remained at the factory until 1898. Later he became one of the founder members of the Deutscher Werkbund.

In 1906, Scharvogel was made head of the Grossherzogliche Keramischen Manufaktur at

White porcelain figure by Ernst Barlach, c. 1908.

Darmstadt, executing not only his own pieces but also those designed by other members of the artists' colony. Other factories also produced work designed by the Darmstadt artists, including Bauscher of Weiden, Krautheim & Adelberg, Josef Bock, Ohme, Meissen, Serapis, the porcelain factory at Burgau, Reinhold Hanke, the Waechtersbacher Steingutfabrik and many others.

Among other Darmstadt artists, Peter Behrens designed porcelain tableware for his own home around 1901, which was manufactured and marketed commercially by Bauscher Bruders of Weiden. In a delicate, angular Art Nouveau style, these pieces are in strong contrast to the overblown stoneware he designed for Franz Anton Mehlem of Bonn around 1900. More interesting are the medievally inspired jugs, usually with pewter mounts, he designed for the firm of Reinhold Hanke of Höhr-Grenzhausen around 1903.

Richard Riemerschmid designed very similar stoneware for Reinhold Merkelbach, another factory in Höhr-Grenzhausen, pieces which are easily confused with those of his colleague Paul Wynand, who had studied with Barlach at the Staatliche Fachschule für Keramik, from 1905. In 1906, Riemerschmid also designed a porcelain table service for Meissen, more traditional in shape than a similar service designed for the same factory by Van de Velde, and with rather clumsy and ugly handles.

Around 1902, Van de Velde designed some superb *flambé* stoneware which was executed by Reinhold Hanke. These pieces, with smooth, rounded bodies and angular but flowing handles, are in contrast to the work of the Darmstadt designers, seeming to bear no allegiance to past styles and reflecting the influence of such architects as Guimard and Horta, who were much admired by Van de Velde. Between 1903 and 1905, he was commissioned to design porcelain tableware by Meissen; these beautifully restrained pieces have moulded decoration and underglaze blue painting and gilding. They must rank among the most successful and beautiful industrial ceramics of this period.

Josef Emanuel Margold designed ceramics for Josef Bock's factory in Vienna and for Ernst Wahliss's Serapis factory in the same city. Ernst Riegel designed figure models which were made by Waechtersbacher Steingutfabrik.

Ceramics were taught at the Weimar Bauhaus, but the workshop was closed on the move to Dessau; it was felt that the teaching of ceramics exemplified a somewhat 'folksy' attitude which was far removed from the school's philosophy. Also, the use of architectural ceramics as an integral part of a building, which had become popular around 1900, was not well regarded by the majority of serious architects in the 1920s.

The Bauhaus pottery workshop was run as a separate studio at Dornburg. The master of form was the sculptor Gerhard Marcks and the master of craft Max Krehan. From 1923, Otto Lindig and Theodor Bogler were given their own design studio. This was when the pottery workshop itself was divided into the workshop for instruction and the workshop for production. Both Lindig and Bogler were Bauhaus journeymen.

Early Bauhaus pottery is surprisingly traditional, both in shape and decoration. Gerhard Marcks' designs in particular are based on traditional German and Flemish salt-glazed stoneware, embellished with 'naive' pictures on cobalt. Many of these pieces are, however, extremely attractive and may be compared with similar work done by numerous traditional American 'crock' houses in and around New York throughout the nineteenth century.

Bogler and Lindig were more concerned than Marcks with producing prototypes for mass production. Although interesting, their table wares do not compare with some of the products of the established factories such as Meissen. Some of Bogler's designs were produced by Velten-

Above Ceramic figure designed by Michael Powolny, *c.* 1906.

Left Covered pottery jug, designed by Reinhold Hanke, *c.* 1906.

Vordamm and others by the Staatliche Porzellan-Manufaktur of Berlin. The majority, however, were produced in quantity from moulds by the production workshop of the Bauhaus itself.

The Staatliche Porzellan-Manufaktur in Berlin was one of the main producers of new design during the 1920s and 1930s. Apart from its association with some of the Bauhaus potters, it manufactured an extremely famous and widely selling porcelain service in 1930 designed by Trudi Petri and called Urbino. Another important service was the '1382' designed by Hermann Gretsch and manufactured by the Porzellaneschirr. Arzberg and first shown at the 1930 exhibition of the Deutscher Werkbund in Paris.

Throughout the period under discussion, the work of the major German factories was of considerable importance. Like Sèvres in France, Meissen and KPM (the Königlichen Porzellan-Manufaktur of Berlin, later the Staatliche Porzellan-Manufaktur) were at the forefront of new techniques and employed many talented outside designers and artists.

Berlin was probably the first factory in Germany to concern itself with new ideas. In 1878, it established a chemical and research department under the directorship of one of the most gifted European ceramic chemists, Hermann Seger, who is remembered primarily today for his invention of Seger cones in 1886, small ceramic pyramids which melted at different temperatures and thus enabled the heat within the kilns to be far better controlled than in the past. Seger also developed a very fine porcellaneous body capable of taking the extremely high temperatures required for the superb range of metallic oxide *flambé* glazes he had perfected. This body was known as Seger-Porzellan; *flambé*-glazed examples were exhibited for the first time in 1880 but were not manufactured commercially until 1883.

Seger continued working at Berlin until 1890. His colleague in the chemical department was Albert Heinicke who had joined Berlin in 1873. His speciality was crystalline glaze, which he had developed to a commercially viable stage by 1885. Sometime after 1900, Heinicke developed a fine porcelain body suitable for underglaze painting. He remained at the factory until 1910.

The artist directorship of the factory was under Alexander Kips from 1888 to 1908, being succeeded in the latter year by Scharvogel's erstwhile partner at Munich, Theodor Hermann Schmutz-Baudiss. The latter retained his directorship until 1926. Under the influence of its chemical and artistic directors, the work of the Berlin factory can be divided into four groups – glaze effects, sculptural Art Nouveau pieces and later figures in the Art Deco style, more formalised pieces which are close in feel to the Viennese work of Powolny, Löffler and others, and table wares.

Schmutz-Baudiss, known for his atmospheric, 'underglaze' paintings, was responsible primarily for the formalised, Viennese approach. In the late 1890s, he had worked at the Ganser factory at Diesen-Ammersee with two other distinguished Hermann potters, Paul Dresler (whose work was influenced by Middle-Eastern ceramics) and Auguste Papendieck. In 1897, he had become a member of the Vereinigten Werkstätten of Mu-

Opposite top Vase with putto filial made at the Königlichen Porzellan-Manufaktur of Berlin, modelled by Fritzsche and decorated by Flad, *c.* 1900.

Opposite bottom A pair of Seger porcelain vases with ormolu mounts, *c.* 1890.

Left Two figures produced by the Serapis Fayence factory in Vienna, *c.* 1925

Below Stoneware bottle designed by Gerhard Marcks and executed by Max Krehan at the Bauhaus pottery workshop at Dornburg, *c.* 1922.

Bottom Stoneware jar and lid made in Vienna by Lucie Rie, 1930s.

nich. Designers at Berlin who were greatly influenced by Schmutz-Baudiss' style included Emil Rutte and Adolf Flad. Later modellers of figures, some of whom worked right through to the Second World War and after, included Paul Schley, Adolf Amberg, Hans Schwegerle, Anton Puchegger, Karl Himmelstross and Eduard Klabena; the last named is particularly well-known for his superbly modelled and brightly coloured birds.

Encouraged by the initiative of the Secessionist potters, Meissen began to produce interesting new work around the turn of the century. In 1903–4, they commissioned tableware from Henry van de Velde, having in 1896 been gratified by the popularity of their first important Art Nouveau service, Krokus, which was designed by Julius Konrad Hentschel.

Other freelance designers included Richard Riemerschmid and C. Paul Walther, and Meissen also cast figures by Ernst Barlach. Their most celebrated modeller during the years between about 1910 and 1930 was Paul Scheurich, who, in the 1920s, modelled attenuated, almost Mannerist, figures which were often cast in white porcelain. He is famous for a series of figures based on dancers in the Ballets Russes which were executed around 1914.

Above Three Meissen
figures modelled by Paul
Scheurich, *c.* 1920.

Right Ceramic clock
designed by Michael
Powolny, *c.* 1910.

Other factories which should be mentioned here
are Nymphenburg, whose artistic director from
1906 to 1909. Josef Wackerle, was one of the best-
known German ceramic modellers, and Rosenthal,
which was founded in 1879. The latter factory
made fine domestic wares, including three famous
services, Darmstadt (1905), Donatello (1907) and
Isolde (1910).

The involvement of the Wiener Werkstätte with
ceramics began initially with the founding of the
Wiener Keramik studio in 1905 under the joint
directorship of Michael Powolny and Berthold
Löffler. Powolny had been a pupil at the Vienna
Kunstgewerbeschule and was one of the founders
both of the Secession and the Werkstätte. He
specialised in faïence figures of cherubs in white,
yellow and black, as well as producing large, neo-
Mannerist figures and animals. Löffler's work is
similar. In 1912, the Wiener Keramik amalgamated with the Gmündner Keramik of Franz
Schliess to form the Vereinigte Wiener und
Gmündner Keramik GmbH.

The role of the Vienna Kunstgewerbeschule
was crucially important in the development of
Austrian ceramics at the turn of the century. In
1876, it had established a separate ceramic workshop with its own technical and chemical laboratory. Around 1900, special ceramic courses were
arranged with workshops for decoration and glazing under Hans Macht. Moser and Hoffmann
taught design, while at the same time having their
own ceramics made by outside firms, of which the
most important was probably the Josef Bock
porcelain factory in Vienna.

From 1909 to 1932, the ceramic classes at the
Kunstgewerbeschule were taught by Powolny,
Löffler and Robert Obseiger, the last named
having been a pupil at the school from 1909 to
1914. Thus the ceramic department of the
Kunstgewerbeschule and the Wiener Keramik of
the Werkstätte were linked by the same directors,
who were also instrumental in gaining the patronage of outside firms for the potters they taught
in the school.

Between 1900 and 1905, before Powolny and
Löffler began teaching, pupils at the Kunstgewerbeschule included Jutta Sikka and Helena Johnova;
at this time, they produced somewhat crude
abstract glazed pots. In the period between 1910
and 1915, there was an immediate change of style.
Pupils like Obseiger, Ludwig Schmidt, Julie Sitte
and Rosa Krenn began to produce stylised figure
models with subtle colouring. At that same time,
these and other Kunstgewerbeschule pupils such
as Fritz Dietl, Anton Kling, Emil Meier, Wilhelm
Schleich and Anton Kleiber began designing for
the Wiener Keramik. Two pupils, Emilie
Schleiss-Simandl and W. Schuhl designed
Gmündner Fayence.

Of the industrial factories associated with the
Kunstgewerbeschule and the Werkstätte, the most
significant was that of Josef Bock. This had been
founded originally by Johann Kutterwatz in 1828
and was taken over by Bock in 1871; he remained
the director of the factory until 1935. Among those
who are known to have produced designs for the

factory are Hoffmann, Moser, Rudolf Hammel, Antoinette Krasnik, Jutta Sikka, Therese Trethan, Hans Kalmsteiner, Johanna Poller-Hollmann, Otto Prutscher, Emanuel Margold and Dagobert Peche.

Particularly good tableware was designed by Therese Trese Trethan and Jutta Sikka around 1900–5 in angular, functionalist shapes. Tableware with simple black geometric ornament on white was designed by Hoffmann around 1908. Eduard Klabena, whose bird figures were produced by Berlin, modelled some pieces for Bock before he started his own Langensdorfer Keramik factory in 1911.

In 1885, Friedrich Goldscheider founded the Goldscheider'schen Porzellan-Manufaktur und Majolika Fabrik, with factories in Vienna and Pilsen. Some of the earliest figures were modelled by Arthur Strasser, who specialised in Middle Eastern subjects and Negro busts. Other figures included draped female forms holding shell-form lamps, some of which were signed 'Doebrich'. Many Kunstgewerbeschule graduates were employed on a permanent or freelance basis.

In 1892, the firm of Reissner, Stellmacher and Kessel was founded in Turn-Teplitz. The wares produced here were marketed under the tradename Amphora; some of the porcelain is simple, with *flambé* glazes. However, the factory also produced elaborate figure sculpture, some of which was decorated with gold and inset with stones (Juwelenporzellan); these reached the height of vulgarity. Kunstgewerbeschule graduates included Michael Mörtl, who modelled animals, some of which were also produced by the firm of A. Förster & Co.; Arthur Strasser also produced designs for Amphora.

Another important Viennese factory was founded by Ernst Wahliss in 1863. Under his sons Hans and Erich, this factory began producing Serapis-Fayence around 1911. The best-known designers were Karl (Charles) Gallé, Franz Staudigl, Karl Klaus and Willibald Russ. Tableware was decorated with scrolling geometric motifs, usually in black and green, with profuse gilding; stylised figure subjects were also produced.

The Kunstgewerbeschule and the various factories described above continued in importance throughout the 1920s and 1930s, with the style of their products varying very little from the prewar pieces. The inter-war years also saw the founding of a small number of important factories, the best known of them being the Wiener Porzellanmanufaktur Augarten, founded in 1922–3. This factory, which produced both table and decorative wares, exhibited a large group of pieces at the 1925 Paris Exhibition, which was awarded a Gold Medal. Designers for Augarten included Hoffmann, Powolny, Prutscher and Valerie Wieselthier. Much important work was also produced by the Wiener Kunstkeramische Werkstätte Busch & Ludescher, which had been founded in 1908. Modellers included Bruno Emmel, Johanna Meier-Michel, Michael Mörtl, Anton Puchegger and Olga Sitte.

The 1930s saw a movement in Austrian ceramics away from the elaborate figure modelling which had by then become characteristic of the Kunstgewerbeschule and its admirers. Although Moser's students at the Kunstgewerbeschule at

Head of a girl, ceramic by Valerie Wieselthier, *c*. 1925.

the beginning of the century had produced simple pieces with strong forms and monochrome glazes, Powolny and Löffler had been responsible for a move towards figure modelling which gradually took on a more elaborate style, finally becoming quite Baroque.

This development reached both its high point and its culmination with the work of Susi Singer and Valerie (Vally) Wieselthier in the mid 1920s. Around 1930, Robert Obseiger, who had by then become the most influential teacher at the Kunstgewerbeschule, began to produce small vessels decorated with matt glazes of rich colour. These pots stand out from the surrounding mass of often whimsical figure modelling, as do those of one of the most brilliant pupils of the Kunstgewerbeschule during the 1920s, Lucie Marie Gomperz, who, as Lucie Rie, became internationally famous as one of the greatest studio potters after she had settled in England in 1938.

Other notable figures in Vienna in the mid-1930s were Gertrud and Otto Nazler, almost self-taught except for a few lessons with the Viennese figurative potter Franz Xavier Iskra. Like Lucie Rie, they had their first international success in Paris; Rie had shown her work in the 1925 exhibition and again in the 1937 show; in the latter, the Nazlers received a silver medal. Their work, like that of Rie and Obseiger at this time, is concerned with glaze and form.

Lucie Rie herself has indicated that the influence of some of the English studio potters, notably Bernard Leach, had spread to Vienna by this time and the English approach to pottery may have had more than a little to do with this new direction in Viennese ceramics. The Nazlers, like Rie, left Austria in 1938, settling in the United States. This new direction in ceramics, begun in England, can also be seen in the work of one or two German studio potters in the inter-war years, notably Richard Bampi and Jan Bontjes van Beek.

Glass

Loetz vase with pewter mount, *c.* 1900.

THE THREE GREAT NAMES connected with Art Nouveau glass are Gallé in France, Tiffany in the United States and Loetz in Austria, although many other factories and individuals were active as makers and designers in the period between approximately 1880 and 1914. Of these three, the least highly regarded today, in terms of the art market, is Loetz, possibly because the glass itself remains 'anonymous' and relates not to an individual but to a corporate image.

The Loetz factory was founded at Klostermühle in 1836 and was named Glasfabrik Johann Loetz-Witwe in 1848 by Suzanne, widow of Johann Loetz. In 1879, Max von Spaun became head of the factory, appointing Eduard Prochazka as works manager. Over the next eleven years, the factory produced seven varieties of decorative glass, many of which attempted to imitate the surface appearance of different hardstones. The first iridescent pieces were produced in the 1880s, and in 1898, the firm showed a major group of iridescent glass in the Vienna Jubilee Exhibition designed by Max von Spaun. Hoffmann, Moser, Prutscher, Peche and Powolny are all known to have designed pieces on commission for the factory, while Loetz executed pieces on commission for the Werkstätte.

Not surprisingly, members of the Werkstätte were involved as designers with most of the leading Austro-Hungarian glass houses at this time, as they were with most of the potteries. Apart from those mentioned in the previous paragraph, other important Werkstätte glass designers included Olbrich, Moser, Wimmer, Löffler, Jutta Sikka, Hilda Jesser, Vally Wieselthier, Reni Schaschl, Mathilde Flögl, Ludwig Jungnickel, Fritzi Löw-Lazar and Julius Zimpel.

Firms for whom the Werkstätte designed, or whom the Werkstätte commissioned to execute their pieces, included Loetz, Meyr's Neffe, Johann Oertel, Ludwig Moser & Söhne, Carl Goldberg and J. & L. Lobmeyr. They also designed pieces made by various glasshouses on commission for the important retailers, Bakalowitz of Vienna.

Of all the major Austrian firms, J. & L. Lobmeyr was considered the most prestigious, followed by Graf Harrach. Both these firms were located in Vienna. Lobmeyr produced table glass of very high quality; they also marketed decorative pieces, including engraved and etched work and superb enamelled pieces in the Middle-Eastern taste, the quality of the enamelling being far superior to that found on similar pieces being produced contemporaneously by Brocard in France.

Around 1910, the firm produced its first pieces designed by members of the Werkstätte. Hoffmann designed what is probably his best known range of decorated glass for Lobmeyr, pieces with opaque black or grey motifs on clear or matt glass, a type of decoration called 'bronzitdecor', which was taken up by other Werkstätte designers, especially Jungnickel. The factory continued to produce new designs by members of the Werkstätte throughout the 1920s and 1930s and even during the Second World War held an exhibition in Vienna which included pieces newly designed by Adolf Loos.

The Harrach glass house is less interesting. In 1898, it exhibited a group of attractive pieces in the Vienna Jubilee Exhibition which were obvious imitations of Tiffany, and in 1900, its display had widened its scope to include cameo glass in the style of Gallé and enamelled pieces decorated with designs after Alphonse Mucha. In 1901, the painter Julius Jelinek became artistic director and he commissioned designs from a number of the leading Czech Secessionists, including Jan Kotěra.

The Wiener Werkstätte was also closely connected with the firm of Ludwig Moser & Söhne of Karlsbad, which had been founded in 1857. Before the First World War, Hoffmann had designed pieces in opaque black or purple glass, faceted or moulded with human figures or foliate decoration.

After the war, other Werkstätte members, including Hilda Jesser, Wimmer, Peche and Zimpel also designed for the firm. Meyr's Neffe, founded originally in 1814, exhibited pieces in the Paris 1900 Exhibition; many of these were iridescent and of Persian shapes. Designers included Moser and Olbrich. In the 1920s, they produced pieces designed by Hoffmann and Moser, and a particularly extensive group by Prutscher. However, by this time they had become part of the Karlsbad Kristallglaswerkshutte of Ludwig Moser & Söhne. Two other firms producing good iridescent and cameo glass were Wilhelm Kralik & Söhne, which until 1881 had been one of the three factories known collectively as Meyr's Neffe, and Pallme-König & Habel.

The firm of Bakalowits in Vienna was the most prestigious retailer of glass, for whom many factories did exclusive work. In the late 1880s, Bakalowits began selling iridescent glass designed by Richard Bakalowits and Kolo Moser, this being made by Loetz. By 1889, they had commissioned designs from a number of younger German artists, including Olbrich, who designed a pair of crystal glass candlesticks. In the Paris 1900 Exhibition, Bakalowits showed pieces designed by Olbrich, Moser and Bertold Löffler, and iridescent glass lamps in curvilinear Art Nouveau metal mounts by Gustav Gurschner. A large group of pieces designed by Moser were shown in an exhibition in London in 1902 organised by *The Studio*.

Kolo Moser himself had spent six months in a glass manufactory before the Werkstätte was formed and had practical experience of production methods. Many of his tableware designs showed the hand of an innovator, his wine glasses, for instance, being made in one piece, as opposed to the usual three-section production. He designed much decorative iridescent glass for Bakalowits which was executed by Loetz, Meyr's Neffe and the Reinische Glashütten

In Germany, there were a number of important Art Nouveau designers, the most significant of whom was probably Karl Koepping. He had trained as a painter and etcher in Munich but began experimenting with glass around 1895. He first took on Friedrich Zitmann, an expert glass blower, to execute his designs, but after a policy disagreement in 1896, his pieces were made by the Grossherzogliche Sachische Fachschule und Lehrwerkstätte für Glasinstrumentmacher und Mechaniker. His tall, spindly pieces, with extraordinary curvilinear stems, were greatly admired and were retailed by Bing in Paris; he also produced elegant and beautifully coloured wine glasses in less outrageous shapes.

Koepping's erstwhile partner Zitmann began producing pieces in a somewhat coarsened version of Koepping's style, which also proved very popular, and around 1897 began making iridescent glass with bubbling and pitting. This was intended to imitate the surface effects of excavated Roman glass, the shapes of which Zitmann also copied exactly. Roman glass of this type was also the inspiration for Tiffany Cypriote glass, first made around 1895–6 (Zitmann may well have been inspired as much by this as by originals), and the Frankfurt firm of P. A. Tacchi was making direct copies of Roman glass with iridescence in the late 1870s. Good Art Nouveau glass was also designed by Desiré Christian for the Meisenthal factory in Lothringia.

The German Seccessionist involvement in glass was not as important as it was in Austria. WMF established a glass factory in 1881, principally to produce the glass liners for its metalwork. However, in 1883 they established a serious factory although the production of art glass did not begin until the 1920s; at this time, they marketed iridescent pieces called Ikora-Kristall and Myra-Kristall.

In the 1920s and 1930s, WMF commissioned designs from, among others, Richard Riemerschmid, Wilhelm Wagenfeld and Paul Haustein.

A collection of Loetz iridescent glass, *c.* 1900.

Above Set of glasses designed by Josef Hoffmann for Lobmeyr, *c.* 1910.

Right Decorated glass beakers designed by Hilda Jesser, *c.* 1920.

Below 'Islamic' enamelled glass vase by Lobmeyr, *c.* 1900.

Below right Two vessels in violet glass, designed by Josef Hoffmann, 1915.

Riemerschmid also designed glass for Ferdinand von Poschinger's Buchenau Glashüttenwerke in Bavaria. This firm produced many examples of Art Nouveau glass around 1900 in different techniques, which owed much to Gallé, Tiffany and Loetz. Another important designer for Buchenau was Betty Hedrich.

A series of tall-stemmed wine glasses produced by the Reinische Glashütten of Cologne around 1900 and similar set by Peill und Söhne datable to around 1910 have been attributed by some writers to Riemerschmid; a glass of the same type is illustrated in the Deutscher Werkbund yearbook for 1912. Some tall simple glass bottles were designed by Behrens around 1898 and may have been made at the glass factory established at Darmstadt, the Grossherzoglichen Hessisches Edelglasmanufaktur. From 1907, this factory was under the directorship of Josef Emil Scheckendorf, a member of the Munich Secession who had exhibited glass with the Vereinigten Werkstätten in 1901.

Another important German glass designer was Wilhelm von Eiff, who had studied briefly under Pankok at Stuttgart in 1913. In 1921, he worked for a short while for a firm established by Stefan Rath, a nephew of the Lobmeyr brothers, at Steinschönau, and in 1922 he became professor of engraving on glass and gemstones at the Stuttgart Kunstgewerbeschule. His engraved glass is of a very high quality, similar in style to that of Orrefors. Glass of the same type was produced by the Sachischen Landesstelle für Kunstgewerbe, designed by Richard Sussmuth, Walter Nitschke, Anton Witt and Imgard Kotte-Weidaner.

In the 1930s, one of the most important designers of glass in Germany was the ex-Bauhaus student Wilhelm Wagenfeld. Glass was not a subject specially taught at the Bauhaus, although Wagenfeld saw, and was obviously influenced by, the glass table wares with metal and wood mounts designed in the metal workshop at Weimar by Krajewski, Tümpel and, most successfully, by Albers.

Wagenfeld remained at the Bauhaus until 1931, after which he became an independent designer specialising in glass and ceramics. In 1932, he designed a fireproof glass tea service for Jenaer Glaswerke Schott und Gen.

This firm had for long been one of the leaders of modern glass in Germany, having produced a simple glass tea service for the Werkbund in 1912 designed by Ilse Decho. If anything, the earlier tea service is of a more satisfactory form, although Wagenfeld's development of heat-resistant glass is of crucial importance. Wagenfeld also designed for the Vereinigte Lausitzer Glaswerke factory, Weisswasser/Oberlausitz, of which he became director, his facet-cut pieces being called Rautenglas; other designs were made for the Rosenthal Porcelain Factory glass division (the actual building for which was designed by Gropius), for the glass division of WMF and for Peill & Putzler. He established the Werkstätte Wagenfeld in 1954 and one of his best-known commissions of recent years was for the cutlery, crockery and trays on Lufthansa airlines. He will probably be remembered as one of the greatest Functionalist architects and interior designers.

Loetz iridescent glass lamp in curvilinear metal mount by Gustav Gurschner, 1900.

Silver, Jewellery and Metalwork

AS WITH FURNITURE, the majority of the members of the main German and Austrian Secessionist groups designed in both precious and base metals, and the Wiener Werkstätte produced a wide range of jewellery, usually designed by Hoffmann, Moser, Prutscher, Czeschka, Peche or Wimmer; known workers (or actual makers) for the Werkstätte included Alfred Meyer, Alfred Wertnik, Konrad and Josef Hessfeld, Adolf Erbrech, Karl Medl, Josef Wagner, Theodor Quereser, Konrad Schindel, Konrad Koch and Karl Ponocny, the last named of whom seems to have made the majority of jewellery designed by Hoffmann and Moser. Another maker was Anton Pribil, who produced many of Czeschka's designs.

The Wiener Werkstätte's metalwork was made in an extraordinary range of styles. This is especially true of Hoffmann's designs. The earliest examples, dating from 1903–4, are often very formal, with simple, very 'modernist' shapes; in some cases, the pieces have a hammered finish. Pieces such as the silver tea service designed in 1904, with its monumental samovar, must rank among the greatest metalwork of the twentieth century. Much of this early work by both Hoffmann and Moser shows the obvious influence of Mackintosh, Ashbee and Van de Velde and, especially in the placement of handles and feet, of Christopher Dresser. Mackintosh's influence can be seen clearly in the open-lattice baskets designed by Hoffmann, which are strongly geometric, and Ashbee's in some flattened covered dishes designed also by Hoffmann and which date from 1908.

The influence of Ashbee on Moser can be seen in a tall stemmed covered cup in silver and lapis-lazuli designed in 1908, and the influence of Dresser most strongly in pieces such as the plain silver sugar bowl of perfectly spherical shape with four smaller spherical feet designed in 1905.

Hoffmann continued to design metalwork throughout his long career. In 1912, he founded the Österreichisches Werkbund and in 1920, he moved more into the realm of industrial design as head of the Gruppe Wien of the Deutscher Werkbund. In the 1920s, he produced many designs of similar monumentality to his prewar pieces but also designed some extraordinary fluted silver, much of which is gilt and some of which reaches the height of neo-Rococo extravagance. He produced many cutlery designs for the Solingen firm of Carl Pott, founded in 1906, and for the last of which he was awarded posthumous gold medals at the Brussels World Fair of 1958 and the Milan Triennale of 1960.

Czeschka also designed some very extravagant silver before the First World War, which is often inset with precious and semi-precious stones and ivory. The inspiration for such pieces seems Romanesque or Byzantine. Wimmer's early style often appears to have a strong Cubist element overlaid with an Expressionist exaggeration of form. This is particularly true of a faceted silver tea service designed in 1912.

In Germany, there was much very ornate Art Nouveau metalwork, especially by firms such as J. P. Kayser Söhne of Krefeld, who manufactured a wide range of pewter under the trade name Kayser-Zinn from 1874, and the Württembergische Metallwarenfabrik or WMF, which was founded in Geislingen in 1853 by Daniel Straub. Around 1900, under the directorship of Carl Haegele, WMF produced some of the most outrageously curvilinear Art Nouveau metalwork, usually in either pewter or nickle-silver, and often with green glass liners, to be found anywhere in Europe. The designer Hugo Leven was responsible for the finest Kayser-Zinn, while Beyschlag was the chief designer for WMF.

Several other firms produced interesting pewter, including the Metallwaren-Fabrik Eduard Hueck of Lüdenschied which founded in 1864 and which employed around 100 workers by 1900. The firm commissioned work from many of the leading Secessionists, including Peter Behrens, Josef Maria Olbrich and Albin Müller, the last named of whom had gone to Darmstadt in 1906, where he remained for the rest of his career. In Cologne, the Kunstgewerbliche Metallwaren-Fabrik H. Feith and A. Floch produced interesting designs under the trade-name Electra and in Nuremburg, an historic centre for the production of pewter, was the Kunstgewerbliche Metallwaren-Fabrik Orion of G. F. Schmidt and Friedrich Adler. The Weihlund had its own pewter workshop at Helltrau, designers of which included K. Kretschmer, Karl Kross, Konrad Hentschel, Paul Hanstein and Wolfgang von Wevin. Much good Art Nouveau jewellery was produced under Georg Kleemann at the Staatliche Fachschule für Edelmetall at Pforzheim.

Other commercial firms producing Art Nouveau silver and plate include M. H. Wilkens & Söhne of Bremen, founded in 1810. In the early years of the present century, they made ornate pieces designed by Heinrich Vogeler, and also simpler pieces by Behrens and Müller. Another Bremen firm, Koch & Bergfeld, employed many designers in its own studio and outside designers included Hugo Leven and Albin Müller. One of

Below Silver-gilt tea service designed by Josef Hoffmann, 1904.

Bottom left Silver teapot, sugar bowl and milk jug, designed by Henry van de Velde, 1903.

Bottom right Pewter tea service designed by Hugo Leven for J. P. Kayser Söhne of Krefeld and marked with the trade name of Kayser-Zinn, c. 1900.

Right WMF silvered metal liqueur set, *c.* 1900.

Below right Jewellery designed by Josef Hoffmann, *c.* 1904.

Below far right Edelzinn pewter jug designed by Josef Maria Olbrich, 1901.

the largest and most important firms was P. Bruckmann & Söhne of Heilbronn, which had been founded in 1805. Designers included Behrens, Friedrich Adler, Paul Haustein, Josef Emanuel Margold, Franz Borès, Rudolf Rochga, George Roehmer and Bernhard Wenig. Bruckmann was also one of the major industrial firms to produce the designs of the Deutscher Werkbund.

The range of metalwork designed by Behrens for AEG should not be forgotten in this context; around 1900 Behrens also designed several ranges of cutlery for the firm of M. J. Rückert of Mainz, as did Richard Riemerschmid. The latter's designs tend to be simpler than those of Behrens, which retained strong elements of curvilinearity.

Possibly the most impressive of metalwork designers active in Germany in the first half of the twentieth century was Henry van de Velde. His early silver is in a style which can perhaps be described as 'geometric-curvilinear'; it may be compared to some of the earliest designs of Georg Jensen. A particularly fine group of Van de Velde's silver is in the Zürich Kunstgewerbemuseum and is of exceptional quality; the majority of it was made by the Grand-Duke's court jewellers at Weimar, Hans and Wilhelm Müller, or by Van de Velde's pupil Albert Feinauer.

Right Bronze lamp with nautilus shell by Gustav Gurschner, 1900.

Left High silver vase decorated with lapis-lazuli (1908) and spherical silver sugar bowl (1905), designed by Koloman Moser.

Below Brass ebony and silver teapot produced by Marianne Brandt at the Bauhaus workshop, *c.* 1924.

One of the most distinctive German silversmiths in the early part of the century was Ernst Riegel who worked at Darmstadt between 1906 and 1912, after which he became head of the Staatliche Werkschule in Cologne. He designed much ecclesiastical silver in an ornate, monumental style, which seemed to owe much to Byzantine or medieval models.

The inter-war years saw few noteworthy developments in the design of German metalwork except at the Bauhaus. The firm of Treusch in Leipzig produced pieces influenced by French designers and by Jensen, and a few individuals, such as Bettina Krumbholtz, who was also active in Leipzig, made simple items often embellished with enamelling.

The metalworkshop at the Bauhaus was started at Weimar by a craftsman called Kopka; he proved unsuitable, however, and his place as master of craft or technical supervisor was taken by Christian Dell. The masters of form were Johannes Itten from 1919 to 1923 and László Moholy-Nagy until 1928; after the latter date, the workshop was incorporated into the Department of Interior Design, although Wilhelm Wagenfeld was placed in charge of metalwork production. From its earliest days, the metal workshop had a number of extremely gifted pupils, including Otto Rittweger, K. J. Jucker, Wolfgang Tümpel, Wolfgang Rössiger, Friedrich Marby, Josef Knau, Marianne Brandt, Josef Albers and Wagenfeld himself. Many of the best Bauhaus designs are associated with the names of Jucker, Brandt and Wagenfeld, the last named of whom subsequently became one of the most important industrial designers in Germany, his work in glass being particularly significant.

The earliest products of the Bauhaus workshop were not far removed from that of a normal craft studio, being principally in precious metals. This ceased after Moholy-Nagy took charge, and from

Below Silver duck on stand with semi-precious stones, designed by Ernest Riegel, *c.* 1910.

Right 'Flame Leaper', figure in ivory and metal by Frederick Preiss, *c.* 1930.

then on most of the things were designed in either nickel-silver or brass, often with black ebony handles. A style soon became evident in the wide range of domestic wares – teapots, kettles, tea set – a style based on the sphere, hemisphere and cylinder. Within this apparently limiting formula, designers such as Rittweger and above all Brandt produced pieces of extraordinary elegance, yet well suited to industrial production.

Another principal function of the metalworkshop was the designing of interior fittings, notably lamps and various lights. The light-fixtures designed at the Bauhaus did become one of the school's most valuable commercial assets. Extremely elegant examples designed by Marianne Brandt, Hans Przyrembel and Karl Jucker were industrially produced by a number of firms, including Schwintzer & Graff and Körting & Matthiesson, the latter marketing the Kandem range.

Attached to the metal workshop was a jewellery workshop which was run autonomously by Naum Slutzky; not surprisingly, it ceased to exist after Moholy-Nagy assumed overall responsibility for Bauhaus metalwork. Slutzky's extremely functional pieces – he designed a ring with a setting which enabled the stone to be changed at will – have had considerable influence, especially on Scandinavian jewellery design, during the years since the Second World War.

Weaving

WEAVING and later wallpapers were two of the most commercially successful fields of Bauhaus production. One of the principal departures of the Bauhaus weaving style was its rejection of the pictorial mode which had dominated late nineteenth-century and Art Nouveau hangings, the majority of which were in traditional tapestry weave. Many of the Bauhaus weavings were designed under the influence of Paul Klee, who took a particular interest in the workshop, but while these and other 'artist' designed pieces show a strong individualism, they are all in abstract patterning.

The products of the weaving workshop can be divided into four groups – individual pieces, commissioned works, series designs made in quantity at the Bauhaus itself and, fourthly, prototypes for industrial mass-production. The workshop was taken over by Gunta Stölzl in 1927 (she had been a Bauhaus student), followed by Anni Albers in 1931, and finally by Lilly Reich in 1932. These three, and other talented designers, including Lies Dienhardt, Martha Erps, Gertrud Hautschk, Ruth Hollos, Benita Otte and particularly Otti Berger all produced splendid work. Firms which produced Bauhaus textiles included Poly-textil Gesellschaft of Berlin and Pausa of Stuttgart. Wallpapers were produced by Rasch in 1930–1.

Above Woven silk tapestry made by Anni Albers at the Bauhaus weaving workshop by Anni Albers, 1926.

Left Cotton carpet designed for a nursery by Benita Otte at the Bauhaus, 1923.

Belgium

by Philippe Garner

Belgian design 1890–1940

BELGIUM, PERHAPS MORE than any other country, in the period 1890–1940, shows the very direct influence on the decorative arts of prevailing political circumstances. In the years before the First World War, under the kingship of Leopold II, Belgium enjoyed a strong and flourishing economy, backed by the wealth in natural resources of her extensive colonies. This new prosperity which was reflected around 1900 in the wealth of Belgian creativity and the strength of her luxury crafts, emerged from a period of considerable social unrest in the 1880s. After the fall of Belgium's Liberal government in 1884, the working class had rallied in 1885 under the banner of the Parti Ouvrier Belge and there had followed a disruptive succession of riots and strike threats.

After 1886, the Belgian socialist cause attracted the support of a number of middle-class liberal intellectuals, professional men such as the lawyer Max Hallet, who were to play a crucial role in the economic growth of the country and also in the conversion to the socialist cause of young artists, architects and designers. They created a rational link between their own socialist ideals and the emergent theories of design that were to harden into a version of Art Nouveau that was propagated and flourished as a truly socialist art, 'L'art du peuple'.

The principles of William Morris thus came to fruition in Belgium whilst failing to have any profound effect in his own country in the somewhat misguided realities of the British Arts and Crafts Movement. Max Hallet and his like-minded colleagues Jules Destrée and Emile Vandervelde formed close links with Henry van de Velde, perhaps Belgium's most important theorist and designer during the 1890s, and it was as a result of their lobbying that the Parti Ouvrier Belge was persuaded to employ the revolutionary architect Victor Horta to create their Maison du Peuple, built between 1895 and 1899. Despite Horta's protest that his selection as architect for the project was not political, the building stood as a monument to the democratisation of the Belgian applied and decorative arts.

The avant-garde of Belgian art had first manifested itself in the 1880s. Octave Maus, a spokesman for the movement, founded his progressive journal, *L'Art Moderne,* in 1881, whilst the most progressive artists formed themselves into the Groupe des Vingt in 1884 under the guidance of Maus. Les Vingt involved themselves at first in the promotion and exhibition of the avant-garde in the fine arts and showed works by Redon, Seurat, Lautrec, Gauguin, Cézanne, Van Gogh and others. The election to their ranks in 1888 of Henry van de Velde marked the beginning of their involvement in the applied arts, which they exhibited after 1891 at the annual salons alongside examples of the fine arts. In 1894 the group reformed as the Libre Esthétique and, at their first salon, the designer Gustave Serrurier-Bovy exhibited a complete range of domestic furnishings.

The Libre Esthétique formed the backbone of Belgian ideological Art Nouveau, embracing notably the work of Van de Velde, Serrurier-Bovy and Horta and reflecting both the principles of pioneer designer Viollet-le-Duc and the English theorists, and the prevalent stylistic preoccupations with Japanese art and with organic form. The import of Japanese artifacts into Belgium, as in England and France, can be traced back to the 1860s and notably to the opening of La Maison Japonaise in Brussels in 1866. Serrurier-Bovy retailed imported Japanese wares through his decorating business, opened in Liège in 1884. The crystalisation during the 1890s of these various elements combined with the rich and fertile thread of symbolism running through art and design, made turn of the century Belgium a major international centre for the arts.

The tide began to turn in the early years of the century. Van de Velde moved to Weimar where, in 1906, he supervised the foundation of the Kunstgewerbeschule. A new generation of designers came very strongly under the influence of the Austrian Secession style and turned their backs on Belgium's own dynamic organic style. In so doing they sacrificed Belgian independence and it seems a highly appropriate symbol of this new lead from Austria that one of Josef Hoffmann's major achievements, the Palais Stoclet, should have been commissioned by a Belgian and built between 1905 and 1911 in Brussels. The circumstances of the First World War made the Belgian arts the victims of political factors just as, in the 1890's, political factors had helped revitalise the applied arts. After 1918 Belgium became a follower rather than a leader in the applied arts; her foremost architects, men such as René Braem and L.-H. de Koninck, showed a very strong debt to the Viennese school; French decorating firms such as Dominique found a market for their designs; it is symptomatic that Herbert Hoffman's seminal 1930 study of international modern interiors devotes only two pages to Belgian designs, illustrating two uninspired Modernist Brussels interiors, one by Victor Bourgeois, the other interior by L.-H. de Koninck.

Left The dining room of the Hotel Solvay, designed by Victor Horta and constructed between 1894 and 1898.

Above Interior by the architect L.–H. de Koninck, 1930.

Below Dining room of a house in the Hague designed by Henry van de Velde, 1898.

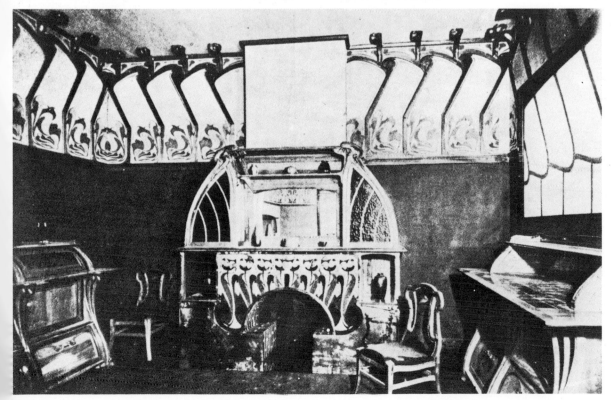

Above Wooden chair by Henry van de Velde, 1898.

Above right Interior of the Paris shop, La Maison Moderne, designed by Henry van de Velde for Julius Meier-Graefe in 1898.

Right Two women's gowns designed by Henry van de Velde, 1900.

Furniture and interiors

Belgium's foremost designers of the Art Nouveau period were architects of total environment, concerned with every aspect of design from architectural structure to the smallest details of furnishings and domestic utensils. Henry van de Velde took this to the extreme of designing the clothes to be worn in his interiors. Their schemes can be compared, despite superficial national distinctions of style, to the concepts of Hector Guimard in Paris, Charles Rennie Mackintosh in Glasgow and Josef Hoffmann in Vienna.

Henri van de Velde was perhaps the most versatile Belgian designer of his generation and the influence of his theories were to help shape the direction of European design through the first quarter of the twentieth century. A self-taught architect, Van de Velde had started his career as a painter working in a broad graphic style reminiscent of Maurice Denis and showing the strong influence of Japanese wood blocks. He expounded and published his theories of design and put them into practice when he designed and fitted out his own home, Bloemenwerf, at Uccle in 1894, achieving an organic whole that made it the embodiment of his principles and a landmark of modern design. Van de Velde's use of robust organic lines,

abstracting not the entire plant form, but only the essential stem from nature, created a distinctive new style. The commissions received by Van de Velde to create four room settings for Bing's Maison de L'Art Nouveau in 1895 and to design Julius Meier-Graefe's influential Paris shop La Maison Moderne in 1898 are evidence enough of its success. The tobacco shop designed by Van de Velde in 1898 in Berlin for the International Havana Company is a perfect example of his fully-developed Art Nouveau style. There is a sense of total unity between the dynamic abstract rhythms of the furniture, the fitted cabinets and woodwork and the stencilled wall decorations.

Victor Horta underwent a formal training as an architect and became a fervent disciple of Viollet-le-Duc's principles of structural honesty. Although his Maison du Peuple served as his most perfect credo, Horta was at his best in the design of private houses with few budgetary restrictions. Like Van de Velde, he conceived both structure and furnishings and, like Van de Velde, he made full use of the abstract curving line. Horta's style was more lush, however, than that of Van de Velde and could create an ambiance of luxury which one does not associate with the more spartan 'honesty' of Van de Velde's furniture and interiors. Horta

Far left The dining room of the Horta House in Brussels, begun in 1898.

Top right Detail of the dining room door moulding.

Above Entrance hall of the Emile Tassel House, by Victor Horta, 1893.

Left Fireplace in the Van Eetvelde house designed by Victor Horta from 1895-7.

was at his peak for a period of some ten years which began with his design of a home for the engineer Emile Tassel in 1893.

Horta's interiors were full of light and the vitality of his ever-present patterns of whiplash curves never detracted from the sense of space which he always conveyed. The metal structure of his interiors was laid bare, but Horta's skill was such that the structure itself came to play a role within the decorative concept of the whole, its lines echoed in the metal whiplashes of light fittings and furniture, in the graphics of window-leading or mural decoration. Horta's masterpiece was his Hôtel Solvay, constructed between 1894 and 1898. His major works include the Van Eetvelde house of 1895-7, his own home, now the Musée Horta, undertaken in 1898, the Aubecq house of 1899-1902 and the house commissioned by Max Hallet in 1902.

Paul Hankar was amongst the more talented of the second rank of Belgian architect-designers working in the shadow of Horta and Van de Velde. He designed homes for a number of artists including a villa for his friend Philippe Wolfers in 1900. Others worthy of note are Paul Saintenoy, Gustave Strauven, a former apprentice chez Horta, Emile van Aberveke and Paul Vizzavona.

Aside from the architect-decorators, the most important furniture designer and decorator was Gustave Serrurier-Bovy. A true product of his age, brought up on the teachings of Viollet-le-Duc and the English Arts and Crafts Movement, Serrurier-Bovy devised a personal, honest style of furniture design in the early 1890s akin to that of Van de Velde and characterised by simple yet emphatic organic lines. He exhibited at the London Arts and Crafts Exhibition in 1896 and at the Paris Salon du Champ de Mars between 1896 and 1903, and, in 1899, opened a factory at Liège for the large-scale manufacture of his designs.

Glass

In the *arts du feu* Belgium's foremost factories in the period 1890-1940 were the glassworks of Val-Saint-Lambert and the Kéramis potteries founded by the Boch family in 1841. With both ceramics and glass, as with other areas of the applied arts in Belgium, it was only before the First World War that production was inventive and worthy of international attention. The successful growth of the Val-Saint-Lambert works dated back to the formation in 1826 of the Société Anonyme des Verreries et Cristalleries du Val-Saint-Lambert. By 1890 the works were featuring prominently in international exhibitions and, during the period 1890-1910, under the artistic direction of Léon Ledru, produced a wide variety of exciting glass-ware ranging from the functionalist pieces designed by Van de Velde to more elaborate coloured and decorated glass showing the influence of innovations made by Emile Gallé in Nancy.

The Kéramis works enjoyed the benefit of the creative directorship of Alfred William Finch for a brief period between 1890 and 1893. Finch, a painter, had been a founder member of Les Vingt and, in 1891, included Kéramis ceramics in the group's Salon. He injected a new vitality into Belgian pottery design and the wares made under his direction reflect the prevailing avant-garde taste for simple graphic motifs abstracted from nature. It is a typical reflection of the international stature of pre-First World War Belgian decorative art that Finch's ceramics were retailed in one of the most adventurous shops in Paris, La Maison Moderne. The Vermeren-Coché potteries, around 1900, made a series of stoneware masks inspired from Belgian folklore after models by the sculptor Isidore de Rudder.

Metalwork and jewellery

Only during the first phase of the period 1890-1940 did Belgium produce any designers or craftsmen of note in the area of metalwork, silver, jewellery and decorative sculpture. Belgium's most distinguished craftsman-designer of the Art Nouveau period, whose work is comparable in quality to the best contemporary French creations and whose technical versatility compares with that of René Lalique, is Philippe Wolfers.

Wolfers was born into a family of jewellers and learned the skills of the craft in his father's workshop. During the 1880s he worked on pieces in eighteenth-century taste before evolving a personal style in the early 1890s. Along with others of his generation he turned to nature for inspiration, stylising plant forms in a manner that betrayed the debt to Japan. Wolfers used plant, animal and human forms in his jewellery designs which were often given extra piquancy by their Symbolist allusions. His jewels could include such details as a medusa mask in carved ivory and gold with staring opal cabochon eyes or a carved ivory nude restrained by gold serpents. Another jewel, for example, a pendant entitled *La Nuit* of 1899, incorporates a naked figure carved in carnelian, with enamelled butterfly wings. Wolfers was a master of the techniques of enamelling and used the *plique-à-jour* process that was enjoying such a vogue in Paris. He favoured unusual contrasts of materials and exploited the colours and irregularities of semi-precious stones. He designed models to be cast in bronze, elaborate contorted Art Nouveau silver mounts for glass vases from the Cristalleries du Val-Saint-Lambert and silver vessels to be richly decorated with enamels. After 1904 he abandoned jewellery to concentrate on the extraordinary multi-media sculpture in which he had started to specialise during the 1890s.

A regular feature in Wolfers' scuplture and in the work of other Belgian decorative sculptors after 1893 was the incorporation of carved ivory. The vogue was encouraged by King Leopold II after the first importation of ivory from the Belgian Congo in 1893. Leopold made gifts of ivory to a group of prominent sculptors and craftsmen and the earliest results of this sponsorship were exhibited at the Exposition Universelle held in Antwerp in 1894. Examples of such work include the symbolist bust, *Sphinx Mystérieux*, of 1897 by Charles van der Stappen; *Orchidée*, Arthur Craco's fluid sculpture in ivory and gilt-bronze of 1894, originally included in the 1894 Antwerp exhibition, and the extraordinary candlestick conceived by Franz Hoosemans as a carved ivory figure of a woman entwined in giant thistles.

Henry van de Velde's dynamic graphic style was well adapted to the design of a variety of metalwork from luxury silverware to the more functional objects that were to become a more major preoccupation during his years in Germany. The design of silver jewellery allowed the opportunity for the unrestrained exercise of his principles of dynamic rhythm and interplays of organic lines and forms. His metalwork masterpiece is perhaps the electro-plated candelabrum exhibited at the Libre Esthétique in the late 1890s and purchased in 1900 by the Musées Royaux d'Art et d'Histoire. In its total synthesis between form, function and decoration this object can be cited as a perfect resolution of the stylistic and theoretical problems which Art Nouveau designers sought to resolve. Van de Velde's designs for domestic metalware ranged from elegant flatware to somewhat cumbersome stoves. Horta and Serrurier-Bovy designed metal furniture and fittings as part of their total vision as *ensembliers*. In future, designers were not to see their artifacts singly, as isolated objects, but as part of a total planned environment.

The architect Antoine Pompe produced a series of designs around 1900 for metal tableware, ironwork and jewellery in a refined Art Nouveau style, but his concepts were never executed. Fernand Dubois created silverware and other luxury objects in a more naturalistic version of Art Nouveau. He had been the pupil of Charles van der Stappen and became a friend of Horta who built a house for him between 1901 and 1906. Like so many other leading Belgian designers he regularly incorporated carved ivory into the works he exhibited at the Libre Esthétique between 1894 and 1899.

Amongst the few exponents of the luxury crafts in Belgium after the First World War was Philippe Wolfers' son Marcel who became an accomplished artist in lacquer. He experimented with the medium on vases and other vessels of simple traditional Oriental forms, achieving unusual effects of texture, unusual natural patternings and added refinements of gilding and mother-of-pearl inlays.

Above Henry van de Velde's electro-plated candelabrum, late 1890s.

Left Lacquered pot and cover by Marcel Wolfers, 1920s.

Right Ivory and bronze head by Julien Dillens, *c.* 1895.

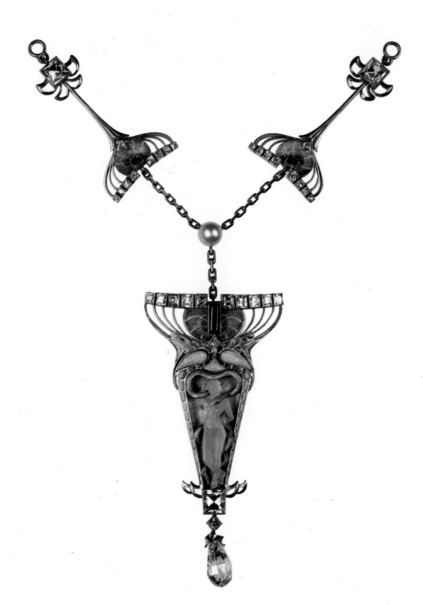

Graphics

Belgian graphics were dominated around the turn of the century by a decorative Art Nouveau style that showed strong affinites with the Paris style as epitomised by Alphonse Mucha. Foremost of the Belgian artists in this decorative vein was Privat-Livemont. He had studied in Paris and returned to Belgium in 1889 to work as a decorator. His first commission to design a poster came in 1890 from the Cercle Artistique de Schaerbeek and during the nineties he showed his strength in such posters as those for 'Absinthe' 'Robette' designed in 1896, 'Bec Auer' of the same year, 'Cacao Van Houten' of 1897 and 'Café Rajah' of 1899. Privat-Livemont's style used themes very similar to those of Mucha, notably Art Nouveau women with arabesques of stylised hair, and as a result he has been accused of plagiarism. However, the two artists evolved independently and Privat-Livemont's graphic motifs and colour schemes were distinctive and personal. The craze for collecting posters developed in Belgium as it did in Paris and the leading retailer, Dietrich, would supply collectors with the work of the foremost designers who included Privat-Livemont, Victor Mignot, Henri Meunier, Adolphe Crespin and Fernand Toussaint. Meunier's style was strong, simple and confident, as can be seen at its best in his poster *Rajah* of 1897. Crespin is perhaps best remembered for his association with the architect Hankar for whom he designed a poster in 1894. Theo van Rysselberghe was a close friend of Octave Maus and figured prominently in Les Vingt and the Libre Esthétique, designing several of their exhibition posters. Armand Rassenfosse founded the *Caprice Revue* with Emile Berchmanns and Auguste Donnay and all three exhibited their graphics at the Libre Esthétique. Perhaps the most significant Belgian poster, certainly the most characteristically Belgian, was Henry van de Velde's 'Tropon' of 1898.

Above 'Eve', a pendant designed in 1901 by Philippe Wolfers; opals, diamonds, emeralds and pearls set on gold.

Right Lithograph by Privat-Livemont, 1900.

Opposite The 'Tropon' poster by Henry van de Velde, 1898.

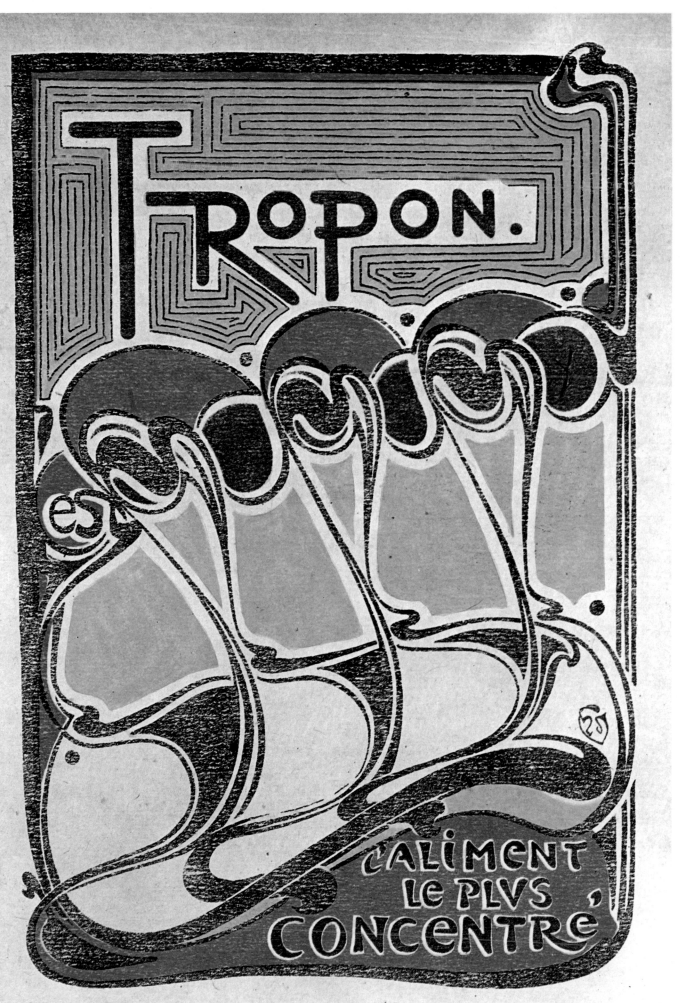

The Netherlands

by Gillian Naylor

The 1890s in the Netherlands

THE IMPETUS FOR DESIGN innovation and reform in Holland, as in most West European countries, stemmed partly from the expansion of trade and industry during the nineteenth century and partly from the activities of a growing and articulate architectural profession. Throughout the period under review, Dutch architects were active as designers, theorists and teachers, demanding and achieving standards appropriate to their various philosophies of form and structure.

The first attempts to examine and establish standards for applied design, for example, came in the 1870s, when the architect P. H. J. Cuypers began working on two important commissions in Amsterdam – the Rijksmuseum (1876–85), which now houses an important collection of Dutch Art Nouveau, and the Central Station (1886–9). Soon after he had started work on the Rijksmuseum, Cuypers, who had studied under the French architect and theorist Viollet-le-Duc, founded the Quellinus school (named after a seventeenth-century Flemish sculptor) in order to train the craftsmen needed for work on the museum; and in 1881 he established two further museum schools: the Rijksnormaalschool voor Teekenonderwijzers, to train drawing teachers, and an Arts and Crafts School (Rijksschool voor Kunstniverheid).

These schools helped to fulfil a need for professional training that had been growing more acute in Holland during the nineteenth century, and were the first of many similar organisations, societies and associations that were founded from the 1870s onwards in order to promote better standards in design, architecture and craftsmanship. In 1871, for example, the Association for the Promotion of Industrial and Handcrafts (Vereeniging tot Bevorderung van Fabrieks-en Hand-nijverheid) had organised an exhibition in Amsterdam on the theme of 'Art applied to Industry', with such disastrous results that in that same year a Museum of Industrial Art was founded in Haarlem. In 1893, several architects who had worked in Cuypers' office (including K. P. C. de Bazel, J. M. L. Lauweriks and J. M. de Groot launched the *Architectura et Amicitia* society, which brought together artists working in various fields; and in 1904 V. A. N. K., the influential Dutch Society of Arts and Crafts (Nederlandsche Vereeniging voor Ambacts-en Nijverheidskunst), was set up in order to combat what was felt to be the 'pernicious' influence of Art Nouveau.

For by this time Art Nouveau, inspired by Belgian precedent, was spreading throughout Holland; and its forms, as well as its philosophy, ran counter to the social and aesthetic ideals established by the Dutch design reformers, ideals which were reinforced by the work and theory of that remarkable and frequently underestimated architect, H. P. Berlage.

Berlage, like Cuypers, was not trained in Holland, and had studied at the Institute of Technology in Zurich, in the department of architecture founded by Gottfried Semper. Although Semper had left Zurich four years before Berlage began to study there, his influence, naturally enough, still predominated. From Semper, Berlage inherited the conviction that architecture aspires to order and objectivity, and that 'style' is determined by structure, which itself is determined by materials and purpose. Semper's thesis, elaborated in his seminal book *Der Stil in den technischen und tektonischen Kunsten* (1860–3), that man-made forms, like natural forms, should be determined by the logic of fitness, function and adaptability, was reinforced in Berlage's case, by the latter's study of contemporary botanists and zoologists, most notably Ernst Haeckel, whose book, *Kunstformen der Natur*, published in 1899, drew analogies between fine art and craft forms and natural forms in marine organisms. Again a further, and in view of subsequent developments, influential dimension was added to Berlage's theory through his preoccupation with Hegelian philosophies, which convinced him of the necessity for 'style', which he defined as the essence, rather than the appearance of architecture. So that Berlage, a Utopian Socialist in the tradition of Ruskin and Morris, campaigned through his work and writing, for the demonstration of a new philosophy of form: a universal 'style' in art, architecture and design that would reflect as well as promote the achievement of social and aesthetic harmony.

Such a style, however, could not, in Berlage's opinion, encompass the vagaries and eccentricities of Art Nouveau which, at the turn of the century, were being promoted by disciples of Henry van de Velde, the Belgian painter turned architect, designer and theorist. In 1898, for example, J. Thorn Prikker, the Symbolist painter (who also worked as an interior designer, producing wallpapers and fabrics, including batik work), and Chris Wegerif, a furniture designer, had opened Arts and Crafts, a shop in The Hague, which, in spite of its British name, sold furniture and objets d'art which Berlagian theorists condemned as 'unhealthy'.

In 1900 Berlage opened t'Binnenhuis, his own

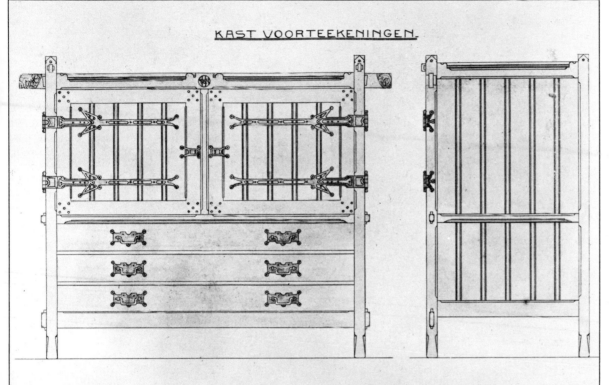

KAST VOORTEEKENINGEN.

Above left Cabinet
by H. P. Berlage, *c.* 1900.
Above Chair designed by
H. P. Berlage *c.* 1904.
Below Linen damask,
by Chris Lebeau, *c.* 1895.

shop in Amsterdam, in order to sell furniture and furnishings designed to demonstrate his belief in the demonstration of structure and truth to materials. His approach to furniture design, which was derived from Semper's *Der Stil*, and which anticipates that of Gerrit Rietveld, was defined in *Over Stijl in bouw-en meubelkunst* (On Style in Architecture and Furniture Design) published in Amsterdam in 1904: 'A piece of furniture', he wrote, 'consists of the composition of parts into a firm whole, of which the parts serve as a framework for the panelling.'

The influence of Berlage on subsequent generations in Holland is obvious; for on the one hand the De Stijl group inherited his preoccupation with the structure and symbolism of space and form, while the Amsterdam School, also working in the 1920s, shared his confident demonstration of materials and texture.

Dutch design 1890–1920

At the same time, however, the achievements of the Dutch Art Nouveau designers, in spite of contemporary condemnation, were remarkable, not only for their invention and refinement, but for their demonstration of a specifically national variant of the style. Art Nouveau elements,

Above 'Delftsche Slaolie' poster by Jan Toorop, 1895.

Right 'Narcissus' design for fabric, by Michel Duco Crop, 1890.

Far right Vase by the Zuid Holland Pottery at Gouda, *c.* 1900.

predictably enough, first began to appear in the work of Dutch Symbolist painters, most notably Thorn Prikker and Jan Toorop who were both associated with the Belgian Les Vingt group; and Art Nouveau tendencies in graphic design and illustration were re-inforced following an exhibition of British graphic art in The Hague in 1893. Toorop, for example produced his famous posters for 'Delftsche Slaolie' in 1895, and these designs, with their tense line, and obsessively two-dimensional vitality, demonstrate a quality of abstraction unique in Art Nouveau graphic design at that time.

A similar abstraction is also evident in Dutch textile design during this period, and a source for these exotic and proto-expressionist patterns can no doubt be traced to Holland's long-established trading links with Java and Indonesia. Dutch traders had, of course, been bringing in work from the colonies in the East Indies since the late sixteenth century; as in other European countries, however, the Art Nouveau renaissance in Holland prompted a new interest in the work of alien cultures (most notably of course, as far as France, England and Austria were concerned, in Japan), and during the last decades of the nineteenth century, several Dutch designers and textile manufacturers 'rediscovered' Javanese batik work, on the one hand experimenting with the traditional craft methods, and on the other adapting and simplifying the complex processes involved for mass-production. Thorn Prikker, for example, produced batik-inspired work for the Arts and Crafts shop in The Hague, and Agatha Wegerif-Gravesteyn, the wife of Chris Wegerif, also experimented with batik in their workshops in Apeldoorn. Several other leading designers, most notably Theodorus Colenbrander, C. A. Lion Cachet, the architect K. P. C. de Bazel and Juriaan Kok also worked in batik, while Michel Duco Crop designed machine-printed textiles for P. F. van Vlissingen & Co. of Helmond in the 1890s; dress fabrics, damasks and moquettes were also produced, those by Jaap Gidding and Jacob Jongert for Leo Schellens of Eindhoven being characteristic of Dutch Expressionist design in the 1920s.

Dutch ceramics, glass and silverware were also remarkable for their variety and invention at the turn of the century. The most celebrated designer specialising in ceramics during this period was Th. A. C. Colenbrander who, in spite of Berlage's dismissal of him as a 'craftsman of little importance', produced a wide range of unique and individual designs throughout his career. His bizarre and delicate work for the Rozenburg pottery in The Hague is well known, and towards the end of his life he designed an equally idiosyncratic collection for the Ram pottery at Arnhem – work which is distinguished by its flame-like and abstract patterning. Juriaan Kok, J. Schellink and R. Sterken also worked for Rozenburg. Other potteries which produced interesting work during this period include that of Wed N. Brantjes at Purmerende, the Zuid Holland at Gouda and the Amstelhoek factory, the latter introduced designs by C. J. van der Hoef at the turn of the century: vases etc, decorated with simple, almost naive, geometric patterns a

Top Tea-set designed by Juriaan Kok for the Rozenburg pottery in the Hague, 1903.

Above Clock by L. W. Nieuwenhuis, c. 1904.

Above right Rozenburg eggshell earthenware vase, c. 1900.

complete antithesis to the sophisticated delicacy of Rozenburg. Among Dutch silversmiths, Jan Eissenlöffel was probably the most inventive, but Frans Zwollo and the architect Johannes Lauweriks also worked in silver, while Berlage and de Bazel designed glassware, the latter for Leerdam.

In comparison with contemporary work in Belgium and France, Dutch furniture design at the turn of the century seems sober, restrained and even monumental, the designers achieving richness and variety from their choice of materials and decoration, rather than from plasticity of form. Dutch bourgeois traditions no doubt influenced design in this area, as well as that respect for sound construction and the honest use of materials recommended by Cuypers and Berlage. The work of Chris Wegerif, for example, for the Arts and Crafts shop in The Hague, has hardly a hint of mannerism, and is reminiscent of that of Voysey, while that of Gerrit Wilhelm Dijsselhof obviously also derives some inspiration from English Arts and Crafts achievements. Dijsselhof designed this furniture for a private client, Dr. van Hoorn, and much of the 'luxury' furniture produced during this period was for special commissions. The Rijksmuseum, for example, has furniture designed by Th. W. Nieuwenhuis, and C. A. Lion Cachet who were working for Van Wisselingh of Amsterdam. The most prestigious of these pieces were for Th. G. Deutz van Schaik, who had a house on the Frederiksplein in Amsterdam.

There is a direct stylistic link between this furniture, with its sobriety of form and richness of decoration, and that produced by the Amsterdam school designers and architects of the 1920s. For the design philosophy of architects such as Michel de Klerk and Piet Kramer was derived as much from the Art Nouveau stress on individualism and experiment, as from Berlage's demonstration of

the nature of materials. So that while the Dutch variant of Art Deco is as lively, idiosyncratic and inventive as its French equivalent, Dutch design in the 1920s was motivated by an ideal of social purpose rather than the demonstration of luxury, 'taste', and conspicuous consumption.

De Stijl and after

A very different interpretation and demonstration of the ideal of social purpose in design, however, was developing in Holland during the First World War, based on concepts of form and commitment that were also derived from the theories of Berlage. For the De Stijl group of architects and designers, who issued their first manifesto in November 1918, believed that art, architecture and design should aspire to universality rather than individuality, and that a universal 'style' was, in fact, emerging, that would both symbolise and precipitate universal harmony.

The initiator and most articulate member of the group was Theo van Doesburg who edited the *De Stijl* magazine from its inception in 1917 until his death in 1931. Van Doesburg was trained as a painter, but in the period immediately prior to the First World War, he worked as an art critic, reporting on the activities of the European avant-garde in various Dutch magazines and newspapers. The revelation of the work and philosophy of the painter Piet Mondrian, however, convinced him that universality and objectivity were attainable in design and architecture as well as painting. (Mondrian, who had been working in Paris, returned to Holland just before the outbreak of the 1914–18 war, and was painting his *Pier and Ocean* series at Scheveningen when Van Doesburg encountered him and his work.) This conviction was reinforced by his discovery of the contemporary work of architects such as J. J. P. Oud, Jan Wils and Robert van t'Hoff, who were all designing buildings with strongly stressed horizontals and

Right Chair by C. A. Lion Cachet, *c.* 1904.

Far right Armchair designed by M. de Klerk, *c.* 1913.

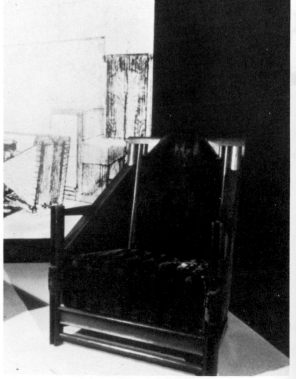

verticals. (Wils and van t'Hoff returned from the States just before the war with first-hand knowledge and photographs of the work of Frank Lloyd Wright, while Oud came back from Germany, renouncing his former Arts and Crafts allegiances for what he described as 'Cubist' architecture.)

The De Stijl belief that progress and perfection, on both a material and metaphysical level, could be demonstrated by means of the new formal and spatial harmonies made possible by the use of materials such as steel, concrete and glass, was of course, shared by designers and architects in France, Germany and Russia, and Van Doesburg travelled widely throughout Europe in the 1920s, exchanging ideas with other like-minded theorists. By 1925, for example, De Stijl had an international membership, Van Doesburg having recruited campaigners from Russia, Austria and the Bauhaus.

The most remarkable and influential of the De Stijl designers, however, was Gerrit Rietveld, a carpenter by training, who studied architecture in evening classes and who designed two of the most famous 'icons' of the Modern Movement: the Red-Blue chair in 1917, and the Schroeder house in Utrecht in 1924.

Rietveld, who was the son of a cabinet maker, set up his own furniture workshop in 1911; his early work is simple and carefully hand-crafted, in keeping with the Dutch Arts and Crafts tradition. In 1916, however, he was introduced first to the painter Bart van der Leck, at that time a member of the De Stijl group, and then to the architect Robert van t'Hoff, who asked him to copy, from photographs, furniture by Frank Lloyd Wright for the *Huis ter Heide* (1916). The Red-Blue chair was designed a few months after this, its formal and spatial innovations no doubt inspired by Rietveld's recent encounters with new attitudes to materials and form. The chair was, in fact, designed as a personal experiment but, following

Above Zig-zag chair by Gerrit Rietveld, 1936.

Left Crate chair by Gerrit Rietveld, 1936.

its illustration in *De Stijl* magazine, it became widely known in avant-garde circles throughout Europe. 'The so-called Red-Blue chair,' Rietveld subsequently wrote, 'the chair made of two boards and a number of laths, that chair was made to the end of showing that a thing of beauty, e.g. a spatial object, could be made of nothing but straight machined materials. So I had a plank sawn into strips and laths; the centre part I sawed into two halves, so I had a seat and back, and then, with the laths of various lengths, I constructed the chair. When making that thing, it never occurred to me that it would prove all that meaningful for myself and possibly for others; that it would even have an impact on architecture.'

Rietveld continued to work as an architect and furniture designer throughout his career (his final work, completed after his death, was the Stedelijk Van Gogh Museum in Amsterdam).

The majority of his furniture designs were experimental, but several, including the 'crate' chair and table (1934), the zig-zag chair (1934), and an upholstered armchair (1935) were manufactured by the Metz retail store well known for its support of modern design and designers.

The need to demonstrate the new ideologies through designs for mass-production was, of course, a primary aim of Modern Movement designers, who also campaigned for the use of materials that would, in their opinion, be light, efficient, durable, and, if produced in sufficient quantities, inexpensive. Tubular steel, which fulfils all these requirements was widely promoted during the 1920s and 1930s, and Rietveld designed several chairs using the material. It was Mart Stam, the Dutch functionalist architect, however, who produced one of the first cantilevered chairs in tubular steel (1924–6), and W. H. Gispen, originally an 'art' metalworker who had opened his own small factory in Rotterdam in 1916, was producing designs for serial production in tubular steel by 1925, as well as promoting functionalist philosophies.

One of the most interesting of the design organisations that has survived since the 1920s, however, is the Weverij de Ploeg, which was first established as an idealistic agricultural community at Best, in Brabant, in the years following the First World War. The original community was dissolved, and in 1923 some of its members, believing that industry must supplement the ideal of agricultural self-sufficiency, set up a small weaving mill in the village of Bergeyk. Their efforts and endeavours were recognised and supported by several cosmopolitan designers, including Mart Stam; and Otti Berger, a weaving instructor at the Bauhaus designed many of their early fabrics. The firm has maintained a remarkably high standard of design since the 1920s, and in 1956 commissioned Gerrit Rietveld to design a new factory, which produces printed textiles as well as weaves, the majority designed in their own studios.

Since the turn of the century, therefore, Holland has produced an active and inventive design profession, whose achievements, while reflecting European as well as international developments, remain essentially national, demonstrating the profession's ability to relate its idealism to practical requirements.

Opposite The Red-Blue chair by Gerrit Rietveld, 1917.

Above Poster by W. H. Gispen, 1921.

Left Hanging lamp of glass and metal by W. H. Gispen, *c.* 1925.

Scandinavia

by Ada Polak

IN THE COURSE OF THE PERIOD from 1890 to 1940, the Scandinavians emerged from being mainly imitative in the decorative arts to holding an important position in European design; in some fields and at certain periods their influence spread beyond their own countries. During the 1930s the expression 'Scandinavian design' came to imply a whole new way of living within the home, widely adopted all over the Western world.

These developments were led by Denmark and Sweden, which could build on centuries of independent nationhood and courtly life, and the high standards of taste and craftsmanship which are the precious adjuncts of a long and stable history. No similar traditions existed in Finland and Norway, which both gained their national independence in the course of our period (the political union between Norway and Sweden being dissolved in 1905, that between Finland and Russia in 1917). Finns and Norwegians were apt to look to their neighbours in general questions of style, though individual artists from both countries could, in inspired moments, produce the very best.

Throughout the period, but especially after the First World War, artists and designers in Denmark and Sweden worked purposefully together to explore the technical and stylistic possibilities of the decorative arts of the age and also to define their role in the modern world and adapt their products to it.

Ceramics before 1920

The first symptoms of rebellion against the expensive style and pomp of European historicism could be seen at the Scandinavian Exhibition in Copenhagen in 1888. Here Bing & Grøndahl's Porcelain Factory (founded in 1853) showed its famous Heron service, which was exhibited in Paris the following year. Designed by the painter Pietro Krohn, it struck a fine balance between the complexities of a naturally observed theme and stylized and disciplined form. The service was produced with the technique of underglaze painting, which had been worked out in 1885 by Arnold Krog for the Royal Porcelain Factory of Copenhagen (founded in 1779). Krog stood as artistic leader of the factory from 1884 to 1916. He had used the new technique himself in a series of vessels of marked Japanese inspiration, and the soft, gentle colouring under the faultless, shiny glaze was finely attuned to the lyrical taste of the *fin-de-siècle*. The underglaze technique did, of course, become an enormous commercial success, and its soft blue-white-grey harmonies are to this day most people's immediate association with the name of Royal Copenhagen porcelain.

In preparation for the Paris Exhibition in 1900, Bing & Grøndahl engaged the painter J. F. Willumsen to do some creative work for them. During his short period as ceramic designer, Willumsen produced some powerful models in high-fired stoneware, which were realized with great technical mastery by the factory's technical staff.

But the most original talent in Danish ceramics at this stage was undoubtedly Thorvald Bindesbøll. He began as a painter, but between 1893 and 1904 he worked primarily with pottery. His exuberant mind overflowed with ideas which he sketched down rapidly on paper, and then realized in earthenware, sometimes with his own hands, sometimes with the assistance of professional potters. Bindesbøll worked first at the pottery of J. Wallman in Utterslev, and later at the Københavns Lervarefabrik (G. Eifrig) in Valby near Copenhagen. He formed his clay into large, simple, powerful forms, and decorated them with wavy lines which divided one large colour area of slip from another. But there is no fashionable dreaminess about Bindesbøll's wavy lines; they are not inspired by mysterious algae or the tresses of sorrowing maidens, but by the clouds of the skies and the waves of the sea.

During the 1890s, the two great Swedish factories, Rörstrand and Gustavsberg, both engaged artists to design for them, in preparation for the great Scandinavian and international exhibitions. Alf Wallander worked for Rörstrand from 1896 onwards and Gunnar Gunnarson Wennerberg for Gustavsberg from 1895 to 1908. The architect Ferdinand Boberg and his wife Anna worked for Gustavsberg from 1909 to 1914 and periodically also for Rörstrand. All these artists produced charming and attractive, though sometimes very complex models of excellent quality in an idiom strongly influenced by international Art Nouveau. They also designed excellent models for serial production.

Between 1897 and 1902, the Anglo-Belgian designer Alfred Finch produced some strikingly simple and well-made pottery for the Iris workshops in Helsinki. The creator and leader of this enterprise was Count Louis Sparre, and some good quality furniture and metalwork, as well as ceramics, were produced there, all in a simple, unaffected style, influenced by progressive tendencies on the Continent. At the Paris Exhibition in 1900, the Iris Room in the Finnish pavilion created quite a sensation by its quiet, inexpensive intimacy, which contrasted strikingly with the opulence of the surroundings.

The ceramic factory of Arabia in Helsinki was

founded in 1876 as a subsidiary of Sweden's Rörstrand. In 1916 it passed into Finnish hands. Thure Öberg had been head designer since 1895, and he produced some very fascinating lamps and vases in a complex and sophisticated Art Nouveau style. The Fennia series of vessels produced from 1902 onwards, have hand-painted decorations in angular, abstract patterns, a curious kind of Art Deco far in advance of its time. It was designed by the progressive architect Eliel Saarinen, but he was most probably initially inspired as a ceramic designer by the painter Akseli Gallen-Kalela, the great moving spirit behind so much of what happened in radical directions in all the arts of Finland at the turn of the century.

Glass before 1920
About the turn of the century, both the two main Swedish factories for tableware and decorative glass, Kotsa (founded in 1742) and Reijmyre (founded in 1810) engaged many of the same artist-designers who had worked in the ceramic industry. Gunnar G. Wennerberg worked for Kosta from 1898 to 1902 and again in 1908. Alf Wallander designed for Kosta from 1907 to 1911 and sporadically for Reijmyre between 1908 and 1914. Ferdinand and Anna Boberg also designed

for Reijmyre. All these artists worked mainly in complex cased glass technique invented by Emile Gallé which was by now being copied all over Europe. Wennerberg in particular had grasped the spirit of the style and gave it a fine and poetic personal interpretation.

Silver and metalwork before 1920
The great name in Scandinavian silver was of course Georg Jensen. He began by making jewellery in a handsome international Art Nouveau style. In 1904 he opened his own workshop in Copenhagen, where he produced vessels and tableware, assisted from 1906 by Johan Rohde, and eventually by several other goldsmiths and designers. The style that gained Georg Jensen international fame was robust and richly decorated, with the ornaments borrowed directly from nature and with a wide use of sculptured detail. Famous models in this style are the teapot with the rose on the cover from 1905 (a complete tea and coffee service with the rose as the common motif grew from the initial model), and the five-branched candlestick of 1921, with its energetic curves and tight clusters of fruit motifs. In 1915 Johan Rohde designed a set of table silver, which is still in production, and which to many people

Earthenware dish produced at Valby by Thorvald Bindesbøll, 1901.

seems to represent the very essence of the George Jensen style.

Thorvald Bindesbøll produced sketches for silver models, some of which were realised before the turn of the century by the Copenhagen firm of A. Michelsen. But Bindesbøll really thought in ceramic terms, and his silver designs had to be substantially adjusted by working goldsmiths to be put into production.

In Sweden Jacob Angmann began his career as silversmith soon after 1900, and worked with great integrity in a personal version of the Art Nouveau style throughout his career. Most of his designs were realised by the big Stockholm firm of Gullsmeds Aktie Bolaget (GAB) (founded in 1867). The Norwegians did their most spectacular work in coloured enamels. Both the great Oslo firms of J. Tostrup (founded in 1838) and David Andersen (founded in 1876) produced some elegantly fragile stemmed cups in *plique-à-jour*, which won both praise and medals in Paris in 1900.

Furniture before 1920
Throughout the period of 1890 to 1920, the Danes were world leaders in this field, and they looked to eighteenth-century England for models. Both Johan Rohde and Thorvald Bindesbøll worked within this idiom, each according to his temperament, Rohde's designs being elegant, simple, exclusive, and Bindesbøll's heavy, robust and intensely personal. The Swedes were more orientated towards the contemporary styles of the Continent. Ferdinand Boberg produced some very fine and expensive furniture for King Oscar's Room in the Swedish pavilion in Paris in 1900 in an international Art Nouveau style. The architect Carl Westman designed interiors complete with furniture and fittings, all in an austere style, with a stress on the rectilinguar, which shows an affinity with the work of Charles Rennie Mackintosh. Of great originality is the furniture in the Thonet bentwood technique, designed by another architect, Carl Bergsten, which makes use of purely geometrical elements.

Textiles before 1920
In Denmark and Sweden, traditional techniques of weaving and embroidery were being rediscovered in and around the new museums, and successfully adapted for use in modern homes. Large-scale tapestries with figure compositions of quality were being produced by two Norwegian artists, Frieda Hansen and Gerhard Munthe.

Frieda Hansen was both designer and weaver. In her workshop in Oslo she created a series of large compositions, many of which were shown at international exhibitions and acquired by museums abroad. She was also technically inventive; her transparent curtains with flower patterns, in which the warp is only partly covered by the woollen weft, came to figure among her most admired products.

Gerhard Munthe, an Impressionist painter of some note, developed advanced ideas on the use of stylization which he put into practice in a long series of cartoons derived from folklore subjects. The tapestries were then made up by professional weavers. He is also notable as a creator of handsome books. When a newly translated edition of the thirteenth-century national epic *Heimskringla* (the sagas of the Norwegian kings) by Snorre Sturlasson was produced in 1898, it was planned by Munthe, who also directed the printers and illustrators, while providing many illustrations and all the borders and vignettes himself.

The Functionalist Ideal 1914–40
Though neutral during the war, the Swedes experienced great restrictions, hardships and changes in their material life, which in their turn led to a deepened consciousness of many social problems. At the same time, echoes of radical new

Below left Vignette by Gerhard Munthe for the 1899 illustrated edition of Snorre Sturlasson's *Heimskringla*.

Below right PH-lamp in copper and brass, designed in 1927 by Poul Henningsen for Louis Poulsen, Copenhagen.

Folding deck chair in teak designed by Kaare Klint for Rudolph Rasmussen, 1933.

made considerable advances in the analysis of the true function of furniture. As professor in furniture design at the Kunstakademi from 1924 and as designer for the highly reputed furniture-making firm of Rudolph Rasmussen from 1928, he had a first-hand knowledge and understanding of theory and practice alike, and enjoyed widespread influence in Sweden as well as in Denmark. Another architect, Poul Henningsen, analysed the table lamp and its functions, and produced a model which won a gold medal in Paris in 1925. Two years later a perfected version was put into production in Copenhagen, and thousands of models of the PH-lamp have served down the years, both in Scandinavia and in many other countries.

Ceramics 1920–40

Patrick Nordström, a potter born in Sweden in 1870, spent a number of years around 1900 in Paris, where he worked closely with the great makers of stoneware, including Delaherche, Chaplet, Carriès and others. He was not the only Scandinavian to be acquainted with these developments, but partly by chance and coincidence, he became the main transmitter of their ideas to the northern countries. By 1911 he was himself making stoneware, and in 1912 he settled in Copenhagen where he spent the rest of his life. In the exciting ceramic circles of Copenhagen, Nordström found the stimulus he needed to put into practice the ideas he had brought back with him from Paris. Between 1912 and 1922 he was attached to the Royal Copenhagen Porcelain Factory, where he began production of stoneware vessels and figures, partly inspired by the Paris potters, but with distinct echoes of Chinese Sung, which have continued to be produced to this day.

In 1930 Axel Salto, one of the most imaginative of Danish potters, as well as an all-round designer of note, began a long partnership with the firm, producing stoneware vessels in a powerful and highly personal style.

During the 1920s some stoneware sculpture was produced, probably influenced by the work of the German sculptor Ernst Barlach in pre-war Berlin. Jais Nielsen and Knud Kyhn, both painter-sculptors, produced an impressive series of figures in stoneware, many of large dimensions and glazed in oxblood red. One of Denmark's most famous sculptors, Gerhard Henning, modelled charming figures to be produced in milky white porcelain between 1909 and 1914 and again between 1920 and 1925. Bing & Grøndahl had produced porcelain models sculptured by Kai Nielsen in the years immediately preceding the war, while Ebbe Sadolin, perhaps most famous as an illustrator, designed some fine tableware for the factory.

The purest expression of Functionalist style in ceramics, however, were the stoneware goods, produced between 1929 and 1969 at the Saxbo workshops in Copenhagen. Its leader and inspiring force was Nathalie Krebs, a chemical engineer who had worked for some time for Bing & Grøndahl, specialising in coloured glazes. When she started her own workshop, she first moved into premises which had been vacated on the death of Patrick Nordström, and where he had worked privately since 1922. For the formation of her pots

ideas on production and style reached Scandinavia from other European countries, and the Swedes began to rethink their ideas on housing and the furnishing of homes within the context of their own situation.

A small group of individuals was instrumental in the thinking out and practical promotion of the new thoughts on style and design in many areas of the decorative arts in Scandinavia.

Gregor Paulsson had spent his formative years in Germany and became the main 'ideologist' of the group, promoting the aims of the group with slogans like 'Better Household Goods' and 'Let the Artists Design for Industry'. Paulsson also inspired the radical reform of the Svenska Slöjdföreningen (Swedish Crafts Association) founded in 1845). In its new guise it became the main instrument for reform in design and production.

Another promoter of the new ideas was Erik Wettergreen, Director of the Nationalmuseum of Sweden, an impassioned lover of the Franco-Swedish styles of the eighteenth century.

Third in the central group of reformers was Elsa Gullberg, a textile designer of note and the only practising artist-craftsman among them. In 1917 the group presented its ideas to the public in tangible form at the Housing Exhibition at the Liljevalchs Konsthall in Stockholm. Here for the first time a series of interiors were shown, not as artists dreamt they might be in some ideal and utopian world, but as homes for ordinary people, furnished with goods of taste and quality. The exhibition drew an enormous and enthusiastic public. The spectacularly beautiful Swedish show in Paris in 1925 introduced the ideas of the group to a wider European public.

A similarly thoughtful approach to design and production can also be found in post-war Denmark, but there the new ideas were spread largely by single individuals, rather than as a part of a national programme. The architect Kaare Klint

Right Lion's head in *chamotte* stoneware by Gunnar Nylund for Rörstrand, 1933.

Left Covered stoneware vase by Patrick Nordström for the Royal Porcelain Factory, Copenhagen, 1922.

Below left 'Argenta' vase with green glaze and silver inlay, designed by Wilhelm Kåge for Gustavsberg, 1930.

Below Stoneware vessel by Axel Salto for the Royal Porcelain Factory, Copenhagen, 1931.

'The Potter', sculpted figure in stoneware with oxblood glaze, by Jais Nielsen, 1925.

Nathalie Krebs sought the assistance of professional potters, such as Gunnar Nylund, the Swede, who worked at Saxbo during the first year of its existence, and the sculptor Erik Rahr and others.

The longest and closest partnership, however, was that with Eva Stæhr-Nielsen, which lasted from 1932 to 1969. Mrs. Stæhr-Nielsen adapted her models brilliantly to carry the exquisite glazes invented by Nathalie Krebs. Paradoxically, these most Functionalist of potters' products are not very useful; at best they can hold a bunch of flowers, and their main function is indeed to stand and look beautiful.

This account of Danish ceramics would be incomplete without a mention of the family firms of potters with a long history and tradition. In such companies modern ideas could be accepted and taken up in the discipline and controlled context of a practical pottery business. Herman A. Kähler learned the craft from his father in the family workshop at Næstved (founded in 1839), and has again taught it to his son, H. J. Kähler, who now carries on the firm. They work mainly in glazed stoneware. The island of Bornholm has rich clay deposits, and has for centuries been a centre for good anonymous pottery-making. In 1859 L. Hjorth set up a small factory for the production of terracotta, figures and vessels, in a Neo-classical style. His son and his sons and daughters still produce fine quality work at Bornholm in a restrained modern idiom.

Gunnar Nylund left Saxbo in 1931 to become head designer of the Rörstrand-Lidköping factory in his native Sweden, where he produced some excellent designs for mass-produced household goods. His co-operation with Nathalie Krebs however, had given him more ambitious ideas and he also produced a series of porcelain and stoneware designs. Some of these are in the austere purist style of his Danish colleague, while others

are directly modelled on Sung ware. He has also produced some impressive sculpture. At the factory of Gustavsberg Wilhelm Kåge worked as designer from 1917, and remained the decisive artistic influence throughout our period and beyond.

According to the Functionalist programme, he began by reforming the serial production of household goods in a modern idiom. But his activities also included the creation of more ambitious genres of decorative ware. He created his Argenta series of green glazed stoneware inlaid with silver for the Stockholm Exhibition in 1930, as well as the Farsta series of stoneware vessels in painted faïence, and his series of large dishes painted with fashionable women's heads was particularly impressive. In 1937, Kåge was joined at Gustavsberg by Stig Lindberg. He introduced a more strikingly modernistic style to the serial production, but his many contributions to Swedish pottery came after the end of our period.

Porsgrunds Porselænsfabrik (founded in 1885) in Norway produced some good porcelain and pottery in a modern idiom, especially during the years from 1927 when Nora Gulbrandson was chief designer. The 1930s also saw the beginnings of original work in Finnish ceramics at the Arabia factory, but the great period in the history of the Arabia factory came after the Second World War.

Glass 1920–40
By far the most spectacular and original contribution in Scandinavian design was in Swedish glass. The new developments were from the first centred on the factory of Orrefors (founded in 1898). In 1916, stimulated by the call from Stockholm of 'Let the Artist Design for Industry', the management engaged Simon Gate as designer, and in the following year Edward Hald also joined them. Both Gate and Hald were painters and neither had previous knowledge of glass. Under

Top Saxbo stoneware vase,
c. 1930.

Above Early Graal glass
by Edward Hald, 1917.

Right Glass vase by Simon
Gate, *c*. 1930.

Below left Early Graal
glass by Simon Gate, 1917.

Below right Furnace-
worked vase of clear glass,
with black foot and rim, by
Simon Gate for Orrefors,
1930.

the expert guidance of the experienced glass-blower, Knut Bergqvist, they soon began to see the potential of the material.

From the very start they worked along three main lines, which were to be followed up to the end of our period with ever greater confidence and sophistication. There were the models in pure furnace work, often produced in one or two colours, black and clear being a fashionable combination. Over the years many handsome table services were also produced, some expensive for Orrefors itself, and others simple and cheap but pleasing to look at and good to handle, for the sister factory of Sandviken. The second line was glass decorated with engraved figures and ornaments. With the help initially of one craftsman, Gustaf Abels, a cutter from Kosta, they began producing patterns for engraving. Gate worked mainly with Neo-classical subjects to be executed in deep and finely graded relief; these had a distinct flavour of Lobmeyr, but possessed a crisp vitality all of their own. Hald chose his subject frequently from contemporary life and had them executed in a sketchy manner, with the engraver's wheel producing more a matting of the surface than deep incisions. There was a gay Parisian air about many of Hald's decorative patterns – he had after all studied with Matisse. The third and final line in Orrefors art glass had coloured patterns inlaid into the glass, the genre being given the proud name of Graal as early as 1916.

The starting point for the Orrefors Graal was Gallé's standardized cased glass vases with flower decorations cut out of the surface, but as the motifs on Graal were enclosed in the glass and received a final heating within its clear casing, they acquired a fluidity and glassiness which made them something quite new and startling. In 1930 the supporting technique of Ariel was worked out.

Compared to what the Swedes did, the contribution to the development of the art of glass-making of the other Scandinavian countries was modest. In Denmark, the architect Jacob E. Bang worked as designer at the factory of Holmegaard (founded in 1825) from 1928 to 1942.

In Finland, Henry Ericsson designed engraved glass for the factory of Riihimäki (founded in 1910) in a style clearly inspired by Edward Hald, and so did Sverre Pettersen for Hadeland in Norway from 1928 until the end of our period and beyond. Arttu Brummer made some good but modest glass with inlaid air bubbles in the style of Marinot, again for Riihimäki. Gunnel Nyman was the pioneer of the great Finnish expansion within the field of art glass during the 1950s and 1960s, although her first experiments with glass had been interrupted by the Second World War. Alvar Aalto, the famous architect, designed glass vases in plain metal, sometimes tinted into one colour, most famous among them being the Savoy series created in 1937.

Silver and metalwork 1920–40

Stylistically speaking, the purest Functionalist silver was made by Wiven Nilsson in his workshop in Lund in Sweden, with an almost Cubist look in his most characteristic pieces. Ernst Fleming in his Atelier Borgila in Stockholm also worked in a radically modern style.

In Denmark Kay Bojesen trained in Georg Jensen's workshops, made extremely shapely models in plain and unadorned silver, and also some very fine table silver. He also worked in wood, making some of the most attractive toys of the period. Kay Bojesen employed outside designers in his silversmith's workshop, among them the architects Magnus Stephensen and Ole Wanscher, the latter more famous as a furniture designer. Sigvard Bernadotte of the Swedish royal family was for many years artistic director of Georg Jensen's workshop. Kay Fisker, an architect by profession, designed some exquisite models for the firm of A. Michelsen.

In Norway, the Functionalist style was introduced in silver by Jacob, and practised with proficiency and charm by Oskar Sørensen, head of the firm of Tostrup. The other great Oslo firm, David Andersen, produced some good Functionalist models from the designs of a team of young designers, the most talented being Torbjørn Lie Jørgensen.

Furniture 1920–40

The central position of Kaare Klint has already been mentioned. Working very much in the same spirit were the architect Ole Wanscher, Mogens Koch and others. Their designs were realized by firms like Jacob Kjær, Fritz Hansen and A. J. Iversen, whose unfailingly high standards of craftsmanship must take much of the credit for the excellence of Danish furniture of the period.

In Sweden a whole phalanx of designers followed the now broadly accepted tenets of Functionalism, and worked sensibly and well to produce good, useful and reasonably priced furniture for a mass public.

Carl Malmsten worked happily in exotic and expensive woods, with inlaid decoration, and frequently with more than a glance back to the Franco-Swedish eighteenth-century tradition.

Gunnar Asplund, active during the 1920s, was another exponent of the gently traditional 'Swedish grace', but after acting as chief architect to the Stockholm Exhibition in 1930, he accepted more radical forms, producing among other things a steel chair of great elegance. Bruno Matthson created his own technique, covering bentwood chairs with hemp webbing.

But the great exploiter of bentwood was of course Alvar Aalto. In 1930, as part of the furnishings for a sanatorium he was building, he produced his first version of the famous armchair of laminated birchwood. In 1933 came another variety, both being realized by his own firm for mass-produced furniture, Artek (founded 1935). Aalto's chairs worked on a completely new technical principle, which exploits the gentle springiness of the construction and the sitter enjoys a pleasant feeling of light movement.

Textiles 1920–40

Much excellent work was done in both woven and printed materials for use in the interior by both Swedish and Danish designers, some working in private workshops, others designing for factories, but the picture is too large and varied for single names to be mentioned. In tapestry weaving some interesting developments took place. In 1919 Märta Måås-Fjetterström opened her own workshop near Lund in Sweden, where she created a very personal kind of tapestry weaving with pictorial subjects, firmly based on folkweave techniques and traditions. She also produced furnishing fabrics. An extraordinarily powerful and original weaver was Hannah Ryggen. Born in Sweden in 1894 and trained as a painter, she settled in Norway in 1923 and devoted the rest of her life to tapestry weaving, her most notable achievement being a series of large-scale, narrative tapestries. The period also saw the beginning of the revival of rya weaving in Finland.

Decanter with stopper, designed by Oskar Sorensen for J. Tostrup, 1938.

Above Tapestry-woven wool rug from the workshop of Märta Måås-Fjetterström, Bastad, c. 1930.

Far left Laminated birchwood chair, designed by Alvar Aalto, 1933.

Centre left 'Lise Lotte Hermann', detail from a tapestry by Hannah Ryggen, 1938.

Italy and Spain

by Ian Bennett

Italy

IN ITALY, the principal influence on the applied arts at the turn of the century was French. In common with most other Mediterranean countries, Italy espoused a violent curvilinear style without, however, the restraining factors of great artistry found among the Nancy and Paris designers. It must be said at the outset that there is very little of early twentieth-century Italian applied art which is of more than passing interest. The exception, though an extremely eccentric one, being the furniture of Bugatti. Only after the Second World War did Italy begin to have a major impact on international design, especially in the fields of interiors and furniture.

The Italian showing at the Paris 1900 Exhibition was considered little short of a disaster. The pavilion itself, designed by Ceppi, was a weird amalgam of the black and white stripes of Siena Cathedral and the Byzantine extravagance of San Marco. The French critics, with the Italian exhibits primarily in mind, coined the phrase *style nouille* or 'noodle style'.

Indeed, it was largely due to the generally hostile reaction to the Italian section of the 1900 Exhibition that it was decided by Italy that the Turin Exhibition of 1902 should be as splendid an affair as possible. The architect Raimondo d'Aronco was chosen to design the principal buildings, and these again were in an ornate, Byzantine style which, despite the enthusiasm of some Italian critics, was not much of an improvement on the 1900 fiasco.

The Italian section at Turin did not, in general, fare much better at the hands of the international critics, one writer in *The Studio* remarking that 'the whole effect of it was that of a huge bazaar, rather than an exhibition of artistic work'.

Not to be discouraged, the Italian Government decided to hold another International Exhibition in Milan, which took place in 1906, an event seemingly dogged by disaster, including the destruction by fire of the Italian Pavilion of Applied Art in August. The designers of the Italian pavilion this time were Bianchi, Magnani and Rondoni, whose edifice bore a remarkable resemblance to the Turin building but without the bravura.

Italy did not lack a few architects capable of interpreting the Art Nouveau style. The best of them was probably Pietro Fenoglio of Turin, who designed a number of important buildings in the years around 1900, the most famous of which was his own house, the Casa Fenoglio, finished in 1902. In this building, the architect sought for the concept of total unity, which was the concern of many of the leading architects of the period. Other interesting architects include Alfredo Premoli of Turin, who was greatly influenced by Guimard, Giovan Battista Comencini of Udine, whose Hôtel de Londres shows an awareness of Mackintosh, Raimondo d'Aronco, who has been mentioned in connection with the 1902 Turin Pavilion and Giuseppe Sommaruga, the most important Italian exponent of the new German style of Behrens and a precursor of the Futurist concept of architecture proclaimed by Sant'Elia in his Manifesto of 1914. Even Sommaruga could not resist embellishing his work with Art Nouveau motifs.

Although no mention is made of his name, it seems possible that one of the aspects of the Italian display at the Turin exhibition of 1902 which so dismayed the English critic of *The Studio*, as it did many others, was the now famous interior designed by Carlo Bugatti, in which he achieved the height of Moresque fantasy in one of the most memorable creations of any single designer at any of the international exhibitions which took place at the beginning of this century (see p. 276).

Bugatti had been designing furniture in Milan for more than fourteen years by the time the 1902 Exhibition took place, furniture which had usually been among Italy's few successes. It was first shown in the Italian Exhibition in London in 1888; it was like no other furniture produced in Europe, the combination of painted vellum, polished copper and brass, carved and painted wood and hanging silk tassels giving it a weird and barbaric appearance.

Bugatti's furniture won a first prize at the London exhibition. In Paris and Turin, he won gold medals, despite the fact that in the former exhibition, his work was described sarcastically by Edmond de Goncourt as typifying 'the yachting style'; at Turin, it was either ignored by the critics or mauled. The German Fritz Minkus, in *Kunst und Kunsthandwerk*, described the Turin interior as producing 'the effect of a newly invented automobile, which cannot be quite comprehended at first glance, of outstanding technical refinement, together with an extremely ugly and ponderous appearance', an ironic remark in view of the fame Carlo's eldest son Ettore was to achieve as one of the greatest automobile designers and manufacturers.

In fact, 'ponderous' is not an entirely unfair description of much of Bugatti's furniture, although in the Turin Exhibition, he had begun to produce more delicate curvilinear pieces with less extravagant ornamentation, a slight change in style

due, no doubt, to the French furniture he had seen in Paris in 1900. In 1905, however, Carlo ceased to manufacture his furniture, selling the rights to do so to the Milan firm of De Vecchi.

Bugatti has become the most famous of the Italian furniture designers at the turn of the century; in many respects, he was the only one to create a unified style, which, for all its occasional excesses, remains the expression of an individual personality.

Among other Italians, the most highly regarded was probably Eugenio Quarti, who was born in 1867 and who worked in Milan until his death in 1931. Quarti's furniture is probably the most restrained attempt by an Italian designer to produce an Art Nouveau style. He was influenced obviously by the curvilinearity of the French exhibits in Paris in 1900, but his own furniture in the period between 1898, when he showed it publically for the first time in an exhibition in Turin, and 1900, is among the most florid of his whole career. There is also evidence, especially in the extraordinary sofa he exhibited in Paris, with its huge rounded back, that he was greatly impressed by his fellow Milanese, Carlo Bugatti, of whom he was a close friend.

By 1902, however, Quarti's furniture had be-

come more restrained and elegant, often painted white and with stencilled flower patterns, the inspiration for which was possibly Mackintosh or, more likely, the Vienna Secession. In the 1906 Milan Exhibition, strong elements of Art Nouveau curvilinearity were still to be seen in his pieces, but they showed the restraint of the German designers Behrens and Riemerschmid, by whom many Italians at this time were strongly influenced.

Quarti's room at the Milan exhibition was destroyed by the fire mentioned above, but it was seen by a number of international critics who found it a refreshing change from the usual eclectic extravagances of the majority of Italian designers. It should be noted that the movement towards simple furniture capable of mass-production and inspired by the German experiments, was known as 'mobile Povero' and designers of it included Ettore Bracco and Pietro Zen.

The latter was born in 1879 and continued working in Milan until 1950; he was the son of another leading Italian Art Nouveau cabinet-maker, Carlo Zen (1851–1918). Carlo's furniture, which appeared at most of the major international exhibitions, starting with Turin in 1898, exemplified the worst in the Italian commercialization of the florid French Art Nouveau style. By

Top Bedroom suite designed by Carlo Bugatti for a London private house, c. 1902.

Above Chair designed by Carlo Bugatti, early twentieth century.

Above Screen designed by
Carlo Bugatti, early
twentieth century.

comparison, the work of his son, which won
considerable acclaim in the Milan 1906 Exhibition, is rectilinear and restrained, with strong
echoes of both English and German design; a
similar restraint can be seen in the work of his
contemporaries Federico Tessio, A. Rigotti and
the important Turin architect and designer, Giacomo Cometti, in whose work one can see the
influence, above all, of Henry van de Velde. Carlo
Zen's preference for the overblown may be seen
also in the furniture of B. Massimino, A. Lauro, A.
Vergani and A. Issel. Valabrega's room at the
Milan 1906 Exhibition was, for him, surprisingly
restrained, although *The Studio* critic remarked on
the deplorable eclecticism of his style.

Italy also saw the development of a strongly
'rustic' or 'peasant' style of craft furniture, which
was often merged stylistically with elements of Art
Nouveau. These elements are seen in particular in
the work of certain Sicilian designers active in
Palermo, notably Ernesto Basile and Vittorio
Ducrot (for whom Basile often designed furniture
and wrought-ironwork). In Rome, the same approach may be seen in the furniture designed by
Duilio Cambellotti and that produced by Aemilia
Ars, a Secessionist group which existed from 1898
to 1903 and which included designers such as
Alfonso Rubbiani and A. Pasquinelli.

The most ornate example of the 'peasant' style,
however, remarkably close in feeling to the products of Russia, Hungary and Finland, was that by
Giorgio Clemente of Sardinia. His furniture was
exhibited in Turin in 1911, and was among the
most popular exhibits.

The furniture of Ducrot and Basile is never as
'folksy' as this; the pieces, usually of mahogany,
are massive and are frequently embellished with
metalwork by Antonio Ugo and painting by Ettore
Maria Bergler. The style seems often to have
echoes of ancient Etruscan or Greek pieces, and
seems prophetic of the monolithic Neo-classical
style popularised by the Fascist regimes in Italy
and Germany during the 1920s and 1930s. This
move towards monumentality became more apparent in Italian furniture design in the years
immediately before the outbreak of the First
World War, especially in the work of Luigi
Brunelli, Giulio Ulisse Arata of Piacenza and in
the designs for the interior furnishings of the
Palace of the King of Siam undertaken by Galileo
Chini between 1912 and 1913.

Of the various Italian applied arts which appear
in the decorative arts journals around the turn of
the century, ceramics are usually singled out for
particular praise. This was especially so in England, where artists and designers like William
Morris and William de Morgan had paid tribute to
the pioneering efforts of various Italian factories in
the second half of the nineteenth century in
reviving painted pottery (majolica) and lustre. Of
these, the two most important were Cantagalli and
Doccia, the former dating from the fifteenth
century and the latter from the eighteenth.

The Cantagalli factory was inherited by Ulisse
Cantagalli from his father Giuseppe in 1878.
Ulisse and his brother Romeo made good copies of
Italian majolica, Persian and Isnik wares and
Hispano-Moresque lustre, developing a fine cop-
per lustre which they called 'Pigeon's Blood'. A

number of talented decorators were employed by the factory, including the brothers Carlo, Giorgio and Torquato Boldrini and B. and F. Sirocchi. All these artists painted work designed by William de Morgan when he was resident in Florence for six months of each year during the 1890s.

The Doccia factory of the Ginori family had exhibited examples of its lustrewares at the Great Exhibition in London in 1851, and is credited with being one of the first to revive this ancient, but lost, art of ceramic decoration. In 1896, the factory merged with the Società Ceramica Richard, which had been founded in 1873 by Giulio Richard; the merged firms became known as Richard-Ginori and went on to become the largest manufacturers of industrial ceramics in Italy. The artistic director was Luigi Tazzini of Doccia, with a staff of designers including Giulio Richard himself and Giovanni Buffa. The factory produced ceramics of every conceivable kind, with a strong leaning towards the more florid aspects of Art Nouveau.

Another important factory in Florence was L'Arte della Ceramica, which was founded in 1896–7 by Galileo Chini. The general manager was the Ferrarese artist Vincenzo Giustiniani and the chief designer from 1902 to 1904 was the influential Domenico Trentacoste. In 1907, the factory moved to Mugello; Galileo Chini was the technical director of the new factory, with his brother Chino as artistic director. The factory lasted until 1955, changing its name in 1907 to Chini & Co.

The most important factory in one of the great traditional centres of Italian ceramics, Faenza, was the Fabricche Riunite de Faenza of Francesco Randone and Pietro Melandro, the former having been a pupil of Theodore Deck in France. The factory began production in 1910 and, mixed with a strong Japanese-Isnik leaning, no doubt derived from Deck, is a sympathy for the 'whiplash' Art Nouveau style; good pieces in both monochrome and lustre were produced by the factory.

Despite Italy's long history as one of the leading European producers of glass, with many of the great factories of Venice and Murano still operating well into the twentieth century, little of interest was produced in the period under consideration. Some delicate floral vases, in a style reminiscent of that of Koepping in Germany were produced by two Venetian factories, Pauly & C., which had been founded in 1863, and Salviati & C., which was founded around 1890 by Antonio Salviati. The latter company specialised in the production of glasses of extraordinary technical difficulty, in which the floral bowl is joined to the slightly domed base by a single incredibly thin strand of glass which follows its natural curlicues, akin to the effect made by a thin stream of treacle when it is allowed to fall on to a flat surface from a height.

Perhaps the major Italian glass designer of the inter-war years was Paolo Venini who in 1924 formed a partnership with Giacomo Cappellin, their firm being known as Vetri Soffiati Muranesi Cappellin-Venini & C. The artistic director of the firm was the Symbolist painter turned applied arts designer Vittorio Zecchin who, in 1913, had begun designing enamelled glass with another painter, Teodoro Wolf Ferrari, these pieces being made by the Murano glassworks of Artisti Barovia.

From the outset, Cappellin and Venini produced simple but elegant tableware in a style obviously based upon early Italian glass but with that emphasis on functionalism found in Philip Webb's glass designs of the 1860s, or those by Riemerschmid and Behrens in Germany in the early part of this century. Unfortunately, the partnership did not endure for long and in 1925, Venini founded his own company, Vetri Soffiati Muranesi Venini & C. Throughout the late 1920s and 1930s, Venini himself experimented with many different techniques as well as continuing his work as a designer of fine glass.

Above Carved sideboard with old Sardinian motifs, exhibited by the Fratelli Clementi in Turin, 1911.

Above left Interior by Vittorio Valabrega, shown at the Milan Exhibition of 1906.

Top Sofa designed by Carlo Zen, 1902.

Below Glass vase c. 1900 by Salviati & Co.

Spain

IN SPAIN, only the name of the architect Antoni Gaudí has become widely known, in contrast to the exceptional group of modern painters the country has produced, including Picasso, Gris, Dali and Miró.

In general, the applied arts of Spain at the turn of the century represented the extreme vulgarization found in other southern European countries, particularly Italy and Portugal. To this extreme decadence, Gaudí's work stands not so much in contrast – for no one could call it peaceful or restrained – but as an example of the fact that the style of violent curvilinearity had not been exhausted by the French and Belgian designers and, in the hand of an intuitively brilliant artist, still retained great originality and potency.

It is incorrect, although typical, to find Gaudí treated as a somewhat isolated phenomenon in Spain; he was, in fact, part of a Catalan movement in the fine and decorative arts centred in Barcelona, a movement which became the Spanish version of Art Nouveau, El Modernisme. The main force of the movement was to be seen in architecture and, as we said at the beginning, very little applied art of any note was produced. Also, the word 'modernism' suggests that the Spaniards were in sympathy with the ideals of many of the

Secessionist architects in Europe, especially in Germany, who were pioneering new methods.

This was certainly not true of Gaudí, however, whose work may, in many respects, be considered the finest flowering of the 'peasant' style of Art Nouveau, with a strong emphasis on traditional materials. Among the turn of the century Spanish architects, perhaps only Luis Domènech y Montaner may be said to represent Modernism in Spanish architecture, although in the work of others, such as Rafael Massó, there can be seen an awareness of the concepts of functionalism associated with architects such as Behrens and Loos.

It is arguable that, architecturally, Barcelona represented the most intense development of curvilinear Art Nouveau to be found anywhere in Europe. Apart from the architects already mentioned, others included Henrique Sagnier, José Puig y Cadafalch, Francesc Folguera, Raspall, Jujol, Moncunill, Granell, Artegas, and Josep Pericas; even today, more than 200 buildings in the 'modern' style still exist.

Catalonia itself was ideally suited for this major Spanish development of the new European style since it was the only area of the country which had attempted to evade the general decline into total decadence and poverty following the loss of Empire in the seventeenth and eighteenth centuries. Certainly it was the only part of Spain in which industry had managed to flourish. It is no surprise therefore that in no other area of the country is there any significant example of Art Nouveau to be found and the few examples that exist are generally by Barcelona architects or their followers.

It was Domènech who pioneered a revival in craftwork inspired by the English Arts and Crafts Movement, a revival which also had its roots in a series of books and articles written in the 1870s by such critics as Sanpere y Miquel and Miquel y Badía, who had toured the leading industrial nations.

For many of his buildings, Gaudí designed extraordinary, idiosyncratic, furniture. Among surviving examples are pieces designed for the chapel of the Colonia Güell in Santa Coloma de Cervelló, near Barcelona (1898–1914), the Casa Calvet of 1898 to 1904, in Correr de Casp, Barcelona, and for the Casa Battló (1905–7).

The style of the furniture is consistent, the Colonia Güell pieces being perhaps slightly starker than those for the Casa Calvet, in which the organic, 'shell-and-bone' forms, are most obvious. One extraordinary piece, the authenticity of which has been called into question, is the ornate prayer

Right Dressing table designed for the Palacio Güell, Barcelona, by Antoni Gaudí, 1890.

Below Wooden armchair designed for the Casa Calvet, Barcelona, by Antoni Gaudí, 1902.

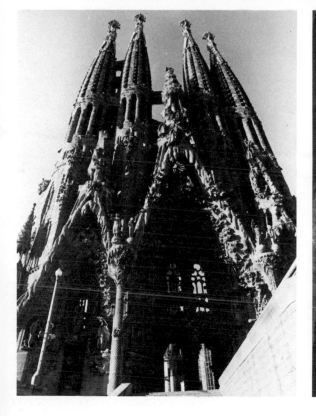

The church of the Sagrada Familia, Barcelona, begun by Antoni Gaudí in 1882 and still unfinished; its spires, façades and buttresses show a rapid movement from the precepts of the Gothic Revival to a highly individual version of Art Nouveau.

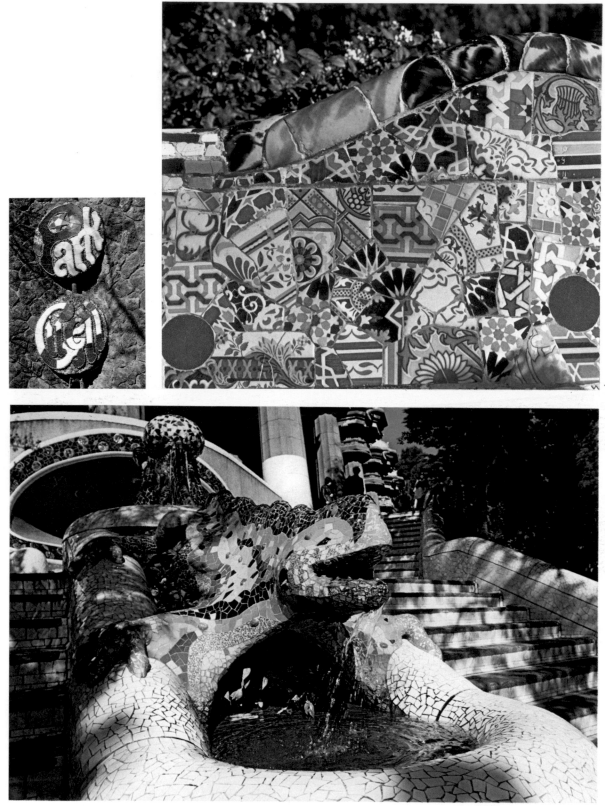

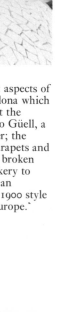

Gaudí's maturity: aspects of the park in Barcelona which Gaudí designed at the request of Eusebio Güell, a local manufacturer; the mosaics on the parapets and fountains include broken tiles and old crockery to achieve as potent an expression of the 1900 style as anywhere in Europe.

stool supposed to have been part of the furnishings of the Battló house which was sold at auction in Versailles in November 1973. The rich 'acajou et bois de loup' base of this piece, with upholstered platforms for the knees and elbows, was surmounted by an amazing edifice of stained glass and wood, embellished by five large gilt-bronze roses. Although very Spanish in feel, this piece bore little resemblance to known examples of Gaudí's furniture.

No discussion of the applied arts in Spain would be complete without mention of another Catalan, Josep Llorens Artigas, unquestionably one of the greatest potters of the twentieth century. Born in Barcelona in 1892, Artigas exhibited his first ceramics, based on traditional Spanish peasant pottery, in 1915. In 1918, he founded the Agrupacció Courbet and in the same year wrote an essay on a member of this group, Joan Miró, in *La Veu de Catalunya*. At this point in his career, Artigas began to show the same concern with understanding the methods and materials of past styles which had characterised nineteenth-century potters such as Deck and De Morgan, and in 1922 published an important book entitled *Les Pastes Ceràmíques: Les esmalts blaus de l' Antic Egipte*.

Eastern Europe

by Ian Bennett

THE DECORATIVE ARTS in Eastern Europe, those countries which today comprise the Communist block, were inspired at the turn of the century by three principal ideas. Firstly, there was a strong sense of historical nationalism. This is evident in Russian art, in Hungarian, Romanian, Yugoslavian, Czech and Polish art, and in Finnish art, which lies outside the scope of this chapter. With the exception of Russia, all the Eastern European states (the present boundaries are, of course, largely the creation of recent history) were under the domination of either Austria, Germany or Russia herself. Yet the various groups of peoples – Magyars, Croats, Slavs – living in places whose names have since disappeared from the map of Europe, such as Bohemia, Moravia, Montenegro, Croatia, Serbia and Bosnia, used their unbroken sense of national and ethnic pride to create unique artistic styles.

In many respects, therefore, the various movements in the decorative arts in these areas were political. Thus it is no surprise that another of the chief influences was the socialist work ethic of William Morris and John Ruskin. Many of the craft communities which grew up in Eastern Europe were founded in the name of these two Englishmen, whose ideas were also strong in the innumerable technical schools and art colleges which were founded in the Austrian and German spheres of influence.

Finally, since so large a part of Eastern Europe was within the Austrian Empire, the influence of Viennese design was also of great importance. French Art Nouveau influences may also be discerned, but to a lesser degree.

Russia

In Russia, the new mood in both the applied and fine arts first became apparent in the early 1880s. In 1880, a group calling itself the Nevsky Pickwickians revolted against the nationalistic, academic, school of painting. This young group included Alexandre Benois, Serge Diaghilev, Valentin Serov (later the designer of *Schéhérazade*), Konstantin Korovine and Léon Bakst. These six individuals, all of whom were to become associated with the Ballets Russes, formed a splinter group under Diaghilev's leadership in 1889, publishing their own magazine *Mir Iskustva*, which continued publication until 1905. Initially painters, they concerned themselves subsequently with the arts of the theatre, while at the same time organising exhibitions of paintings and sculptures and the applied arts, to which foreign contributors were invited. An exhibition held in Moscow in 1906, for instance, included the work of Charles Rennie Mackintosh.

The *Mir Iskustva* group was keen to awaken an interest in Russian folklore, and their aim was shared by three other groups dedicated to the revival of traditional Russian crafts – Abramtsevo, Trocadero and Talashkino. Abramtsevo, near Moscow, was the first of these groups. It was founded by Savva Mamantov and his wife to give useful work to the local young peasants during the winter months. Mamantov was a railway magnate who surrounded himself with literary and artistic personalities. His aim of making art socially useful was a deliberate challenge to the St. Petersburg Academy of Fine Arts and to the somewhat decadent cultural milieu of the Court.

The second community – Trocadero – was founded by Elena Polenova in 1884. She was a close friend of the Mamantovs and, with her considerable knowledge of Russian folk crafts, had been one of the main inspirational forces behind the founding of the first community. The third group was founded in 1887 by Princess Sviatopolk-Tchetvertynska on her estate at Talashkino. It was later reorganised and run by Princess Maria Tenicheva, who had financed the magazine *Mir Iskustva* and who was herself greatly influenced by Elena Polenova.

All four new groups attracted many of the same artists and designers and thus their joint work coalesces into the Russian contribution to new design at this time – the Russian version of Jugendstil or Arts and Crafts. One of the leading figures at Abramtsevo was Mikhail Vrübel, the son of a Polish cavalry officer in the Russian army. Vrübel had studied under Ilya Repin, the leading Russian academic painter, but showed his idiosyncratic approach to art in 1885 when he organised the building of a cathedral as a communal project, the interior and exterior of the building being covered in ceramic mosaics and tiles. Vrübel introduced the Mamantovs to another leading member of the Diaghilev group, Valentin Serov. At Abramtsevo, Vrübel painted icons and designed and painted ceramics. He became subject to violent fits of religious mania and died blind and partly paralysed in an asylum.

At Trocadero, Elena Polenova had assembled an impressive collection of old Russian crafts to be used for study purposes. She designed pieces in a similar style to be carved in wood by the boys attending her school. Among the designers and artists who worked with her were Marie Jacomichikov-Wéber, Nathalie Davidov, Victor Vaznietzov, Constantin Korovine and Serge Malioutin. Furniture, pottery, embroidery, book-binding and illustrations, wallpapers and toys were all designed and executed in the workshops. Surrounding villages well-known for particular crafts were also utilised; thus embroideries designed by the group were given to peasant women in the village of Solomenka. This village, famous for its embroideries, produced its own dyes, executing work in a characteristic palette of indigo, madder and green.

The communities at Abramtsevo and Talashkino both designed and built their own theatres, projects enthusiastically carried out by members of the *Mir Iskustva* group. These were not the usual crude and amateurish theatricals, but had scenery, costumes and accessories designed and painted by professionals.

The most important of the Russian craft communities was unquestionably Talashkino. There was a sculpture studio under Serge Malioutin, an artist deeply influenced by old Russian folk tales and legends. Malioutin designed the Talashkino theatre and painted scenic backdrops for it. Other architects and designers who taught there included A. Zinoviev and V. Beketov, and much of the furniture was designed by an artist later to become internationally famous with the Ballets Russes, Nicholas Roerich. Roerich is remembered principally today for his costume designs for the first performance of *Le Sacre du Printemps*.

Furniture was also designed by the painter Apollinaris Vaznietzov, brother of Victor; Apollinaris also designed furniture for the small avant-garde atelier in Moscow called Zemstro, where the sculptor Innokenti Joukov created works inspired by Russian historical and peasant subjects. Talashkino, obviously inspired by Vrübel's example, also built its own church in traditional Russian style.

Princess Tenicheva had an important collection of both traditional Russian crafts and also modern design, including work by Colonna, Tiffany and Gallé; the pupils, who were taught embroidery, furniture-making, woodcarving, ceramics and enamelling, were thus aware of current stylistic developments in Western Europe and the United States. The Princess herself was a skilled enameller and had her work in this medium exhibited at the Salon of the Société des Beaux-Arts in Paris. She also designed costumes for her theatre and, with other painters, produced some of the painted balalaikas which were features of all the Russian communities and which were especially admired by foreign critics.

The work produced in Abramtsevo and Talashkino was exhibited in the Paris Universal Exhibition of 1900, together with an extensive group of traditional folk crafts provided by the Russian Ministry of Agriculture, which had received instructions in 1888 to foster the continuance of these crafts among the Russian peasantry. Both the new and the old work was enthusiastically received, especially by the British who, in the true spirit of William Morris, applauded the medieval continuity of a folk tradition apparently unspoiled by industrialization (the English attitude to Japanese art was much the same).

Faced with the sturdy honesty of the Russian craft communities' work or the brilliant

Right Decorated armchair designed by Princess Tenicheva at the Talashkino community, 1890s.

Below Settee designed by Nicholas Roerich at Talashkino, 1890s.

of extraordinary workmanship; multi-coloured and multi-textured gold was combined with semi-precious and precious stones (the former were preferred) and superb enamelling, both matt and translucent. A wide range of snuff boxes, cigarette cases, photograph frames and nécessaires were produced, as well as carved hardstone animals, birds and human figures and extraordinary sprays of flowers resting in rock-crystal vases cut so as to appear half-filled with water. There were also the famous enamelled and jewelled eggs which the Russian Royal Family exchanged at Easter.

The unquestionable technical brilliance and perfectly orchestrated use of materials act as strange counterpoints to the utter artistic sterility of almost all Fabergé's work. The agate pig, the chalcedony pigeon, the crocodilite chicken, the enamelled eggs and bejewelled flower sprays are, in many respects, the rich man's plaster ducks.

Apart from the products of the craft communities, Russian ceramics of this period are of little interest. The Imperitorskii Farfor Zavod (Imperial Porcelain Factory) had been founded in St. Petersburg in 1744 and throughout its history has been controlled by central government, first under the Tsars and latterly under the Communist régime. Some attempts were made to instil life into it in the mid nineteenth century when Tsar Nicholas I brought over the designer Derivière from Sèvres, but the Russian work remained derivative and uninspired. In the 1880s Alexander III, under the influence of his Danish wife, imported designers and painters from Royal Copenhagen, but despite some good underglaze painting in the Danish manner by Linberg, the Tsar unfortunately insisted on choosing the models the factory should produce, and the artists were allowed no freedom.

During the 1920s, some Suprematist artists turned to painting on porcelain. Most important of these artists was Nikolai Mikhailovich Suetin.

exuberance of Diaghilev and his group, it is difficult to be objective about the concurrent products of the Fabergé workshops at St. Petersburg and Moscow. The House of Fabergé was founded in 1842 by Gustav Fabergé; his son Carl Peter, born in 1846, became head of the firm in 1870. The house exhibited for the first time at the Pan-Russian Exhibition of 1882 in Moscow and won a Gold Medal. Two years later, Carl Fabergé received a Royal Warrant from Alexander III.

The principal influence on Fabergé's work was French eighteenth-century vertu. The St. Petersburg branch specialised in small jewelled objects

Right Bronze and enamel bird made at the workshops of the Talashkino community, 1890s.

Opposite top left Porcelain inkstand designed and painted in Suprematist style by Nikolai Suetin, 1923.

Opposite bottom Fabergé silver mounts on a Tiffany peacock vase, c. 1900.

Opposite far right Jewelled flower by Fabergé, formerly in the Strauss Collection, c. 1900.

Many of his painted pieces, such as two whole tea services now in the Hermitage, Leningrad, were executed on St. Petersburg porcelain blanks, the shapes and painting making uneasy partners. However, while director of the Lomonsow Porcelain Factory, Suetin designed pieces of Suprematist shape with painted designs. Such pieces must be considered among the few successful integrations of modern art and ceramics. Other Suprematists who painted and designed porcelain were Ilja Chashnik, who also worked at Lomonsow, and the best known painter of the Suprematist group of artists and designers, Kazimir Malevich.

Hungary

If French Art Nouveau had any strong influence on the applied arts of the Eastern European countries, Hungary was the country which was most inspired by it. At the beginning of this century Hungary had assumed the unfortunate status of a province of the Austrian Empire. Magyar nationalism was, of course, fervent and many of the leading young designers were also keen to emphasise the influence of Oriental cultures on the historical Hungarian style. The combination of Byzantine and Turkish styles on traditional Magyar art thus produced a unique blend of historico-romantic symbolism seen at its most exaggerated on the Hungarian pavilion for the Turin International Exhibition of 1911, and in Aladár Körösföi-Kriesch's murals for the Academy of Music in Budapest executed at about the same time; these show historical and legendary Hungarian events in a strange stylistic mixture of Byzantine monumentality and wilting symbolism.

Pure Art Nouveau in the French manner can be seen in the Reök Palace at Szeged designed by Ede Magyar and built between 1896 and 1897; this is in contrast to the 'official' architectural style, a version of Viennese Baroque exemplified by the Török Bank in Budapest designed by Armin Hegedüs. Around 1910, the architect István Medgyaszay, an important pioneer of functionalist architecture in Hungary in the 1920s and 1930s, designed his first buildings.

Not surprisingly, the most fervent 'Magyar' style was to be seen in the pavilions erected for the international exhibitions, for these were the buildings which would generate the greatest worldwide critical response. The pavilion at the 1905–6 Milan Exhibition was designed by Geza Maróthi in the Magyar-Turco-Byzantine style. The interior and furniture were designed in a similar style by Maróthi, Odon Faragò and Ede Thorokai Wigand. Most of the furniture was inlaid with metals and upholstered in red cloth. Wigand, an architect by profession, had been designing furniture since 1898; his first pieces were in a somewhat angular style, and with a use of costly materials, clearly influenced by Hoffmann and the Viennese school. Later pieces, such as those in Milan, were in the nationalistic peasant style.

Wigand also designed stained glass; his most famous commission in this medium is a set of six windows (four others were designed by Sándor Nagy) in the House of Culture at Marosvásárhely, Romania, executed between 1911 and 1913 and illustrating Hungarian legends and traditional ballads. Nagy, also an architect and designer of applied arts, had drawn cartoons for carpets shown in the Milan pavilion, these being executed by his wife. Other carpets in the same show were designed by Aladár Körösfoi-Kriesch and made by Leo Belmonte. One of the most popular features of the Hungarian section in the Milan Exhibition was the carved wood toys, many of which had been designed by G. Weszely, head of the Royal Hungarian School of Toymaking at Hegybánya-Szélakna.

The apogee of the Hungarian nationalistic style was the pavilion for the 1911 Turin Exhibition. Designed by Emile Tory and Maurice Pogány, it was the most extraordinarily powerful mixture of traditional Magyar and Byzantine influences. The façade was ornamented with huge sculptures of crusaders by Nicolas Ligeti, the turrets were lined with dull copper and the interior light filtered through stained-glass windows designed by Miksa Róth. The hushed, cathedral-like atmosphere was carefully nurtured, as was the effect created by the historico-symbolism of the paintings and sculptures by Geza Maróthi, Eduard Telcs, Louis Greff, Louis Bansky and Aladár Körösföi-Kriesch. The pavilion and its contents were intended as a mystical, holy, symbol of an independent Hungarian people.

Unfortunately, most of the pavilion and its contents were destroyed by the fire which raged

Below A dining room in the Hungarian style designed by Ede Wigand for the Hungarian pavilion at the Milan Exhibition of 1905–6.

Below right The Hungarian pavilion at the 1911 Turin Exhibition, designed by Emile Tory and Maurice Pogány, showing an extraordinary mixture of Magyar and Byzantine influences.

through the Turin Exhibition complex. Among the most important of the destroyed Hungarian exhibits was a dining-room ensemble, including furniture, tapestries, glass and a dinner service by Zsolnay, designed on commission for Count Tivádar Ándrássy by Rippl-Rónai. Only one piece, a tapestry called *Girl in a Red Dress* survived from the suite.

The most important of the Hungarian craft communities was the Gödöllö Atelier. The formation of this group was inspired by Morris and by the Russian experiments described above. One of the leaders of the group, Aladár Körösföi-Kriesch, was in regular correspondence with Leo Tolstoi. Originally only for weaving and embroidery, Gödöllö soon broadened its scope, producing designs for ceramics, glass, metalwork, sculpture and book-bindings, as well as holding regular exhibitions of paintings and undertaking commissions for murals. Indeed, much of the work previously mentioned in connection with new Hungarian design emanated from Gödöllö.

The example of Hungarian Jugendstil best-known internationally is Zsolnay pottery. The factory was founded in 1862 by Vilmos Zsolnay at Pêcs, and in its early years produced earthenware in a semi-industrial, semi-folk style. In 1893, Vinsce Wartha was appointed artistic director of an experimental studio and it was he who developed with Zsolnay the famous iridescent lustre glaze called Eosin. The inspiration for this glaze was certainly Massier's work in France.

Stylistically, Zsolnay's products can be divided into six main groups – those in traditional style, those in lustre resembling Tiffany or Loetz glass, the figures, the dishes painted with flowers and landscapes in red, green and blue, the pots with animals sculpted in high relief, and pieces made in the twentieth century which show the influence of the Vienna Secession. After 1900, many examples were made in porcelain as well as earthenware.

In artistic terms, the designer Joszef Rippl-Rónai marks the high point of the factory's history. His designs are determinedly Art Nouveau, with flowing floral patterns close in style to the work of Maurice Ranson and Walter Crane (the latter had visited the factory in 1900). Rippl-Rónai designed many pieces for execution in the Eosin glaze; the design was etched onto a ruby ground and made to stand out by the addition of gold lustre. Like Clément Massier, Zsolnay and Wartha also experimented with a muted sparkle and ruby or silver lustre through a matt or crackled base of tin glaze.

Apart from Rippl-Rónai, designers for the factory included the sculptors Sandor Apáti Abt and Lajos Mack, small figures by both of whom were exhibited by Zsolnay at the Paris 1900 Exhibition, and Vilmos' children Miklos, Terez and Julia. Another member of the family, László von Mattasovsky-Zsolnay, designed and decorated earthenware in his own studio. The factory received great acclaim at the international exhibitions, and still exists today.

Czechoslovakia

In the 1890s, the Prague Royal School of Art Craftsmanship was founded under the directorship of Professor Stribel; this was the first of many

A side altar and embroideries designed by Kastner at the Royal School of Art Craftsmanship, Prague, c. 1900.

small art and technical colleges founded throughout the country.

The leading figure in the Prague school was Jan Kotera, who was born in 1873 in Brünn, capital of Moravia. He studied architecture in Vienna under Otto Wagner and exhibited paintings at the official Prague Salon, the Rodolfinium. He continued to show work with the Vienna Secession and when the Marischer Kunstverein opened in Brünn in 1911, its exhibitions were dominated by the Viennese. Brünn became, next to Prague (the capital of Bohemia, the Czech part of the state) the leading cultural centre of what is now Czechoslovakia.

At the Prague Art School, the students were taught by a number of talented architects, painters and sculptors. The ceramic class was under Professor Kloücek, who designed earthenware for manufacture in peasant potteries; such pieces, similar to Horti's work in Hungary, were produced under the same circumstances, although Kloücek seems to have favoured raised floral decoration, not incising.

Most of Kotera's pieces were made of ash with metal inlays, and were inspired by English models, especially Baillie Scott and Voysey. Kotera also designed glass for Harrach's Glass Manufactory

Right Green lustre vase made at the Zsolnay factory, c. 1900.

Below Hungarian Zsolnay vase in lustred stoneware, designed by Joszef Rippl-Ronai, c. 1890.

at Neuwelt. He was also one of the most important members of the Mánes Union, the principal Secessionist body in Prague, which had its journal aptly named *Volné Směry* (Free Trends).

Another extremely influential teacher at the Prague school was Jan Beneš, who devised a system of teaching design based upon plant forms which he called 'Stylisierung'. The ideas behind this was to 'replace the fruitless copying of historical forms by the study of nature as the real source of all form and colour.' Beneš was also artistic director of the Chamotte Textile Manufactory at Rakonitz, where Helená Johnová was one of the designers.

Johnová had studied at the Prague School of Arts and Crafts and in 1907 was a founder member of the Prague group of artists and designers called Artel. From 1909 to 1911 she studied ceramics under Powolny at the Vienna Kunstgewerbeschüle and in 1919 was appointed professor at the Prague School of Ceramic Art; in this capacity, she was closely involved with the development of modern ceramics in Czechoslovakia.

The Mánes Union mentioned above, included artists like Alphonse Mucha. It was concerned with new developments in modern European art. It organised the exhibition of Rodin's work in Prague in 1903, and its direction was influenced principally by French Impressionism and Post-Impressionism.

Poland and Other Countries

The main Polish dissident group of artists and designers, the Sztuka, was centred on Cracow, the German part of Poland (Galicia). It included the painters Jácek Malczewski, Ferdynand Rüszczcuz and Josef Chelmonski. The sculptor Konstanty Lászczko exhibited with this group, as did Stanislaus Wyspianski, a painter and designer of stained-glass, and Julius Makárewicz, who was responsible for the restoration of the Imperial Palace at Warsaw. The Sztuka held regular exhibitions of painting and sculpture but also placed importance on the applied arts. Kasimir Sichülski, who had exhibited with the Vienna Secession, designed tapestries, and the exhibitions included furniture, metalwork and stained glass designed by Edward Wittig and Konstanty Lászczko.

Various schools of arts and crafts were set up in Romania, including one at Craiova, founded by Gheorghe Chitu and in Bucharest (the School of Fine Arts). Probably the most famous graduate from both these institutions was Constantin Brancusi, who exhibited for the first time in Bucharest in 1908. Brancusi also exhibited in Prague in 1914 in an exhibition called 'Modern French Artists'. It need hardly be said that his influence on the development of French decorative styles is crucial, if not yet properly documented.

The Byzantine-peasant style can also be seen in the work of the various areas which today constitute most of Jugoslavia – Bosnia, Dalmatia, Croatia, Serbia. The Serbian pavilion at the Turin 1911 Exhibition was designed by Branko M. Tanásević and decorated by Ch. Inchiostu; it was in the Byzantine style, with the type of furniture familiar from the Russian craft communities (although, ironically, the Russian pavilion at Turin was in an anachronistic neo-Greek style).

PART THREE

THE
BACKGROUND
TO THE
DECORATIVE
ARTS

1890-1940

The Great Exhibitions

by Lynne Thornton

NINETEENTH-CENTURY international exhibitions were intended to be living encyclopedias of man's achievements, a balance-sheet of scientific, technical and moral progress. They were used to impress other nations with the host's political and industrial might and to act as a showcase for commerce. Each exhibition tried to surpass the one before in a gigantic, self-congratulatory display. Emphasis was laid on volume, weight, size and cost, each country in competition to produce the biggest and the best. The millions of visitors were probably rather more overwhelmed than instructed or morally elevated, after acres of Baroque palaces, Neo-classical temples, mosques, pagodas and chalets; they were, however, offered many entertainments and distractions, whipped cream on the solid pudding of worthiness. From the extensive coverage of the artistic press of the period, we today have the impression that Art Nouveau was the centre of interest. It had, on the contrary, a hard struggle amongst the heavy machinery and ostentatious objects of technical virtuosity produced by important manufacturers.

By the twentieth century, a hitherto unshakeable confidence in the future and in progress for progress's sake had been undermined by social unrest, wars and recessions, so that international exhibitions could never be the same carefree and ever-expanding affairs that they had been. The necessity of using them as an opportunity for studying the problems of urban planning was understood and there was some attempt at specialisation. The old tussle between industry and good design, artist and craftsman went on, but there was an insistence on original creation, compared to the formerly acceptable pastiches of past styles. The halls were designed by well-known architects and interior decorators and the furniture and objects were better integrated into a general Plan for Living. By 1939, however, the year of the New York World Fair, industry and science had again triumphed and the decorative arts were relegated to the background or were absorbed by production on a large scale.

Of the thirty or so international exhibitions held between 1890 and 1940 in places as far apart as Riga, Hanoi, Rio, Adelaide, Moscow and Istanbul, eight stand out as being of particular interest: the early ones, since they helped the spread of Art Nouveau, the Paris 1925 Exhibition, as an unrepeatable celebration of quality and luxury in the decorative arts, and those of the 1930s, since they had a profound influence on our habitat today.

Exhibitions before 1890

Although the first large commercial exhibition was held in Paris in 1798, it was the 1851 Crystal Palace Exhibition in London which inspired later World Fairs. Throughout the fifties and sixties, the critics complained of the slavish imitation of past styles, that the craftsman had become an animated machine and that, although the exhibits were ingenious and often technically brilliant, there were no modern creations; everything was subordinated to the clients' taste for luxury and the manufacturers' greed.

At the 1878 Paris Exposition Universelle, there were glimmerings of an artistic revival, but the glass shown by Jean, Rousseau, Gallé and Brocard and the faïence by Deck was heavily marked by their interest in Japanese, Egyptian or Persano-Arab art. At the 1889 Exhibition in Paris, the precursors of Art Nouveau were more clearly distinguishable from the mass of copyists. Chaplet showed his porcelain with flambé glazes, Taxile Doat his *pâte-sur-pâte* and Delaherche his rustic stoneware. Rousseau and his collaborator Léveillé exhibited their crackled glass and Gallé was highly praised for his enamelled, engraved and tinted vases, both for their technical innovation and their high artistic merit. Gallé and the future School of Nancy were also notable in the furniture section, although they were overshadowed by the pseudo-

La Caresse du Cygne, statuette in ivory and bronze by Philippe Wolfers, exhibited at the Exposition Internationale, Brussels, 1897.

Ethnographical room by
Paul Hankar at the
Exposition Internationale,
Brussels, 1897. The
woodwork and furniture are
in *bilinga nauclea*.

Tiffany magnolia vase in silver, gold, enamels and opals, exhibited at the World Columbian Exposition, Chicago, 1893.

eighteenth-century veneered commodes and heavy oak buffets in the Henri-Deux style. As a result of this exhibition, Gustave Sandoz created the Comité Français des Expositions à l'Etranger and a group of artists, collectors and manufacturers founded the Société d'Encouragement à l'Art et à l'Industrie, both of which helped to raise the status of creative decorative arts.

World Columbian Exposition, Chicago, 1893

The exhibition in Jackson Park, 'the biggest in the world', proved the vitality and growth of American industry. Chicago, still a village in 1830 and a city only in 1857, was famous for its flour-milling, slaughter-houses, canned meat and tanneries. The gum-chewing, tobacco-spitting public were unashamedly proud of the progress their country had made and were inclined to criticize the foreign exhibits as being too refined and namby-pamby for their taste.

Opulence was the keynote of the American exhibits (which included ice-cream soda fountains and saloon bar fixtures) sent from all over the United States by decorating and furnishing companies. Tiffany & Co. had their own pavilion, which combined Spanish and Renaissance elements, the interior resembling a Byzantine church. They showed silver and plate with Japanese, Indian, Moorish and Egyptian motifs, some of the magnificent chased and enamelled pieces being priced at $10,000. While the Tiffany furniture was composed of thousands of squares of natural woods in different colours, most pieces in the exhibition were either revivals of the Colonial 'Old World' styles or debased forms of an earlier Eastlake conception (Charles Lock Eastlake had been instrumental in introducing the ideas of William Morris and Ruskin into the United States).

These were, however, now offset by some good American arts and crafts. There were a few interesting pieces in the glass section: Thomas Webb sent cameo glass from England, and Léveillé crackled glass from France. The Daum brothers, however, had the misfortune to be badly displayed, while Gallé did not participate at all. The ceramic section was richer, with contributions from the Austrian, Ernst Wahliss, the Dane, Hermann Kähler, and Royal Copenhagen, and stoneware and faïence by Doultons and Maws. France sent Chaplet, Muller, Bigot and Delaherche; the latter was to have a profound effect on American ceramists, particularly on William Grueby. Among the American art potters of note were Mary Louise McLaughlin (who had already showed in Philadelphia in 1876 and in Paris in 1878), Maria Longworth Nichols (her Rookwood Pottery had won a gold medal at the 1889 Paris Fair) and Mrs. C. A. Plimton, a leading member of the Cincinnati pottery club. Chicago, then, was eclectic but erratic.

Exposition Internationale, Brussels, 1897 (Colonial Section)

The main part of the exhibition was situated in the Parc du Cinquantenaire and included the Palaces of Fine Arts, Sciences and Belgian Industry, as well as the foreign pavilions. The colonial section was twelve kilometres away, at

Turveren. It was destined to bring the Belgian Congo to the public's notice and to encourage artists to use imported ivory and exotic woods, in particular *bilinga nauclea*. Paul Hankar, Gustave Serrurier-Bovy, Henry van de Velde and Georges Hobé, were commissioned to design furniture and interiors to house the exhibits.

The sculpture section was especially interesting. There had been a flourishing ivory market in Antwerp since 1888 and some ivory statues were shown at the Antwerp Exposition Universelle in 1894. At Turveren, there were eighty pieces, Symbolist, Art Nouveau or traditional, some set off by silver, gold and precious stones, by thirty-eight artists, including Craco, de Rudder, Rousseau, Khnopff, Meunier and Van der Stappen. Philippe Wolfers, who had a remarkable selection of crystal and silver in the Palais des Beaux-Arts, showed fourteen pieces including a remarkable vase in ivory and bronze, *La Caresse du Cygne*. The decorative arts were completed by eight large embroidered panels by Hélène de Rudder representing the past and the future of the Congo. The quality of the exhibits was remarkably high and many are now in the Musée Royal de l'Afrique Centrale in Turveren.

Stoneware vase by Adrien-Pierre Dalpayrat with ormolu mounts by Keller, exhibited at the Paris 1900 Exhibition.

Above Interior in painted parchment and metal by Bugatti for the Exposizione Internationale, Turin, 1902.

Left Mahogany display cabinet by Bernhard Pankok, exhibited at Turin in 1902.

Right 'The Rose Boudoir' by Charles R. Mackintosh and Margaret Macdonald Mackintosh for the Turin exhibition of 1902.

Exposition Internationale, Paris, 1900

The 1900 World's Fair set out to embody the ideal of peace, progress and civilisation. By the time the last certificate, medal and prize had been handed out, it was already being seen as a crucial point in the decline of European optimism. More than forty nations participated, including Imperial Germany, but only the Shah and the King of Sweden accepted the official invitation; the other crowned heads saw Paris as a hotbed of anarchist plots, and there was a general anti-French feeling after the Dreyfus affair. In spite of this, nearly fifty-one million visitors filed past all the marvels of science and technology, paintings past and present, the Quai des Nations with its decorative palaces in indigenous styles and the numerous amusements, which included Loïe Fuller's dancing, Sadda Yakko's theatre and the Big Wheel. They travelled by the newly-opened Métro with entrances by Guimard, but avoided the *trottoir roulant*, the moving sidewalk destined to carry them over the 350 acres. The exhibition was breathtakingly pompous, with a mass of over-lavish ornamentation run wild.

Every well-known name in the Art Nouveau movement was there: Lalique and Vever with their Baroque jewels, furniture by the Six, Hoentschel, the School of Nancy, Bing's L'Art Nouveau and Meier-Graefe's La Maison Moderne; ceramics by Chaplet, Bigot, Cazin, Dalpayrat, Muller, Lachenal, Massier and the School of St. Amand, the American art potters, the German and Scandinavian ceramic factories and egg-shell earthenware by the Dutch firm of Rozenburg. There were Tiffany windows, Gallé symbolist vases, glass by Léveillé, Loetz and Koepping; enamels by Thesmar and Feuillâtre, silver by Cardeilhac and Christofle; tapestries after Burne-Jones, Grasset, Gustave Moreau, Lévy-Dhurmer and Rochegrosse; carpets, book bindings, pewter, medallions, embroideries, lace, and so on.

Exposizione Internationale, Turin, 1902

Breaking with tradition, the organisers stipulated that the exhibits must be original works displaying a marked tendency to an aesthetic renewal of form and that imitations of historical styles or industrial productions lacking in artistic inspiration would be refused admittance. There was a distinct bias towards Germany, artists from the Low Countries and British Arts and Crafts.

Germany had the largest section after Italy and showed thirty-eight interiors designed by Behrens, Pankok, Paul, Olbrich and Berlepsch-Valendas, with ceramics by the Berlin Manufactory, Schmuz-Baudiss, Lauger and Scharvogel. Holland exhibited furniture by the group t'Binnenhuis and Lion Cachet, textiles by Dysselhof and graphics by Nieuwenhuis.

Scandinavia sent examples of ceramics by their leading manufacturers, Kosta crystal and textiles by Alf Wallender; the United States sent Tiffany stained glass windows, lamps and Favrile glass, metalwork by the Gorham Manufacturing Co. and Rookwood pottery. France had a relatively small section, which included Lalique, the major ceramists, the School of Nancy, L'Art Nouveau and La Maison Moderne, Charpentier, Selmersheim and Plumet. English Arts and Crafts designers were there in force: Voysey, Day, Ashbee, Crane, Anning Bell, Benson, De Morgan, etc., but it was the School of Glasgow which won the day. The Scots showed furniture, objects and embroidery in three rooms decorated in mauve, rose, bright green, black and white. Many of the pieces had already been seen at the Glasgow International Exhibition and at the Vienna Secession in 1901 (the Secessionists, who had done so much to help the School of Glasgow to be better known on the Continent, did not exhibit at Turin). Although there were 250 contributors to the Italian section, they did not have much originality or sense of harmony and most of the exhibits were in a bastardised Liberty style. While the Italian architecture was influenced by the Secessionists and the Darmstadt colony, the decorative arts had all the frills of rococo Art Nouveau, without its spirit or basic form. The one exception was Carlo Bugatti, whose remarkable and highly individual furniture in parchment and metal was independent of all current styles.

Louisiana Purchase International Exhibition, St. Louis, 1904

The Fair was held to celebrate the centenary of the purchase of the State of Louisiana by Thomas Jefferson. For the occasion, St. Louis was relandscaped, streams diverted, hills levelled off, lagoons dug and Tyrolean alps raised. The exhibition area was twice the size of Chicago's (1897), three times that of Paris (1900) and ten times Buffalo's (1901). There was a Palace of Varied Industries, a Temple of Fraternity, a Palace of Art and numerous pavilions for each state and foreign country; one palace alone cost a million dollars.

St. Louis saw the confirmation of the importance of the American art pottery movement, which had started in the 1870s. After having begun in an amateur sort of way, the ceramists had by now made great advances. Technical help had been given in the form of the treatise by the Sèvres ceramist Taxile Doat, which had been published in 1903 by Adelaide Alsop Robineau in the influential *Keramic Studio*. Until then, there had been a certain amount of artistic inspiration taken from Oriental and French ceramics seen at international exhibitions, but the work of the dozens of small American firms showed that they had now found their own style. William Grueby exhibited his matt glazes (he had won three medals at the Paris 1900 Exhibition), Mrs. Robineau her carved porcelain, Rookwood vases with vellum glazes (in contrast to their usual shiny finish), Artus van Briggle his moulded faïence with symbolist motifs, and the Tiffany Furnaces Favrile Pottery their first ivory-tinted porcelain, which was not commercialised until 1905. Besides this wealth of ceramics, Tiffany showed Favrile glass and there was a selection of American Arts and Crafts furniture, including that of Charles Rohlfs, which had been seen at Buffalo (1901) and Turin (1902).

Despite the fact that Alphonse Mucha designed a poster of a rather plump woman holding the hand of a Red Indian to advertise the Fair in France, the French section, directed by Alfred Picard, the long-suffering organiser of the Paris 1900 Exhibition, was of little interest: St. Louis remained a truly American success.

Chest of drawers in fumed oak by Charles Rohlfs, exhibited at Buffalo (1901), Turin (1902) and St. Louis (1904).

Exposition des Arts Décoratifs et Industriels, Paris, 1925

The 1925 Exhibition gave rise to a spate of books, catalogues and articles on how to appreciate and understand the contemporary decorative arts. Through these publications and recent exhibitions, notably that held in the Paris Musée des Arts Décoratifs in 1976–7, we can delight in the diversity, richness and high quality of the exhibits. The 1925 Exhibition saw the triumph of the decorators or *ensembliers*, particularly in the Pavillon d'un Collectionneur (Ruhlmann and his group), L'Ambassade Française (Groult, Dunand, Selmersheim, Dufrène, Follot) and the Pavillon de la Compagnie des Arts Français (Süe et Mare). Although some rooms in L'Ambassade Française were decorated with simplicity, even austerity, by Roux-Spitz, Chareau, Mallet-Stevens and Jourdain, the remainder were filled with furniture in shagreen, lacquer, exotic woods and ivory.

There was a series of coloured plaster boutiques built on the Pont Alexandre II for Sonia Delaunay, Lalique, Heim, Herbst, Jourdain, Cheuret and Hébrard; Paul Poiret showed his brilliantly-coloured Martine interiors on his three barges moored on the Seine, and Rateau exhibited his green-patinated bronze furniture designed for Jeanne Lanvin in the Pavillon de l'Elégance. The big department stores showed work by their studios in separate pavilions – Studium (Louvre), Pomone (Bon Marché) Primavera (Printemps), La Maîtrise (Galeries Lafayette), while other pavilions were financed by Sèvres, Christofle, Baccarat, Luce and Lalique. Although wrought-iron doors, screens, lamps and console tables by Edgar Brandt were to be found all over the exhibition, most of the applied arts, metalwork, jewellery, ceramics, glass, book binding, tapestries and lighting appliances, were shown either in the building organised by the magazine *Art et Décoration* under the heading of Artistes Français Contemporains, or in the Grand Palais, classed according to the different techniques.

Amongst this wealth of colour, comfort and luxury, the rationalism of the Pavillon de l'Esprit Nouveau (Le Corbusier, Ozenfant, Jeanneret, Cubist paintings and furniture by Thonet) seemed very cold indeed. The traditionalist organising committee had tried to ban them from the exhibition and it was only by a ruse that they were able to show their work at all.

Twenty-one foreign countries and the French colonies participated, with abstentions from the United States, Germany, Australia and Norway. Many of the buildings and their contents were a mixture of 'modern' Neo-classicism and academism, except for the striking Soviet pavilion painted a fiery red, in which the Constructivists exhibited side by side with Russian rural handicrafts. Sweden showed Orrefors glass, Denmark showed Jensen silver and ceramics by Royal Copenhagen, Jean Gauguin and Bing & Grøndahl; Austria was represented by Hoffmann's Wiener Werkstätte and Belgium by Horta's furniture, Val-Saint-Lambert crystal and 'Kéramis' ceramics. Gio Ponti, founder of the architectural revue *Domus* was the star of the Italian section, while Holland, deprived by the organisers of the collaboration of the architectural group De Stijl, sent established

artists already famous in the 1900s. Britain, exhausted by the British Empire Exhibition at Wembley in 1924, half-heartedly showed eighteenth-century pastiches and furniture by Gordon Russell and Ambrose Heal.

Just as Brinkmann had done for the Hamburg Museum at the 1900 Paris Exhibition, so Edward J. Moore bought a selection of the finest Art Deco pieces, which are now in the Metropolitan Museum, New York, many of the other exhibits being in the Paris Musée des Arts Décoratifs.

After the 1925 Exhibition began the decline of a purely ornamental style for the élite and the rising influence of the modernists. Although many of the celebrated Art Deco *ensembliers* and artists were to work throughout the 1930s in a 'transatlantic liner' style, the innovators, rejected by the traditionalist Salon des Artistes Décorateurs, formed the Union des Artistes Modernes in 1930, which completed the schism between the 'decorative' and the 'functional'.

Exposition Coloniale, Paris, 1931

Reconstructions of mud huts, mosques and Far Eastern temples, animated by people in their native costume, were nothing new at international exhibitions. 'Voilà nos esclaves!' wrote Eugène Melchior de Vogüé in 1889, ironically summing up the general feeling of pride at 'owning' these strange apparitions from the far-off colonies. The 1931 Exhibition was important in showing the advance that had been made in the greater understanding of the indigenous arts and culture of France Outre-Mer. The fine arts were ahead of the applied arts in succumbing to the exoticism of the colonies. French painters and sculptors had for many years been showing their work at the Salons of various Orientalist societies and the influence of Oceania and black Africa on the School of Paris from 1905 on is well known. Although Chareau, Legrain, Coard, Dunand, da Silva Bruhns and other designers had been working in the colonial idiom during the twenties, 1931 was the first year in which there was such a large showing of furniture, ceramics, textiles and jewellery inspired by exotic prototypes.

The exhibition, directed by Maréchal Lyautey, was held in the Park of Vincennes, around Lake Daumesnil. The participating countries included Denmark, Portugal, Belgium, Italy, the Low Countries, Brazil and the United States. There were displays of every aspect of colonial life, pavilions in native styles and superb reconstructions of monuments such as the Angkor Wat, enlivened by dramatic floodlighting and coloured fountains.

The fine and applied arts were exhibited in the Musée Permanent des Colonies (now the Musée des Arts Africains et Océaniens). The façade has a magnificent frieze sculpted in low relief by Janniot; it took his two collaborators and thirty craftsmen three years to complete the sea of stylised figures representing the different colonies. The furniture designers were torn between making special exhibition pieces or catering for an expatriate clientèle. In the first case, they made full use of the exotic woods available: palissander, amaranth, teak, red padouk, bilinga, bubinga, wacapo and Macassar ebony, or Far Eastern

Above Ceramic vase by René Buthaud, exhibited at the Exposition Coloniale, Paris, 1931.

Above right Bas-relief by Alfred Janniot, symbolising the forces of the Earth, on the façade of the Palais de Tokyo at the Trocadero, Paris, 1937.

lacquer, enriched with ivory and mother-of-pearl. Furniture for export had, however, to conform to the spirit of local colonial architecture, to be easily transportable, collapsible if necessary, and to be in materials which would easily support a hot climate. Besides, the buyers from abroad had leanings towards Empire, Louis-Quinze or the Dutch Colonial style, rather than contemporary creations. The problem was solved by showing luxury pieces side by side with a cheaper range.

Among the *artistes-décorateurs* were Ruhlmann, Prou for Pomone, Guillemard for Primavera, Kohlmann for Studium, Montegnac, Renaudot, Leleu, Chéuret, Fréchet, Djo-Bourgeois, Domin for Dominique and Groult. Jean Dunand exhibited lacquer panels and inlaid metal; there were fountains and lights by Sabino, Etling, Perzel and Lalique; glass by Colotte, Sabino, Luce, Marinot, Walter, Daum, Baccarat and Saint-Louis; ceramics by Decoeur, Besnard, Massoul and Buthaud; carpets by da Silva Bruhns; textiles and wallpaper by Bonfils and Follot; metalwork by Brandt, Serrière, Linossier, Daurat and Subes. Hamm showed small objects in ivory, horn and mother-of-pearl next to cigarette cases and boxes in lacquer.

In the jewellery section, there were brooches and clasps of Algerian inspiration, onyx, coral and lapis pendants in the form of African masks, tiger and panther claws mounted in enamelled gold, and necklaces which mixed Negro Art with Cubism. Fashion, too, was touched by this vogue for exoticism: Marcel Rochas designed squared shoulders inspired by the costumes of Balinese temple dancers and the low necklines and softly draped bodices of many 1931 dresses closely followed the lines of Buddhist robes.

The critics of the time felt that this vogue would only last a short time but that the designers had made a much appreciated gesture towards the Colonies, so important to the French economy.

Exposition Internationale des Arts et Techniques, Paris 1937

The aim of the exhibition was to show that the beautiful and the useful were compatible, that art and technology should and could go hand in hand and that rationalism, simplicity, elegance and harmony in everyday life would help the spiritual well-being of man. It was a national morale-booster after the Depression, which had left so many unemployed in consumer trades.

One of the most striking features was the Palais de Chaillot, its curved Neo-classical structure replacing the ugly heterogeneous building designed by Haussmann in 1878. The Trocadero's complex of museums overlooking the Seine, the Champ de Mars and the Eiffel Tower today still offers one of the most beautiful perspectives in Paris. The two major pavilions were those of Germany and the U.S.S.R. in symbolic confrontation on either side of the Champ de Mars. Of the forty-five or so participating nations, many mixed a false 'modernism' with the rustic and traditional. Scandinavia and the Low Countries exhibited furniture and objects which were uncomplicated, and relatively cheap, being designed for a large market. Austria (whose Wiener Werkstätte had closed down in 1932 with Hoffmann's retirement), and Britain, who had a poor showing of period revival furniture, were considered too 'cosy'.

The gardens and most of the façades of both the temporary buildings and permanent museums were enriched by sculptures and bas-reliefs by Janniot (who had been prominent at the 1931 exhibition) the Martel brothers, Gimond, Orlandi, Landowski, Dejean, Drivier, Niclausse, and Sarabezolles. The interiors were decorated with engraved *verre eglomisé* panels by J. J. K. Ray and Max Ingrand and large painted decorations by some of the most representative artists of the 1930s. There were posters and publicity by

Cassandre ('Dubo, Dubon, Dubonnet'), Carlu and Cappiello, and myriads of fountains and jets which rose and fell and turned pink, mauve, blue and green according to the music played on a giant piano.

Mallet-Stevens designed the Pavillon de la Solidarité, the Pavillon de l'Hygiène and the Palais de l'Electricité (which housed Dufy's giant panorama 'La Fée Electricité'). He also presided over the avant-garde Union des Artistes Modernes, who exhibited silver, textiles, furniture, ceramics, book-binding, graphics and sculpture. The Société des Artistes-Décorateurs showed fashionable interiors of the year 1937, with sprigged wallpaper, furniture in carved oak or figured fruitwood, sideboards faced with leather, mirror glass or *verre eglomisé*, panels, quilted and fringed satin upholstery and draped curtains. Its members included many well-known names from the 1920s, Dunand, Süe, Montegnac, Dufet, Mercier, Renaudot, Groult, Rapin, Prou, Dominique, Printz, Adnet and Fréchet. They were joined by Porteneuve, Ruhlmann's successor, Arbus, anti-functionalist, who had brought back the curvilinear in the early thirties, and Jean Royère, who was to create entirely new forms during the fifties. The same feeling for discreetly lit, enveloping interiors for a chosen clientèle, was to be found in the Pavillon de l'Ile de France decorated by Dominique, Frank, Follot, Leleu, Adnet and Pascaud.

The taste in the late 1930s for Surrealism and the theatrical was most obvious in the Pavillon de l'Elégance organised by Jeanne Lanvin, the unusual disposition of the models in arcades and dramatic lighting having an equal success at the 1939 New York Fair.

We have seen that, at the exhibitions of the late nineteenth century, designers and craftsmen of originality had to struggle for recognition; even at the Paris 1900 Exhibition, the Art Nouveau artists were nearly submerged by the generally incoherent, over-ornamented mass. Although Turin (1902) was the first specialised international exhibition, it was not until Paris (1925) that the words 'Decorative Arts' found their way into the official title, from which the name of the style Art Deco was taken. Almost immediately after the status of the decorative arts had been established, there came a split between the *ensembliers* and the 'Modernists' which became definitive in 1930. In 1935, at the Brussels Exposition Internationale et Universelle, the divergence of these two movements were very clear, the Salon des Artistes-Décorateurs with their 'foyer de la famille française' on the one hand, and the Union des Artistes Modernes on the other. Even then, the U.A.M. which had done so much to change the French habitat, was criticised for not working enough with industry, as had done the members of the Bauhaus, disbanded in 1933. Although the 1937 Paris Exhibition was organised to encourage the collaboration of art and technology, the decorative was still opposed to the functional. At the 1939 New York World's Fair, however, there were few signs of individual creations. The aim: to present a synopsis of human activities and possible future developments; the theme: 'The World of Tomorrow'. The age of mass-production was on its way.

Top 'Salle de la haute couture', arranged by Jeanne Lanvin for the Paris 1937 Exhibition.

Above A music room arranged by André Arbus for the Paris 1937 Exhibition.

Photography and Cinema

by Philippe Garner

THE HISTORY OF PHOTOGRAPHY between 1890 and 1940 is both rich and varied. The fifty-year span is, of course, an arbitrary one and, if the wealth of material available for study is to be more fully explained, might more appropriately be deemed to have started in 1888. The introduction by George Eastman in August of that year of the world's first easy-to-use roll-film camera, the Kodak, marked the beginning of a significant new era of photography, an era of popularisation with the practical possibility of simple, instantaneous photography for professional and amateur alike. Amidst the almost infinite diversity of output and creativity which followed, the study of the history of photography after 1890 is perhaps best broadly divided into two parts, though overlaps inevitably occur. The subject divides itself fairly naturally between instantaneous, documentary photography and the self-conscious aesthetic evolution of photography, with its parallels and associations within other areas of the arts.

The most pertinent application of the new fast films and hand-held cameras that were now commercially available on a wide scale was in the newly-created genre of 'snapshot' photography. The freshness and spontaneity of this new genre found a notable exponent in the 1890s in the British photographer Paul Martin. An otherwise mundane professional photographer, Martin took his snapshots in his own time, as a hobby, and it is on these that his reputation has survived. It has been said of him that, 'He was content to record what he saw and pleased him, and his snapshots have more significance than much of the work of "concerned" photographers of today.' George Ruff Jnr., another British photographer, proved his talent as a gifted amateur with snapshots of unusual vitality dating from the early years of the century. In France the young Jacques-Henri Lartigue, given his first camera in 1901, entered into a lifelong devotion to capturing the everyday elements of life in snapshots imbued with a very personal warmth and *ingénu* humour.

Documentary photography had, by 1890, already established its own tradition, bringing forth the occasional spark of inspired observation amidst the sea of commercial picture-making.

The pattern continued after 1890 with such talents as Eugène Atget, Horace Nicholls, Lewis Hine and, later, Walker Evans, who distinguished themselves by their ability to instil a personal point-of-view into the subject matter of their photography.

The Frenchman Eugène Atget worked painstakingly and discreetly during the first quarter of the century documenting Paris life and architecture, the backstreets, shop-fronts, brothels and parks that other photographers overlooked. His sharp, gold-toned prints have a remarkable sense of intimacy. British photographer Horace Nicholls made lively photo-documents of Edwardian life and a vivid record, first of the Boer War and subsequently of the First World War. Lewis Hine's poignant documentation of the abuse of child labour in America in the early years of the century helped alleviate conditions.

Walker Evans came to photography in 1928. Reacting against the artiness of soft-focus pictorialism that had dominated the photographic scene, Evans gave a sharply-defined beauty to the mundane. His most notable work was his documentation of the poverty of America's mid-West in a series of some four hundred photographs taken as part of a Farm Security Administration project between 1935 and 1937.

Photo-journalism was one new facet of documentary photography to evolve in the period in question, finding its fulfilment in the 1930s in picture magazines such as the German *Müncher Illustrierte Presse*, launched in 1929, the British *Picture Post*, launched in 1938, and the American *Life*, launched in 1936; its first cover was a dynamic photograph by Margaret Bourke-White. The new breed of photographers pursued picture-stories with a human interest that would fascinate a very large public, using the new small-format 35mm cameras such as the Leica.

Amongst the most distinguished photojournalists were Henri Cartier-Bresson, Robert Capa, best remembered for his documentation of the Spanish Civil War, Felix Man, Erich Salomon, and Bert Hardy. Bill Brandt's early, stark, visual essays on industrial England were published in *Picture Post*. Brassaï's remarkable documentation of Paris night life appeared in book form in *Paris de Nuit* of 1933 and *Voluptés de Paris* of 1935. The extraordinary New York photographer Weegee slept fully dressed and with a police radio by his pillow, always at the ready, first on the scene to capture the aftermath of crime or accident with his 4 × 5 Speed Graphic and harsh direct flash.

The increased facility of the photographic process after 1890, a facility which both encouraged mass-market amateur use and allowed a new directness and realism to the professional, inspired a natural reaction on the part of those who respected photography as an art-form. Photography by no means heralded the death of painting, as had been forecast by certain critics; on the contrary, photography liberated painting from the

Snapshot by George Ruff Jnr.,
Brighton, *c.* 1905.

practical necessities of documentation and pictorialism, allowing a more rapid evolution towards abstraction.

By 1890, however, photography was in need of aesthetic revitalisation. Commercialisation had debased the idealism and achievements of the 1850s and 1860s. During the 1880s British photographer Peter Henry Emerson had fought virtually single-handed to win acceptance for his pictorial style, which he dubbed Naturalism. In the wake of an ultimately disenchanted Emerson came the establishment in 1892 in London of the Linked Ring, a society whose aim was '. . . the complete emancipation of pictorial photography . . . from the retarding bondage . . . of that which was purely scientific or technical . . . its development as an independent art.' The founder members included Henry Peach Robinson, George Davison and Henry Hay Cameron, son of Julia Margaret Cameron. Perhaps the most talented member of the Linked Ring was Frederick H. Evans, whose warm subtle-toned platinum prints are amongst the most beautiful examples of British Pictorialism.

The concept of photography as a fine art, however, found no greater advocate than the American Alfred Stieglitz. Founding the Photo-Secession in 1902 with a small group of photo-

Right Alfred Stieglitz, photographed by Alvin Langdon Coburn, published in *Camera Work*, January 1908.

Below Analytical close-up by Edward Weston, 1930s.

graphers who shared his ideals, Stieglitz created a rallying point for American Pictorialism. The galleries of the Photo-Secession at 291 Fifth Avenue became known after 1905 not only for the regular exhibitions of both American and European photography but as a showcase for the avant-garde in American and European art, Stieglitz refusing to isolate photography from the other arts. 291 displayed the work of Picasso, Matisse, Braque, Picabia, Brancusi and others and introduced examples of the primitive African carvings that were causing such excitement in Parisian artistic circles. Stieglitz exhibited the work of American artists John Marin, Arthur Dove, Marsden Hartley, Abraham Walkowitz and Max Weber and, before the Armory Show of 1913 which won the avant-garde a wider recognition, he was virtually alone in encouraging and promoting their talent.

The founder membership of the Secession included photographers John G. Bullock, Frank Eugene, Gertrude Käsebier, Joseph T. Keiley, Edward J. Steichen and Clarence White. Amongst the subsequent membership, the most distinguished talent was perhaps that of Boston photographer Alvin Langdon Coburn. The work of members and selected guests was published in fine-quality gravure reproduction in the pages of Stieglitz's quarterly journal *Camera Work*, a fifty-part work, the first issue of which appeared in January 1903.

The most characteristic Photo-Secessionist work used soft-focus effects in painterly compositions that demonstrated their status as art by imitating traditional concepts of painting. As painting, however, took rapid steps towards abstraction, the pictorialists found themselves in an impasse. A critic of 1912 remarked, 'Now, however, that it (painting) is seeking to render a vision of things not as they are palpable to the eye but as they impress the imagination, Mr. Stieglitz proves what he has known all along, that photography is powerless to continue its rivalry with painting.'

Although Pictorialism died a by no means sudden death, lingering through the twenties and thirties as the most popular style for both amateur and professional aiming at self-consciously artistic effect, by the 1920s it was no longer associated with the avant-garde. The Linked Ring dissolved in 1910, while 291 held its last show in 1917. A new direction was required and in America emerged in the analytical work of the West Coast School, finding its greatest exponent in Edward Weston and its rallying point in the f – 64 Association established in 1932.

The f – 64 group included Weston, Ansel Adams and Imogen Cunningham. They took their name from the aperture they used to achieve maximum definition. This pursuit of definition united them in a reaction to the soft Pictorialism from which some of them had evolved. Weston wrote in his daybooks that 'The camera should be for a recording of life, for rendering the very substance and quintessence of the thing itself, whether it be polished steel or palpitating flesh'. Working with a 10×8 plate camera he gave a philosophical dimension to landscapes, nudes or objects as diverse as seashells, vegetables or his austere and beautiful 'Bedpan' of 1930. Imogen

Cunningham specialised in the study of flowers and other natural forms, most usually in close-up, sharply analysing pattern and texture and discovering an extraordinary sensuality. Ansel Adams specialised in studies from nature and dramatically lit visions of the American landscape. Working to this day, he has made an industry of the production of his meticulously exposed and flawlessly printed images.

Minor White emerged in the late 1930s as perhaps the most intellectual exponent of the American analytical school. Frederick Sommer made analytical studies of often bizarre and distasteful subject matter using the techniques of the f – 64 group. Paul Strand was a New Yorker influenced at first by the ideals of Stieglitz but soon evolving his own principles of objective, analytical photography. His 'The White Fence' of 1916 represents an important landmark in this evolution.

In Europe, as in America, Pictorialism enjoyed popular favour. Popularisation brought about a lowering of standards, as can be seen, after the First World War, in much of the work illustrated in annual reviews such as *Photograms of the Year* and the *Salon International d'Art Photographique de Paris*. The analytical style that subsequently found favour in the United States was perhaps not

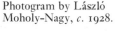

Photogram by László Moholy-Nagy, *c*. 1928.

Right Kiki of Montparnasse, photographed by Man Ray, *c*.1930.

Below 'Bewegungs Studie' by Rudolf Koppitz, 1926.

Below right 'Wet Veil II' by Erwin Blumenfeld, 1937.

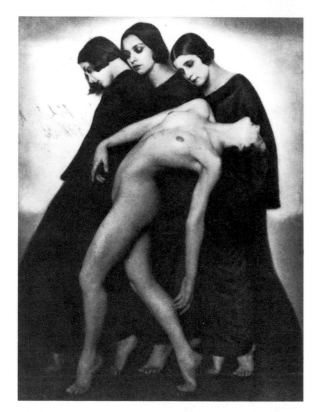

suited to the European mentality and very little distinguished work in this vein was produced in Europe. An exception was the German Albert Renger-Patzsch whose work was published in a series of books during the 1920s and 1930s. Creative photography in Europe during the inter-war years presents a multiplicity of interests, very often closely linked to other facets of the arts, notably in such manifestations as the Surrealist photography of Man Ray and the teaching of photography at the Bauhaus by László Moholy-Nagy. European trends seemed somehow more fluid, more varied and less easily defined.

Moholy-Nagy taught photography at the Bauhaus at the invitation of Walter Gropius between 1923 and 1928. He revived the photogenic drawing process of creating images on light-sensitive paper without the use of a camera, a process first used by William Henry Fox Talbot in the 1830s. Moholy-Nagy's photograms, as the results of these experiments were called, used patterns of light and shade in abstract compositions with a dynamism evocative of Constructivist paintings. He encouraged a freedom of technique that could embrace multiple exposure and montage. Perhaps the greatest exponent of this latter technique was German-born John Heartfield, co-founder in 1919 of the Berlin Dada group, but best known as the creator of virulent anti-fascist montages that incorporated both graphic and photographic elements.

A strong sense of composition often allied with a slightly ponderous symbolism characterised the work of certain mid-European photographers, such as the Austrian Professor Rudolf Koppitz, whose masterpiece is his 'Bewegungs Studie' of 1926, and the Czechoslovakian Frantisek Drtikol.

Perhaps the most central, yet enigmatic figure in creative European photography was the American Man Ray who moved to Paris in 1921 and became a key force in the Dada and Surrealist movements. Man Ray created his own version of the photogram which he dubbed the 'rayogram'; he discovered and exploited the process of solarization, giving a bizarre quality of light to his portraits, nudes and still-lifes. He recorded the features of the artistic giants of the day, Picasso, Picabia, Duchamp, Ernst and others, as well as those of various personalities related to the arts – minor poets, performers, patrons or beauties such as the young Lee Miller, who, inspired by Man Ray, took up photography herself. His portraits bring to life the rich group activity of the Paris of the twenties and thirties. If Man Ray, Lee Miller or Maurice Tabard, chose to examine the nature of objects through the camera, it was as poets, by allusion rather than analysis, in contrast to the emerging American mode. Paris created the climate in which the young German-born Erwin Blumenfeld created a remarkable series of metamorphic images of nudes, before moving to the United States in the late thirties to a successful career as a fashion photographer.

The new directions of European photography and their contrast with prevalent American work were noticeable at the show at the Julian Levy Gallery in New York in early 1932 entitled 'Modern European Photography'. The contributors comprised Man Ray, Lee Miller, Roger Parry, Eli Lotar, Ilse Bing, Ecce Photo, Florence Henri, Emmanuel Sougez, Maurice Tabard, André Kertesz and Brassaï from Paris, Walter Peterhaus, Peter Weller, Herbert Bayer, Otto Umbehr, Walter Hege, Helmut Lerski, Alice Lex, Oscar Nerlinger, Lucia Moholy and László Moholy-Nagy from Germany.

Fashion photography as a creative form came into its own in the early years of the century and, by the late 1920s, had spawned some exceptional talents. The first successful fashion photographer was the Frenchwoman Mlle. Reutlinger, though her work is formal and lacks the poetry to be found in the work of the Baron Gayne de Meyer, the first truly creative fashion photographer, who concocted a romantic fantasy world using soft, diffused lighting, halos of back-lighting, intangible surfaces, sleek and flawless models. It has been claimed that de Meyer's skilful use of artificial lighting was copied by the cinema industry. For a number of years de Meyer was the star of Condé Nast's *Vogue*.

De Meyer's top position at American *Vogue* was taken over by Edward Steichen, formerly a key figure in the Photo-Secession. Steichen worked for *Vogue* between 1923 and 1938, though his first fashion work, and the first published fashion photographs in colour, was his series published in

Nancy Cunard photographed by Cecil Beaton, c. 1930.

Art et Décoration in 1911, illustrating the creations of Paul Poiret. Steichen's lighting was harsh by contrast with that of de Meyer but seemed particularly effective in his modernistic images, using cut-out black-white geometric backgrounds and the aloof looks of his favourite model, Marian Moorehouse.

George Hoyningen Huené joined Paris *Vogue* in 1925 and was soon its chief photographer. A man of great taste, Huené conveyed a sleek and soft sense of movement and romance and was at his best photographing the fluid fashions of the early 1930s. Huené discovered the talent of the young Horst P. Horst who became one of *Vogue*'s foremost photographers after 1932.

English photographer Cecil Beaton evades all attempts to categorise his talent, turning with ease from travel or documentary work to society portraiture or fashion. He produced a comprehensive portfolio of portraits of all the characters that made up the elusive international *Beau Monde* of the twenties and thirties. At first influenced by de Meyer, he found his own style of fashion photography in the neo-romanticism of the mid thirties. Martin Munkasci, working for *Harper's Bazaar* in the 1930s was instrumental in bringing fashion photography from the confines of the studio into the open air.

Spectacular setting from D. W. Griffith's *Intolerance*. 1916.

The development of the movie film has its roots in two threads of nineteenth-century invention which came together in the early 1890s in Thomas Edison's first projections. The alliance was between the evolution of optical 'persistence of vision' toys, such as the Zootrope and Praxinoscope, and the refinement of rapid consecutive exposure techniques, such as those used so effectively in the documentation and analysis of consecutive phases of movement by pioneers Eadweard Muybridge, Etienne-Jules Marey and Ottomar Anschütz. The first American copyrighted motion picture was the Edison Kinetoscopic Record of a Sneeze registered on 7 January 1893. It was Louis Lumière who made the first European projection of moving pictures in 1895.

A period of some twenty years elapsed, however, before the complexity and variety of skills required to produce good-quality moving pictures were appreciated and brought together, enabling the birth of an industry that was to enjoy an ever-increasing popularity during the twenties and thirties. The cinema is a truly popular medium demanding wide public support at the box office to keep the wheels of the industry in motion. It is an industry that has evolved countless genres, but the vast majority of films, however, were spawned by the demand for entertainment, far fewer by the truly creative sensibility of author or director. Those avant-garde films that are acknowledged today as amongst the most exciting of their period often found inadequate appreciation with their contemporary public. The more commercial productions of the cinema can nonetheless, on occasion, be a marvellous reflection of tastes and styles, exaggerating fashions almost to the point of caricature and creating a distinctive celluloid style that, in turn, can be seen as the most perfect reflection of its era. There is no better mirror of a society than the fantasies it creates for itself and there is no more perfect world of illusion than the cinema.

D. W. Griffith is generally regarded as the first significant director to emerge in the history of the cinema. He started his career with the Biograph Company in 1908 but it was with *Birth of a Nation* of 1915 and his *Intolerance* of 1916 that he made his name. Griffith and, subsequently Cecil B. de Mille with spectacles such as *The Ten Commandments* (1923) greatly enlarged the technical scope of the new medium. The artistry of film production owed a great deal to European talent in the early years of the cinema. *The Cabinet of Dr. Caligari* by Robert Wiene of 1919 is an extraordinary landmark in its use of distorted perspectives and shadow patterns for dramatic effect, Sergei Eisenstein's new and imaginative editing techniques have made classics of such films as *The Battleship Potemkin* and *Ten Days that Shook the World*.

The world centre of the film industry was establishing itself positively in southern California, however, and attracting some of the best foreign talent, including Eisenstein who went under contract to Paramount, Sweden's leading director, Victor Sjöström, who changed his name to Seastrom and numerous others, including the Germans Josef von Sternberg and Fritz Lang. It was in 1926, before his move to Hollywood, that

Left Brigitte Helm in Marcel L'Herbier's *L'Argent*, 1927; jewellery design by Raymond Templier.

Far left and below Two Modernist settings for Fritz Lang's *Metropolis*, 1926

Right The eye-cutting scene from *Un Chien Andalou*, directed by Luis Buñuel in collaboration with Salvador Dali, 1928.

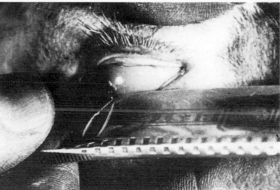

Lang made his masterpiece, *Metropolis,* a nightmare vision of Modernism as a grotesque capitalist paradise, a stylish garden of Eden atop futuristic skyscrapers, feeding on the human sacrifice to the Machine monster of the dehumanised working class.

It was, similarly, a few years later, the more artistically fertile European background that encouraged the remarkable collaboration of Salvador Dali and director Luis Buñuel in their two important Surrealist films, *Un Chien Andalou* of 1928 and *L'Age d'Or* of 1930. Julien Levy, who struggled to gain recognition in America for the best avant-garde films as well as still photography from Europe, brought both of these films to New York for projection in his gallery. Their shock value attracted a notoriety and hence the attention which his other offerings, including Man Ray's *L'Etoile de Mer,* Fernand Léger's *Ballet Mécanique* and Marcel Duchamp's *Anemic Cinema,* had failed to inspire. Out of Levy's Film Society was to grow the film library of the Museum of Modern Art.

The advent of synchronised sound in the late 1920s was a major breakthrough in the evolution of commercial film production. This factor, combined with the demand for escapist cinema after the financial disasters of 1929 and the availability of cheap labour as a result of the Crash, engendered the Hollywood genre that is associated with the early 1930s, the lavish musical. M.G.M.'s *Broadway Melody* of 1929, which won an Academy Award as the Outstanding Film of the Year, was one of the first successes in this field. Warner Bros. achieved considerable success with the series of films directed for them by Busby Berkeley whose name is synonymous with the slick and inventive choreography of large casts exemplified in his *Golddiggers of 1933.* Rival production company R.K.O. combined the talents of Fred Astaire and Ginger Rogers in a delightful series of films which include some of the most stylish sets and dance routines conceived in Hollywood.

The obvious fear of fashion overtaking filming schedules explains the general tendency for set designers to avoid the too-obviously fashionable. Producers were fully aware that the public's need for the cinema as a projection of popular dreams was perhaps best satisfied through the star system and in many cases the stars became more important than the films in which they were cast. Their appearance was imitated and their life-styles envied. The glamorous portrayal in publicity photographs of a studio's crop of stars became an important by-product of the film industry.

The beginnings of the lavishly choreographed musical: M.G.M.'s *Broadway Melody* of 1929.

Busby Berkeley's
choreography in *Golddiggers
of 1933.*

Painting and the Decorative Arts

by Marina Henderson

TO EMPHASISE THAT TOOROP's *Three Brides* was painted only five years before Picasso's *Demoiselles d'Avignon*, that ten years separated Horta's Hôtel Solvay from Loos' Steiner House, that Marcel Breuer's tubular steel and canvas chair dates from the same year as the triumph of Ruhlmann at the Paris Exhibition of 1925, is to dramatize some of the rapid changes that took place in the fine and decorative arts between 1890 and 1940. Just as radical as these respective changes in style was the change in relationship during this period between painting and sculpture on the one hand and architecture and design on the other. Although many developments in art were absorbed after varying lapses of time into the popular decorative idiom, the progression of painting and sculpture in the first decades of the twentieth century was essentially that of a withdrawal from a mass-market society, that of architecture and design of an effort to cater for it.

The cause of this fundamental divergence was cogently stated by Henry van de Velde, the Belgian architect and designer who was one of the most influential international exponents of Art Nouveau. In an address at the Cologne Exhibition of 1914, he stated that 'the artist is a fervent individualist, a free spontaneous creator. He will never voluntarily submit to a discipline forcing on

him a type, a canon.' This public protest against the direction of architecture and design towards mass-production and therefore standardization can be seen as heralding the international Modern Style, in much the same way that the 1900 Paris Exhibition heralded the decline of Art Nouveau.

Although Art Nouveau was so brief a phenomenon (when McKnight Kauffer wrote his history of posters in 1924, he did not even mention Alphonse Mucha) it is significant in the history of art as the first art movement that consciously and deliberately sought to create a new style. The 1890s, the decade of Art Nouveau, was also the height of the Symbolist movement and a peak period of Post-Impressionist activity. And although primarily associated with architectural, graphic and object design, Art Nouveau is linked in a complex and sometimes contradictory relationship to contemporaneous and future developments in painting.

In reaction to the optical realism of the Impressionists, the Symbolists aimed to depict 'the idea in sensuous form' and, in protest against the increasing industrialization of society, drew their subject matter from legend, literature, religion and the occult. Distinguished by a shared attitude rather than a common pictorial style – the movement included artists as diverse as Gustave Mo-

Below right Jan Toorop: *The Three Brides*, 1893.

Below Pablo Picasso: *Les Demoiselles d'Avignon*, 1907.

Above *The Carnation*, poster by Alphonse Mucha, 1897, showing the influence of the Symbolists' sensuous, organic painting.

Left James McNeill Whistler: *The Little White Girl: Symphony in White No. II 1864*, showing the strong Japanese influence on late nineteenth-century art, another stylistic source of Art Nouveau.

reau, Odilon Redon, Puvis de Chavannes, Ferdinand Khnopff – Symbolist painting recorded not the observation but the sensation, the intuitive experience of the artist. In both the aim to communicate emotion and in the subject matter employed to do so, much Symbolist painting, despite a totally opposed aesthetic philosophy, is allied to Art Nouveau: the use of undulating line, the proliferation of the female figure with flowing hair, as in the works of Gustav Klimt, insects, peacocks, water, decorative accessories or symbolic iconography. The work of Emile Gallé is perhaps the most direct example of Symbolist influence in applied design. Sharing the essentially literary inspiration of the painters, Gallé translated the decadence of Huysmans and the melancholy of Mallarmé into highly-wrought glass of sensuous organic form and inlaid, textured furniture, recalling the jewelled canvases of Gustave Moreau, and embodying an idea, an emotion.

The somewhat decadent elegance which typifies Symbolist painting became the hallmark of Art Nouveau in France: it informs the posters of Mucha, the jewellery of Lalique, the ironwork of Guimard, the furniture of Louis Majorelle. But the flowing, flaring, asymmetrical line employed by Art Nouveau designers was linked to a variety of art sources. In retrospect, Holman Hunt's *The Lady of Shalott* can be described as a proto-Art Nouveau painting, and the work of the Pre-Raphaelites became widely known in Europe towards the end of the nineteenth century. Later, in the work of Aubrey Beardsley, two of the main stylistic sources of Art Nouveau design were triumphantly united, the Pre-Raphaelites and the art of Japan as transmuted by Whistler in his paintings, to create the quintessence of Art Nouveau graphic design.

In the work of the Post-Impressionists, Bonnard, Seurat and Toulouse-Lautrec, the influence of Japanese prints was also assimilated to create stylistic features which became part of Art Nouveau's decorative vocabulary. Asymmetrical composition, flat, simplified areas of colour, a flowing linear surface pattern, curvilinear movement; these features, seen in Bonnard's famous screen, painted when he was exhibiting with the Nabis, Seurat's *Le Cirque* and Toulouse-Lautrec's colour lithographs, dominated Art Nouveau graphic design, especially in posters which were produced by virtually every leading artist at the time. Posters were one of the few art forms not attempted by Gauguin, although his *cloissonisme* was popularized in the designs of Grasset.

An important branch of Art Nouveau which was to persist, though transmuted, when the decorative elegance of the French school withered, can clearly be traced to him. While at Pont-Aven, between 1888 and 1891, Gauguin was inspired through the teaching of William Morris, to experiment in crafts. It is perhaps to this inspiration, helped by the influence of another William Morris disciple, Henry van de Velde, who had turned from easel painting to architectural, graphic and industrial design, that we can trace the origin of the expressive, essentially abstract use of line.

In Gauguin's *Vision after the Sermon*, the brutal and emotional use of line becomes the structural focus of the composition and, reinforced by flat areas of arbitrary colour, arouses a response independent of the subject matter. This definitive use of line rapidly spread in Belgium. Its immediate effect can be seen in Lehman's catalogue for the influential 1891 Les Vingt exhibition in Brussels. Through Van de Velde's designs for textiles, furniture, architectural accessories, lectures and writings, this influence was felt all over Europe and became a distinguishing feature of the German Jugendstil and, subsequently, the Expressionists.

When his influential book *From Delacroix to Neo-Impressionism* was published in 1899, Signac remarked that the basis of modern art must be the abstract organization of colour and line. It was not, perhaps, until Kandinsky's first purely abstract watercolour in 1910, that this was logically fulfilled, but the way had been paved by the Art Nouveau development of abstract and stylised organic forms. Van de Velde's metalwork or *Tropon* poster are essentially abstract conceptions.

The rapid decay and vulgarization of Art Nouveau lay in the contradiction that while – following the tenets of William Morris – it was meant to be a new style for a new industrial age, in practice it became one in which a handful of artist-designers created individual artifacts which shared a common decorative language for a short time. As such, it was the last coherent style in which both the decorative and fine arts found close identity. But, since it was not a style susceptible to standardization and mass-production, it was ill-suited to the demands of a mass society dominated by technological change.

One of the most flamboyant efforts in the fine arts to come to terms with this society was that of the Italian Futurists. In their Manifesto of 1910, they extolled urban life and machines, stating that the task of the artist was to 'put the spectator in the centre of the picture', to make him participate in the artistic experience which was no longer merely to be the privilege of the artist.

The Futurists employed some of the technical language of Cubism, not in an attempt to explore form but rather to arouse emotion. Glorifying speed, movement, action, crowds, the Futurists' work became rapidly known over Europe through exhibitions held from 1911 onwards in Paris, Brussels and London. As a group whose aim was direct communication, it is apt that their influence was most clearly seen in poster design, where several features of their painting became virtual clichés: the use of chaotic typography (anticipating Dada), of dramatic linear perspective, of simultaneous presentation of successive aspects of movement, first used by Balla in his charming *Dynamism of a Dog on a Lead*. In such posters as

Above The sense of curvilinear movement embodied in Georges Seurat's *Le Cirque*, 1890–1, became a major stylistic device for Art Nouveau graphic artists.

Opposite Holman Hunt: *The Lady of Shalott*, 1886, showing the flowing, asymmetrical lines later to be more closely associated with Art Nouveau.

Top Gustav Klimt: *Salome*, 1909.

Above Paul Gauguin: *The Vision after the Sermon*, 1888; the expressive use of line in this painting was taken up especially by Belgian Art Nouveau designers, as in the wood engraving (left) by Henry van de Velde, 1893.

Right Both the Futurists and the later Dadaists were fascinated by the possibilities of conveying the sense of moving streamlined forms in their paintings, as in Marcel Duchamp's *Nude Descending a Staircase*, 1912.

Below The smooth lines of the decorative sculptures of the twenties reflect the concern of the fine arts with streamlined forms; female form in bronze by V. Brecherel, *c.* 1925.

Cassandre's great *Etoile du Nord*, the Futurist faith in the new technology is combined, within a Cubist organization of space, with a dynamism and communicated sympathy that would even have satisfied Marinetti, the founder of the movement.

The Futurist extolling of speed and dynamic action also became a commonplace in object design in the later twenties and thirties. Seen at its best in Lalique's famous *Victoire* mascot, at its most commonplace in the straining lines of the decorative sculptures of improbably healthy girls popular during the twenties and thirties. The curious passion for streamlining the most inappropriate objects, radios, cookers, cocktail cabinets, may also ultimately be traced back to the Futurist example.

The most important element in early twentieth-century design, however, was the search for structural order, for form independent of accidental appearance. Cézanne had found this in 'the cone, the cylinder, the sphere'. In their early Cubist works, Picasso and Braque followed Cézanne in their analysis of the subject matter into abstract components. Their object was not to recreate pictorially the subject as it is seen at a particular moment or in a particular place, but as it is known in its many aspects simultaneously. By 1910, Cubism had resolved the subject matter into a linear geometry of interlocking planes. It was this analytical stage of Cubism that was transmitted through De Stijl, Suprematism and Constructivism to the Bauhaus, where its abstract geometry was absorbed into the development of the international Modern Style.

From 1912, when they first introduced collage, onwards, Picasso and Braque's Cubism became progressively more decorative, a trend which culminated in the lyrical elegance of Juan Gris' synthetic Cubism, the illustrative realism of Duchamp, and the colour abstraction of Kupka and Delaunay. It was these variants of Cubism that were attacked by Le Corbusier and Ozenfant in their book *After Cubism*, published in 1918, when they accused current Cubist painting of having degenerated into elaborate decoration.

De Stijl, an association of artists, architects and designers, took its name from the review founded by Theo van Doesburg and Piet Mondrian in 1917 shortly after Mondrian's return from Paris, where his painting had been revolutionized under Cubist influence. Mondrian's variant of Cubism, Neo-Plasticism, was restricted to primary colours and square or rectangular shapes, the interaction of verticals and horizontals. He considered Neo-Plasticism not as a personal conception of the individual artist, but as 'the logical development of all arts, ancient and modern' and the basis for a future rational architecture and industrial design.

Mondrian's theory that 'less is more' was most successfully applied in architecture, notably in the work of Mies van der Rohe, as in the elevation and plan for a Brick Country House in 1923, and in graphic design, such as Piet Zwart's posters. In applied design, the insistence on the limited mathematical interaction of planes paradoxically resulted in a certain fussiness. Rietveld's desk and chair of 1917 are both formally and functionally unsatisfactory. Van Doesburg himself compro-

Left Modernist interior: impersonal, geometric and devoid of ornament, *c.* 1930.

Below El Lissitsky; *Proun 99, c.* 1924; the teaching of El Lissitsky and Moholy-Nagy at the Bauhaus on the importance of abstract forms was of central importance in the development of the international Modern Style.

mised with the original strict tenets of the movement and his use of horizontals in the mural decorations for the Café de l'Aubiette led to a break with Mondrian.

In his Suprematist painting, *White on White*, Malevich carried Cubist geometry to its ultimate logical conclusion of complete abstraction. He applied this conclusion in his experiments with the problem of form in three dimensions, treating architecture as an abstract visual art. Developments in Suprematism and Constructivism at the Bauhaus, especially in their concern with forms in space and movements and the application of new materials to sculpture and design, followed the teaching of El Lissitzsky and Moholy-Nagy. Basic Cubist geometry was of central importance to the ultimate emergence of the international Modern Style, impersonal, geometrical, devoid of ornament. Whether executed sumptuously, as in Mies van der Rohe's Tugendhat House of 1937, or brutally, as in Le Corbusier's Weissenhoff Housing Project of 1927, the style, in architectural and applied design, parallels an earlier, fundamental, trait in the fine arts during the first decades of the century: the reduction to apparent simplicity through the exploration of fundamental form.

Art Deco was not principally concerned with form but with ornament, exquisite craftsmanship and expensive elaboration. Becoming less elaborate, though nonetheless expensive, during the twenties, the stylistic conventions of Art Deco which had been drawn from a variety of sources, including the Wiener Werkstätte.

The most obvious example is the decorative use of Cubist geometry from the mid 1920s onwards. The influence is exemplified in the textiles of Sonia Delaunay, the rugs of da Silva Bruhns and Marion Dorn, the bindings of Pierre Legrain, the silverware of Jean Puiforcat and the jewellery of Gérard Sandoz, Paul Brandt, Jean Fouquet and Raymond Templier. Reduced to bold geometrical shapes juxtaposed for visual effect and colouring which was often crude, the popular adaptations of Cubism, especially in the mass rather than designers' market, seem far removed from such achievements as Braque's profound examination of structure in even his most decorative pictures like *The Café Bar*. But even when apparently far removed from developments in the fine arts,

Above Lacquer panel by Gustave Miklos, 1922.

Right Design for a carpet by Marion Dorn, *c.* 1935.

objects intended for a mass market do display certain family relationships, as can be seen when we compare the pared-down purity of Brancusi's *Mademoiselle Pogany* with the decorative stylization of much derivative object design.

A similar visual affinity had linked the work of Art Deco artists with the paintings of Matisse. Matisse's elimination of detail and his reduction of line and colour to their elements had an immediate decorative appeal that was exploited by such designers as Lepape, Georges Barbier and (with a judicious mixture of Cubism) Charles Martin, in their immensely popular *pochoirs*, fashion plates and luxury book illustrations. Modigliani's sensuous distortion of the female form can equally be seen in much illustrative work of the time and was popularized by decorative artists such as Jean Dupas, whose posters, especially, educated the eyes of a mass audience in both France and England.

The most consistent popularizer of contemporary fine art developments, however, was the theatre. Bakst's stupendous designs for *Schéhérazade* and *Cléopatre*, which had such an immediate effect on fashionable taste, had been the West's first opportunity to appreciate the blend of Russian folk art with assimilated Western influence that had inspired the *Mir Iskustva* movement; Diaghilev continued to use outstanding artists to design décors and costumes for his ballets; these include Picasso, Matisse, Rouault, de Chirico and Cocteau. It was through a ballet, *La Chatte*, of 1927, designed by Gabo and Pevsner, that Constructivist developments were first intro-

duced to France. Similarly, Miro's whimsical abstract patterning reached a wide audience in his brilliant designs for Massine's *Jeu d'Enfants*, 1932. Conversely, in the mid 1930s, theatre designers like the neo-romantic Christian Bérard in Paris, the Bauhaus-trained Joseph Urban in New York and the whimsically nostalgic Rex Whistler in London, were amongst the most influential interior designers, contributing to the markedly theatrical flavour of chic room décors at the time.

This theatricality, emphasized by the returning fashion for Baroque, also owed a good deal to Surrealism. In 1924, proclaiming the death of Dada, a hectically vociferous movement stressing the illogical, absurd and chance elements in art, André Breton hailed the advent of an art that was 'to resolve the previous contradictory conditions of dream and reality into a . . . super-reality'. The fantasy, figurative detail and elaborate visual narrative, illustrating both the conscious and subconscious level, of Surrealist painting, were welcomed at a time when people were becoming weary of the economic austerity of the Depression and the aesthetic austerity of the international style. Truly Surrealistic designs, like the famous 'leg' console table by Robsjohn-Gittings or Dali's fantasies for Schiaparelli and Edward James (which included a room in which the furniture and décor was based on parts of Mae West's body) were produced for the delectation of a few. But through advertisements, as in the photographs of Peter Rose Pulham for Victor Stiebel, window displays like those by Artur Gumitsch and the habit of expensive fashion magazines like *Vogue* and *Harper's Bazaar* of commissioning painters to design their covers (these included Dali, de Chirico, Laurencin), Surrealist influence reached a wider public.

Van de Velde's prophecy had been correct. In an increasingly affluent and demanding urban society, which was necessarily dependent on large-scale industrial production to supply its needs for housing, furniture and every other sort of utensil, the architect-engineer, not the artist-designer or even the craftsman-designer, became the creator of style, both in architecture and design.

Above left Carpet designed for Radio City Music Hall, New York, c. 1925.

Left Robert Delaunay: *Hommage à Blériot*, 1914, a development of Cubism which was to have a profound influence on interior design.

Above Surrealist photograph by Angus McBean, 1930s.

Literature and the Decorative Arts

by Isabelle Anscombe

Below Dante Gabriel Rosetti (1828–82).

Below centre Portrait by G. F. Watts of William Morris, 1870.

Bottom Oscar Wilde (1854–1900).

Opposite A page of typographic experiment from *Blast*, the manifesto of the Vorticist movement, founded by Wyndham Lewis.

IN TRACING A RELATIONSHIP between the literature of a period and its decorative arts one immediately runs into a problem of classification. True, there are areas where a direct association can be shown, as in the line drawings of Aubrey Beardsley and the design of the *Yellow Book* or the typography used in *Blast*, where the signatories of Vorticism were putting their names as much to a style as to the Manifesto itself. However, in such cases there is only a narrow line between decorative and fine arts. Even where an attempt is made to write from a similar philosophical or aesthetic position to the artist, the problems remain, for either the philosophy stems principally from the fine arts or has little to do with the actual products of the decorative arts.

The treatment of decorative arts in writing relies on description; the problem of classification is therefore in the place of description within the body of work of a particular author. Traditionally, returning now to the rules of rhetoric, description (*ekphrasis*) is a detachable and inessential part of narrative and serves only as a jewel, highlighting the writer's skill. It is the passage in a book which can be skipped over without losing the thread of the story.

However, many of the novels of this period would all but cease to exist if that view was maintained. Proust's *A la Recherche du Temps Perdu* or Virginia Woolf's *Mrs Dalloway* or *To the Lighthouse* rely on description for the narrative to exist at all; Henry James's. *The Golden Bowl* uses description as the key to the novel's themes, while James Joyce employed absolute particularity of description to heighten the narrative to a plane of anti-realism. The problem of classification is defined not in relation to placing writers in specific categories but in observing the changing role of the descriptive passage throughout the period.

The first impetus for decorative art in the nineteenth century came from John Ruskin, although the legacy of his writings gave rise to ideas which he would never have espoused himself. Ruskin saw himself as a seer who would draw attention to the infinite and essential in nature, who would bring an unhappy populace back to the truths of nature through their own moulding of their environment. He extolled the freedom of the workman's expression in Gothic edifices and denounced the cult of conventionalisation upheld by the organisers of the 1851 Great Exhibition as being the very opposite of his essential truths.

In some ways, his most apt exponent could be said to be Charles Dickens whose descriptions of the degradation of London streets and paucity of inspiration in the commercial system fully supported Ruskin's criticisms. In *Hard Times* little Sissy Jupe is ridiculed with all the force of Ruskinian scorn for preferring realistic flowers for a carpet pattern rather than the scientifically correct conventionalised motif. In fact, however, Ruskin's truest followers were the Pre-Raphaelites and William Morris.

Morris took Ruskin's advocation of medieval society to heart and combined it with his socialist theories in *News From Nowhere* to depict an England after the revolution as a society of craftsmen and agriculturalists who lived by the clean waters of the Thames. Morris wanted to persuade by the charm of his descriptions of healthy people living fulfilled lives, yet *News From Nowhere* is closer in spirit to the descriptions of medieval communities in his Prose Romances than to Karl Marx. Nor are Morris's ideas far removed from Oscar Wilde's *The Soul of Man Under Socialism* or Wilde's American lectures where he rejected socialism for the doctrine of Individualism. The ideals are the same; give the artist freedom to express himself, encourage a country to find an art among its own resources without recourse to ancient models, let man express his individuality through his surroundings, whether it be his own beloved blue and white china or Morris's bright colours of medieval heraldry.

The Pre-Raphaelites adapted Ruskin in their attention to the details of nature and the accurate depiction of medieval scenes. Dante Gabriel Rossetti was by nature, however, unsuited to the bluff innocence of Morris and his paintings and writings show a preoccupation with the prevailing sensual tastes. His *Sonnets for Pictures* are an attempt to correlate the two arts almost in the tradition of Baudelaire's Swedenborgian 'correspondances'. If material objects are uncoded symbols for spiritual values, one must attempt by the suggestion of association to penetrate the parallel spiritual world. One brief example of Rossetti's desire to marry the two arts of painting and poetry is these lines from *Lilith (For a Picture)* where the alliteration heightens the dreamy, almost mystical qualities of his own paintings:

> 'The rose and the poppy are her flowers; for where
> Is he not found, O Lilith, whom shed scent
> And soft-shed kisses and soft sleep shall snare?'

For Rossetti, a description of colours, of scents, of dresses or landscapes, adds a depth to a painting which insinuates that there is more to one's choice of decoration than mere taste.

There is also found in Rossetti the beginnings of

Below Portrait of Georges Rodenbach by Raffaëlli.

Bottom Medallion by Lalique of Sarah Bernhardt, one of the prototypes of La Berma in Proust's *A la Recherche du Temps Perdu*, c. 1900.

Opposite top Cover design by Aubrey Beardsley for the *Yellow Book*, which began publication in 1894.

Opposite centre Helleu's sketch of Robert de Montesquiou, the original of Huysmans' Des Esseintes and Proust's Baron Charlus, 1890s.

Opposite bottom Marcel Proust (1871–1922).

the romantic leanings towards Italy which remains present not only in the English maiden tourist's predilection for the 'pensione', but in the writings of Browning, E. M. Forster and Henry James; its enduring importance for English sensibilities is summed up by T. S. Eliot:

'In the room the women come and go
Talking of Michelangelo.'

The curious mixture of virginal beauty and lush sensuality which the British find in Italy began with the publication of Walter Pater's *Studies in the History of the Renaissance*. In the Preface he defined the questions proper to the aesthetic critic as:

'What is this song or picture, this engaging personality presented in life or in a book, to *me*? What effect does it really produce on me? Does it give me pleasure? and if so, what sort or degree of pleasure? How is my nature modified by its presence and under its influence?'

In his Conclusion he answers these questions:

'To burn always with this hard gem-like flame, to maintain this ecstasy, is success in life . . . . While all melts under our feet, we may well catch at any exquisite passion, or any contribution to knowledge that seems, by a lifted horizon, to set the spirit free for a moment, or any stirring of the senses, strange dyes, strange flowers, and curious odours, or work of the artist's hands, or the face of one's friend.'

What is crucial in Pater is the passion of his writing, the quality of his descriptive passages. What Pater's aesthetic critique calls for is precisely the description, in detail, of the effect of experience upon the individual's sensibility. What the aesthetes, the later heroes of Pater's cult, were to do was to describe their reactions to objects or events. What became precious was not so much the quality of an experience, but the constant refinement of their sensibilities. From this came the cult of the artificial, the search for the exotic,

the establishment of the private world for the cultivation of the sensibility.

This development laid new emphasis, therefore, not only on the quality and type of one's surroundings, but also on the quality of one's description. In France, a parallel development had grown out of Théophile Gautier's call for 'l'art pour l'art'. There, in reaction to the successive revolutions and the rise of bourgeois politics, it was Paris itself which became the subject matter. The writer became the 'flâneur' described by Walter Benjamin; the *flâneur* was the man who wandered the illuminated arcades of Haussmann, who treated the city as his own interior where he could observe and spy on life; the writer became the figure of the disinterested detective reconstructing the city by reference to his own sensibilities. Thus Baudelaire, in *Le Cygne* in the Paris section of *Les Fleurs du Mal*, can mourn the passing of the Paris he admired, yet the city is *his* and the poem returns to his own sensibilities:

'Paris change! mais rien dans ma mélancolie
N'a bougé! palais neufs, échafaudages, blocs,
Vieux faubourgs, tout pour moi devient allégorie,
Et mes chers souvenirs sont plus lourds que des rocs.'

Likewise in Georges Rodenbach's *Bruges-La-Morte* the description of Bruges is a central part of the novel, reinforcing by the description of the quiet town with its still waters and humdrum streets the widower's grief:

'Une équation mystérieuse s'établissait. A l'épouse morte devait correspondre une ville morte. Son grand deuil exigeait un tel décor.'

In translating Edgar Allan Poe, Baudelaire felt that he had found a truly kindred spirit. In Poe's *Philosophy of Furniture* what begins as matter-of-fact advice on the choice of carpets and other fixtures, not dissimilar to Eastlake's *Hints on Household Taste*, turns into a description of a way of life:

'The proprietor lies asleep on a sofa – the weather is cool – the time is near midnight: we will make a sketch of the room during his slumber.'

The room is decorated in silver, crimson and gold, containing 'landscapes of an imaginative cast', portraits of 'female heads of an ethereal beauty . . . . four large and gorgeous Sèvres vases, in which bloom a profusion of sweet and vivid flowers . . . . a small antique lamp with highly perfumed oil . . . . two or three hundred magnificently bound books' and a lamp which 'throws a tranquil but magical radiance over all.' The room is almost that which one would imagine behind Baudelaire's *Le Balcon* or *Harmonie du Soir* and could be a prototype for Huysmans' Des Esseintes or Wilde's shallow copy, Dorian Gray. What is central is the weight given to objects in the description of the interior because it is those objects which create – define and place – the aesthete who inhabits it.

All these ideas find their master in Marcel Proust. In *A la Recherche du Temps Perdu* description is no longer a means to an end within the structure of the narrative, nor is it the creation in fiction of a particular 'type'; description is an end in itself. In *The Image of Proust*, Walter Benjamin

wrote that:

'The image of Proust is the highest physiognomic expression which the irresistibly growing discrepancy between literature and life was able to assume .... Proust's method is actualization, not reflection. He is filled with the insight that none of us has time to live the true dramas of the life that we are destined for. This is what ages us – this and nothing else. The wrinkles and creases on our faces are the registration of the great passions, vices, insights that called on us; but we, the masters, were not home.'

In *Le Temps Retrouvé* Proust exclaims:

'Ah! que le monde est grand à la clarté des lampes! Aux yeux du souvenir que le monde est petit!'

It is this making-small in the actualization of remembrance which is the central point of Proust's description, reinforced by the constant search for resemblances. Thus it is, in *Du Côté de Chez Swann*, among the Chinese porcelain, screens and Japanese silk, and the lamps, plants and orchids of Odette's room, that Swann can desire to kiss Odette because of her resemblance to a Botticelli portrait:

'. . while the kiss, the bodily surrender which would have seemed natural and but moderately attractive, had they been granted him by a creature of somewhat withered flesh and sluggish blood, coming, as now they came, to crown his adoration of a masterpiece in a gallery, must, it seemed, prove as exquisite as they would be supernatural.'

Here is no longer the dandy seeking new and vivid pleasures from perversity, no longer an artificial setting up the stage for a chosen experience – as Des Esseintes created the black scenario for the celebration of the death of his virility – but the weighing up of all experiences through resemblance to augment the consistency of experience.

The circle drawn by the lamplight of Proust's memory is static and given; reflection is powerless to create or produce. Therefore, like Poe's description of a room at midnight, while the occupant slumbers, the furniture, artifacts and decoration which are described have a peculiar permanence. If one sees Proust's writing as the culmination of the doctrine of 'l'art pour l'art' and the cult of the dandy it is possible to read a 'correspondance' between the qualities of Proustian description and the decorative essence of Art Nouveau. Where William Morris called his designing his 'bread and cheese work' and incorporated his own patterns in his descriptive writing, Proust is at one remove from actual production and Art Nouveau was precisely the design aspect which relied upon the linear movements of growth in the sinuous stems and unfurling leaves to give, paradoxically, an impression of a static luxuriousness, the exotic moment caught in time.

Similarly, one can look at the writings of Virginia Woolf and see an association with the art which was produced by her own sister, Vanessa Bell. Duncan Grant, whom Vanessa regarded as the superior artist, had been influenced by early visits to Italy and combined his admiration for Italian fresco with the precepts of Post-Impressionism. Many of the murals or decorative designs for furniture or needlework produced by Vanessa Bell and Duncan Grant for the Omega

Workshops or for the Woolfs' house at Rodmell or their own house, Charleston, show an Italian appreciation of colour and form as well as theme.

The products of Omega have been criticised for their poor finish, yet what was most important was the final effect, the fact that everything in a room had been considered and decorated within the same mode. Virginia Woolf's writing can be considered from the same viewpoint. In *To the Lighthouse* is this description of an artist painting on the quay:

'. . . in Panama hat and yellow boots, seriously, softly, absorbedly, for all that he was watched by ten little boys, with an air of profound contentment on his round red face, gazing, and then, when he had gazed, dipping; imbuing the tip of his brush in some soft mound of green and pink. Since Mr Paunceforte had been there, three years before, all the pictures were like that she said, green and grey, with lemon-coloured sailing-boats, and pink women on the beach.'

Virginia Woolf writes with the same brush and palette, creating a whole picture through the essential impression:

'Her voice, her laugh, her dress (something floating, white, crimson).' (*Mrs Dalloway*)

Interiors are of the utmost importance, especially

Above Scene from the film of Jean Cocteau's *Les Enfants Terribles*, 1950.

Right F. Scott Fitzgerald (1896–1940), with his wife Zelda.

in the description of women, as the odd impressions of the background are vital to the delineation of character.

How far Pater's ideals had drifted down into G. E. Moore's *Principia Ethica*, which the Apostles discussed in Bloomsbury, is impossible to say, but there remains a lingering similarity in the concluding chapter of Moore:

'. . . personal affections and aesthetic enjoyments include *all* the greatest, and *by far* the greatest, goods we can imagine.'

When such a philosophy is here translated into descriptive prose it is no longer against the background of Beardsley and the *Yellow Book*, but amid discussions of Post-Impressionism. These are the concerns of Virginia Woolf's novels and her criticism too, in *The Common Reader*, rejected analytic examination in favour of a description of her own sensibilities amid aesthetic enjoyment. The techniques of description have changed as much as those of painting. To return to the painter on the quay in *To the Lighthouse*:

'But her grandmother's friends, she said, glancing discreetly as they passed, took the greatest pains; first they mixed their own colours, and then they ground them, and then they put damp cloths on them to keep them moist.

So Mr Tansley supposed she meant him to see that that man's picture was skimpy, was that what one said? The colours weren't solid?'

Wyndham Lewis's hatred of Bloomsbury and his rejection of the Omega took almost the same lines:

'. . . art-for-art's sake . . . is nothing to do with art – it is a spectator's doctrine, not an artist's: it teaches how to enjoy, not how to perform.' (*Men Without Art*)

The symbol of the Vortex was for space, for classical permanence, and not for time and the enjoyment of the romantic flux. Although concerned with the decorative arts, his writing shows no concern for the depiction of art; as *Blast* so forcefully demonstrated, it was a matter of directness, of the design of a page, not of description. The designs of Grant and Bell for the Hogarth Press show a much gentler echo of the text in contrast to Lewis's didacticism, which was designed to disturb. A writer whose descriptive prose came closest to Lewis – and also to the Surrealists – is Edward Upward, such as in *The Railway Accident*:

'Outside the station the air would be warm and I should remember clock-golf in the rectory garden, or there would be heavy snow recalling the voluntary ascetic life I had often planned: there would be crocuses or vultures, it would not be the same as it was here.'

Somewhere in the middle, as it were, comes the poetry of T. S. Eliot, whose meticulousness in describing objects and interiors is equally shocking, but has an internal coherence in its imagery quite unlike Upward's 'crocuses or vultures'. Eliot writes in the Prufrock Cycle:

'Her hand twists a paper rose,
That smells of dust and eau de Cologne,'

In a different sense, Jean Cocteau also created whole interiors which, by their unreality, allowed

for the apparent normality of fantasy actions, as in *Les Enfants Terribles*.

In the work of Henry James the importance of the object, the satisfaction of one's sensibilities in relation to artifacts, is paramount and his very style is an attempt to assimilate the completeness of the treasured object, as in *The Golden Bowl*. In the Preface to *The Spoils of Poynton*, he gives the definition of:

'. . . life being all inclusion and confusion, and art being all discrimination and selection.'

The writer is therefore the image of the collector, the connoisseur. Adam Verver, in *The Golden Bowl*, is precisely that:

'Nothing perhaps might affect us as queerer, had we time to look into it, than this application of the same measure of value to such different pieces of property as old Persian carpets, say, and new human acquisitions.'

A final, and somewhat surprising, example of the last remnants of Romanticism, in discovering lost symbols and illusions of the spiritual in parallel everyday objects, is found in F. Scott Fitzgerald. Here, James's connoisseur has given way to the rich American for whom the lights of Broadway shine. Brought up on Keats, Fitzgerald believed in the romantic hero whose vision would imbue his surroundings with an inner light; but all his heroes were doomed to failure. Nevertheless, the light is there in Fitzgerald's descriptions, even if it is bound to fade again. In *The Beautiful and Damned*, perhaps his most poignant novel, is this description of Broadway on Armistice night, 1918:

'Under these bright lights glittered the faces of peoples whose glory had long since passed away, whose very civilisations were dead – men whose ancestors had heard the news of victory in Babylon, in Ninevah, in Baghdad, in Tyre, a hundred generations before; men whose ancestors had seen a flower-decked, slave-adorned cortège drift with its wake of captives down the avenues of Imperial Rome.'

But for the individual, as for Fitzgerald himself, the illusion fades with age:

'At thirty an organ-grinder is more or less a moth-eaten man who grinds an organ – and once he was an organ-grinder! The unmistakeable stigma of humanity touches all those impersonal and beautiful things that only youth ever grasps in their impersonal glory.'

Anthony and Gloria Patch are reduced to drink to conjure up the lost magic and the novel ends with their departure for Europe, too depleted now ever to enjoy it.

The fate of Anthony and Gloria Patch symbolises the end of the cult of the beautiful object. Their quest for happiness was dependent on money and at last the taint of production has entered the world constructed by Pater, Wilde, Huysmans and Proust. The description of the beautiful room, the objet d'art, is lost in the description of the struggle to attain those things. Design itself changed from the luxuries of the Paris 1925 Exhibition, the extravagances of Art Deco to a consciousness of utility and economy. The end of the great era of the decorative object, of Art Furniture, coincided with the end of the description in prose of those lost rooms and forgotten collectors.

AALTO, Alvar (b. 1898)
Scandinavian architect and furniture designer, best known for his bentwood designs.

ALBERS, Josef (1888–1977)
German painter and designer who worked at the Bauhaus.

ANGMAN, Jacob (1876–1942)
Swedish architect and furniture designer.

ARGY-ROUSSEAU, Gabriel (b. 1885)
French Art Deco glass designer.

ARTIGAS, Josep Llorens (b.1892)
Spanish potter.

ASHBEE, Charles Robert (1863–1942)
British Arts and Crafts architect, designer and writer; he founded the Guild of Handicraft in 1888.

BAILLIE SCOTT, Mackay Hugh (1865–1945)
British architect and designer, he worked extensively abroad.

BAKST, Léon (1886–1925)
Russian theatre designer who introduced bright colours and oriental motifs into his sets and costumes for the Ballets Russes.

BARLACH, Ernst (1870–1938)
German sculptor, graphic artist and ceramist.

BARNSLEY, Sidney (1865–1926)
British furniture designer and craftsman working in the Cotswolds.

BAUDELAIRE, Charles (1821–67)
French poet, art critic and journalist, he also translated the works of Poe and de Quincey. *Les Fleurs du Mal* was published in 1857.

BEARDSLEY, Aubrey (1872–98)
British decadent writer and illustrator.

BEATON, Cecil (b. 1904)
British photographer.

BEHRENS, Peter (1868–1940)
Austrian architect and designer and member of the Deutscher Werkbund.

BEL GEDDES, Norman (1893–1958)
American industrial designer.

BELL, Vanessa (1879–1961)
British painter, muralist and interior designer.

BENSON, William Arthur Smith (1854–1924)
British architect, designer and metalworker; he was encouraged to start his metalwork shop by William Morris.

BERLAGE, Hendrik Petrus (1856–1934)
Dutch architect, theorist and designer.

BINDESBØLL, Thorvald (1846–1908)
Danish ceramist and designer.

BING, Samuel (1838–1905)
German writer and entrepreneur who opened his shop, La Maison de l'Art Nouveau, in Paris in 1895.

BRACQUEMOND, Félix-Henri (1833–1914)
French painter, etcher and ceramist.

BRANDT, Edgar (1880–1960)
French metalwork designer.

BRANDT, Marianne (b. 1893)
German metalwork designer who worked at the Bauhaus.

BRANGWYN, Frank (1867–1956)
British graphic artist and designer.

BREUER, Marcel (b. 1902)
Hungarian architect and designer who studied in Vienna; became director of the Bauhaus furniture design department in 1924.

BRIGGLE, Artus van (1869–1904)
American studio potter; he worked at Rookwood and subsequently set up his own pottery in Colorado.

BUGATTI, Carlo (1855–1940)
Italian furniture designer and craftsman.

CHAPLET, Ernest (1835–1909)
French ceramist.

CHARPENTIER, Alexandre (1856–1909)
French Art Nouveau designer and decorator; he was associated with Samuel Bing.

CHERMAYEFF, Serge (1900)
Russian architect and designer working in Britain.

CLIFF, Clarice (1899–1972)
British ceramic painter working in Stoke-on-Trent.

COATES, Wells (1895–1958)
Canadian architect and designer working in Britain.

COCTEAU, Jean (1889–1963)
French novelist, dramatist, critic and illustrator; he was closely connected with many of the leading theatre designers of his time.

COLENBRANDER, Theodorus A. C. (1841–1930)
Dutch ceramist.

COLONNA, Edward (1862–1948)
German designer and decorative designer working in U.S.A. and France.

COOPER, John Paul (1869–1933)
British architect, silversmith and jeweller, influenced by Henry Wilson.

LE CORBUSIER, Charles-Edouard Jeanneret (1888–1966)
French architect and designer whose work pioneered Modern Movement.

CRANE, Walter (1845–1915)
British designer, painter, illustrator and writer; a socialist, he was president of both the Art Worker's Guild and the Arts and Crafts Exhibition Society.

CZESCHKA, Carl Otto (1878–1960)
Austrian painter, architect and designer; member of the Wiener Werkstätte.

DALI, Salvador (b. 1904)
Spanish artist; the leading figure of the Surrealist movement.

DAUM, Auguste (1853–1909)
DAUM, Antonin (1864–1930)
French glass designers, brothers.

DAY, Lewis F. (1845–1910)
British arts and crafts designer and writer; he started his own business in 1870, was a founder member of both the Art Workers' Guild and the Arts and Crafts Exhibition Society.

DECK, Theodore (1823–91)
French art potter.

DECOEUR, Emile (1876–1953)
French ceramist.

DELAHERCHE, Auguste (1857–1940)
French ceramist in the Art Nouveau style; he was associated with Samuel Bing.

DELAUNAY, Robert (1885–1941)
French painter and designer, he designed sets for the Ballets Russes.

DOAT, Taxile (1851–1938)
French ceramist working at Sèvres and the University City Pottery, U.S.A.

DORN, Marion (1900–64)
American textile designer who worked in Britain 1922–38. She pioneered the Modernist rug.

DRESSER, Christopher (1834–1904)
British industrial designer; after achieving a doctorate in botany he turned to design for industrial production.

DREYFUSS, Henry (1904–72)
American industrial designer.

DUFRÊNE, Maurice (1876–1955)
French designer; worked for Julius Meier-graefe who opened his 'La Maison Moderne' in 1898. He emerged as a leading Art Deco designer.

DUFY, Raoul (1877–1953)
French painter and textile designer, he worked for Paul Poiret.

DUNAND, Jean (1877–1942)
Swiss Art Deco furniture designer, metalworker and lacquer-worker, working in France.

EAMES, Charles (b. 1907)
American architect and designer.

EASTLAKE, Charles (1836–1906)
British designer and writer; his *Hints on Household Taste* was enormously influential in America.

ELMSLIE, George Grant (1871–1952)
Scottish architect and designer working in Chicago.

ENDELL, August (1871–1925)
German architect and designer.

ERP, Dirk van (1860–1933)
American arts and crafts metalworker.

ERTÉ, Romain de Tirtoff (b. 1892)
Russian graphic artist and theatre designer working mainly in Paris. He is best known for his drawings for *Harper's Bazaar*.

FABERGÉ, Carl (1846–1920)
Russian jewellery designer; jeweller to the Russian Imperial Court.

LA FARGE, John (1835–1910)
American stained glass designer and artist.

DE FEURE, Georges (1869–1928)
French Art Nouveau decorative artist and designer.

FINCH, Alfred William (Willi) (1854–1930)
Belgian ceramist working in Finland.

FISHER, Alexander (1864–1936)
British Arts and Crafts enameller; he studied in France and subsequently set up his own school in Kensington.

FOLLOT, Paul (1877–1941)
French designer who developed his style from Art Nouveau to Art Deco.

FRANKL, Paul (1886–1958)
Austrian architect and furniture designer, he settled in America in 1914.

FRY, Roger (1866–1934)
British painter, critic and designer; he opened the Omega Workshops in 1913 to apply Post-Impressionism to the decorative arts.

FURNESS, Frank (1839–1912)
American architect working in Philadelphia.

GAILLARD, Eugène (1862–1933)
French Art Nouveau designer and writer, connected with Samuel Bing.

GALLÉ, Emile (1846–1904)
French designer; his Nancy workshops produced some of the finest productions in glass and furniture within the Art Nouveau style.

GALLEN-KALLELA, Akseli (1865–1931)
Finnish painter and designer; pioneer of nationalistic Finnish art.

GATE, Simon (1883–1945)
Swedish glass designer.

GAUDÍ, Antoni (1859–1926)
Spanish Art Nouveau architect and designer.

GAUDIER-BRZESKA, Henri (1891–1918)
French artist and designer; associated with Omega workshop.

GAUGUIN, Paul (1848–1903)
French painter, sculptor and graphic artist; leader of the Pont-Aven group.

GILL, Eric (1882–1940)
British sculptor, typographer and writer; he founded a Catholic guild to promote the revival of religious attitudes to art and craftsmanship.

GIMSON, Ernest (1864–1919)
British architect and designer; he set up his own workshops in the Cotswolds with Ernest and Sidney Barnsley and Peter Waals.

GOMPERZ, Lucie Marie (Lucie Rie) (b. 1902)
Austrian artist potter.

GRANT, Duncan (1885–1978)
British painter, muralist and designer.

GRASSET, Eugène (1841–1917)
Swiss architect, writer and designer working in France in the Art Nouveau style.

GRAY, Eileen (1879–1976)
British designer working in Paris. Known for her lacquerwork.

GREENE, Charles Sumner (1868–1957)
American architect and designer. He worked with his brother Henry, showing an eclectic appreciation of Arts and Crafts ideals.

GROPIUS, Walter (1883–1969)
German architect and designer; director of the Bauhaus 1919–28.

GRUEBY, William H. (1867–1925)
American potter known for his use of a matt glaze.

GUIMARD, Hector (1867–1942)
French architect and designer working within the Art Nouveau style to create the total environment.

GULLBERG, Elsa (b. 1886)
Swedish textile designer.

HALD, Edward (b. 1883)
Swedish glass designer.

HANSEN, Frieda (1855–1931)
Norwegian textile designer.

HEAL, Ambrose (1872–1959)
British furniture designer. He entered the firm of Heal and son in 1893. Vice-President of the D.I.A.

HENNINGSEN, Poul (1896–1967)
Scandinavian architect and designer.

HOFFMANN, Josef (1870–1956)
Austrian architect and designer; a founder member of the Vienna Secession, he founded the Wiener Werkstätte in 1903.

HOLIDAY, Henry (1839–1927)
British painter and stained glass designer; a member of the Pre-Raphaelite circle.

HORTA, Victor (1861–1947)
Belgian architect and designer in the Art Nouveau style.

HUBBARD, Elbert (1856–1915)
The founder of an arts and crafts community, the Roycrofters, in America, where he organised workshops, lectured and wrote.

IRIBE, Paul (1883–1935)
French designer and illustrator.

JAMES, Henry (1843–1916)
American novelist and critic.

JENSEN, Georg (1866–1935)
Danish silver and jewellery designer.

JOEL, Betty (b. 1896)
British furniture and textile designer.

JOUVE, Paul (1880–1973)
French designer.

KAUFFER, Edward McKnight (1890–1954)
American artist who worked in Britain between 1914 and 1938. He pioneered Cubist style in posters and designed rugs and interiors.

KLIMT, Gustav (1862–1918)
Austrian painter and designer, associated with Vienna Secession.

KLINT, Kaare (1888–1954)
Danish architect.

KNOX, Archibald (1864–1933)
British silver designer who was the inspiration behind Liberty and Co.'s 'Cymric' and 'Tudric' lines.

KOEHLER, Florence (1861–1944)
American arts and crafts jewellery designer.

KOEPPING, Karl (1848–1914)
German Jugendstil glass designer.

KROG, Arnold (1856–1931)
Scandinavian ceramist attached to the Royal Porcelain Factory of Copenhagen.

LALIQUE, René (1860–1945)
French designer, trained as a goldsmith. He was best known for his jewellery and glass designs. He opened his own glassworks in 1909.

LAEUGER, Max (b. 1864)
German architect and art potter.

LEACH, Bernard (b. 1887)
British ceramist who studied pottery in the Far East, returning in 1920 to St. Ives with Shoji Hamada.

LEGRAIN, Pierre (1889–1929)
French Art Deco designer.

LEWIS, Wyndham (1884–1957)
British painter, writer and designer, a founder of Vorticism.

LIVEMONT, Privat (1861–1936)
Belgian graphic artist and poster designer.

LÖFFLER, Berthold (b.1874)
Austrian painter, designer and graphic artist.

LOOS, Adolf (1870–1933)
Austrian architect and designer and pioneer of Modernism.

LURÇAT, Jean (1892–1966)
French painter, ceramic artist and leading tapestry designer.

MACDONALD, Margaret (1865–1933)
MACDONALD, Frances (1874–1921)
Scottish artists and designers of the Glasgow Four.

MACKINTOSH, Charles Rennie (1868–1928)
Scottish architect and designer; leading figure of Glasgow Four.

MACKMURDO, Arthur Heygate (1851–1942)
British Arts and Crafts architect and designer; he founded the Century Guild in 1884.

MAJORELLE, Louis (1859–1926)
French designer and cabinet-maker in the Art Nouveau style.

MAN, Ray (b. 1890)
American photographer who lived in Paris; an important member of the Dada and Surrealist Movements.

MARCKS, Gerhard (b. 1889)
German sculptor and potter who worked at the Bauhaus.

MARINOT, Maurice (1882–1960)
French glass designer.

MARTIN, Robert Wallace (1843–1923)
The Martin brothers (Robert, Walter, Edwin and Charles) began producing stoneware at Fulham, moving to Southall in 1878.

MATHEWS, Arthur F. (1860–1945)
MATHEWS, Lucia K. (1870–1955)
American artists and muralists, they founded the Furniture Shop and Philopolis magazine in San Francisco.

MATHSSON, Bruno (b. 1907)
Swedish designer.

MATISSE, Henri (1869–1954)
French painter and sculptor.

McGRATH, Raymond (b. 1903)
Australian architect and designer working in Britain.

McLAUGHLIN, Mary Louise (1847–1939)
American pottery and porcelain decorator.

MOHOLY-NAGY, László (1895–1946)
Hungarian designer and photographer who taught at the Bauhaus and developed the photogram.

MOORE, George E. (1873–1958)
British philosopher, mainly concerned with ethics and aesthetics.

MORGAN, William de (1839–1917)
British ceramist, closely connected with William Morris and known for his lustreware.

MORRIS, William (1834–96)
British writer, poet and designer; founder of Morris and Co. and the Kelmscott Press; leader of the Arts and Crafts Movement.

MOSER, Koloman (1868–1918)
Austrian painter, designer and graphic artist; involved in the founding of both the Vienna Secession and Wiener Werkstätte.

MUCHA, Alphonse (1860–1939)
Czech artist and poster designer.

MUNTHE, Gerhard (1849–1929)
Norwegian furniture designer.

MURRAY, Keith (b. 1893)
British architect and designer.

MUTHESIUS, Hermann (1861–1927)
German architect and designer; influenced by a lengthy visit to England. He founded the Deutscher Werkbund in 1907.

NASH, Paul (1889–1946)
British painter and designer.

NEUTRA, Richard (1892–1970)
Austrian architect working mainly in California.

NILSSON, Wiven (1870–1942)
Swedish silver designer.

NORDSTRÖM, Patrick (1870–1929)
Swedish potter, at the Royal Porcelain Factory of Copenhagen.

ORBRIST, Hermann (1863–1927)
Swiss designer working in Germany.

OBSEIGER, Robert (1884–1940)
Austrian designer and potter.

OLBRICH, Josef Maria (1867–1908)
Austrian Art Nouveau designer, architect and artist. Co-founder of the Vienna Secession.

PABST, Daniel (1826–1910)
American furniture designer and cabinet-maker, working in Philadelphia.

PARRISH, Maxfield (1870–1966)
American graphic artist and poster designer.

PATER, Walter (1839–94)
British writer, he evolved his own aesthetic critique.

PECHE, Dagobert (1887–1923)
Austrian artist and metalwork designer; co-director of the Wiener Werkstätte.

PICASSO, Pablo (1881–1973)
Spanish Cubist painter and sculptor working in France.

PICK, Frank (1878–1941)
British poster designer and typographer; he was responsible for design for the London Underground.

POE, Edgar Allan (1809–49)
American writer whose work was seized upon by French and English decadents.

POELZIG, Hans (1869–1936)
German architect and designer.

POIRET, Paul (1879–1944)
French theatre, interior designer and costumier, he founded the Atelier Martine in Paris in 1911.

PONTI, Gio (b. 1891)
Italian architect and furniture designer.

POWOLNY, Michael (1871–1954)
Austrian pottery decorator and teacher.

PROUST, Marcel (1871–1922)
French novelist; the original eight parts of *à la Recherche du Temps Perdu* were published 1913–1927.

PRUTSCHER, Otto (1880–1949)
Austrian architect, furniture designer, jeweller and designer. Worked at the Wiener Werkstätte.

PUIFORCAT, Jean (1897–1945)
French Art Deco Silversmith.

QUARTI, Eugenio (1867–1931)
Italian furniture designer working in Milan.

REDON, Odilon (1840–1916)
French painter, lithographer and etcher and an associate of the Symbolists.

RIEGEL, Ernst (1871–1946)
German Jugendstil gold and silversmith.

RIEMERSCHMID, Richard (1868–1957)
German architect and designer and founder member of the Deutscher Werkbund.

RIETVELD, Gerrit Thomas (1888–1964)
Dutch designer and architect; a member of the de Stijl group.

ROBINEAU, Adelaide Alsop (1865–1929)
American ceramist; she edited the *Keramic Studio* and worked with Taxile Doat at the University City Pottery.

ROHE, Mies van der (1886–1969)
German architect and designer and last head of the Bauhaus.

ROHLFS, Charles (1853–1936)
American furniture designer and craftsman working within the Art Nouveau idiom.

ROSSETTI, Dante Gabriel (1828–82)
British painter and poet and leading light of the Pre-Raphaelites. Also involved in the formation of Morris, Marshall Faulkner and Co.

ROUSSEAU, Clément (b. 1872)
French Art Deco furniture designer.

RUHLMANN, Emile-Jacques (1879–1933)
French designer and 'ensemblier' in the Art Deco style.

RUSKIN, John (1819–1900)
Influential British social critic, his writings were the main inspiration for the Arts and Crafts movement.

RUSSELL, Gordon (b. 1892)
British furniture designer and craftsman; began designing in the Arts and Crafts idiom, then absorbed the ideas of Modernism.

RYGGEN, Hannah (1894–1970)
Swedish textile designer working in Norway.

SAARINEN, Eliel (1873–1950)
Finnish architect and designer.

SAARINEN, Eero (1910–1961)
Finnish designer working in America.

SALTO, Axel (1889–1961)
Danish potter.

SCHIAPARELLI, Elsa (b. 1896)
Italian fashion designer working in France and America.

SCOTT FITZGERALD, F. (1896–1940)
American novelist and short story writer.

SERRURIER-BOVY, Gustave (1858–1910)
Belgian architect and designer influenced by Arts and Crafts Movement ideals.

SPARRE, Louis (1866–1964)
Swedish furniture designer.

STAITE-MURRAY, William (1861–1962)
British ceramist and teacher, influenced by Far Eastern techniques.

STAM, Mart (b. 1899)
Dutch architect; he designed the first cantilevered chair.

STICKLEY, Gustav (1857–1942)
American writer and furniture designer; he founded *The Craftsman* magazine in 1901, publicising arts and crafts ideals.

STIEGLITZ, Alfred (1864–1940)
American photographer who founded the Photo-Secession in 1902.

SULLIVAN, Louis (1856–1924)
American architect; the pioneer of the modern office block and father to the Prairie school of architecture.

TAYLOR, Ernest Archibald (1874–1951)
Scottish artist and designer, he worked within the 'Glasgow Style'.

TAYLOR, William Howson (1876–1935)
British ceramist who founded the Ruskin Pottery in 1898.

TEAGUE, Walter (1883–1960)
American industrial designer.

TIFFANY, Louis Comfort (1848–1933)
American designer and interior decorator; he specialised in stained glass and art glass as well as mosaics, jewellery and metalwork.

TOOROP, Jan (1858–1928)
Dutch painter and poster designer.

TOULOUSE-LAUTREC, Henri de (1864–1901)
French painter and poster designer.

UPWARD, Edward (b. 1903)
British writer belonging to the Marxist tradition of the 1930s.

VELDE, Henry van de (1863–1957)
Belgian theorist and designer; he helped found the Kunstgewerbeschule in Weimar in 1906.

VIOLLET-LE-DUC, Eugène-Emanuel (1814–79)
French writer and architectural theorist.

VOYSEY, Charles Annesley (1857–1941)
British Arts and Crafts architect and designer.

VUILLARD, Edouard (1868–1940)
French painter; member of Les Nabis.

WAGENFELD, Wilhelm (b. 1900)
German functionalist architect and industrial designer; he worked at the Bauhaus.

WAGNER, Otto (1841–1918)
Austrian designer; member of the Deutscher Werkbund.

WALTON, George (1867–1933)
Scottish Art Nouveau designer.

WEBB, Philip (1831–1915)
British architect and designer; he was associated with Morris and Co. from their foundation. He designed many country houses.

WHISTLER, James MacNeil (1834–1903)
American artist living in London; one of the first to recognise the importance of Japanese design.

WILDE, Oscar (1854–1900)
British poet, novelist and playwright; in both his life and his work he espoused the aesthetic ideal. His American lectures propagandized the Aesthetic movement there.

WILSON, Henry (1864–1934)
British Arts and Crafts architect, sculptor and silversmith.

WIMMER, Joseph Eduard (1882–1961)
Austrian designer and metalworker; co-director of the Weiner Werkstätte.

WOLFE, Elsie de (1865–1950)
American interior designer.

WOLFERS, Philippe (1858–1929)
Belgian Art Nouveau jeweller and sculptor.

WOOLF, Virginia (1882–1941)
British novelist and literary critic.

WRIGHT, Frank Lloyd (1867–1959)
American architect, writer and interior designer, pioneering and integral, structural style of interior decoration; he was the first major 'modern' American architect.

WESTMAN, Carl (1866–1936)
Swedish architect and decorative designer.

ZEN, Carlo (1851–1918)
Italian Art Nouveau cabinet-maker.

ZEN, Pietro (1879–1950)
Italian modernist furniture designer.

Select Bibliography

I Styles and Influences in the Decorative Arts 1890–1940

ART NOUVEAU
AMAYA, MARIO: *Art Nouveau*, London and New York, 1966
BATTERSBY, MARTIN: *The World of Art Nouveau*, London, 1968
RHEIMS, M.: *The Age of Art Nouveau*, London, 1966
RHEIMS, M.: *L'Art 1900*, Paris, 1965
SCHMUTZLER, ROBERT: *Art Nouveau*, London 1964
TSCHUDI MADSEN, S.: *Art Nouveau*, translated by R. I. Christopherson, London, 1970
WARREN, G.: *Art Nouveau*, London, 1972

ART DECO
BATTERSBY, MARTIN: *The Decorative Twenties*, London, 1969
BATTERSBY, MARTIN: *The Decorative Thirties*, London, 1971
CLOUZOT, HENRI: *Le Style Moderne dans la Décoration Moderne*, Paris, 1921
DESHAIRS, LÉON: *L'Art Décoratif Français, 1918–25*, Paris, 1925
DESHAIRS, LÉON: *Intérieurs en Couleurs*. France, Paris, 1926
EMILE-BAYARD: *Le Style Moderne*, Paris
FONTAINES ET VAUXCELLES: *L'Art Français de la Révolution à nos jours*, Paris; *Encyclopèdie des Arts Décoratifs et Industriels Modernes au XXème siècle*, Paris, 1926
HERBST, RENÉ: *Modern French Shop Fronts*, London, 1927
HILLIER, BEVIS: *Art Deco*, New York, 1969
HILLIER, BEVIS: *The World of Art Deco*, London, 1971
MOUSSINAC, LÉON: *Etoffes d'Ameublement Tissés et Brochés*, Paris, 1925
QUÉNIOUX, GASTON: *Les Arts Décoratifs Modernes*, Paris, 1925
ROCHAS, MARCEL: *Vingt-Cinq Ans d'Elégance à Paris*, Paris, 1951
ROCHAS, MARCEL: *Le Jardin du Bibliophile*, Paris, 1930
ROCHAS, MARCEL: *Livre d'or du Bibliophile*, Paris, 1925

MODERNISM
COLLINS, PETER: *Changing Ideals in Modern Architecture, 1750–1950*, London, 1967
LE CORBUSIER: *Towards a New Architecture*, London, 1927 (Paris, 1923)
PEVSNER, NIKOLAUS: *Pioneers of Modern Design: From William Morris to Walter Gropius*, London, 1936 (new ed. 1977)
PEVSNER, NIKOLAUS: *An Enquiry into Industrial Art in England*, London, 1937

SURREALISM AND NEO-BAROQUE
ALEXANDRIAN, SARANE: *Surrealist Art*, London, 1970
JEAN, MARCEL: *Histoire de la Peinture Surréaliste*, Paris, 1959
WALDBERG, PATRICK: *Surrealism*, London, 1965

REVIVALISM
BATTERSBY, MARTIN: *The Decorative Twenties*, London, 1969
BATTERSBY, MARTIN: *The Decorative Thirties*, London, 1971
ADBURGHAM, ALISON *et al*: *Liberty's 1875–1975*, Catalogue of an exhibition at the Victoria and Albert Museum, London, 1975
HITCHCOCK, HENRY-RUSSELL: *Architecture: Nineteenth and Twentieth Centuries*, Pelican History of Art, London, 1958
'The Studio' Year-books of Decorative Art, London, 1906–30

INDUSTRIAL DESIGN
BALFOUR, MICHAEL: *The Kaiser and his Times*, London, 1964
BANHAM, REYNER: *Theory and Design in the First Machine Age*, London, 1960
BEL GEDDES, NORMAN: *Horizons*, Boston, 1932
BUSH, DONALD J.: *The Streamlined Decade*, New York, 1975
DUMAS, F. G. and DE FOURCAUD, L.: *Revue de L'Exposition Universelle de 1889*, Paris, 1889
EISLER, MAX: *Österreichische Werkkultur*, Vienna, 1916
GIBBS-SMITH, CHARLES H.: *Clement Ader, His Flight-Claims and His Place in History*, London, 1968
GIEDION, SIEGFRIED: *Mechanization Takes Command*, New York, 1948
HOLME, GEOFFREY: *Industrial Design and the Future*, London and New York, 1934
Jahrbuch des Deutschen Werkbundes, Jena, 1912–14, Munich, 1915

LE CORBUSIER: *Le Corbusier et Pierre Jeanneret: Oeuvres Complètes de 1910–29*, Zurich, 1948 (5th edition)
LE CORBUSIER: *Towards a New Architecture*, London, 1927 (Paris, 1923)
LETHABY, W. R.: *Form in Civilisation*, London, 1922
PEVSNER, NIKOLAUS: *An Enquiry into Industrial Art in England*, Cambridge, 1937
PEVSNER, NIKOLAUS: *Studies in Art, Architecture and Design*, London, 1968
READ, HERBERT: *Art and Industry*, London, 1934
ROUSSELET, LOUIS: *L'Exposition Universelle de 1889*, Paris, 1893
SINGER, CHARLES, HOLMYARD, E. J., HALL, A. R., WILLIAMS, TREVOR (editors): *A History of Technology. Volume V. The Late 19th century c.1850–c.1900*, Oxford, 1958
VAN DE VELDE, HENRY: *Geschichte meines Lebens*, Munich, 1962
VAN DOREN, HAROLD: *Industrial Design*, New York, 1940 (2nd edition, New York, 1954)
The Year Book of the Design in Industries Association, London, 1922, 1924–25, 1926–27, 1929–30

II Designs and Designers 1890–1940

FRANCE/Furniture and Interiors
Ancienne Collection Jacques Doucet – Mobilier Art Déco, Provenant du Studio Saint-James à Neuilly, Hotel Drouot Sale Catalogue, 8 Nov 1972
ANDRÉ MARE et La Compagnie des Arts Français (Süe et Mare), Exhibition Catalogue, Strasbourg, 1971
BATTERSBY, MARTIN: *The World of Art Nouveau*, London, 1968
DUNAND, JEAN, GOULDEN, JEAN: *Exhibition Catalogue, Galerie du Luxembourg, Paris, 1973*
Exposition Retrospective E.-J. RUHLMANN, Musée des Arts Décoratifs, Paris, 1934
Les Folles Années de la Soie, Exhibition Catalogue, Musée Historique des Tissus, Lyon, 1975
GALLÉ, EMILE: *Écrits Pour l'Art*, Paris, 1908
GARNER, PHILIPPE: *Emile Gallé*, London, 1976
HERBST, RENÉ: *Pierre Chareau*, Paris, 1954
HERBST, RENÉ: *25 Années U.A.M.*, Paris, 1955
HOFFMAN, HERBERT: *Intérieurs Modernes de Tous les Pays*, Paris, 1930
L'Oeuvre de Rupert Carabin 1862–1932, Exhibition Catalogue, Galerie du Luxembourg, Paris, 1974
OLMER, PIERRE: *Le Mobilier Français d'Aujourd'hui (1910–1925)*, Paris, 1926
OLMER, PIERRE: *La Renaissance du Mobilier Français*, Paris, 1927
Wendingen, special issue devoted to Eileen Gray, 1924

FRANCE/Glass
BLOUNT, BERNIECE and HENRY: *French Cameo Glass*, Iowa, 1968
Catalogue des Verreries de René Lalique, Paris, 1932
DERMANT, JANINE BLOCH: *L'Art du Verre en France 1860–1914*, Lausanne, 1974
FOURCAUD, LOUIS DE: *Emile Gallé*, Paris, 1903
GALLÉ, EMILE: *Ecrits Pour L'Art*, Paris, 1908
GARNER, PHILIPPE: *Emile Gallé*, London, 1976
GROVER, RAY and LEE: *Carved and Decorated European Art Glass*, Vermont, 1970
HILSCHENZ, HELGA: *Das Glas des Jugendstils*, Dusseldorf, 1973
PAZAUREK, GUSTAV: *Moderne Glazer*, Leipzig, 1901
POLAK, ADA: *Modern Glass*, London, 1962
ROSENTHAL, LEON: *La Verrerie Française depuis cinquante ans*, Paris, 1927
STERNER, GABRIELE: *Die Vasen der Gebrüder Daum*, Munich, 1969

FRANCE/Ceramics
ALEXANDRE, ARSÈNE: *Jean Carriès*, Paris, 1895
BORRMANN, RICHARD: *Moderne Keramik*, Leipzig, 1902
D'ALBIS, JEAN: *Ernest Chaplet, Les Presses de la Connaissance*, Paris, 1976
FARE, MICHEL: *La Céramique Contemporaine*, Strasbourg-Paris, 1954

JEAN, RENÉ: *Les Arts de la Terre*, Paris, 1911
VALOTAIRE, MARCEL: *La Céramique Française Moderne*, Paris, Brussels

FRANCE/Metalwork
Ancienne Collection Jacques Doucet – Mobilier Art Déco, Provenant du Studio Saint-James à Neuilly, Hotel Drouot Sale Catalogue, 8 November 1972
Art-Deco, Schmuck und Bücher aus Frankreich, Exhibition Catalogue, Villa Stuck, Munich, 1975
Bijoux et Orfèvrerie par Jean Fouquet, Paris, c. 1930
CLOUZOT, HENRI: *La Ferronerie Moderne*, Paris, c. 1925
EMILE-BAYARD: *L'Art Appliqué Français d'Aujourd'hui*, Paris, c. 1925
Hector Guimard Fontes Artistiques, Exhibition Catalogue, Galerie du Luxembourg, Paris, 1971
LALIQUE, MARC and MARIE-CLAUDE: *Lalique par Lalique*, Lausanne, 1977
Le Bijou 1900, Exhibition Catalogue, Brussels, 1965
QUÉNIOUX, GASTON: *Les Arts Décoratifs Modernes*, France, Paris, c. 1925
RAPIN, HENRI: *La Sculpture Décorative à l'Exposition des Arts Décoratifs de 1925*, Paris, 1925
VERNE, H. and CHAVANCE, R.: *Pour Comprendre l'Art Décoratif Moderne en France*, Paris, 1925

FRANCE/Graphic Art
MORNAND ET THOME: *Vingt Artistes du Livre*, Paris 1950
MORNAND, PIERRE: *Onze Artistes du Livre*, Paris 1938

FRANCE/Theatre and Ballet
GADAN ET MAILLARD: *Dictionnaire du Ballet Moderne*, Paris, 1959

FRANCE/Fashion
BEATON, CECIL: *The Glass of Fashion*, London, 1954
CHARLES-ROUX, EDMONDE: *Chanel*, New York, 1975
ERTÉ: *Things I Remember*, London, 1975
Fashion–An Anthology by Cecil Beaton, Victoria & Albert Museum Exhibition Catalogue, 1971
GARLAND, MADGE: *The Indecisive Decade*, London, 1968
GARLAND, MADGE: *The Changing Face of Beauty*, London, 1957
La Gazette du Bon Ton
Harper's Bazaar
HORST: *Salute to the Thirties*, London, 1971
POIRET, PAUL: *En Habillant l'Epoque*, Paris, 1930
SCHIAPARELLI, ELSA: *Shocking Life*, London 1954
Vogue

UNITED KINGDOM
ADBURGHAM, ALISON: *Liberty's: A Biography of a Shop*, London, 1975
ANSCOMBE, ISABELLE and GERE, CHARLOTTE: *Arts and Crafts in Britain and America*, London, 1978
ASHBEE, C. R.: *Collected Letters and Journals*, in King's College Library, Cambridge, by kind permission of Miss Felicity Ashbee
ASLIN, ELIZABETH: *The Aesthetic Movement, Prelude to Art Nouveau*, London, 1969
BATTERSBY, MARTIN: *The Decorative Twenties*, London, 1969
BATTERSBY, MARTIN: *The Decorative Thirties*, London, 1971
BOE, ALF: *From Gothic Revival to Functional Form*, Oslo, 1957
CRANE, WALTER: *William Morris to Whistler*, London, 1911
DRESSER, CHRISTOPHER: *The Art of Decorative Design*, London, 1862
GARLAND, MADGE: *The Indecisive Decade*, London, 1968
HENDERSON, PHILIP: *William Morris, his Life, Work and Friends*, London, 1967
HOWARTH, THOMAS: *Charles Rennie Mackintosh and the Modern Movement*, London, 1952, new edition 1977
MACCARTHY, FIONA: *All Things Bright and Beautiful, Design in Britain, 1830 to Today*, London, 1972
MACKAIL, J. W.: *The Life of William Morris*, 2 vols., London, 1899
NAYLOR, GILLIAN: *The Arts and Crafts Movement*, London, 1971
READ, HERBERT: *Art and Industry*, London, 1934
RUSSELL, SIR GORDON: *Designer's Trade*, London, 1968
SHONE, RICHARD: *Bloomsbury Portraits*, London, 1976
TILBROOK, A. J.: *The Designs of Archibald Knox for Liberty & Co.*, London, 1976
TODD, DOROTHY and MORTIMER, RAYMOND: *The New Interior Decoration*, London, 1929
WILDE, OSCAR: *Art and Decoration: Being Extracts from Reviews and Miscellanies*, London, 1920

UNITED STATES
ANDERSEN, MOORE and WINTER: *California Design – 1910*, Exhibition Catalogue, California, 1974
BROOKS, H. ALLEN: *The Prairie School; Frank Lloyd Wright and his Midwest Contemporaries*, Toronto, 1972
CLARKE, ROBERT JUDSON: *The Arts and Crafts Movement in America 1876–1916*, Exhibition Catalogue, Princeton, 1972
Aspects of the Arts and Crafts Movement in America, Record of the Art Museum, Princeton University, Vol. 34, No. 2, 1975
CRANE, WALTER: *An Artist's Reminiscences*, London, 1907
Daniel Pabst – Philadelphia Cabinet-maker, Museum Bulletin, Philadelphia Museum of Art, Vol. 73, No. 316, April 1977

EVANS, PAUL F.: *Art Pottery of the United States*, New York, 1974
KOCH, ROBERT: *Louis C. Tiffany, Rebel in Glass*, New York, 1974
Mathews: Masterpieces of the California Decorative Style, Exhibition Catalogue, Oakland Museum, California, 1972
SCHAEFFER, HERWIN: *The Roots of Modern Design*, London, 1970

GERMANY AND AUSTRIA
Apocalypse and Utopia, A View of German Art 1910–1939, Fischer Fine Art, London, 1977
ARNOLD, K.-P.: *Gestaltete Form in Vergangenheit und Gegenwart, Möbel aus Hellerau*, Museum für Kunsthandwerk, Dresden, 1973
Bauhaus, Royal Academy, London, 1973
BAYER, HERBERT with WALTER GROPIUS and ILSE GROPIUS (eds.): *Bauhaus 1919–1928*, Museum of Modern Art, New York, 1938 (new ed. 1975)
BOTT, GERHARD (ed.): *Jugendstil*, Kataloge des Hessischen Landesmuseum Nr. 1, Darmstadt, 1973
BURCKHARDT, LUCIUS: *Werkbund Germania, Austria, Svizzeria*, Venice, 1977
EISLER, MAX: *Dagobert Peche*, Vienna, 1925
EISLER, MAX: *Gustav Klimt*, Vienna, 1920
ENGELHART, JOSEF: *Ein Wiener Maler erzählt*, Vienna, 1943
ERICKSEN-FIRLE, URSULA: *Figürliches Porzellan*, Kataloge des Kunstgewerbemuseums, Köln, Band V, Cologne, 1975
GRIMSCHITZ, BRUNO: *Österreichische Maler vom Biedermeier zur Moderne*, Vienna, 1963
HOFMANN, HELGA D.: *Kleinplastik und figürliches Kunsthandwerk aus den Beständen des Münchner Stadtmuseums*, Munich, 1974
HOLME, CHARLES (ed.): *The Art Revival in Austria*, London, 1906
Jan Bontjes van Beek, das Keramische Werk, Neue Sammlung, Munich, 1974
KLEIN, ADALBERT: *Moderne deutsche Keramik*, Darmstadt, 1956
KLEINER, LEOPOLD: *Josef Hoffmann*, Berlin, 1927
Kunsthandwerk und Industrieform des 19. und 20. Jahrhunderts. Staatliche Kunstsammlungen, Dresden, 1976
LÖFFLER, FRITZ and EMILIO BERTONATI: *Dresdner Sezession 1919–1925*, Galleria del Levante, Munich, 1977
MRAZEK, WILHELM: *Die Wiener Werkstätte, Modernes Kunsthandwerk von 1903–1932*, Österreichisches Museum für Angewandte Kunst, Vienna, 1967
MUTHESIUS, HERMANN: 'Kunst und Maschine', in *Dekorative Kunst*, vol. 9, 1902, pp. 141–7
Mutz-Keramik, Ernst Barlach Haus, Hamburg, 1966
MYERS, BERNARD S.: *Expressionism*, London, 1957
NATZLER, GERTRUDE and OTTO: *Ceramics*, Catalogue of the Collection of Mrs. Leonard M. Sperry, Los Angeles County Museum of Art, 1968
NEUWIRTH, WALTRAUD: *Österreichisches Keramik des Jugendstils*, Munich, 1974
NEUWIRTH, WALTRAUD: *Wiener Keramik*, Braunschwig, 1974
NOVOTNY, FRITZ and JOHANNES DOBAI: *Gustav Klimt*, London, 1968
Österreich auf des Weltausstellung Paris 1900, Vienna, n.d. (1900)
OZZOLA, LEANDRO: *L'Arte contemporanea all' Esposizione di Roma*, Rome, 1911
POWELL, NICHOLAS: *The Sacred Spring, The Arts in Vienna 1898–1918*, London, 1974
RADEMACHER, HELMUT: *Das deutsche Plakat von den Aufgängen bis zur Gegenwart*, Dresden, 1965
ROCHOWANSKI, LEOPOLD WOLFGANG: *Wiener Keramik*, Vienna, 1923
SCHMIDT, RUDOLF: *Das Wiener Künstlerhaus*, Vienna, 1964
SEKLER, EDUARD F.: 'Mackintosh and Vienna', reprinted in *The Anti-Rationalists*, London, 1973
SELZ, PETER: *German Expressionist Painting*, Los Angeles, 1957
SPIELMANN, HEINZ: *Der Jugendstil in Hamburg*, Hamburg, 1965
Tendenzen der Zwanziger Jahre, 15. Europäische Kunstausstellung, Berlin, 1977
Vienna Secession, Art Nouveau to 1970, Royal Academy, London, 1971
VERONESI, GIULIA: *Josef Hoffmann*, Mailand, 1956
VERGO, PETER: *Art in Vienna 1898–1918*, London, 1975
VON HARTMANN, G. B. and WEND FISCHER (eds): *Zwischen Kunst und Industrie des Deutschen Werkbunds*, Die Neue Sammlung, Munich, 1975
VON TRESKOW, IRENE: *Die Jugendstil-Porzellane KPM Berlin*, Munich, 1971
WINGLER, HANS M.: *The Bauhaus*, Boston, Mass., 1969

BELGIUM
Art Nouveau Belgium/France, Exhibition Catalogue, Institute for the Arts, Rice University, Houston, 1976
BORSI, FRANCO: *Bruxelles 1900*, Brussels, 1974
DUMONT-WILDEN, L.: *Fernand Khnopff*, Brussels, 1907
HENRION-GIELE, SUZANNE: *Musée Horta*, Brussels, 1972
HOFFMAN HERBERT: *Intérieurs Modernes de Tous les Pays*, Paris, 1930
LENNING, H. F.: *The Art Nouveau*, The Hague, 1951
Pionniers du XXe Siècle, Guimard, Horta, Van de Velde, Exhibition Catalogue, Musée des Arts Décoratifs, Paris, 1971
The Sacred and Profane in Symbolist Art, Exhibition Catalogue, Art Gallery of Ontario, Toronto, 1969
Henry van de Velde, Exhibition Catalogue, l'Ecuyer, Brussels, 1907
WOLFERS, MARCEL: *Philippe Wolfers*, Brussels, 1965

THE NETHERLANDS

H. P. Berlage: Nederlandse Architectuur, 1856–1935, Catalogue of an exhibition in the Gemeente Museum, the Hague, 1975
The Amsterdam School, catalogue of an exhibition in the Gemeente Museum, the Hague, 1975
JAFFE, H. L. C.: *De Stijl*, London, 1970
OVERY, PAUL: *De Stijl*, London, 1969
SINGELENBERG, PETER: *H. P. Berlage, Idea and Style*, Utrecht, 1972

SCANDINAVIA

BOULTON SMITH, JOHN: *The Golden Age of Finnish Art (Art Nouveau)*, Helsinki, 1976
HUGHES, GRAHAM and others: *Georg Jensen*. Special double issue of the monthly *Mobilia*, June–July 1966
POLAK, ADA: *Norwegian Silver*, Oslo, 1972
Royal Copenhagen Porcelain, 200 years of. Catalogue of an exhibition circulated by the Smithsonian Institution, 1974–1976
STAVENOW-HIDEMARK, ELISABET: *Svensk Jugend*, Stockholm, Nordiska Museet, 1964
THUE, ANNIKEN: *Frida Hansen*, Oslo, Kunstindustrimuseet, 1973
WETTERGREN, ERIK: *Modernt svenskt glas*, Stockholm, 1943

ITALY AND SPAIN

BAIRATI, ELEONORA, with ROSSANA BOSSAGLIA and MARCO ROSSI: *L'Italia Liberty, Arrademento e arti decorative*, Florence, 1964
BOHIGAS, ORIOL: 'Luis Domènech', reprinted in *The Anti-Rationalists*, London 1973
BOSSAGLIA, R.: *Il Liberty in Italia*, Milan, 1968
BOSSAGLIA, ROSSANA: *Il 'Deco' Italiano, Fisionomia dello Stile 1925 in Italia*, Milan, 1975
BROSIO, V.: *Lo Stile Liberty in Italia*, Milan, 1967
CIRLOT, JUAN EDUARDO: *El Estilo de Siglio XX*, Barcelona, 1952
Il Liberty a Bologna e nell'Emilia Romagna, Galleria d'Arte Moderna, Bologna, 1977
MACKAY, DAVID: 'Berenguer', reprinted in *The Anti-Rationalists*, London 1973
NICOLETTI, MANFREDO: 'Art Nouveau in Italy', reprinted in *The Anti-Rationalists*, London, 1973
PELLICER, A. CIRICI: *El arte modernista catalán*, Barcelona, 1951
PELLICER, A. CIRICI: *1900 en Barcelona*, Barcelona, 1967
PICA, A.: *Storia del Triennale 1918–1957*, Milan, 1957
PIERRE, JOSÉ and JOSÉ CORREDOR-MATHEOS: *Miró & Artigas, Céramiques*, Paris, 1974
PIRRONE, G. and F. SCIANNA: *Palermo Liberty*, Rome, 1971
PRATS VALLÉS, J.: *Gaudí* (with a preface by Le Corbusier), Barcelona, 1958
SWEENEY, JAMES JOHNSON and JOSEP LLUIS SERT: *Antoni Gaudí*, London, 1960
VIANELLO, G.: *Galileo Chini e il Liberty in Italia*, Florence, 1964

EASTERN EUROPE

L'Art 1900 en Hongrie, Exhibition Catalogue, Le Petit Palais, Dec. 1976–Feb. 1977
DANILOVICZ, C. E.: 'Princess Teniches' School of Russian Applied Art', *The Studio*, vol. 41, no. 172 July 1st. 1907
Die Kunstismen in Russland, 1907–1930, Exhibition Catalogue, Galerie Gmurzynska, Cologne, May–June 1977
Fabergé, 1846–1920, Exhibition Catalogue, Victoria and Albert Museum, 1977
GRAY, CAMILLA: *The Great Experience, Russian Art 1863–1922*, London, 1962
LEVETUS, A. S.: 'The Royal Hungarian Arts and Crafts School', Budapest, *The Studio*, vol. 60, no. 247, 1913
MILANI, ALFREDO: 'Hungarian Art at the Milan Exhibition', *The Studio*, vol. 38, no. 162, 1906
PEACOCK, NETTER: 'The New Movement in Russian Decorative Art', *The Studio*, vol. 22, no. 98, 1901
Russian Avant-garde, 1908–1922, Exhibition Catalogue, Leonard Hutton Gallery, 1971
SCHANZER, HEDWIG: 'The Teaching of Design at the Prague Arts and Crafts School', *The Studio*, vol. 54, no. 226
VALLANCE, AYLMER: 'Russian Peasant Industries', *The Studio*, vol. 37. no. 157, 1906

III   The Background to the Decorative Arts 1890–1940

THE GREAT EXHIBITIONS

ALLWOOD, JOHN: *The Great Exhibitions*, London, 1977
BRINKMANN, Dr. JULIUS: *Die Ankaüfe auf der Weltausstellung Paris 1900*, Hamburg, 1901
BRUNHAMMER, YVONNE: *1925*, Paris, 1937
COMTE, JULES: *L'Art à l'Exposition Universelle de 1900*, Paris, 1900
D'UCKERMANN, P.: *L'Art dans la Vie Moderne*, Paris, 1937
FUCHS–NEWBERRY: *L'Exposition Internationale des Arts Décoratifs Modernes*, Darmstadt, 1902
HERBST, RENE: *25 Années Union des Artistes Modernes*, Paris, 1955
HOENTSCHEL, GEORGES: *Le Pavillon de l'Union Centrale des Arts Décoratifs à l'Exposition Universelle de 1900*, Paris, 1900
ISAY, RAYMOND: *Panorama des Expositions Universelles*, Paris, 1937
MANDELL, RICHARD: *Paris 1900: The Great World's Fair*, Toronto, 1967
MOUREY, GABRIEL: *Histoire Générale de l'Art Français de la Révolution à Nos Jours: l'Art Décoratif*, Paris, 1925
QUÉNIOUX, GASTON: *Les Arts Décoratifs Modernes*, France, 1925

PHOTOGRAPHY AND THE CINEMA

BEATON, CECIL and BUCKLAND, GAIL: *The Magic Image*, London, 1975
Cecil Beaton's Scrapbook, London, 1937
BRANDT, BILL: *The English at Home*, London, 1936
BRASSAÏ: *The Secret Paris of the 30s*, London, 1967
The Daybooks of Edward Weston, Vols I and II, New York, 1961 and 1966
DOTY, ROBERT: *Photo-Secession-Photography as a Fine Art*, Rochester, 1970
EISNER, LOTTE H.: *Fritz Lang*, London, 1976
EISNER, LOTTE H.: *The Haunted Screen*, London, 1969
GERNSHEIM, HELMUT and ALISON: *The History of Photography*, London, 1969
HORST: *Salute to the Thirties*, London, 1971
HOYNINGEN HUENE, Exhibition Catalogue, University of Southern California, Los Angeles, 1970
JENKINSON, P.: *The Busby Berkeley Book*, London, 1973
KOSTELANETZ, RICHARD: *Moholy-Nagy*, New York, 1970
LAMBRICHS, GEORGES: *Les Plus Belles Images du Cinema*, Paris
LEVY, JULIEN: *Memoir of an Art Gallery*, New York, 1977
Man Ray Photographs, 1920–34, New York, 1973
MARTIN, PAUL: *Victorian Snapshots*, London, 1939
MASCLET, DANIEL: *Nus*, Paris, 1933
NEWHALL, BEAUMONT: *Frederick H. Evans*, New York, 1973
NEWHALL, BEAUMONT: *The History of Photography*, London, 1969
SCHARF, AARON: *Art and Photography*, London, 1968
WALKER EVANS: *Photographs for the Farm Security Administration 1935–38*, Library of Congress Catalogue, New York, 1973
WEEGEE: *Naked City*, New York, 1946
WEIGHTMAN, J. (ed.): *Masterworks of the French Cinema*, London and New York, 1973

PAINTING AND THE DECORATIVE ARTS

ALEXANDRIAN, S.: *Surrealist Art*, London, 1970
ARNASAN, H. H.: *Modern Art*, London, 1969
BAYER, H., GROPIUS W. and GROPIUS I.: *Bauhaus 1919–1928*, Boston, 1959
CASSOU J., LANGUI E. and PEVSNER N.: *The Sources of Modern Art*, London, 1962
FRY, E.: *Cubism*, London, 1962
JAFFE, H. L. C.: *De Stijl*, London, 1970
PEVSNER, N.: *The Sources of Modern Architecture and Design*, London, 1968

Contributing Authors

Philippe Garner, the consultant editor of the encyclopedia, has published several works on modern decorative arts, including *Edwardiana, Art Nouveau for Collectors* and the standard critical work on the French glass artist, Emile Gallé. He has also published articles in *The Connoisseur* magazine on Eileen Gray, Jean Dunand and Pierre Legrain.

Roger-Henri Guerrand teaches at the Ecole Supérieure des Beaux-Arts in Paris. His books include *L'Art Nouveau en Europe*.

Martin Battersby is both a theatre designer and a painter, as well as being a leading authority on international Art Nouveau and Art Deco. His most notable books are *The Decorative Twenties* and *The Decorative Thirties*.

Gillian Naylor is an acknowledged expert on the Modern Movement in design and is currently writing a book on the subject. Her books include *The Arts and Crafts Movement* and *The Bauhaus*.

Malcolm Haslam is currently working on a book about the Martin Brothers, art potters. His previous publications include *English Art Pottery 1865–1915, Marks and Monograms of the Modern Movement* and *The Real World of the Surrealists*.

Stuart Durant is Senior Lecturer in the History of Design at Kingston Polytechnic, London. He has published a book on *Victorian Ornamental Design* and has organised numerous exhibitions on the decorative arts.

Lynne Thornton was formerly an expert with Sotheby's, specialising in Art Nouveau. She is now a recognised expert for the major Paris auction rooms and has made a speciality of the study of late nineteenth- and early twentieth-century ceramics.

Ian Bennett is the author of numerous books on the fine and applied arts, including the recently published *Rugs and Carpets of the World*. He is also a keen collector of modern art ceramics.

Isabelle Anscombe, after a period spent working for a London decorative arts business, now devotes herself entirely to writing on the modern applied arts. Her book on the *Arts and Crafts Movement in America* is to be published in 1978.

Ada Polak is the Deputy Curator in Britain of the Arts and Crafts Museum of Norway. She has published articles on the decorative arts in a number of journals, and her book *Modern Glass* is one of the standard works on the subject.

Marina Henderson, who has contributed a special essay on the relationship between the fine and applied art of the twentieth century, is the author of a book on Dante Gabriel Rossetti.

Glossary

AMBOYNA Exotic mid-to-pale coloured wood with a rich natural grain pattern.

BIAS CUT Garments cut 'on the bias' exploit the natural flexibility in the diagonal of the fabric, and the criss-cross pattern of the weave runs diagonally to the body as opposed to the traditional horizontal/vertical cloth pattern.

BOISERIES Wood panelling and other fitted wooden elements of an interior scheme.

CAMEO GLASS Glass in which the decoration stands in relief, cut or etched through layers of different coloured glass.

CIRE PERDUE PROCESS Literally, and actually, the 'lost wax' process in which a mould is made around a wax model which is then melted and drained to be replaced by molten bronze or glass (as in Lalique's early experiments).

CLOISONNISME A style of painting in which strongly defined outlines retaining blocks of colour evoke the technique of cloisonné enamel work.

CLOISONNÉ ENAMEL Enamel in which the design is defined by raised outlines retaining the areas of different coloured enamels.

CRACKLEWARE (CRAQUELÉ) Terms used to describe ceramics with glazes characterised by an intentional and controlled crazing.

DINANDERIE Work in non-precious metals.

EBENE DE MACASSAR A dark exotic hardwood characterised by a natural streaky marking.

ENSEMBLIER Designer/decorator responsible for creating every element of a room setting.

ETCHED GLASS Glass in which the relief of a cameo design, the surface texture or a monochrome graphic design is achieved by the controlled effort of corrosive acid.

FAUTEUIL GONDOLE Tub chair.

FAVRILE GLASS The word 'Favrile' was adopted as a trademark for Tiffany glass to remind customers of the element of craft or handwork.

FLAMBÉ GLAZES Glazes achieved by firing at a very high temperature.

GALUCHAT See Shagreen.

GESSO Gesso work involves the building up of a picture in low relief using a kind of plaster, often enriched with gilding and other materials including mother-of-pearl or stones in addition to paints.

LACQUER A resin drawn from certain Oriental trees and capable of creating a rich, even, lustrous surface when applied layer upon layer to a wood or metal base.

LIMED OAK Oak in which the natural open grain pattern is emphasised by white lines left after rubbing lime into surface.

MARQUETERIE SUR VERRE A process introduced by Gallé in 1897 of inlaying semi-molten glass details of decoration into the hot, soft body of a glass object.

MARQUETRY Technique of inlaying one or more woods into another to render a graphic design on flat elements of furniture and woodwork.

MARTELÉ A particular style of carving glass, peculiar most notably to the products of the Daum factory, giving a broad facetted surface reminiscent of hard-hammered metal.

MEUBLE D'ENCOIGNURE Piece of furniture designed to fit into a corner.

MODELAGE À CHAUD The process of working glass while it is still soft from the heat of the furnace.

PARURE DE CORSAGE Elaborate jewel designed to adorn the chest.

PÂTE-D'ÉMAIL A more brittle, more fragile variant of the *pâte-de-verre* process.

PÂTE-DE-VERRE Glass made by the fusion at a relatively low temperature of pulverised glass bound into a paste and with an admixture of metallic oxides to give colour.

PÂTE-SUR-PÂTE Method of decoration developed in France which consists of building up a low relief by repeated applications of layers of slip and then carving into them to form relief. Very expensive and painstaking technique.

PLIQUE À JOUR Enamel *plique à jour* is translucent enamel fired within an openwork metal design.

POCHOIR PROCESS A process of multiple hand-colouring using stencils, particularly popular in France in the 1920s.

RED PADOUK Burmese wood resembling rosewood.

REPOUSSÉ METALWARE Repoussé wares have the decorative motifs hammered out in relief.

SABOTS Literally 'clogs', a term applied to the terminal elements of furniture legs, often in bronze or, in the case of Ruhlmann, ivory.

SALT-GLAZE At stoneware temperature (1250–1300°C.), salt vitrified to form a glaze when thrown into the kiln.

SANG-DE-BOEUF Term used to describe a deep blood-red colour.

SGRAFFITO Method of decoration, scratching through a layer of slip to expose colour of clay body below.

SHAGREEN Tough, hard skin from sharks, usually tinted pale green, very pale blue, pink or a natural shade of cream. Similar in appearance to lizard skin but with a more regular pattern.

SLIP WARES Earthenware decorated by means of slip (clay, often tinted, diluted to the consistency of cream), applied in a manner similar to that used to decorate an iced cake. Much used by seventeenth- and eighteenth-century Staffordshire potters and modern studio potters.

SOUFFLÉ WARES Type of glaze, usually in a single colour, occasionally with slightly mottled surfaces. Used by Edward Taylor (Ruskin).

STANNIFEROUS GLAZE Ceramic glaze using tin-based oxides.

VERRE ÉGLOMISÉ Term used by Gallé to describe an internal effect of white chemical inclusions in glass.

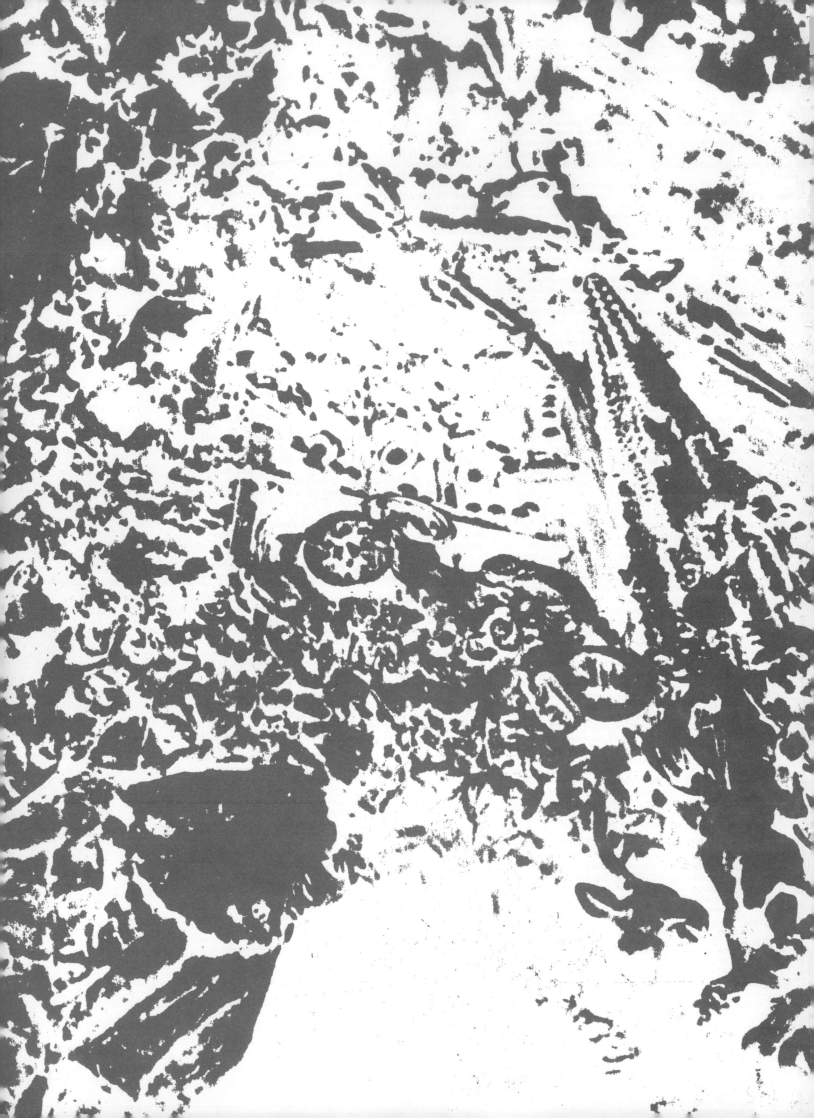